Acclaim for Sandwiches Should NEVER Taste Like Cow Crap

'The world, according to Dave Lowe, is a dangerous place – full of sadistic customs agents, decaying airplanes and toothlessly grinning old women. It is therefore also a wonderful, hilarious place, the kind of world you'd visit yourself if only you had Lowe's wit, open-mindedness and unerring penchant for disaster.'

Matt Gross, *The New York Times' Frugal Traveler*

'Dave Lowe's writing is fast, funny, and so full of life that you can only imagine how from now on everyone will do anything they can to imitate his style.'

Tahir Shah, author of *The Caliph's House* etc.

'Dave Lowe spares you the humdrum of life on the road that plagues so much travel writing today. Instead, he cuts right to the chase with the sort of outrageous highlights you'd want to hear if you were lucky enough to saddle up next to him at the bar.'

Doug Lansky, author of *The Last Trout In Venice*

'From chair throwing Frenchwomen to machete-wielding Vietnamese baguette makers, Sandwiches Should Never Taste Like Cow Crap is proof positive that travel only starts to get real interesting when things go wrong.'

Peter Moore, author of *Swahili for the Broken Hearted*

'Some travelers have to go out of their way to find adventure, but for Dave Lowe, the opposite seems to be true: adventure seems to seek him out instead. Through his highly readable madcap episodes, readers are there, right beside him, taken along for one wickedly funny, turbulent flight.'

Pilot Guides, Ltd., creator of the award winning TV series, *Globetrekker*

'Who doesn't love reading emails from that wanderlust friend you always think about when you're stuck sitting at your desk pushing paper? Dave Lowe's humourous and shockingly real tales from the road suck you into the trials of being a travel junky, and make you want to ask when the next trip is and if you can come along with him!'

Shanti Sosienski, author of Women Who Run

'Dave Lowe's book shows that having the right attitude has a lot to do with the enjoyment of travel. Despite frequent falls off the proverbial horse, Lowe saddles back up with wit and passion for more. The stories in his book are marvelous and memorable.'

Justine Shapiro, documentary filmmaker and host of Globetrekker

'Dave Lowe's new travelogue Sandwiches Should Never Taste Like Cow Crap is an exciting and refreshing read. He has a writing style that is all his own: fresh, personable, and peppered with his own humorous observations and antidotes. As I read the episodes, I felt less that I was reading travel book, and more that I was sitting with a good friend, listening to one hilarious travel tale after another. I could hardly wait to find what happened next.'

Wade Brackenbury, author of Yak Butter and Black Tea

'Sandwiches Should Never Taste Like Cow Crap wends its way as far off the tourist track as one could possibly imagine while maintaining a deliciously madcap, hair-raising yet often hilarious, sense of high adventure. Bless him for taking his readers where I suspect the majority of us would fear to tread.'

Jay Koren, author of The Company We Kept

'At last--a travel narrative that dispenses with movie-of-the-week reverence and gives us the straight dish. Travel, down and dirty, from amorous camels to AK-toting Khmer-Rouge. Stow your trays, get your seats in the upright position, and get ready for a helluva ride.'

Gregg Hurwitz, author of The Kill Clause

DAVE LOWE

SANDWICHES SHOULD NEVER TASTE LIKE COW CRAP

...and other lessons from life on the Lowe Road

ANTA PRESS

SANDWICHES SHOULD NEVER TASTE LIKE COW CRAP

13 Digit ISBN: 978-0-9797898-4-7
10 Digit ISBN: 0-9797898-4-2

Published by Manta Press

1117 Desert Lane, Suite 1966
Las Vegas, Nevada, USA
89102

Telephone: (702) 425-7845

www.mantapress.com

Library of Congress Control Number: 2007943790

Cover painting based on photo by Brandon Roy
(read 'Lightless in Little Tibet')

Cover design: Sebastian Serandrei

Cover photo: Jake Catlett

To **Wile E. Coyote** and his ability
to survive ACME anvils and exploding
ACME dynamite sticks, growing his fur
back again and again for his next adventure.

Contents

Contents

Djibouti, Ethiopia, Kenya and Tanzania

Nepal, India and the Maldives

Contents

Preface

Delhi Train Station, 2 p.m.

It's 45 degrees Celsius, I'm as slick with sweat as a greasy New York hot dog, and I've just been elbowed in the ribs by a woman in a canary yellow silk sari who then spat out a gooey wad of betel nut onto the pavement next to my feet.

A pair of small hands moves towards my shoe and I step back instinctively: a plop of dog shit misses my left foot by an inch and lands on the steaming cement, not far from the splattered betel nut.

Delhi Dog Shit Man looks up at me and grins evilly.

Maybe it was the brain melting heat, or the immense weight of my time spent in India, but instead of screaming, I just start laughing, patting Delhi Dog Shit Man on the back and say, 'Better luck next time dude.'

In the spirit of recycling, Delhi Dog Shit Man scrapes the crap off the sidewalk and lopes off into the crowd in search of other victims.

Sometimes the Travel Gods send you white sand beaches, swaying palm trees or mind expanding enlightenment that sends you on your way, reborn.

And at other times, they just send you the Delhi Dog Shit Man.

Sandwiches Should NEVER Taste Like Cow Crap serves up a tasty stew of lessons learned through adventures, disasters and situations – some good, some bad, some mundane and others unbelievable from Japan to Vietnam, Nepal to Tanzania, and Djibouti to the Maldives.

Looking back at the kaleidoscopic, psychedelic swirl of colorful locals, travelers, saints, sinners, madmen and madwomen encountered on the road, I can't help but wonder: Am I cursed? Could my size 13 shoes be spreading bad luck with every step I take? Or have I somehow landed on the Shit List of the Travel Gods, forever condemned to endure flightmare after disaster after catastrophe?

The jury is still out.

At 19, I never set out for Asia like a modern Marco Polo in search of Eastern riches, a fountain of youth, a white whale or a Holy Grail, I didn't go to find myself on top of the Himalayas, get a spiritual makeover and return home, transformed.

I did, however, learn on my very first trip to Asia that in the world of independent travelers, India loomed large as an Emerald City or Mecca or Las Vegas or Shangri-La, where redemption and rapture went hand in hand with stink and scams, a place down the rabbit hole where you simply had to venture, where you just had to go, in order to consider yourself a serious traveler.

In order to belong.

So on I traveled to South America and Africa and Australia with India always dancing in the distance, taunting me through the windshield.

In late 2004, I finally did it.

I gritted my teeth, plugged my nose and pulled open that trapdoor and fell down into that Universe that is India, and four months later, after enduring saddhus and saints and cows and chaos, I stepped out onto the tarmac in the Maldives, eyes wild, head spinning, and almost sank to my knees like a Pope to kiss the sun drenched and sterile asphalt right then and there.

Grateful to be free of that beast.

Having just scaled the steep sides of the independent travelers' Mt. Everest, I enjoyed the postcard perfect paradise that is the Maldives, thinking my Indian sojourn was over. Behind me. History. Hermetically sealed in my laptop's hard drive as tack-sharp photos and in my brain as vivid memories.

But it wasn't. On an island the day after Christmas I learned a lesson so far undiscovered. My journey had actually just begun. That's the beauty of travel: with the horizon always remaining where it is, every trip is never really quite over, and the next one is already underway. Travel is all around us, constant, wrapping us in it's fingers, never letting go.

And for this lesson, oh Travel Gods, I am most grateful.

After years on the road I now know these Travel Gods have a very keen sense of humor. Or at the very least, are very, very bored. What else can explain the cast of characters I have collided with, including a satanic customs agent in Japan, a horny camel called Raj in India, a demonic taxi driver in Ethiopia, a beaming Dalai Lama in India, or that woman in a burka who punched me in Djibouti?

Not to mention a sandwich filled with cow crap. (That wasn't served to me, scouts honor)

So. After scraping the dog crap off the sidewalk, did Delhi Dog Shit Man head to the nearest sandwich shop and surreptitiously serve it to some unsuspecting traveler in India, unfamiliar with the revenge some waiters love to inflict on hated customers?

Only the Travel Gods know for sure.

January 26th 2008

Japan & Korea

July 22nd, 1992
5:26 P.M.
Osaka, Japan
Pachinko Balls

Hey Annette.

You know that image of Japan, full of bowing people and bullet trains and kimonos and cherry blossoms and Zen temples?

Well, please replace it with images of body cavity searches and public humiliation and expiring travel documents and clubs everywhere you look.

How on earth could one of the world's most orderly countries throw me such curve balls? I've only been here three days, and what I have learned is that the tourist brochures don't tell you getting strip searched at customs can be followed by acute embarrassment and endless cultural rules that of course you don't know until you've broken them.

I'm sitting right now in this noodle joint in Kyoto that's popular with salarymen and office workers, though I can't hear a word they are saying, next door is one of those Pachinko parlors and the shiny balls clanging around are drowning out practically all noise with this crescendo that sounds like a metallic waterfall.

Which is kind of nice, especially the way I feel right now.

The cook/waiter/owner of this place practically ignored me (even though I bought the right ticket from the vending machine OUTSIDE on the street to pay for my food) when I walked in I had to sit patiently for like fifteen minutes before he would even look in my direction.

Welcome to Japan, Land of the Rising Confusion.

Whoa, Let me back up a bit.

As planned, I got the night ferry from Pusan to Osaka, that arrived right on schedule at 10.14 a.m. the next morning, with the crew standing on deck tapping their watches with white gloves.

I was pretty grateful to get off the boat to put the long, eerie overnight journey behind me. The ship was almost empty of passengers, and I was the only person booked into a room with fourteen bunks. Hours after I boarded the ship at sunset in Korea, I had wandered around the cavernous, rusty ship, looking for any signs of the living, but found only crew, who ignored me as they went about their work, orange jump-suited, clutching clipboards and walkie-talkies, chattering away in rapid fire Korean.

On one deck, I found a long line of black and white photos from Interpol pasted on the wall, and because I was bored to tears, studied their faces and read the details of their crimes as the ship's hull creaked and groaned all around me.

In Osaka port the next morning, orders in English, Japanese, Korean and Chinese were broadcast through the faint intercom for passengers to clear customs and immigration, so I dragged my bags down the gangplank and into the tiny customs hall, expecting a quick stamp and away I would go.

I was the only westerner there. I haven't traveled in Asia long, and this is something I am slowly getting used to. As I filled out the customs form, I heard a loud shout. I looked up to see a customs agent with arched, angry eyebrows, motioning for me to follow him.

'You! Over here! You!' he barked.

I picked up my bag and nervously took a step towards him. Did I fit the profile of one of those Interpol criminals I had seen on the ferry? The Japanese standing in front of me must have taken my look of confusion and mistranslated this into 'I'm a wanted axe murderer' because they took a step back as though I were a shiny package with a label that read, SENT FROM THE CHERNOBYL NUCLEAR REACTOR.

When I reached the white haired man I was then gruffly pushed into a small private room. With the door firmly closed to prying eyes, Fucking Evil Customs Guy (he had no name tag, and it seems like a perfect nickname) motioned to four of his inferiors to gather behind my back, forming a tight semicircle.

FECG proceeded to shout at me in broken English accusing me of using a tourist visa to teach English illegally in Japan. A shaky 'no' slipped from my lips and I pulled out my plane tickets and travelers checks to prove I was leaving Japan in four weeks. The bright blue logo of Korean Air stared up at me from the desk, which wasn't good, considering the bad blood between the two counties.

But it was the destination printed inside that made FECG's eyebrows arch in anger.

'Los Angeles?' he hissed.

'Los Angeles,' I whispered.

'LOS ANGELES?' FECG shouted, slamming his fist on the table. Remember those images a month ago, of men toting AK-47's on rooftops all over L.A.? Well, FECG seemed to remember them well.

Make that really well. I would have looked less suspicious if I had possessed a return ticket to Beirut for god sakes.

I swallowed. Hard.

I opened my mouth to speak, but nothing came out. With a snap of his fingers, FECG sent a minion off to photocopy my passport. The rest of the minions filled the space he had vacated, still breathing down my neck.

As the minutes passed, there were more shouts, more screams, and more fist pounding theatrics from FECG, mixed in with more insults and accusations:

> I was here to sell trinkets on the street in Tokyo.
> I was here to work in a backpacker bar in Roppongi.
> I was here to sell fake telephone cards from Iran.
> I was here to smuggle pirated goods from China.

FECG's animated eyebrows were almost vertical now. As calmly as I could, I sat in front of his desk deflecting each accusation with a bellowed 'NO' followed by swear words under my breath.

At any moment I expected my next port of call to be a dark, clammy jail cell. Japan was supposed to be the Land of the Rising Sun, not the bloody Hanoi Hilton. Months of planning and language practice were slipping through my fingers as this nightmare unfolded. A vision of that dank jail cell floated above my head as my documents were fingered and recorded in a thick ledger.

When the minion came back, FECG was still entering all the serial numbers of my student ID cards, traveler's checks, passport and drivers license into the ledger, muttering the numbers in Japanese under his breath. His eyebrows had stopped dancing.

For now.

'AMERICAN EXPRESS!' he screeched, holding up a check

to the light. A vein throbbed on his neck from all the shouting, and I prayed for it to pop.

'Student saved from jail sentence after customs agent's massive aneurism,' newspapers around the world would scream. 'Blood was spurting everywhere,' student says of his harrowing experience.

The minions shifted their feet restlessly.

Then FECG stood up and gave my suitcase a sharp kick. And another. And another. Spit was flying out of his mouth and a wisp of hair stood straight up to the ceiling from what I guessed to be from all the static electricity he had built up.

Did he expect drugs to fall out, like a piñata from the Midnight Express cast party?

With a sharp flick, he unzipped my suitcase and poked around, lifting up clothes and books and socks like they were contaminated with asbestos. Then he dumped all my things onto the floor, and I shouted at him to put them back.

'Shut up!' he yelled, and I was ordered to sit down and wait with a tremulous point of his stubby finger, the color of old ivory chopsticks.

Ten minutes later, with the contents of my suitcase artistically splattered all over the ground, nothing unusual had been found. Well, they did find some clothes that I had neglected to wash.

I was as guilty as charged for that. Absolutely guilty. No contest. I was beginning to think he was going to convict me for this traveler's crime and send me to prison for this inexcusable mistake.

Unhappy at the lack of drugs falling out of my bag, FECG gave my suitcase a final kick and then ordered me to stand up. And so I did, knees shaking.

And then, before I could even protest, he ordered the unthinkable.

Come again?

I was getting strip-searched.

Gulp.

With visions of jail cells dancing in my hypoglycemic, rapidly spinning head, I did as I was told. All sorts of things fly through your head at a time like this. Thoughts you would never imagine....

Is my underwear clean?
Should I invoke my Geneva Convention rights at this point?
Do I have B.O.?
Will I appear on a milk carton?
Are my friends going to see me on CNN?
Am I about to become an Amnesty International poster child?

With my jaws as firmly clamped shut as the Tin Man, FECG slipped on some gloves and then began a very thorough search, uh, rummaging and pilfering around in very private places, looking for drugs, or something else illicit, as my brain screamed: 'JUST HOW FAR AM I WILLING TO GO TO SEE JAPAN?'

I mean, Japan was getting a pretty good glimpse of me at this point and FECG was getting beyond second base. Way bloody beyond. We're talking parallel universe, black hole, sixteenth dimension kind of base here.

Well, at least things couldn't get any worse I thought. He wasn't finding anything illegal stuffed up some convenient orifice.

But then they did get worse. Biblically worse.

Suddenly the door swung open with a bang, and right in front of me was the immigration line I had so innocently been standing in just a few short minutes before. The orderly line of very prim Japanese ladies, who had watched in horror as this 'criminal' had been led away to the backroom suddenly got a lot more than they paid for, a view of some things they had probably never seen. As looks of shock and fascination swept the line with the speed of a college campus mononucleosis outbreak, and as hands flew to faces to cover gaping mouths, FECG continued to go about his job as though we were safely hidden behind a white hospital curtain.

I managed a weak smile to the crowd, a smile that a terrified gladiator might have flashed in Rome's coliseum before being devoured by a lion in front of thousands.

But then a minion broke ranks and kicked the door shut with a slam.

Floorshow's over.

Well, not quite. About thirty very slow seconds of examination continued and no condoms stuffed with cocaine were discovered. FECG's monstrous temper evaporated like a spring mist off Mt Fuji, and the English teacher/smuggler/barman allegations were dropped. In the middle of returning to the safety of my clothes, my passport was handed back, inked with a fresh entrance stamp, valid for ninety days.

'Welcome to Japan!' beamed FECG as though I were now his best friend. He gave me a friendly slap on the back and shook my hand up and down as I sheepishly pulled on my shoes.

When I snatched my passport back I wanted to slap him across the face and then punch his lights out.

I've got lots more to tell you, but give me some more time to process it all. I can say that everything I thought about Japan is wrong, and I'm a geisha hair's width away from taking the next ferry OUT of here. Before I make that decision, here are more reflections on fresh underwear:

1. Because it is an important linchpin that keeps that oh so thin fabric of society together.
2. Because you never know when some mad, white haired fucker is going to make you remove them.

If I do stay, I am going to keep score. Although it is a pretty dismal showing at the moment.

Japan 1, Dave 0.

OK, I'm leaving this restaurant before the sound of those crashing Pachinko balls drives me round the bend. But before I go, remember this lesson:

When going through Japanese customs, be sure to wear fresh underwear.

Love, Dave

July 24th, 1992
6:38 P.M.
Kyoto, Japan
Tani House

Japan 1, Dave 0.

You better believe I'm keeping score.

Hey, Annette.

Right after the Osaka Strip Show I boarded the free shuttle bus to the railway station. Rows of wide-eyed faces peered at me with pity when I slunk into my seat, my face still burning cherry blossom pink from embarrassment.

A stony silence settled inside the cabin. But then a twenty something Japanese woman spoke up. 'I'm terribly sorry for that terrible display of anger,' she said like a safety video on some robot airline. 'This is not the image of Japan we want you to come away with.'

Image? I think my first image of Japan was now lower than that of a roll of sushi squashed underneath the body of a belly flopped sumo wrestler at this point.

A few Japanese ladies sitting in the row behind me nodded in agreement but they could not make eye contact with me after the floorshow they had just seen.

It turned out Kumiko was also a traveler, she had just finished a two year trip around the world that had taken her to the wilds of Africa and the very tip of South America. She was on her way home to her small village, a stop on the train line between Osaka and Kyoto, and was visibly nervous about returning to the suffocating, traditional world she had left when she was twenty-five.

'My mother will be waiting for me at the station with my favorite dinner at home,' she said with a nervous smile. 'My father, too.'

The bus dropped us off at the foot of some tall escalators leading up to the platform. At the top, a massive, lit-up television screen displayed the entire Osaka rail network.

But only in Japanese.

As I stood underneath this shiny Bladerunneresque monstrosity, all blinking lights and octopus tentacled Kanji script, the white gloved, uniformed attendant behind the glass ignored me like I was a ghost.

I looked down at the buttons, even they were in Japanese, and as I fumbled for some coins, my knees were shaking and FECG's shouts were still echoing in my ears. Even though my passport stamp wasn't even dry, I already had another obstacle in my way.

Maybe Japan wasn't the place for me, I thought, maybe I should just turn right around and run screaming down the escalators then get the hell out of this place before something else happened. Like an ACME anvil dropped from the clear blue sky.

Land of the Rising Sun?

It was more like Land of the Rising Confusion.

Kumiko suddenly appeared at my side, pulled out the right coins, punched the right keys, and when the chewing gum sized ticket popped out from the machine, she validated it and then handed it over to me with a little flourish reserved for a crisp thousand-dollar bill.

Taking refuge under Kumiko's wing, I followed her to the platform and as we took our seats on the train, Kumiko's face froze.

It was nine o'clock. Rush hour. All around us were tired salarymen, exhausted looking high school students, sullen mothers pushing prams and stone faced elderly men reading newspapers that rustled like dead autumn leaves.

In the total silence of the train, Kumiko seemed disoriented, out of place, even though she was going home.

So she started talking.

'Returning, is difficult. Some Japanese think that people who have been away for a year aren't Japanese anymore. I was gone more than two years.'

The train pulled away and soon we were zooming through bland suburbs full of cubist apartment blocks, grey freeway overpasses and glassed-in office buildings. As the stations passed, one after the other, Kumiko kept on talking, hardly pausing for a breath, becoming more and more agitated, fingering the buttons on her jacket, smiling bravely at me from ear to ear.

I thought she was going to hyperventilate, pass out cold, leaving me alone to fend for myself in this Japan that was not at all what I had expected. Months of planning and language practice had already gone down the drain, and I felt exactly the same as that British college student I met in Taiwan who had spent six years studying Mandarin at Oxford.

It's not Chinese.

He had arrived in Taipei, cockily expecting to slip into local life with a snap, regaling the locals with his voluminous vocabulary, his grip on grammar, his complex conversation skills, get a girlfriend, get a job, and ultimately achieve every expatriate's dream to build a new life.

But three hours after arriving, he hit a brick wall.

On his first outing into the shopping districts of central Taipei, pedestrians and shopkeepers bluntly waved him off with a flick of their wrists, faces crumpling as he asked them question after question in Mandarin, getting angrier by the minute as his requests went unanswered.

'They must be from Hong Kong,' he said brightly, hoping it was their ignorance of the Mandarin dialect that was causing him to lose such a spectacular amount of face in such a spectacularly short amount of time. When he finally found a petite college student who spoke English, and who was definitely from Taipei, she wrinkled her forehead and asked, 'What language are you speaking? It's not Chinese.'

The look on the British guy's face was exactly like what I felt inside at this point, riding towards Kyoto. Bruised. Lost. Confused.

It's not Chinese.

What the hell was I doing here?

Snapping me out of my daydream was Kumiko, who kept on talking as she drew a map of the train station and the suburban subway lines in Kyoto. 'I am not yet married, but my parents are worried. I am twenty-seven years old.' Kumiko looked at me expectantly. Did she want me to get down on my knee and propose so she could return home with a husband? It wouldn't have surprised me.

Kumiko was becoming more Japanese by the second,

sitting more upright, smoothing out the creases in her jeans, re-arranging her backpack just so.

People were still giving her disapproving looks, seeing her talking to a foreigner in fluent English and nursing a battered backpack, suddenly, gone was the hippie traveler I had seen on the ferry. In her place was a woman in her late twenties, face set stoically, her hair just so, shoes placed firmly on the floor in front of her, back straight.

It was a fascinating transformation.

Then, an announcement was broadcast through the train compartment, Kumiko stopped drawing, and her back stiffened. The train was about to arrive in Kumiko's hometown and familiar houses were now flashing past the windows. She had expected a few more minutes of freedom before colliding full speed back into a life she had left behind.

The train screeched to a halt on the tracks. Kumiko gasped. Her parents, grey haired, dressed soberly in dark blue sweaters and grey slacks, were standing on the platform right outside the window.

Kumiko quickly handed me the map, stood up, fumbled with her large bag and gingerly stepped over the gap between the train and the platform, from her new life and back into the old one. At the last moment, Kumiko turned around, smiled, and said in a whisper, 'Enjoy Japan,' and then she disappeared into the summer light where her parents were waiting to take her home.

I had been in Japan less than two hours at this point, and if it hadn't been for Kumiko, I would have turned right round and gone back to Korea. Hell, my underwear was still in an awful twist from pulling them back on so fast, but with the proper looking people sitting all around me, it didn't seem appropriate to readjust them.

In an attitude I was getting used to quickly in Japan, I sat there in my twisted underwear, resisting the urge to shift for comfort and relief.

Man was it hard.

Was this the secret to Japanese culture? Were all these people around me sitting in twisted, uncomfortable underwear, yearning to breathe free?

I had four weeks to find out.

Thanks to Kumiko's well drawn map, complete with several smiley faces that she had sketched in the margins to cheer me up, I had an easy time navigating through the Kyoto train station and onto a subway line out to the northern suburbs where a short walk down a quiet, tidy street brought me to Tani House, recommended by the Lonely Planet as the best place to stay in the city.

Let me digress about Lonely Planet.

Until a month before I left for my first trip to Asia, I had never heard of it, and the in-the-know student who had recommended this 'miracle' guidebook looked at me strangely when the name did not ring a bell.

In the universe of independent travelers, it seemed, knowing what Lonely Planet was determined if you were part of The Tribe or not. In other words, it also confirmed if you did, or didn't, speak the language of travel correctly.

It isn't Chinese.

Clearly, by the look of her wrinkled lips, I was the pimply new kid on the block with skinny legs waiting to get picked for the football team, chosen last because no one else wanted him.

And that was my introduction to Lonely Planet.

It gave a breezy recommendation to Tani House as a good place to stay, and like all independent minded travelers/sheep everywhere, I followed the map to the right street where Tani House was located.

And it was there where I abruptly slammed straight into a Japanese institution that I had heard spoken about only in whispers amongst travelers.

The Tatami Dragon Lady.

I had been warned that all over Japan that these Dragon Ladies ran ryokans and other guesthouses for foreigners, and they ran tight ships. Some really tight ships. Often serving as accommodation for English teachers, life as a conscript under a sadistic drill sergeant was meant to be easier than living with these women, who looked at it as their cultural duty to not only introduce Japan to foreign guests, but often to rub their noses in their inability to reach the high standards of social mores their country required.

Mrs. Tani was a large woman by Japanese standards, and she welcomed me into her two story wooden home wearing a blue yukata robe pulled around her ample waist. (If you can picture a baby from the resulting union between a sumo wrestler and a third grade Sunday school teacher, you'll have a perfect image of Mrs. Tani)

She wasted no time in finding out how I had heard of her, or her home, the steady stream of Lonely Planet readers seemed to keep her house full most of the time, making for a pretty easy existence. And for Mrs. Tani, the steady flow of money through her front door from a book published half way around the world suited her fine.

Just fine in fact.

As soon as I put my bag down, Mrs. Tani let out a wail.

'NO SHOES IN MY HOUSE!'

Japan 2, Dave 0.

To the strains of a John Denver song playing in the background, Mrs.Tani explained the rules in her house as she gave me a tour.

There was a communal room for women and a communal room for men, she told me sternly, and a single room rented out to married couples only. The garden was a simple, gravel patch surrounded on all sides by a wall of thick, jade-green bamboo that clattered together like chopsticks whenever the wind blew.

'Please use the correct tatami room. Don't go into ladies tatami room. Also, use the bathroom on the second floor, not downstairs. That is for my husband and I only,' she ordered with a shudder, dreading the thought of some barbarian fouling up her pristine bath water.

Because Mr. Tani spoke not a word of English, he happily ignored most of the guests in his house. He was a slight, tiny man, who looked even smaller next to his massive wife, giving them a distinct Boris and Natasha quality.

Most days he was found sprawled on the downstairs tatami room, reading a newspaper and slurping up a bowl of soup. Mrs. Tani handled all the money in the house, and stuffed each day's rate of one thousand Yen from each guest into a neat little fold of her blue yukata robe with stubby, sweaty fingers.

'I am here every day, except Tuesdays, when I go to Osaka

to visit my sister, who lives there with her family. If you have questions, please ask me Monday night, because the house is empty all day Tuesday.' And with that, Mrs. Tani gave me a lumpy pillow, a white duvet, and a map of Kyoto and then warned me never to ring the bell after eleven p.m.

'Tani House is locked till six a.m.,' she said soberly.

I carried my shoes upstairs when Mrs. Tani let out a terrific, ear splitting shriek.

'Remember, no shoes in my house! Put shoes on outside!'

Japan 3, Dave 0.

My mistake earned me a repeated, and heated, explanation of the rules at Tani House. I felt like an ant as she went through her spiel yet again, and when I nodded my head, bent in shame and knees still clattering after that morning's experience with FECG, I was released on my own recognisanse to go and explore.

I was finally free.

With most of Kyoto's temples spread out along the outer edges of the valley, it was a long walk, but the sky was clear and the weather was good. And then, I met another sub species of the Japan resident, the Know It All English Teacher, who treated me like a baby once she knew she had been in Asia a full month longer than I. Her name was Helen, she came from New Zealand and had lived in Kyoto for all of three months.

Ah, the pecking order among expatriates. Invariably this is the first question any foreigner will ask you in Japan, or anywhere in Asia: 'How long have you been here?'

I hate it.

As a virtual virgin to travel in Asia, with only two months under my belt, it is always earning me The Lecture, the annoyingly long talk expatriates give you to convince themselves that they are superior to you through the simple fact that their passport has an older visa/entry stamp than yours. A smug Brit told me in China, 'Some time in a third world country like India would do you a lot of good.'

Thanks buddy. Thanks very much.

Being under twenty years of age doesn't help either. An Australian girl, when she heard how old I was, snapped, 'Nineteen? Huh! I know what I was like when I was nineteen. Bloody stupid. And you're a Yank too. Why the bloody hell do you say 'power outage' when it's a fucking blackout?' she fumed, referring to the Ameri-centric textbooks she was forced to teach with.

Anyway, back to Helen. Though she spoke only ten words of Japanese, she thought she had Japanese culture down cold.

'As a westerner, we can do anything here,' she said to me imperiously, stopping to pick a beautiful flower, the only problem was, the flower was in a pot sitting on a porch in front of some unsuspecting housewife's home.

'I mean, people are so polite here, they will never speak up against you.' She twirled the flower around and placed it behind her ear and gave me a smile reserved for small children.

I didn't say anything. Then Helen walked right up to a wall outside a convenience store, plastered with advertisements.

Many American actors/singers/sports stars make millions of dollars from goofy advertisements seen only in Japan. Michael Jordan for a dishwashing liquid, Joe Montana for an instant coffee, that sort of thing. Taped up outside this convenience store was none other than Arnold Schwarzenegger himself, selling a brand of soy sauce. The Terminator was wearing a hat that was actually a bottle cap.

To my horror, Helen walked right up and ripped down the Schwarzenegger sign and said that no one would care anyway because Japanese were so polite, and on and on she went until I wanted to turn her in to FECG for immediate deportation back to Auckland, pronto.

That would flip the traveler pecking order right on it's head.

As we walked away a window flew open and a matronly grandmother scowled at me, motioning to the blank space that now gaped on her wall. The angry expression flooding her face showed clearly she believed me to be the ripping suspect, but my lame shrug left her unconvinced of my innocence. She scrunched up her face and slammed the window.

Japan 4, Dave 0.

When I learned Helen had to run back home and get ready for her evening lessons at a cram school across town, I was relieved, finally able to ditch her. She wrote out her address and then said in a patronizing tone, 'Don't worry, you'll understand Japan eventually,' and with that she patted my arm like a mother reassuring her child that their first summer camp would be an exotic adventure.

Later that evening, after I had walked my feet flat, I slipped into the bright Tomato convenience store around the corner from Tani House. As I paid for some snacks the woman behind the counter bowed deeply to me and uttered some long sentence of thanks in Japanese. I bowed awkwardly, took my change and left.

It was only when I had crossed the street that I realized I hadn't bought an international phone card, and instead of going back across the street to Tomato, I found another neon-bright convenience store right in front of me called Force.

No sooner had I paid for the phone card at Force, when so long a flood of complements and bowing proceeded that I wondered if the woman was a humanoid robot. No, she was just the mother of the family that had just opened this store right across from Tomato, in direct competition. Before I left, she reminded me by pointing to the wall that Force was open till ten p.m., a full hour later than Tomato. With that, I smiled, bowed deeply, and the woman gave me a broad smile.

Had I actually done some thing correctly in the Land of Rising Confusion?

Japan 4, Dave 1.

I'm now sitting here in the garden at Tani House, alone, listening to the wind blow through the bamboo in the garden. It is a distinctly 'Japanese' sound, the bare trunks are clattering together and rubbing off the green skin, the gravel is covered in bark shed from the bamboo, and there is a small stream trickling near my feet.

The distinctly 'un' Japanese sound I am also hearing is John Denver playing from inside the house.

Pure evil.

I have not decided what I am going to do yet, stay or go back to Pusan. The next letter you get may be from Korea.

Love, Dave

July 28th, 1992
10:32 P.M.
Kyoto, Japan
The Disgruntled Expatriate Club

Hey Annette,

OK. I'm staying.

Sometimes revenge can come through an innovative use of cat hair, at other times it can come via the unlikely assistance of a kind, white haired lady.

Either way, it's always sweet.

Before I go into the details, a little more about Tani House.

It is a Tuesday and most of the residents are teaching so it is as quiet as a graveyard. Early this morning Mrs. Tani stuck her head in the tatami room and announced, 'Today I go to Osaka. Please pay for your rooms now.'

So each of us pulled out a one thousand Yen note and handed them over to the Tatami Dragon Lady. She then stuffed these bills inside a small pocket stitched into her blue yukata, and then she looked at me.

'No men in women's tatami,' she growled, pointing to the door.

Japan 5, Dave 1.

And with that the Tatami Dragon Lady left her house for Osaka.

As soon as she was gone I snuck back into the Ladies tatami room and hung out with Judy, the blonde American divorcee cycling around Japan who was lying on the floor reading a book.

'Hey Judy, are you going out today?' I asked her.

She shook her head. Kerstin, a Danish exchange student who was traveling for a month before she headed home to Copenhagen after living in Osaka for a year, also shook her head. They looked at each other and giggled.

Private joke, I thought.

OK, back to my Japan Rail Pass and the kind, white haired lady.

Yesterday afternoon I hopped on a suburban train to Nara, Japan's ancient capital, where I went to the JR office to validate my Japan Rail Pass. When I got to the front of the line, the girl looked at me blankly and pushed the ticket back at me.

'Expired,' she said softly, as though the pass was a cat that had died.

'What?'

'Japan Rail Pass expired. You can't use it.' She looked at me and then down at her hands.

'It was bought in April,' I said, remembering that the passes were valid for one year.

'Ninety days,' she said, pulling out a new brochure printed in English.

There, about halfway down the page, the words were printed:

Japan Rail passes will only be valid for ninety days after purchase. After ninety days, no refund will be given, and no responsibility taken by Japan Rail. Thank you.

My jaw dropped. My entire trip to Japan had been built around this pass, train travel is outrageously expensive in this country and there was no way I was going to see any part of Japan with the kind of budget I had.

Suddenly I wished I had never met Kumiko and just took the next ferry back to Korea, China, or Russia; anywhere but this place. Japan was nothing like I had expected, and it was getting worse by the hour.

'Where is the manager?' I asked, shaking with rage.

The girl reluctantly got up and walked over to a middle-aged man with glasses. He looked over at me, frowned, and walked over to the desk where I was sitting.

My stomach fell.

If there is one thing I am learning very very quickly in Japan, it is that out of all the clubs that rule here, the Suburban Mom's Club and especially the Middle Aged Salary Man's Club was never going to admit me as a member. (The Elderly Grandmother's Club was a different story. More on that later)

And right in front of me was not only a card-carrying member of the Middle Aged Salaryman's Club, but judging by the sour expression molded onto his wrinkled face, he was a lifetime member, too.

And now Middle Aged Man (or MAM, for short) was standing in front of me, more than happy for the opportunity to drop a shiny guillotine to slice off my head, fuck up my trip, and send me packing back to my home country. Wherever that was.

MAM wouldn't even touch my Japan Rail Pass, lest I contaminate him with my unacceptable-ness.

Whatever. Let's get this over with buddy, so you can gloat over my humiliation, and I can get on with my life.

Before MAM even opened his mouth, I knew exactly what was going to happen next.

'Sir, this pass is not valid,' MAM said, as his subordinate looked at a convenient place between her toes.

I tried a short phrase of Japanese, but it came out so garbled I think I told him to go climb Mt. Fuji then jump off the top of it. As soon as MAM heard these mangled words, he shrunk back in horror.

Japan 6, Dave 1.

A last ditch effort was in order here, a sort of kamikaze, contract signed in blood kind of thing.

'But when I bought this pass, the validity was one year,' I protested, waving the now useless piece of paper like a white flag of surrender.

'Not valid,' MAM repeated with a just a hint of a smile. He bowed and walked back to his desk. There, MAM picked up the phone and dialed a number, chattering away as though I no longer existed.

Somewhere in Osaka, FECG was not laughing. Oh no, he was rolling around on the floor of the Osaka port, white hair

33

pointing into the air, face crumpled in a guffaw so boisterous even his minions were probably cracking smiles.

The girl continued to bore a hole with her ashamed eyes between her toes, and without another word, lifted her arm to signal the next customer to her desk, case closed.

Japan 7, Dave 1.

With my trip to Japan sinking fast, I went to Nara Park where I ate a cheap bento box lunch, and to lick my deep wounds. In Japan, it seemed, epic disasters seemed to follow me like a dark cloud, a faithful dog. (Make that a rabid, mangy, flea bitten Cujo to be exact)

As I dug into the rice ruefully with my chopsticks, a young teacher passed in front of me chirping cheerfully into a megaphone, trailed by three-dozen ten year-olds, all members of the Young Children's Club.

The teacher stopped walking, looked over and gave me a sharp, shocked look. Did I have blood on my face, I wondered, feeling my skin for a hot dripping liquid.

But she was looking into my lap, not at my face.

I looked down - I had absently pushed my chopsticks into the rice and I remembered too late that this symbolized incense in a funerary bowl. I yanked the chopsticks out, but the look of derision on the teacher's face all but confirmed my careless blunder.

Japan 8, Dave 1.

Forget bull in a china shop, I was coming to the rather shaky conclusion that I was like a fire-breathing dragon in a pyrotechnics factory. What else could possibly go wrong at this point?

Then the children broke out of their perfect lines and ran screaming around the grass, where dozens of the famous Nara deer munched in peace. Fearful at first, a few bold boys came up to me and saluted, staring at my half finished lunch. Had the gaijin really eaten it with chopsticks? One by one they gathered closer, making whispered comments until a sharp reprimand from the smile-starved teacher brought them back under her command.

But not for long, the boldest boy ran off to harass a male deer, poking it with a stick and lifting his arms over his head and shrieking bloody murder. The male deer ignored him for about a minute. Then, lowering its head and pawing the dust, the beast charged forward and crashed full force into the boy's chest. It hit him with just enough strength to knock the wind out of him and send him screaming back to his teacher.

When the teacher caught me laughing, she shot me the meanest, coldest look that even FECG probably couldn't have mustered.

Japan 9, Dave 1.

Fire-breathing dragon indeed.

That night the foreign residents of Tani House were gathered all around me in the small tatami room for women, where I was getting plenty of sympathy about my situation.

Most of them were long term residents, either working in bars or teaching in Japan and were therefore forbidden from traveling on Japan Rail Passes. But Maureen, the Irish yoga teacher who had openly admitted to using her blonde hair to get exactly what she wanted from Japan, immediately offered to have some Shinkansen tickets issued for herself, which she would hand over to me; they weren't printed with names on them, though they came with a warning.

'These tickets would be just for destinations south of Tokyo,' she said, 'because the train station attendants never cross check passports with Japan Rail tickets, but in Tokyo, and further north, you'll never get past them.'

Reassured that all was not lost, that at least I might get to see southern Japan, I was really nervous about ripping off the Japan Rail System and getting into even deeper trouble, maybe earning me a rematch with FECG.

Because the last thing I wanted was a Mr. Fix on my ass.

I thanked Maureen and said I'd get back to her.

Not a moment later Mrs. Tani herself came into the room herself, then shot her finger in my direction.

'Sit on the floor,' she ordered.

I looked down and realized I was not sitting on a bench but her dining room table. Oops.

With that, Mrs. Tani stormed out, closing the paper screen door behind her with a Godzilla slam.

Japan 10, Dave 1.

At nine p.m. the residents of Tani House went out to a bar frequented by English teachers, who filled us in on their lives as 'human computers,' the way one teacher from Long Island put it. It was there, in the smoky haze of that tiny, closet-sized bar where the members of the Disgruntled Expatriate Club gathered each week to let off steam about the country and culture that simultaneously overcompensated them with large salaries and at the same time denied them human rights that even captured prisoners were granted under international agreements.

'You fill one bucket with gold, and the other with shit,' someone told me.

The Disgruntled Expatriate Club did not restrict its memberships on the basis of gender, age, or profession like other clubs in Japan; like a cult, all were welcome to join. All you had to have was some experience that had happened to you in Japan that proved you were a second-class citizen.

'Man, they just make me stand in the corner all day and order me to show them pronunciation techniques with my tongue,' a teacher wheezed, spreading boozy fumes in my direction.

'I heard some foreigner was sent to the vet when he was sick,' remarked another.

'Yeah, when I go to the public baths I might as well be a gorilla by the looks I get,' shouted someone else.

A few drunken salarymen were there too, tongues and

ties loosened by too much alcohol, attracted by the hopes of scoring with a foreign girl. Their reserve, stripped away by the cover of darkness and a belly full of Asahi beer, still had gotten them nowhere, and though they were dancing around the room, they nervously slurred into our ears that they were really worried their dicks were too small to ever get a western girl to go to bed with them.

But no sooner had the Disgruntled Expatriate Club heard of my strip search in the port of Osaka, followed by the problem with my Japan Rail Pass, all in less than forty eight hours, I became their instant poster child, their most revered saint, a sort of Jesus figure to this international gang.

And they all had advice on what to do.

'Just go home,' snarled an Irishman, 'Just go the fuck home. Forget Japan even existed.'

'No, just take the buses, they are cheaper than the trains, though still expensive, but you will get to see something,' offered a Canadian.

It was a while later when a British guy, sober, sitting on a bar stool in the corner, had an idea.

'Just get it re-issued in the Kyoto Tourism Office. They are staffed by these little old grandmas who love foreigners. They bend over backwards for travelers there, mate, and then get your trip back on track. Trust me.'

And that's where that kind, white haired lady stepped in.

So the next morning I marched into the Tourism Information Center located in the main railway station and expected a big fight.

But instead, within five minutes, I was standing outside holding a freshly reissued Japan Rail Pass in my hands. All thanks to the Elderly Grandmothers Club.

I was learning that despite cultural mistakes and my neck snapping height, I had earned instant and honorary member status with the Elderly Grandmothers Club, who doted on me everywhere with broad, toothless grins, reaching out for my arm as we stepped off crowded trains, even helping me survive the manic street crossings they navigated with ease. Amidst the swirling currents of modern, urban Japan, they paused to question me on how I found their country, asked if I could eat with chopsticks, and inquired whether I had seen

Mt. Fuji yet.

And as luck would have it, Tourism Information Centers were the beat for many of these women, including a kind white haired woman behind the counter who, upon hearing my story, took pity on me, printed a new Japan Rail Pass on the spot, no questions asked. She didn't even want to see my passport.

Japan was on.

Instead of validating it right then and there, I hopped on the first suburban train I could catch back to Nara, where as luck would have it, I sat down right in the same spot as the day before. If I was going to continue my cult status as a reluctant hero amongst the Disgruntled Expatriates Club, this was where I was going to do it.

When the girl looked up from behind the counter and saw me slide my new rail pass across the table at her, she looked as though she wanted to cry. But when she saw with her own eyes it was a completely new piece of paper stamped in the right places, she reluctantly handed me a form that needed to be filled out.

Before I had gotten even halfway down the page, I detected a second presence in front of me.

It was Middle Aged Man.

MAM was back.

He spat out a rapid-fire sentence that made the girl stand up and drop her head to her chest. He snatched up my new Rail Pass, looked at me, and then looked at the Rail Pass again, aghast.

A grin slipped out of my lips.

Then, MAM picked up a phone and made a call while I sat there, patiently waiting as the girl stood there with her head hung to her chest.

Two minutes later, after a few long pauses, some rapid fire Japanese, and then a few more pauses, MAM replaced the phone, whispered something to the girl, and he handed the paper back to her. She then gave it back to me. MAM slunk back to his desk like a defeated jackal without another word.

I almost felt sorry for him. I'm sure his twisted underwear was riding up and feeling pretty uncomfortable at this point.

But I didn't feel sorry for him for long.

With my small victory I had permanently secured my place as a principal God to be forever worshipped by the

Disgruntled Expatriate Club. Just wait till the gang hears about this, I thought to myself as I stood up, bowed, and left.

Japan 10, Dave 2.

Sometimes Annette, revenge can be sweet, very sweet, and can be accomplished with the most unlikely of allies. That little old lady was one woman whose knickers weren't in a twist at all.

My trip is back on, and I'm off tomorrow on a day trip to Osaka, then up north to Tokyo and beyond: Suruga Bay, Mt. Fuji, Nikko, etc.

I'm glad I didn't run screaming back to that ferry and retreat to Korea. Don't wait for that letter in the mail, because:

You will never be sent an invitation to join the Middle Aged SalaryMan Club.

Love, Dave

July 31st, 1992
2:32 P.M.
Nikko, Japan
Tatami Dragon Lady II

Hey Annette,

Hello from Tokyo.

I'm in Harajuku, this mad neighborhood where all the Japanese schoolgirls go when they want to let their hair down. (Or untangle knots in twisted underwear)

But even here amidst the I'm-cooler-than-you vibe, mixed in amongst the plaid Catholic schoolgirl chic, gothic hairstyles, and impossibly high-heeled shoes there is a club like atmosphere. Girls smile and flash harmless peace signs to photographers, who, if they were in central London, would receive the middle finger if they even aimed their camera in the direction of a punk.

It's no coincidence that most of the girls are wearing secondhand school uniforms from St. Mary's Prep school, fitting in even as they let go of their frustrations with their tightly wound culture.

And everywhere I have been in Tokyo confirms the clubs in this country. No matter where I go I am being judged, accepted, rejected and denied entry to the numerous, tightly knit clubs that rule Japan from childhood to senior citizenhood. The principal ones were:

The Children's Club thought I was freakish, free entertainment,

The Teenage Boys Club worshipped me like a Hollywood actor,

The Teenage Girls Club thought I was the perfect addition to their albums,

The Suburban Mom Club viewed me as a bad influence on their kids.

I've told you about the toughest of them all, the Middle Aged Salaryman Club. Though I had scored one delicious victory in Nara against this suit and tie brotherhood, Tokyo seems to be crawling with members. On subways, while waiting for buses, in department stores, and eating in small restaurants, the ranks of their prolific members view me with heavy suspicion, noses wrinkled, eyebrows arched, a hint of fear mixed with a twinge of envy.

No matter what I do, however many Japanese phrases I memorize, or how many bows I perfectly executed, I have just about given up. The Middle Aged Salaryman Club was a group that I was never to see eye to eye with.

OK, back to my trip. With my Japan Rail Pass back on again, I was off, using Tani House in Kyoto as a convenient, centrally located base, I've been leaving on the first Shinkansen train each morning and returning on the last Shinkansen each night, shooting down to Osaka, up to Tokyo, the Izu Peninsula, even over to Shikoku island.

And every night I have been getting home before Mrs. Tani turned the key and locked her house each night at eleven p.m.

However, in typical Dave fashion, there have been a few close calls.

Two nights ago I had to run top speed from the train station, skidding around corners (almost colliding with some drunken salarymen who pointed at me and cackled with laughter before throwing up in a gutter) to catch the last subway car to Mrs. Tani's neighborhood. If I had missed the last train, it would have been a six thousand Yen cab ride or a two hour walk.

Hey, almost forgot. I can update you on two wars, the first being the one between Mr. and Mrs. Tani and the second being the one between Tomato and Force, the two convenience stores around the corner from her house.

You're going to love both of them.

A piece of free rice paper candy is now being handed out after each purchase at Force, and Tomato fought back and is now giving two. Then free phone cards followed, and then even cash back. The residents of Tani House are comparing all the loot and perks they are getting out of this weird convenience store war. My money's on Tomato as emerging the winner, but Judy, who I told you about, thinks it is going to be Force.

Hard to believe, but I am a week deeper into my trip through Japan and I actually don't have any fresh disasters to report. I can't add any more points to my side of the keeping score thing, I have been holding my own as of late, picking up some Japanese and even beginning to inch my way up the expatriate ladder. I met a couple of teachers who have been in Japan only a week. Boy did I feel like giving back what I had been given by other expats, but I didn't.

And then there is the civil war between Mr. and Mrs. Tani.

According to the residents of the house, Mr. and Mrs. Tani have been having daily afternoon feuds allowing no one time for a quiet nap. Apparently it begins with an intense volley of Japanese swear words, always from downstairs of course, which is followed by chopsticks and other kitchen utensils being hurled against the walls. The problem this causes, is that the staircase out of the house is blocked by flying objects, some of them sharp. Maureen from Ireland compares it to the almost clockwork eruptions of the volcano she visited in Kagoshima, in southern Japan.

'The eruption only lasts an hour, but you can set your watch by it, just like the fights between the Tanis,' she said in her classic Irish brogue.

Though I wasn't there for their afternoon brawls, one evening things were just a bit different. I was returning home at around seven p.m. from a long trip south to Himeji castle. As soon as I turned left down the alley where Tani House is located, tucked behind three other suburban homes, from one hundred meters away I could already hear the shouts from Mr. and Mrs. Tani. After I pulled off my shoes and slipped upstairs, I asked Judy for an update.

'Not much, just the usual,' she said with a laugh and pointing to downstairs with her finger. 'Hey did you feel the earthquake today?'

'No,' I said, 'what time was it at?'

'Five thirty,' Judy said, looking at her watch. 'The whole house was going back and forth. The bamboo made the coolest sound, and Mr. and Mrs. Tani actually stopped screaming at each other for thirty seconds.'

'Now that is something I wish I had seen!' I started to laugh, but stopped abruptly as Mrs. Tani appeared in the doorway to the room, clad as always in her blue yukata. She shot me a look befitting every self respecting Tatami Dragon Lady.

'No men in women's tatami room!' she spat out as though her mouth was full of spicy wasabi.

Japan 11, Dave 2.

I'm on my way back to Osaka after visiting Nikko, the place that is famous for three monkeys carved on a temple frieze in the 'see no evil, hear no evil, speak no evil' pose.

It was my first extended trip north beyond Tokyo, and I can now say that Lonely Planet listings should come with a warning label. You can get seriously burned.

I wound up an invited guest of Mrs. Tani's slim, petite, evil twin sister who also ran a ryokan for foreigners there, and if I knew then what I know now, I would gratefully have returned to the port of Osaka for a rematch with FECG instead of being yet another guest of a Tatami Dragon Lady.

Honest.

The Shinkansen train left Kyoto at exactly 9.48 a.m. and glided smoothly past the other shiny blue and white bullet trains about to whiz off to points south and north in Japan. Two hours later we passed Mt. Fuji, the snow capped cone free of clouds, piercing the clear blue sky.

With time to kill in Tokyo station between trains, I got in line behind some sober looking Japanese ladies and waited my turn to order a bento box lunch for the next leg of my journey.

At the front of the line was an Australian man absolutely furious at the demure salesgirl who was wrapping his tiny sandwich in two layers of paper, a layer of plastic, another layer of paper before placing it all in a huge crinkly plastic bag that could have easily carried a bushel of potatoes.

He watched her angrily, his eyes bulging, and then he

43

whirled around, eyes wild, and slapped his head as his eyes locked with mine. Instantly recognizing a possible member of the Disgruntled Expatriates Club, he bellowed, 'They are killing the planet!' before he threw up his hands in disgust.

After dumping some Yen coins on the counter, he grabbed his lunch and flew out the door. The girl just smiled sweetly and then called out the next number in a warbly, high-pitched voice like a hostess in an airline safety video.

Back in Tokyo station, I quickly got lost in the cavernous space, feeling like a large rock in the middle of a violent white water current of commuters that included young school children, exhausted looking salarymen and matronly grandmothers zooming around me, faces blank and sober as they went about their way, making no eye contact at all.

I felt invisible.

With no policeman or information booth in sight, I looked around for someone to ask for help. There were no teenagers who I had learned were the most likely to understand my rapid English (and who would not run off in panic when approached by a foreigner so tall he seemed to scrape the ceiling) so I picked out my next best target, a late middle-aged woman who I knew zealously took English classes for fun.

The Late Middle Aged Women's Club was one step below the Elderly Grandmother's Club, and though I was not always granted honorary membership, at least I knew if I was lost in a dark alley at two in the morning, about to have a digit from my pinky chopped off by a group of Yakuza gangsters, a member of the Late Middle Aged Woman's Club could be stopped, asked for directions on how to escape from those Yakuza gangsters, (while she calmly adjusted her British looking purse on her arm to hang just so) I would be quickly pointed in the right direction, save my pinky from decapitation and my ass as well. Then the woman would then walk off, her sensible shoes clicking on the cement, later alligator.

The Late Middle Aged Women's Club was way cooler than they looked.

It didn't take long to find one. There, up ahead of me was a woman of the right age with three dead giveaways: a conservative hairstyle, black nurses shoes, and a handbag hung over her forearm in a way not unfamiliar to Queen Elizabeth II.

I stepped cautiously towards this savior, careful not to

frighten her.

'Sumimasen?'

Though the woman literally jumped a foot off the ground, eyes bulging, she did regain her composure (along with her handbag, which jumped into the air right along with her) very quickly, and once she was on solid ground again, replied to my question.

'Hai, dozo.'

I smiled my best I'm-not-a-serial-killer smile, then showed her my ticket which was printed with the platform number. She leaned forward, read the number under her breath, then turned around and pointed in the right direction with the primness and confidence of an experienced teacher.

The Late Middle Aged Women Club to the rescue once more.

'Arigato gozaimus,' I said with a big smile and a deep bow.

'Hai, domo,' she replied as she bowed back to me again and again as I picked up my bags and went on my way.

Japan 11, Dave 3.

Like a virus, the conformity I encountered everywhere in Japan was catching, just like that song by The Vapors. Even after only a few days, I found my brain self-censoring, self-correcting, self-reprimanding, like:

How to stand correctly in line waiting for a bullet train on a train station platform,
How to hand money to sales people with the perfect bow,
How to remove my size thirteen shoes at a temple entrance without looking like a barbarian.

So once I was on the right platform, waiting for the 1.09 p.m. Shinkansen to Utsunomiya, 1.09 p.m. had come and gone, it was now 1.13, and I looked at my watch to see if it had stopped. Ahead of me some salarymen were scowling at their watches too, unhappy to be sharing their train with a foreigner who was:

Not an English teacher
Not an Iranian selling fake phone cards
Not a barman working in Roppongi
Not selling smuggled Chinese goods from Shanghai

Their eyes narrowed. Just where did this foreigner fit, anyway? Before they had time to find the answer, an American businessman a few meters away threw up his hands, recognized me (I was getting used to this) as a member of the Disgruntled Expatriate Club, and shouted in a Texas drawl, 'Oh, come on! This is bullshit!'

Apparently, if you are a member of the Disgruntled Expatriate Club, this gives you carte blanche to walk up to any suspected member and introduce yourself.

Roger was well aware of this rule.

Sticking out his hand he said, 'Hi, I'm Roger. Roger Frankston. I've been living here in Tokyo for a while now. You traveling in this country? Groovy.'

Apparently being a member of the Disgruntled Expatriate Club also grants you the ability to invade other members' personal space and grab at their belongings.

Mi casa es su casa, that sort of thing.

Roger snatched my train ticket and said, 'Oh, you're in the same car as mine, but different row. No problem, Japanese are so polite, they won't ever get angry if you're sitting in their seat.'

I had heard that story before.

Before I could protest our train arrived and my new friend took me to his seat and we sat down. When you weren't ignored by other foreigners, they pulled you in close (claustrophobically close) eager for a conversation at New York speed where the only topic was Japan itself. Complaints spewed continuously and furiously as expatriates related in mind numbing detail the latest inconvenience they had experienced or cultural clash they has endured. And for long-term residents, telling you their life story was de rigueur.

Roger had been in Japan seven years he explained, was an ex-hippie, now married to a Japanese woman, with whom he had a two-year old daughter. Developing a cheap international telephone service for expats in a land where he barely spoke the language had nearly cost him his marriage, his sanity, and his savings, he was now relying on loans from his Japanese in-laws as a way to keep the creditors away and his business afloat.

'I'm about six inches away from dying from karoshi, death from overwork,' he lamented.

The train pulled away, but not before Roger's correct seatmate arrived. Pointing to my seat and pecking his ticket with an angry finger was another member of the Middle Aged Salaryman Club, mouth sewn closed with contempt. Roger uttered some garbled Japanese words, the man bowed and then walked away. 'Told him you were a work colleague and we needed to discuss business,' he said.

Roger began talking at bullet train speed, revving up faster and faster, able to converse freely in English for the first time in months. I was learning that there is a new kind of black hole in the universe. It's located not far from these expat's mouths.

'My wife doesn't like foreigners, and my in-laws don't speak English, so I don't get out too much,' he said, looking at the Tokyo suburbs fly past the window as the words flew from his mouth like frantic bats escaping a cave at dusk.

Then, he dropped a bomb.

'Hey, why don't you stay here and work with me and my wife? We could use a white face in the company!' He reached into his bag and pulled out a brochure packet, a bunch of business cards, and a rumpled folder with his business plan.

'Take a look,' he wheezed, slapping me on the back.

So I did, all the way up to Utsunomiya, grateful for the silence, but then, when the sleek train whispered into the station, I stood up and shook Roger's hand. He slipped me three of his business cards, and dodging Roger's job offer with a mumbled sentence, I got off and walked over the pedestrian bridge to the tracks for the normal JR train up to Nikko.

An hour later I got off at the small station there and walked the six blocks to the ryokan I had booked by phone the day before. As soon as I arrived, the lady of the house threw open the door and my mouth fell.

Standing in front of me was a compact, petite woman with a heavily made up face and a wardrobe of dark woolen clothes, nothing like the woman I had imagined when I had spoken to her on the phone.

'Yesssss,' she asked suspiciously.

'I booked yesterday, ryokan, two nights,' I said slowly, trying not to frighten the lady who probably had as volatile a temper as Mrs. Tani.

'Ryokan?' she repeated, questioning.

'Ryokan,' I said again, pointing to her house, smiling that bright I'm-not-a-serial-killer smile.

Without a word, she slammed the door in my face and for several seconds there was no noise. I took a step back to look at the house number again. Was I at the wrong one? Maybe if I just went next door, there would be a white haired woman from the Late Middle Aged Women's Club, and I would be safe.

But that fantasy was not to be.

The door flew open again with a bang, and the woman shuffled out, and she looked up at me with her hand covering her eyebrows and said, 'You, Mr. Day-vit?'

'Yes, Mr. Dave. Lowe.'

'Low?' she said, looking at the ground.

'Lowe,' I repeated, pointing to myself, getting irritated.

'But, seven p.m.'

I was five hours early. Apparently, amongst Tatami Dragon Ladies, this was a grave sin.

Japan 12, Dave 3.

'I took an earlier train.'

'Early train?'

'Early train.'

She digested this for a moment. 'Come inside, please. I am Mrs. Yuka.' She wiped her feet in an exaggerated way, and eager to please, I copied her. She smiled when she saw

48

this and nodded her head in approval. Maybe she wasn't Mrs. Tani's evil twin sister after all.

Japan 12, Dave 4.

I followed Mrs. Yuka into the pitch-blackness of the foyer where I banged my head against a thick wooden beam so violently I saw stars. I staggered forward, taking two steps further into the house to regain my balance, jaw clenched in a frozen curse.

'Aaahhhhh!' screamed Mrs. Yuka, pointing at my feet. I hadn't taken my shoes off, and after that first grave offense Mrs. Yuka's demeanor changed immediately.

Japan 13, Dave 4.

'Sorry,' I said through tight lips, dropping my bag, and pulling my boots off. When my eyes had adjusted to the darkness, I saw a living room as prim and proper as a country house in Surrey, England. Lace and chintz was spread out over every surface. Mrs. Yuka pulled out a guest book, I filled in my details, and she rattled off the rules.

No strange guests. No shoes in the house. No cooking in the bathroom. No washing clothes in the sink. No smoking. No alcohol. No drugs. No sleeping with other guests. No singing. No loud music. No lights on after ten p.m. No lights on before seven in the morning. Dinner is required each night, but the fee was extra.

Tani House in Kyoto was looking more and more like a Club Med by comparison.

I nodded my head and was shown to my room, a bunk in a shared dormitory where the bath was down the hall. I dropped my bag, and Mrs. Yuka growled.

'Suitcases are kept inside a separate room,' she said, reaching for my bag, which she lifted as easily as though it was empty. I was beginning to think these Tatami Dragon Ladies weren't human at all, but were in fact some mutant species of robotic women, iron fisted, cold hearted and with a strangely fierce devotion to John Denver. Was Mr. Denver the patron saint of Tatami Dragon Ladies?

When Mrs. Yuka had safely locked my bag away, I grabbed my backpack, slipped on my shoes again, and fled to see the town.

Nikko was famous for the Tosho-Gu shrine, home of the see hear and speak no evil carved monkeys, and was packed with busloads of high school students and sullen teachers gripping megaphones. It was raining a little, so I took refuge with the only other western tourists there, a family from Atlanta who had traveled up from Tokyo while their father attended a conference in Tokyo.

'Oh mah gawd, those wihmen are sayo tienee and puhteet, I just cayn't gayt over eyt!' wheezed the mother, snapping pictures as she spoke.

'Ah know,' her daughter said, pointing at the giggling schoolgirls who were gathering up the courage to speak to them, their faces red. 'Weyve guht our entourage, riyt over theyre,' she laughed. 'Liyke little China dowlz.'

I shrunk away and walked back to the town, getting a bowl of soup at a traditional restaurant under dark gray slate tile roofs. The proprietor was so taken back by this tall foreigner, slurping soup amongst her usual customers that she sat at my table to make sure I used the chopsticks correctly. She patted my shoulder lightly when she saw that I didn't need any help.

Japan 13, Dave 5.

Later that afternoon, while waiting out an even larger rainstorm in the lobby of a hotel packed with high school students, I was dripping wet, and even worse, trapped in the foyer with an exasperated, megaphone-clutching English teacher, exhausted after days of trying to entertain her charges. I later learned that a large number of Japanese schoolteachers wound up as patients at insane asylums, driven over the edge by their difficult students.

'AAHHH!' she shouted, seeing my light colored hair. 'BRONDE!!!!!'

A moment of silence swept through the room, as the students stopped talking.

'BRONDE!!!' the teacher repeated, slapping her thigh for emphasis, walking over and pointing at my head.

The students didn't hesitate another second. 'BRONDE!!' they shouted, and then in an instant I became one of those living props those English teachers complained about.

'BACK PACKU!!'

'GUIDU BOOKU!!'

'SHORTSU!!'

'T-SHIRTU!!!'

Each word was repeated three times as I stood there, dripping water on the carpet, the liquid pooling larger and larger around my feet.

'SOCKSU!!'

'WATCHU!'

Suddenly fed up with being a breathing robot, I clenched my teeth, waved my hand goodbye and reached for the door handle as a resounding chorus of 'GOODBYE!! GOODBYE!!!' followed me outside and out into the falling rain.

Back at Mrs. Yuka's mad ranch, I rang the bell. It was ten minutes before she slipped her face through a window crack, gasped, muttered something angrily to herself before she slammed the window shut. It was a full five more minutes before the front door opened, and Mrs. Yuka shot me a mean, stern look, perfected by grandmothers around the world to discipline insolent grandchildren.

'Dinner!' she moaned. 'Dinner! Every night! Here! At my house!'

I slapped my forehead. SHIT. I had completely forgotten.

Japan 14, Dave 5.

As she continued to whine in my ear like a pesky mosquito, I slipped my shoes off and followed her into the dining room where eight foreigners were sitting around a low table in total silence. They had already eaten every course, and I sat down at an empty place, and smiled.

No one smiled back at me.

In fact, even the lively Brazilian lady staying there with

her Cuban boyfriend had not a shred of cheer as Mrs. Yuka brought out a tray laden with miso soup, a bento box and cups of sake. She forbid anyone from leaving the table until I had finished eating, and everyone watched me as I dug in with chopsticks and slurped up the soup.

When Mrs. Yuka had left for the kitchen an Irish guy leaned in and hissed, 'Hurry it along, mate, we don't want to be here all night!'

Just then Mrs. Yuka came back and sat herself down, forcing everyone to introduce themselves, giving their age, occupation, nationality, and most important of all, their opinion about Japan.

They say England creates the strangest breed of eccentrics, well trained on a strict diet of tea and biscuits, of scones and jam, of order, and proper. But Japan is also an island, also separated from the continent it calls home, also a nation of drivers-on-the-left, consumers of carefully decorated seasonal dishes, from iced udon noodles in summertime, to lip-numbing Fugu puffer fish in wintertime. Japan is certainly no less prolific a factory for strangeness.

And Mrs. Yuka was Exhibit A.

When it came to my turn, I half wanted to scream out about strip searches and expiring travel documents and more, but I was afraid of Mrs. Yuka. Make that very afraid. So I turned back to my food. I had still not eaten all the dinner put before me, and eight pairs of eyeballs bored into my skull, pleading with me to set them free. I took one last bite and pushed the tray away.

Mrs. Yuka then brought out a guitar, and as she broke one of her rules (methinks Tatami Dragon Ladies can break any rule they like) the real torture was about to begin. We were urged (make that forced) to sing John Denver songs.

Two hours later, after singing her way through every last one of the greatest hits of John Denver, we were finally allowed to go to bed.

It was only eight thirty in the evening.

The next morning, the words to 'Country Roads' still spinning in my brain, I woke up, showered, and tiptoed to the front door, hoping I could slip out and avoid breakfast. But the front door was locked tight. And Mrs. Yuka was nowhere to be found.

I hunted around for an alternate exit. Were there any windows I could slip out of? Sliding wooden panels I could manipulate? Any paper screens I could dash through?

As I pushed against one windowpane just to be sure, there was Mrs. Yuka, carrying a tray, her mouth twisted into a sneer.

'Day-vit?' she said.

'Lowe,' I replied sheepishly, removing my hand slowly from the window. But I was too late.

'What are you doo-ing?'

'I need to catch the train to Tokyo, and the front door is locked.'

'Toh-kyo?'

I nodded my head, and she put down her tray. 'Tokyo is verrrrrrrry dangerous place,' she told me gravely. 'Many gangster, Yakuza clan.' She made a bang-bang motion with her hand, like she was holding a gun.

I nodded, eager to face any tattooed Yakuza clan if it meant freedom from this mad woman and the wholesome ballads of John Denver. Like a hardened jailor at a maximum-security prison, she reluctantly unlocked the front door and I was free: the bright neon lights of Tokyo were just a short train ride away.

I had so much fun in Tokyo that when I tried to get to the main station it was rush hour. I didn't see any white-gloved attendants pushing people into train cars, but I did have a nasty rush of claustrophobia as commuters piled in and squeezed in close all around me.

By the time I arrived back at the Central Station, I had missed my train back to Nikko, and by the time I was walking down the quiet, suburban lane to Mrs. Yuka's house, it was pitch dark, and like a naughty child, I knew I was going to get it. As I walked on through the cold darkness, images of a dungeon beneath Mrs. Yuka's house floated above my head. Somehow, I think medieval torture implements matched with songs from a 1970's singer would create the ultimate Amnesty International situation.

The house was locked up tight, and not even one light was on. As I stumbled through the garden, I walked straight into a massive spider's web, and staggering around, gasping from the shock, I frantically waved my arms around hoping that the monster arachnid was nowhere near my face.

I guess my yelp woke Mrs. Yuka, because a light had now come on in the house, and I heard her muttering in that way that confirmed I was in for it. It was a slow five minutes before she opened the door, and she didn't even stick her head out the window.

Mrs. Yuka already knew who it was.

'DAY-VIT!' she shouted when she saw me standing there, still shuddering from the spider web encounter. Mrs. Yuka dragged her finger across her lips, then whacked me over the head with an old newspaper, and ushered me off to bed, my stern lecture no doubt waiting for the morning.

The next morning, I heard a faint creak from the floorboards. It was so early that the sun hadn't even risen yet, and before I knew it, the lights flicked on and a voice screamed, 'OHAYO GOZAIMUS!!!'

It was so close to my ear that I sat up and bashed my forehead on the wooden beam above my head. Then, Mrs. Yuka ripped open the curtains and grabbed my pillow so quickly that my head bonked backwards onto the tatami mat.

As she rushed around the room, sweeping madly, lifting blankets and getting ready to start her day, I was beginning to think Mrs. Yuka was one of those school teachers that had been driven round the bend by her students, only she had escaped from her insane asylum to terrorize foreign travelers.

She might have driven even her very own children to flee from this madwoman, or worse, her husband was probably either buried under the back garden or chopped up into sushi and stored in the freezer.

Suddenly the meat from the dinner I ate the night before began to look mighty suspicious.

I looked at my watch. It was 5.45 a.m. I knew there was a JR train at the station, going somewhere, anywhere, as long as it was away from this awful place, and this Tatami Dragon Lady, who I suspected was the Travel God's minion based in Nikko.

So with the words 'Japan Rail, take me home, to the place I belong, Tani House' I pulled on my clothes, stuffed my suitcase with the rest, grabbed my backpack, slipped on my shoes, clutched my Japan Rail pass firmly in my hand, clenched my teeth, and fled.

Sometimes you can get burned by Lonely Planet.
   Right well toasted, actually.
   Sometimes what is listed in that traveler's Bible can actually be a prison in disguise run by a nutcase with an unnaturally strong obsession with John Denver. Sometimes you have to ignore the urge to travel in a paint-by-numbers-fashion and strike out on your own.

   As soon as I slip up, all I have to do is to remember Mrs. Yuka, because:

   If you don't like John Denver songs, never be a guest of a Tatami Dragon Lady.

   Love, Dave

August 04, 1992
10:12 A.M.
Hiroshima, Japan
Paper Cranes and Atomic Bombs

Hey Annette,

I'm back in the relative safety of Tani House after my last day trip south to Hiroshima. Today is Tuesday, and after a short trip to some temples in Kyoto, I am relaxing at Tani House that is as quiet as a Zen temple.

Back at the house, I slipped my shoes off and paused. It seemed very quiet.

Too quiet. I couldn't even hear John Denver singing. Something was definitely wrong.

I cautiously tiptoed upstairs into the Ladies tatami room. Judy was lying on her duvet cover, reading a book and looking relaxed.

'Did you even go out today?'

She shook her head.

'Why is it so quiet?'

'You forgot,' said Kerstin. 'Mrs. Tani has gone to Osaka.'

We all laughed, but just then Mr. Tani poked his head in the room and smiled. Judy motioned to him and he came in, and after she had rolled over on her back, Mr. Tani started to give her a shoulder massage.

Time to hit a coffee shop.

So that's where I am now. OK, back to my trip to Hiroshima.

My Rail Pass is halfway through its validity, and I have to make careful plans to fit in the rest of the country before it, and my Yen, runs out.

Here is where the culture clash between Japan and Korea came into focus yet again. I have spent quite a bit of time trying to convert $400 dollars I had exchanged into Korean

Won in Seoul, and no bank in any town, or even Tokyo itself, will touch it. I would probably have an easier time cashing in Monopoly money than Won in this country. So, with only a limited amount of Japanese Yen left, I have to tighten my travel belt to survive, skipping meals, walking instead of buses, that sort of thing.

After being strip-searched, almost denied access to the Japan Rail network, and countless gaffes and problems, what, really, is just one more thing? The Travel Gods are definitely having a good laugh right now.

Really. Somewhere in Osaka, FECG along with thousands of Middle Aged Salarymen everywhere are having a very good laugh and toasting my misfortune with tiny cups of warm sake.

But they might not be laughing at me in Hiroshima. After a day trip there, my view of this country is tempered yet again by an unexpected experience.

It was the second of August and the anniversary of the bombing of that Japanese city was a few days away. Hordes of school children wearing identical baseball hats were swarming around my ankles, eyes shining brightly, the teachers desperately trying to maintain order in the chaos as they moved towards the Memorial Park.

Just then an old, wrinkled man, waving a flag saw me, pointed and yelled, 'Atom bomb! Atom bomb! Atom bomb!'

I hunched down as though I had just seen FECG again. For over three weeks I had moved about Japan almost as invisible as a ghost, six foot three and towering over everyone by at least a foot, I had gotten used to both being ignored like a leper and then simultaneously frightening small children and little old ladies as I came around street corners.

I mean, even the foreigners in Japan ignored you, nowhere else in Asia did I get cold shouldered so steadily by fellow travelers, nowhere else did I actually see foreigners turn their heads away when they saw me coming down the street, as if they wanted to edit me from the Shoji screen. What only surprises me more is when I catch myself doing the same thing.

Then the old man, closer now, shouted again, even louder.

'Atom bomb! Over here! Atom bomb!' He pointed to a streetcar that was filling up with people. I boarded, bought a ticket and took my seat. I looked up and realized the man was actually the driver.

Instantly, I felt like I was in a parallel Japan.

In Hiroshima I felt like a ghost that had gotten used to being invisible, had gotten used to the ability to slip through walls undetected. When suddenly recognized by the living, however, that ghost had to re-adjust accordingly to this strange new realty.

Because that's what Hiroshima felt like.

For the first time in the country, the normal Japanese reserve was gone, university students looked at me blankly, even middle aged-men who wouldn't have given me the time of day in Tokyo eyed me levelly as we waited to leave the station. Aunties stared at me coolly, and grannies that would have smiled at me and pinched my cheek, made eye contact only briefly before looking away, tired.

The streetcar left the station and for fifteen minutes we weaved through an average looking Japanese city with concrete office blocks, shiny shopping malls, fluorescent lit entrances to subway stations, neon billboards and large, clean streets with spotlessly clean taxis.

Suddenly the streetcar stopped, the driver snapped his neck around, threw up his hands and shouted at me, 'Atom bomb!'

I stood up as sheepishly as well, a sheep, thanked him in my shaky Japanese, and got off the tram, avoiding the stares of the passengers who were still looking at me. I was grateful when the tram pulled away, and I was left alone on the sidewalk.

But where was I?

I was used to feeling lost in Japan, practically all the time in fact, but it didn't stop the feeling of anger that rose up inside me, lava-like, because I could see nothing indicating the direction I was supposed to go.

I knew I was in the middle of a bland urban street. So I walked a block, but found only more anonymous buildings and office towers, I walked back in another direction and found the same thing.

Then, I turned left, and thirty seconds later I turned another corner, and modern Japan vanished. I was looking at the iconic cement building with the metal dome roof that had survived the atomic blast.

I waited for the light to change and walked across the street towards the building that was surrounded by a green park. The plaza was full of paper cranes, flapping in the breeze, made by Japanese children from all across the country to honor a little girl who vowed to make 1,000 cranes before she died to remember the dead from the bombing.

I entered the museum and wandered around the exhibits, shocked into silence. There was a stone step where a faint outline of a person was visible who had died instantly when the bomb had exploded, burned clothes and audio accounts of survivors. I was offered polite smiles by the staff of volunteers who led me around. For the next half an hour, they gave me details about the day that an entire city had disappeared. Afterwards, I sat in the park surrounded by hundreds upon hundreds of those flapping cranes, enjoying the silence. And then an old man sat down next to me.

'America?' he asked.

I nodded.

He wasted no time in asking me any of the usual questions, about my dexterity with chopsticks, or my thoughts on the beauty of Japanese girls, or whether I had seen Mt. Fuji. This was rare in Japan; everywhere I went I was subjected to giving answers to personal and random questions asked by strangers, so much so that it was like being interviewed over and over again by the same quirky journalist with boundary issues.

He began explaining the history of his life in simple, short sentences that he spat out like tokens from a subway ticket machine.

Both his parents had died in the blast, and he was waiting for the cancer many of his friends and neighbors had already succumbed to.

He was seventy-two.

His wife had already died, but not from cancer, just old age. His children lived in Tokyo, and he saw them each just twice a year, once in summer, and once in winter. He was about to see his grandchild for the first time, and he was excited.

His spiel didn't last long, not more than five minutes, and for the first time in Japan, the constant push and pull of cultural rules, the oil and water situations that had left me exhausted since I had arrived in the country were gone.

Something had shifted.

As soon as he had told me his life history, he stood up, shook my hand and crunched his way over the gravel to a tree where he pulled a string of paper cranes towards him.

He pulled one off, walked back to me and handed it over with a deep bow. I stood up and bowed the way I was supposed to. I had been in Japan enough time to have somewhat perfected this most ubiquitous of Japanese gestures.

The old man smiled at me broadly in approval before turning around and walking back under that tree branch hung heavy with paper cranes.

And then he was gone.

Japan 14, Dave 6.

Like the kind white haired lady at the Tourist Information Center in Nara, this man was also wearing underwear that wasnt twisted up at all.

Tomorrow I'm off again on my last trip away from Kyoto, south to Kyushu. My Yen is still tight, but somehow, here in the Land of the Rising Confusion, it seems appropriate.

Now I have to perfect the financial concentration one reserves for observing Japanese gardens. Being one with the raked gravel calmness. Perfecting Zen-like breathing techniques as I skip meals and walk.

I know FECG wouldn't have had it any other way.
The scorecard continues.
Losing weight with a smile.

Love, Dave

August 9th, 1992
8:02 P.M.
Aso, Japan
Down Unzen's Throat

Annette, I'm sitting on the left side of a Shinkansen, tray table pulled down, and if I close my eyes I could be on a plane out of here. I'm getting ready to leave; yet another travel plan has been nixed by Japan.

Maybe it's a guy thing, but before I leave Japan I had to see a volcano. Not an extinct one, but one that was active, spewing lava. Perhaps it was a Godzilla thing, too.

One that was alive.

So southward I went in search of one.

In the Kyoto train station I booked my last pack of tickets with a white-gloved station attendant, and the next day I boarded an early morning Shinkansen, the blue and white car gliding up as promised in the Railways of Japan timetable at precisely 8.57 a.m.

I found my seat, wedged between two businessmen who probably cursed their luck at their seat assignments that placed them a mere elbow's length away from a member of the Independent Travelers Club, and for the next three hours we passed through stations that had now become like old friends: Shin Osaka, Osaka, Kobe, Okayama, etc.

As the train sped through the warm morning, the car rocked uncharacteristically from side to side and the conductors raced to the front. Then there was a screech of brakes and the bullet train stopped dead on the tracks. But the car was still shaking. It was actually an earthquake, 6.5 on the Richter scale, triggered deep beneath the earth in Osaka Bay.

We stayed stationary for about thirty minutes. Tiny robot machines were sent along the tracks, checking for damage, explained the animated college student across the aisle. The two members of the Middle Aged Salaryman Club looked on in shocked silence by twisted underwear as we talked.

There were lengthy announcements in Japanese and passengers gathered up their things and moved towards the exits, a minute later, the train slowly crawled to the next station and we were ordered off by more white-gloved Japan Rail staff. Within fifteen minutes, an empty Shinkansen appeared, we re-boarded, and were sent on our way.

My volcano plan imploded when I was told that Kyushu Island didn't honor Japan Rail passes to the country's southernmost city, Kagoshima. I would have to shell out 13,000 Yen for an extra ticket. My rapidly shrinking budget didn't allow for that. Funny, the last time I checked Kyushu is still part of Japan, so why does it not honor the Japan Rail Pass? I never got an answer to this question.

After that brief redemption in Hiroshima park full of paper cranes, my trip kept on swerving back and forth like a needle on some cultural Richter scale.

Truth be told, I had slipped up a bit in the Cultural Adaptation Department and had made several blunders that pushed my losing streak to new 'Lowes.' The most glaring of which was in a Kyoto temple where I stepped over a barrier, thinking it was just a temporary rope cordoning off a newly washed floor. In fact it was an off limits section that sent security guards scurrying for their superiors, who returned, red-faced and horror stricken at the fresh size thirteen shoeprints on the floor, spluttering out a lengthy, and well deserved, dressing down.

Japan 15, Dave 6.

So Kagoshima was off.

I ended up going to Nagasaki instead, where I had access to Mt. Unzen, also an active volcano on the island, it had erupted just the previous year, and was still smoking.

Nagasaki reminded me of San Francisco, steeply sloping hills descended to meet the sea, there was a clean, busy harbor, and the bright sky was cooled by ocean breezes. The city's role as the first contact point to the west also mirrored San Francisco's history as a jumping off point to foreign lands.

After stops at the Hypocenter Park, where the atom bomb was dropped above a northern suburb of Nagasaki, I took a bus to Glover Garden where reconstructed Dutch houses surrounded large ponds with a great view of the city.

At sunset, I sat down at a park bench and less than two seconds later a friendly security guard walked up to me, turned bright red, and stuck out his hand. He sat down, introduced himself as Hiroshi and started to ask me the usual laundry list of question I was getting used to answering in Japan. Having satisfied his curiosity, he pulled out a rolled up English textbook and we ploughed through a few exercises relating to irregular past participles and future perfect tenses.

And that was where I met the first member of the Nobody Club, those who fell between the widening cracks opening up across all levels of Japanese society.

Unlike ordinary Japanese, these club members looked at me not as a pariah or a leper, but as a savior, a saint, a convenient Jesus. They bombarded me with questions about America and life in the west where they hoped to live one day, clinging to me like a life preserver in a sea of their society's rejection that surged menacingly all around. Rejection I had tasted loud and clear myself.

Then the book was put away and Hiroshi told me about his one overseas experience, his honeymoon in Hawaii with his wife, three years before. Just seventy-two hours in Waikiki had awakened his interest in all things American. Especially rock music. All thanks to the Hard Rock Café, where he had gone for dinner one night.

'Do you know Sting? Beatles? Madonna?'

I nodded.

Hiroshi looked at me and shook my hand up and down, grinning from ear to ear. 'American rock, NUMBER ONE!!!'

Like a lot of Japanese, when they do something, they go all the way. Hiroshi spent all his free time and money on collecting every tape, magazine, record, or poster from his hobby, and it took up all his spare time after work and on weekends. His dream was to visit all the Hard Rock Cafes around the world, much to the disappointment of his loyal wife who has been working for ten years as a simple tea lady in a bank.

More than somewhat embarrassed by her husband's passion he devoted towards his hobby she had stopped bringing him to official functions, but he didn't care because that just gave him more time to listen to Voice of America broadcasts. She had even refused to have a baby with him before he gave up his interest, but so far the topic hadn't been resolved because he didn't want children.

Hiroshi went on and on, throwing up his hands, gesticulating about lyrics and music videos he had seen on MTV, and even quoted English passages from interviews that his favorite singers had given to Japanese magazines.

When I looked at my watch, Hiroshi looked sad, but it was time to go, the last bus to the city was leaving, and it was too far to walk in the dark. As I stood up, Hiroshi saluted me and shook my hand.

'Rock and roll, number one, man,' he said quietly as he went back to his post, his English textbook, his rock music, and his isolation.

The next morning I caught an early train to Aso, the town closest to Mt. Unzen, one of the most active volcanoes in Japan. A year earlier the volcano had erupted, and according to recent reports, it was still smoking.

Perfect.

I know I was tempting fate here, had I decided to scale Mt. Fuji, it would probably have erupted, smothering me in ACME ash and then burying me in hot ACME lava. But I decided to tempt fate anyway. The Travel Gods must have a day off sometime, right?

After checking into my ryokan in the town that was mercifully managed by an easy going member of the Elderly Grandmother's Club and not a mutant relation of Mrs. Yuka, her extremely animated explanation was pantomimed and punctuated with grunts and mutterings so explicit I knew that for my safety, and her reputation, I was not to get too close to the volcano.

So off I went.

Less that five minutes after leaving the hotel a light rain started falling and I pulled out my umbrella. In the gutters running along side the road, I saw something that I had never seen before. Large, red-clawed crabs were walking sideways along the ground, dipping their bodies in the running water. It wasn't Christmas Island, but there were hundreds of these crabs marching down the muddy hillsides, jumping into the rushing water.

A few minutes later I overtook a foreigner who was also walking up the road under an umbrella.

'Rainin' pretty heavily, eh mate?' said the Australian who introduced himself as Jake. It turned out he was heading for the volcano too, and we followed the signs to the trailhead. Water was gushing down the path, but we hiked on anyway, as heavy drops of water continued hitting our umbrellas with fat plops.

For the next hour we hiked deeper into the forest while Jake gave me an earful about what it was like being married to a Japanese.

In a matter of a few short weeks, this itinerant wanderer's life had ground to a halt and the chips had fallen firmly and permanently into place, he met his wife, a secretary at the English college where he taught, ending his nonstop wandering around the world. He had been living in the country for more than ten years now, teaching English and explained that he was hiking alone because his wife and her parents were at the hotel with their new baby who was two months old.

'Not speaking the same language is a plus, mate, you can't fight,' he laughed. Turned out that Jake could only speak about fifteen words in Japanese.

'The in-laws can be a bit of a nightmare, but I just ignore 'em. They can't speak Australian, anyway.' His voice boomed off the rain soaked tree trunks.

Jake pressed on with why he chose to live in Japan rather than Australia, even though he found the country 'primitive' and the people lame.

'You're a knight in shinin' armor here, mate. All the girls want a piece of you.' As we hiked on, he turned and looked at me.

'Have you been to India yet?'

I shook my head, remembering the comment from the Brit about going to a third world country like India would 'do me some good.' And then Jake's jaw sped off into top gear, recounting in minute detail every bowel-churning episode of his twelve months on the ground in the subcontinent, including run-ins with Saddhus and saints and all sorts of gods and monsters and viruses and hallucinations. Having been beaten up by Japan for weeks, I was keen to give Mother

India a miss, what on earth would I experience there if for me Japan was strip searches and public humiliation?

Brainwashed by Saddhus, most likely, I would probably wind up on a Lonely Planet milk carton, 'Have you seen me?' printed on its side, distributed in Bali and Goa and along Khao San road.

NO. I was NEVER going to India.

'Aw, mate you just have to go!' wailed Jake, slapping me on the arm. 'I nearly died there. Three times! Train crashed on the way to Calcutta! Bus lost a wheel going to Rajastan! And the cows, well they didn't like me I can tell you!'

I looked down at my feet, hoping for a subject change: my shoes were squishing at every step, and I was getting tired of this vampire-like company of random foreigners that the universe kept on dealing to me, like dud cards in a poker game.

Though we kept climbing, the volcano was nowhere to be seen. The rain clouds had descended so far we were now in the mist that wrapped us in a deep, grey chill.

Then, a large white sign in English and Japanese warned people not to go any further, the caldera was over the ridge, and we were ordered to turn back.

'C'mon, lets go.' Jake hopped the fence and he squelched down into the thick mud on the other side of the low barrier.

'I don't think so,' I said with great hesitation.

'Aww, mate, the volcano is safe, hasn't been an eruption in ages!'

I knew a year didn't count as 'ages' but I reluctantly hopped over, expecting ACME pitchforks and ACME anvils at any moment. We pushed on through the fog. The next thing I knew my foot that I put out in front of me was not contacting the ground, dangling uselessly in the air. It was the jagged lip of the caldera, the fog had erased all boundaries.

I grabbed a tree trunk and watched Jake start sliding down the steep slope, using nothing for support. The air began to stink of sulfur, and I started to cough.

Against my better judgment I followed, but a moment later, I felt a strange warmth heating up my feet. It wasn't my shoes, it was the ground itself. Not only was it hot, it was steaming, and even through the thick soles of my shoes I could feel the heat of the magma soaking up through the rain sodden earth. When the breeze changed direction, I could smell sulfur even more strongly.

Time to head back.

I yelled down to Jake, who had now disappeared in the mist and he just shouted back calmly, 'Take care mate!' before he climbed down deeper into the active, smoking throat of Mt. Unzen's caldera, mercifully taking his crazy stories from India with him. I hopped back over the fence and hiked back to my hotel as the cherry red crabs continued their sideways creeping and crawling through the gushing creeks, no ACME pitchfork or anvil in sight.

I've only got one more stop to go before I leave the Land of Rising Confusion, Iki Island, off the north coast of Kyushu. The weather reports are talking of typhoons, so I have no idea what this will mean for my plans.

Love, Dave

August 14th, 1992
12:37 P.M.
Iki Island, Japan
Crooked Teeth

Hey Annette,

I'm in Fukuoka train station and a typhoon is blowing fiercely outside.

Trains are cancelled.

It has been going on for, um, ten hours, and the last time I poked my head outside I saw the umbrellas of two ladies invert, practically carrying them away as swiftly as Mary Poppins.

The ferry back to the mainland got me here just in time, and it was a narrow scrape, an extra day in Japan and I would be financially fucked, as I mentioned about the Yen and Won situation. So I'm on track to get back to Tani House tonight.

But first, Iki Island.

I've been in Asia less than three months, but I have now learned that the less the Lonely Planet book says on a place, the better they are.

Iki Island hasn't even got half a paragraph about it.

Exactly what I needed. I could choose only one more place to go before leaving Japan, and I wanted to get off the beaten track, really off, and a recommendation by that student on a random train was all I needed.

After counting my Yen to see if they would stretch that far, and found that they did, I boarded a small train for Hakata, the jumping off point for Iki Island.

Iki is just a speck of land between Japan and Korea, two hours by ferry from a small port east of Fukuoka. The trip over was to be my last collision with the Teenage Boys Club, and the closely related Teenage Girls Club: the tiny ship was packed with giggling Japanese high school students who crowded around me to translate from a tiny dictionary.

Pressed in on all sides by questions I had been asked over and over again during my stay in Japan, I patiently endured my latest group of admirers as the sea breeze blasted us and the boat heaved through the blue waves. The sober conformity of their school uniforms reflected the almost textbook questions I could now answer in my sleep -

'How do you find Japan?'
'Can you eat Japanese food?'
'Can you use chopsticks?'
'Do you speak Japanese?'

It's funny in this country, once you give answers to these questions, the smiles continue but the interest fades, being a gaijin must be how a shiny toy feels like the day after Christmas.

Old news.

After arriving in the tiny harbor the students still managed a cheery goodbye and piled into their buses. As I walked up the hill, I looked back to see them peering at me through the large windows with looks of genuine concern. My guidebook didn't even have a real chapter on Iki, I was on my own, without a reservation, and virtually no Japanese.

What business did I, a foreigner, have out here in the middle of nowhere, all alone? It was a question I had been asking myself since I had arrived in Japan, and had yet no answer to.

I was relieved when their buses roared off in a cloud of exhaust, the students frantically waving from the windows, their faces like yin and yang symbols, half smile, half scowl.

A half an hour later I had exhausted all my connections in the small harbor, filled mostly fishmongers wives, their wet arms were buried deep into tubs of smelly squid. They spoke no English, and no one had any idea where a confused, sweating foreigner could spend the night.

Then, a short grandma came wobbling down the road, clacking by on wooden shoes, gesticulating wildly. My face brightened. I was an honorary member of her club, and was sure to be welcomed with open arms.

I wasn't wrong.

It turned out her family had a traditional ryokan run by her son's wife. After I was introduced to them, the daughter-in-law took over, and through Japanese and furious head nods, broad grins and bows, we negotiated a price and I was given a large room on top of the house with sliding paper screens and a view of the blue sea.

Then they rented me a sturdy Chinese bicycle to get around the island. There were no public buses or taxis. It was still early in the morning, and the mother gave me a lengthy explanation in Japanese, punctuated with furiously explicit hand motions to explain the layout of the roads on Iki island. From her spiel I gathered the hills would be difficult, but clean, empty beaches would be my reward.

I walked the bike through the small town and leaned it up against the wall of a shop to buy some lunch. Inside were two local students who quickly introduced themselves. As soon as they called their friends on a payphone to inform them that a rare, live gaijin was in town, in five minutes flat I was signing autographs and posing for pictures.

Pressed with the same questions as on the ferry, I was finally released, free to explore Iki. I took my boxed bento lunch and took off for the hills.

Huffing and puffing up steep twisting roads and coasting down steep valleys, the going was harder than the Japanese mother had demonstrated with her hand motions, there were very few people out here, and all I found were long, deserted beaches fringed with rice fields that sighed in the breeze.

I did come across some tiny villages dotting the hilltops, with lines of snow-white laundry flapping in the wind.

But there were more cats than people.

I never saw another bicyclist, and only a few cars passed me with polite toots of their horn and respectful bows, as deep as their steering wheels would allow, of course.

At one beach, a group of friends were having a picnic and invited me to eat. One guy handed me an Asahi beer, and we clinked cans. I spent the next two hours getting drunk with these new friends:

No English, just basic Japanese and grunts.

No personal questions, just beer and food.
No bows, just belches and farts.

Things were going great and underwear was untwisted all round.

That is, until dessert.

Then a large yellow banana became a convenient prop, and soon one of the more inebriated men was trying to imitate a particularly private part of a foreigner's anatomy, wagging the fruit in front of my face. Then he garbled on and on, pointing to his ass, which he seemed happy to show off. To prove it, he turned his back to us and dropped his pants, mooning me and his friends who stood there horrified and apologized under their breath to me like Kumiko had done at the Osaka port after my run in with FECG.

Clearly this man belonged neither to the Middle Aged Salaryman's Club, nor the Nobody Club - he was simply the treasurer for the Drunken Jerks Club.

Later, after escaping from the party, I cycled up more tiring hills and found stunning views across the straits of Japan to Korea, my next destination.

I stopped for a rest and a chance to catch up on my letters, so I chose a wooden bench perched over a gurgling stream irrigating a rice field. I also knew I had to gather my strength for the three large hills I had coasted down earlier in the day, I would have to pedal like mad to reach the town again before dark.

As I sat, absorbed in my writing, from over my shoulder, I heard muttering, a cackle, and then a laugh.

Was the drunken guy back with his banana?

No.

It was a woman, bent nearly double with age, who literally appeared out of nowhere. When her mouth opened in a huge grin, it revealed her few remaining teeth pointing crazily in all directions. Without a formal greeting, she just sat down next to me and peered at my writing that to her looked as exotic as Arabic. She chatted with me in the lilting southern dialect of Japanese as if I understood her every word.

We sat there for almost an hour, the old woman and I, and I dug out postcards and guidebooks from my trip to show her. As the sun crashed into the sea, dark clouds on the horizon announced the arrival of the fierce summer typhoon that would come ashore two days later, churning the sea so badly that the ferry service back to Kyushu would be cancelled for two days.

I realized that if I didn't get a start back to town now, I would arrive back in the harbor after dark and I wasn't keen on riding through the pitch-black night.

So I decided it was time to go.

As I closed my journal, I said goodbye in Japanese and the old woman looked at me sadly as I zipped up my backpack and got to my feet.

Then I realized the second seat on the bike was large enough to give her a ride. In an elaborate explanation I tried to explain I could offer the woman a lift, the island was small, there was no public transport, and she couldn't live that far away. The woman with the crooked teeth had been such good company that I just didn't want to leave her behind.

At first she couldn't understand at all, and her face crinkled up in confusion.

But then the Yen coin dropped.

She stared up at me, her mouth open at what I was offering her, looking at the seat in horror. She started to bow again and again, shaking her head at me in a violent refusal, as though in the presence of a vampire who was kindly asking for permission to bite her neck.

Saddened, I hitched my backpack on, and prepared to cycle back alone.

But then she stopped and looked around. There would be no one here to witness the sight of her riding on the back of a tall foreigner's bike, so why not give it a go?

This was one woman whose underwear wasn't twisted into an uncomfortable knot, and recognizing a kindred spirit, I patted the spare seat with a smile.

The old woman grabbed my arm, hiked up her skirt, and I stabilized the bike as she got on. She gingerly reached out and grabbed my waist, unsure of what she was getting herself in for.

Before she could say no, I jumped into the seat and was off, coasting down the hill towards the bottom of the valley. The front wheel wobbled, the brakes were weak, and the bike lurched from side to side, and I almost dumped that poor woman into a muddy rice field.

She hung on desperately as I pedaled up the next hill, struggling to reach the top. I glanced back. The old woman was muttering silently to herself, as if she was praying. But a grin was stretched clear across her face, revealing that row of crazy, crooked teeth.

Over the next few hills, I struggled up, pedaling furiously, then coasted down, wobbling wildly, and all along the way we laughed our heads off. The woman never fell off, although it came close a few times. No car or any pedestrian saw us, and if they had, what could they have done to stop us from having so much fun?

I continued on, pedaling up the last hill before the harbor. And then came the tap on my shoulder that I had been dreading all along, we had reached the tiny road where her house was, and the old woman needed to get off.

Flooded with sadness, I braced the bike as she hopped down. As she reached the safety of the ground, the old woman collapsed into a series of deep, respectful bows. In the most honorific Japanese way, she was thanking me, and I returned the gesture as best I could with a shaky bow.

So we stood there in the golden yellow light of the setting sun, that old lady and I, bowing low to each other like two old friends, in the middle of that black asphalt road, on that tiny speck of land off the coast of Japan.

We were two people from completely different cultures, ages, lives and religions, not wanting to say goodbye. In an instant, all of my frustration was gone. It seemed the old woman, on behalf of Japan, had forgiven all of my awful cultural mistakes and stupid gaffes I had committed in her country, erasing them with a single, crooked-toothed grin. And with my shaky bow, I had forgiven FECG and the cast of characters that had made my trip in her country so difficult.

It was one of the most touching displays of thanks I had ever received.

As I hopped back on the bike and coasted down the last hill, I looked back to see the old woman still bowing low to the ground, that broad grin still spread across her face from ear to ear, those crooked teeth still pointing at me.

Finally, just as I'm about to leave Japan, I've done it. I've broken the curse. I'm still in the Fukuoka train station, and I've just been told I can catch a bullet train heading back to Kyoto in an hour, and should be there by evening.

In time to beat Mrs. Tani and her nightly lockdown, of course.

For the mean time, I'm passing the hours sitting on the floor of the huge train station. It's rush hour, and I'm surrounded by Salarymen of all stripes.

But none seem to be looking at me like they used to. In fact, not one is giving me any sort of look of disapproval. One of them even smiled. You see, they are trapped here by the same typhoon, and we are all in the same boat. For once, underwear, all round, is not in a twist.

After that encounter on Iki, I have decided to stop keeping score.

The score is 28:7, by the way.

A total washout in favor of Japan.

Of course.

As I watch the students, the mothers, the salarymen, and all the other passengers walk by, I'm wondering, did FECG make my entry into his country difficult to catch my attention, to make me more aware, more appreciative of what his country was going to teach me? Did Mrs. Yuka have the same intentions with her inflexible, rigid ways?

Nope. I think she is just a madwoman, plain and simple.

This is my last letter to you from this country. Next up is Korea. That is, if my Yen doesn't run out and I am forced to sell fake telephone cards from Iran on the street.

Who knows. I may have caught the Travel Gods napping on Unzen, but something tells me they are wide-awake and very, very angry.

If you come across an old lady in Japan with crooked teeth, give her a lift.

Love, Dave

August 16, 1992
11:44 A.M.
Kyoto, Japan
The Udon Noodle Truce

Hey Annette,

Though my trip through Japan is almost over, and I have been here nearly a month, there was one contact in this country that I had yet been able to make.

Michael was the brother of my Scout Master in California who had been living in Kyoto for a few years, and though I tried his phone number several times, I was continually unable to reach him.

As my trips north and south unfolded, I thought I wouldn't get a chance to meet him before I left Japan, though the day after returning to Kyoto from Iki Island, I managed to get in touch with him and arrange to meet at a convenient street corner in the north of town.

Up to this point, my experiences with foreigners in Japan have been pretty hit or miss. (focus on the miss) In fact, when I agreed to meet Michael, I expected to meet yet another foreigner, swaggering in and blathering on about their 'deep' understanding of Japanese culture, their 'clear' idea of their own superiority, extremely happy for a fresh pair of ears (mine) to spew bile and venom about their adopted homeland. (That they never left, of course)

But when he turned up riding a 100 CC Honda motorbike, Michael quickly shook my hand and asked, 'Are you up for some food?'

I said sure, and without another word, Michael handed over his only helmet for me to wear, I hopped on the back, and off he tore through the back streets of Kyoto, me clinging on as best I could while he weaved and zigzagged through the alleys, the yellow beams of his headlights reflecting off walls and windows and a cat or two.

At one intersection, while waiting for a traffic light, Michael turned around and said, 'I've just got to stop off at a festival market, where my friends are having an art exhibition. Do you mind if we stop there?'

I shook my head, and when the light changed, Michael took off again, roaring through the streets and gliding past houses, shops and small parks. Then we pulled up at an intersection and Michael waved at three Japanese standing behind a folding table covered in ceramic sculptures they were packing away into boxes.

After we were introduced, I half expected to see the oil and water, foreigner vs. local battle play itself out. But as I stood there in the fading light of the setting sun, I didn't see it. Surely it will begin eventually, I told myself.

Just wait.

But wait I did, and nothing happened.

Michael and the artists chatted away in Japanese, and then, when the boxes were full, a car arrived and they were loaded up and the three Japanese artists smiled, shook my hand and were gone.

Michael pointed to a restaurant across the intersection where the front door was covered by a royal blue cotton panel painted with koi fish. 'Let's eat over there,' he said, and I grabbed a table inside while he parked his motorbike outside.

When we had ordered, Michael told me more about his life in Kyoto. As my stomach growled, I half expected the all too familiar vicious spew of anti-Japanese tirade to launch itself at any moment, but as I sat there, fainter and fainter from hunger, and from the shock of not hearing a single negative word about Japan, here was a foreigner who was not a member of the Disgruntled Expatriates Club who had forged his own path and was doing quite nicely.

Two steaming bowls of Tempura Udon finally arrived and we quickly dug in.

'So how do you like Japan?' Michael asked abruptly as the waitress dropped off two cups of boiling hot tea.

I stopped breathing. I was holding my chopsticks in the air, and the bundle of noodles clutched between them dripped heavy plops of soup back into the bowl. Just as I was about to spill out all the things that had happened to me, like whooshing air escaping from a punctured gas bag, recounting strip searches and public humiliation and expiring travel documents and Mrs. Tani and MAM and Mrs. Yuka, and how I had stumbled and blundered since Day One in Japan, I swallowed. I looked down at the Udon noodles in front of me and changed the channel.

'I love it,' I said, shocked at the words falling out.

After taking another mouthful of noodles, I let forth a flurry of sentences extolling the beauty of Mt. Fuji and the peace of the Zen gardens in Kyoto. And then I took another mouthful of noodles and enthused about the small neighborhoods full of wooden houses I had explored in Tokyo, and earthquakes on the Shinkansen and about that little old lady on Iki.

Consider it the Udon Noodle Truce.

The torrent of words was probably a bit much coming from someone so new to Japan, and Michael's eyes widened as I put down my waving chopsticks and replaced them with my arms that flew around over my head as words kept tumbling from my mouth.

There was nothing else I could talk about. After hearing and seeing his deep devotion to all things Japanese, there was no need to fill him in on the fact madmen ran the Port of Osaka and that madwomen ran many a ryokan from Kyoto to Nikko.

I'm sure he had heard it all before anyway.

When Michael dropped me off at Tani House, I took off the helmet, shook his hand, and said goodbye.

As I walked back inside the mad suburban world of Mr. and Mrs. Tani, I quietly thanked him for showing me yet another layer of the onion that is Japan.

Still have a few days left in Japan..... then, Korea.

Love, Dave

Hello Annette,

I couldn't leave you hanging about the drama at Tani House and the Convenience Store War, could I?

No way.

So I'm squeezing in one last letter from Japan, sent from Korea.

You're going to love this.

As luck would have it, my last day in Japan was a Tuesday. My Japan Rail Pass had expired the day before, my trip back from Iki was to be my last in the country. I just calculated how much the Shinkansen tickets would have cost if I had bought them: $2,500 dollars. (Now you know why I locked horns with MAM)

After I had wandered around Kyoto's old quarter, the river, and watched Japanese mothers and their daughters clip clop past me in wooden shoes to get photographed under weeping willows, I returned after dark to find Tani House still lit up bright as day, the front door/paper screen pulled open wide, and loud shouts and banging were coming from the downstairs living room.

Though I couldn't understand them, the insults seemed more heated than usual. I slipped off my shoes and tiptoed upstairs to find the foreign guests huddled in the corner of the women's tatami room, as though taking shelter from some imminent typhoon. They all winced as another chair bounced off the wall beneath us.

Kerstin whispered to me. 'Mrs. Tani's sister was ill, so she came back early from Osaka. She found Judy being massaged by Mr. Tani, and all hell broke loose. She's been screaming at Mr. Tani for five hours!'

'Where's Judy?'

She shot me a look. 'Where do you think?' She indicated in the direction of where her backpack used to be. Suddenly the private joke made sense.

Apparently Mr. Tani had quite the racket going, every Tuesday, with his wife away, and a house full of young western women eager to learn about Japan, he had quite the available harem at his disposal. The old man it seemed, even without a word of English, had found quite the Underwear Untwisting Scheme, once a week, every week, like clockwork.

'Mrs. Tani kicked her out?'

She nodded her head and another hail of screams came from downstairs. A book bounced off a wall, then another - Mrs. Tani was hurling her small library at her husband, irate as a snake. It was four more hours before the fight subsided, and we could all get some sleep.

And then there is the war between Tomato and Force, and like the Tani House situation, that war is far from over.

Force and Tomato have both gone twenty four hours, and residents of Tani House have reported that both places are handing out more and more loot, cash back, free phone cards, they are practically feeding themselves for free on the gifts as the two stores continue their customer retention program.

What's next?

No one knows.

Don't you ever judge an ordinary Japanese suburb by its cover. Because there might not be a mad, John Denver obsessed Mrs. Yuka around, but there is bound to be her evil twin, an equally John Denver obsessed Mrs. Tani or two lurking around offering rooms to unsuspecting foreigners, lured in by benign Lonely Planet listings.

I have exactly 510 Yen left.

I am still unable to exchange the Korean Won I have, even at the largest fucking bank in Tokyo. This means I am a wooden shoe step away from begging on the streets, the banks here treat the money of their closest neighbor like its stone money from Yap.

Well, I'm not surprised, the bank's employees are all members of the Middle Aged Salaryman Club anyway, and we are talking about a very twisted underwear situation.

What does it mean to have 510 Yen left in your pocket in one of the most expensive countries in the world? I'll tell you what it means:

It means no breakfast.
It means eating a plain bowl of rice for dinner.
It means no buses.
It means no subways.
It means relying on my size 13 feet to get around Japan.
It also means FECG is laughing his head off in Osaka port.

Despite the two amazing days on Iki, and the meeting with Michael over that bowl of Tempura Udon noodle soup, I am so ready to leave Japan.

I have bought the ferry ticket back to Pusan, and have carefully added up the costs of getting to the Kyoto station by subway, then an ordinary train to Osaka Port. I will have exactly 140 Yen left. All coins of course.

It was going to be close.

If I miss the boat, the 140 Yen will allow me to get back to Osaka itself, but not back to Kyoto and the relative safety of Mrs. Tani's house.

In short I will be fucked.

Not as fucked as missing the last helicopter out of Saigon, but in pretty deep shit indeed.

Somewhere, deep in the port of Osaka, FECG is rolling around on the floor, clutching his stomach, howling in hysterics.

Wish me luck.

Love, Dave

August 21, 1992
6:44 P.M.
Straits of Japan
Typhoon Interpol

If you think I was going to leave Japan without a bang, think again.

Hi Annette.

I'm in Pusan on my way to Seoul tomorrow, and before I go on, some first impressions of Korea....

While n Japan, hair is tightly wound up, coiffed just so, admired with twittering voices, checked carefully with frequent furtive glances in a full length mirror, here in Korea, you can let your hair down and exhale.

Koreans are direct, boisterous, and un-self conscious, total strangers lean in on planes, subways and on the street to wheeze a kimchi scented hello, cars swerve crazily around corners and run red lights, taxi drivers give back change in their bare hands, rural bus drivers stop to chat with their colleagues, and women in Pusan's seafood market did little dances to welcome me to their country.

But before I even got here, I left Japan with one more story. Of course.

The ferry to South Korea left Osaka harbor the same way I arrived: on time, and in daylight. I didn't, however, get the intimate welcome I had received a month earlier from FECG, my passport was stamped and then a white-gloved customs agent pointed me up the gangway which I climbed as quickly as I could, wary of falling ACME anvils that could have tumbled down from the blue sky. I'm sure that the 140 Yen (exactly as much as calculated) I had left wouldn't have covered the hospital bill for that injury.

When I found my cabin in the stomach of the trembling ship, I realized I was aboard the same vessel I had traveled with over from Korea four weeks prior. After successfully dodging disaster after mishap while traveling through one of the world's most orderly countries, I still couldn't believe the wonkiness that had followed me so closely and so faithfully.

If it had been a dog, I would have shot that Cujo dead.

But that damn dog was about to follow me one step further.

On the top deck, I passed a few university students who giggled at me, and I was pressed with a few questions as we watched the ropes get untied and the ship drifted away from the dock. For the last time I was politely asked the same questions everyone wanted to know in Japan, and when it was over, I was almost sad. The islands in the Sea of Japan passed as the sun set, the sky darkened, and the stars came out.

But not for long.

They disappeared underneath a thick layer of cloud, a cold wind started to pick up and the ship started to rock from side to side. Whitecaps formed in the waves, and the ship's orange jump-suited crew ran around me, securing lines and tarps.

I went back to my cabin. It was still empty. There was a tiny TV but the picture showed only snow. A crumpled copy of the Japan Times was stuffed in another drawer.

Bored, I staggered down the hallway. The ship was listing so far to each side I almost tripped on the carpet. For the next hour, I walked the length of the ship, down to the boiler room and along the wall where the same Interpol posters still hung, detailing the crimes of the world's most wanted criminals.

Dinner was served in a cavernous room where the tables hummed and the chopsticks vibrated from the roar of the engines. I tried to buy a bento box from a vending machine with my last Yen.

But I didn't have enough, so I had to use my Won instead. A bento box. That is how close I came to begging on the streets in Japan. Or selling fake phone cards on the street from Iran.

Where were all the passengers? Even the college students were gone. I ate alone as a couple of cleaners mopped the rusting floors.

Then I went for a walk up on deck, but it didn't last long; it was raining now and flashes of lighting lit up the slick surfaces of the ship. Some of the corridors were now dark as the lights had been switched off.

Back in my cabin, I chose the top bunk and quickly fell asleep; there was simply nothing else to do.

A few hours later, I woke up to find the drawers and cabinets flying open and closed like they were possessed by an evil spirit, my suitcase and backpack had rolled off the bed, the lamp was banging against the wall, and only the railing was keeping me from being flung to the floor.

As I squinted my eyes in the darkness, I could see water running in under the door and sloshing in the room.

Were we sinking?

Throwing on my clothes, I climbed down from the bunk, pulled my bags out of the icy water, and opened the door.

The lights were flickering in the hallway, and I groped my way down to the staircase. There I climbed up as the ship tossed from left to right in the huge waves.

I guessed that the ship had passed through the Straits of Japan and was in the middle of the open ocean where a typhoon was roiling the sea.

Seawater and rain was gushing down the steps from upper decks, and as I got nearer to the top, a fresh whirl of wind flexed the glass windows in and out. I noticed a steel door flapping back and forth, unlatched, letting in a roaring torrent of water and silvery flashes of white lightning.

When I reached it, I pulled the handle towards me, and the door was closed, when it suddenly flew open again, the door yanked me with it, and I smashed my nose against the glass before it slammed closed, cutting off the wind, sealing out the rain and seawater.

I looked down to see an extra pair of hands that was also holding the door closed. They belonged to an orange-jacketed crewmember standing next to me, who was securing the latch that had come undone in the storm.

The man saw me smile sheepishly, but he began to scream at me in Korean, blaming me, I guessed, for the door opening in the first place, he thought I was stupid enough to have decided to take a walk during the typhoon and had unlatched the door myself.

Then he looked closer at my face and then over his

shoulder at the long line of Interpol photos posted on the wall, the same posters I had seen on the ship on my journey from Korea. He peered at my face even more closely and then ran over to the wall, where he pointed at one photo of a man wanted for murder. Then he shouted and pointed back.

He thought it was me!

I turned and ran back down the stairs as the orange-jacketed crew member chased me, but I was fast enough to out run him and after a few bolts down long corridors, and flying down iron staircases, out of breath, I reached my cabin. I slammed the door and locked myself inside.

So, I told you I left Japan with a bang, and my time in Pusan was no less fraught with problems. I thought I had left the Land of Confusion behind.

Guess not.

More news on that in the next installment.
Love, Dave

August 26th, 1992
11.17 A.M.
Pusan, South Korea
Lost in Translation

Hey Annette.

I'm at the airport in Pusan waiting for my flight to the capital, Seoul. I got a standby seat for $40, and I just finished talking to some US soldiers who told me what life was like on the American army base near the DMZ.

Two days ago, I staggered off the ferry in Pusan harbor, squinting in the dawn light, knees weak from the storm and my previous night's collision with the crew.

Hauling my bag down the rickety gangplank to sweet, solid ground, it took a few minutes before I got my balance, and more than four hours for the queasiness in my stomach to subside from the overnight journey. As I got my bearings in yet another unfamiliar city in yet another foreign country, I pushed through milling crowds and clouds of strong smelling squid to find a place to stay.

I questioned a friendly looking teenager for directions to my hotel. She grunted and seized the guidebook out of my hands in a very un-Japanese like manner, as though retrieving a bone from a naughty puppy. She brought the book to her face, but there wasn't a scrap of Korean written on the pages and she shoved the book back at me, shook her head, and walked away.

I eventually found a taxi. The driver craned his neck around to look at me closely, as though a foreigner had never sat in the back seat before (one probably hadn't) and he wanted to make sure I was real. To check, he reached between the seats, pinched my knee, and giggled.

I read off the address for my hotel and the driver's mouth dropped. His hands came off the steering wheel, he whirled around, and before I could even react, he grabbed my guidebook clean out of my hands for the second time in two minutes.

The book confused this man even more. He turned the book around in his hands until it was upside down, and then he pressed the text right up to his glasses. Mumbling softly, he looked at me and then back at the book and slammed it shut.

'PUSAN!!' he screamed brightly.

'Yes, Pusan,' I replied calmly, 'Pusan.'

When I realized from the map that his car was only about fifteen blocks from the hotel, I pointed through the windshield and the man started driving, whirling around every two seconds to see if I was still sitting in the back seat. When he saw that I was, he pinched my knee again.

Five minutes later, the driver pulled down an anonymous alley where the tiny guesthouse sat up a flight of stairs in a concrete apartment building, tucked off the boulevard that ran parallel to the sea. I smiled, paid the driver, and he screamed, 'PUSAN!' one more time before he pinched my knee for the last time.

I was greeted at the top of the stairs by the Korean equivalent of the Japanese Tatami Dragon Lady, a late middle-aged woman with thick glasses wearing an apron, a permed hairstyle and an iron-grip handshake that could easily have crushed Superman's fingers. She spoke no English, and looked me up and down thoroughly, muttering just like the taxi driver.

'Mrs. Kim,' she said in a harsh tone, pointing at herself.

With vigorous hand gestures and head nods she laid out the rules and regulations of her home, and snatched my passport from my hands like a customs official and then spent twenty minutes flipping through it trying to find the details she needed for the registration form.

I was exhausted and my eyelids sank closed. Just as I was dreaming of sleep, Mrs. Kim smacked me with her arm, she had leaned in and was peering at me closely, and it wasn't until I looked in a mirror that I realized my skin was a pale shade of green.

Finally I was released to my room where a simple mat stretched across the floor, covered with a thick blanket. I could smell salty air seeping in through the windows, and Mrs. Kim had followed me in, and was now chatting away at me in Korean, as though I were fluent, watching me unpack my bags. She remained there for ten minutes until I used the trick I had learned in Japan to get rid of Tatami Dragon Ladies, I started to unbutton my shirt and she ran off like the wind.

I don't remember even falling asleep. I just remember waking up, still in my clothes and realizing the light was all wrong. When I had arrived it was a bright morning, and now the light was fading fast. I looked at my watch. It was nearly seven o'clock in the evening. Feeling better, I took a quick shower and walked down the hall where I saw a group of western foreigners sitting in a semi-circle around a Japanese guy in the tiny living room.

They ignored me as I walked across the room, where Mrs. Kim, ever the serious hotel matron was watching the scene intently, hovering around the doorway nervously, her brows arched in confusion.

The three westerners were in their early twenties, probably college students, all the same age as their Japanese friend. They hung on his every word, and it was like watching cult members in the presence of their leader, bowing down and kissing his feet. When they spoke, it was only in Japanese, they covered their mouths when they laughed, and even their body language was Japanese. I turned to stare, but they didn't even blink an eye.

I had heard of foreigners who had gone off the rails in Japan, thinking they were Japanese, speaking only Japanese, eating only Japanese food, even dressing in traditional samurai's clothing, cutting off all ties with their previous lives.

As I pulled on my shoes Mrs. Kim gave me a nervous look. Things were not going according to her wishes, and I think she wanted these strange people out of her house.

As I pulled the door open to leave, I finally got some acknowledgement - the westerners looked at me like I was evil, some un-Japanese devil that had come in and polluted the air.

Out in the street, a chilly, salt soaked wind was blowing as people walked home. Shops were already closing, their owners were busy pulling large iron roller doors down that were then locked, obscuring the front door, including the house number.

I followed the boulevard towards the port, passing the dock where the ferry had tied up after crossing from Japan. It was already gone. The berth was now filled with squid boats polishing the large glass lights they used to attract their catch, so bright they were even visible from space.

Then, I tumbled down some steps and found a massive underground shopping center, brightly lit by neon, where restaurants and stores were still bustling and humming despite the late hour. I wandered around for almost two hours amongst the jostling, pushing people that swirled all around me.

'SOLDIER!' screamed an elderly man, running up to pump my arm up and down.

I shook my head, and he looked disappointed.

'American soldier?' he said in a whisper, looking closer at my hair, which he realized was several inches too long to satisfy the rules of the US military.

I sat down to eat a bowl of soup. As I ate, my daypack was snatched away, opened, and rifled through. Then it was dropped on the floor.

I surfaced from this underground world at an exit where the salt spray tickled my nose. I was in a huge fish market where slick plastic buckets were full of seething eels, ink squirting squid, snapping shrimps, and furious crabs, while teenagers and college students were screaming and jumping up and down, spilling out of the bars and clubs lining the slippery cement.

I walked past one group and before I knew it was pressed with alcohol from a heavy dark bottle, putrid fumes blown in my face as they begged me to take some. After I drank, the gang tossed one of their smaller friends up and down like a rag doll. I watched them do this for a few times taking a few polite sips, before they dropped their unfortunate friend right on his head.

Then, two pairs of arms snagged me and I was hustled into a dark bar, and soon alcohol was served all round. I learned the gang was celebrating one of their friend's last night of freedom before he entered the Korean Army, and they had six hours to party before he had to report to base.

As I was introduced, each guy patted me on the back and shook my hand for longer than was necessary. It was weird, after a month in Japan, where you floated through public areas as though you were invisible, here I was met with intense eye contact, arms were thrown over my shoulder, and one of the taller guys, suavely dressed in a pink Lacoste shirt, looked at me and said, 'I like sex.' After slicking back his hair with his fingers, he added, 'I have seen last day Basic Instinct. Very sexy lady!'

Then, a dreaded karaoke machine was switched on and wailing and croaking commenced, I was trotted out onto the tiny stage, laughed at, pelted with peanuts and ordered to sing. So sing I did, luckily lubricated by enough alcohol to subdue my hatred of this truly evil form of entertainment. (fortunately, no one sang John Denver songs)

Two hours later, we wandered outside into the cold air and I was taken to a street stall where a tank was full of small octopus swimming around in panic. I expected some kind of calamari, but instead was served a live octopus, whose tentacles were reaching out of the bowl of water, searching for a safe passage back to the sea.

But it didn't have long to live. One of the more red-faced guys grabbed it, stuffed the head into his mouth and as the tentacles frantically hung on his face and his glasses, he devoured it like some spectacled Jabba the Hutt. Before he swallowed it, the last tentacle snatched his glasses and they fell to the floor.

He offered one of the arms to me, that was still wriggling furiously on the table, but I was finally able to make an easy escape, two of the guys threw up simultaneously in a gutter, causing the proprietor to kick us out of his restaurant with a volley of bellows. After my goodbyes, I fell back down into the underground shopping mall. It was 11.45 p.m. Though I figured I could guess where I had first entered the mall, to my alcohol soaked brain, the entire shopping mall was now a rat maze with Mrs. Kim the piece of cheese at the end.

Completely lost, I eventually picked a flight of stairs where I guessed Mrs. Kim's house was. When I stepped outside, I took a look around me and cursed to myself, not one building, house, street corner or shop looked familiar, everything had been transformed, first by the darkness, and second by those metal doors that covered all the house numbers. I had no idea how far away Mrs. Kim's house was.

Like Hansel and Gretl, I was bereft of breadcrumbs. I had taken no business card with Mrs. Kim's phone number, I had no guidebook, no key, not even my passport, not even my plane ticket, which I was due to use the next day. How was I going to find all my documents, money and bags in time for my noon flight the next day?

Fifteen minutes later a man walked by wearing a police uniform. I stood up and introduced myself and he shrank back against the wall like I was Jack the Ripper, he scrunched his brow, shouted in Korean and waved me off, hoping I would disappear.

I turned around, walked back to the main road and tried again to retrace my steps to locate Mrs. Kim. I was now even more confused and sat down again on a curb, dejected. It was almost 12.30 a.m.

Then a man walked by wearing a hotel uniform. He looked over at me and smiled.

'Fuck you, man.'

For this guy, the F word seemed to be lost in translation. However, if he had looked closely at my face he could have seen that I knew I was, indeed, pretty fucked. I stood up and tried to explain to him the word hotel by bringing my hands together and pressing them against my ear and motioning with my hands to imitate a key turning in a lock.

'11 o'clock, I need to be at airport.'

He looked at me smiled again, and started to walk away. I followed him like a lost kitten. We walked along the empty streets, deserted and quiet with not a soul around. I kept repeating my story to him like a broken record, complete with sound effects for emphasis until he whirled around and shrieked, 'HOTEL??'

'Hotel, yes HOTEL!' I shouted back. 'I'm lost!!'

'Rost?'

'Lost,' I said with emphasis, saying it slowly.

His brow furrowed, and then we turned a corner and he shouted, 'Fuck you, man!' again at the top of his lungs to no one in particular.

Then we reached his hotel where a serious faced front office manager was standing behind his desk, thinking his young employee had brought with him a new customer. His face fell a mile when he knew I was not a new customer and that I needed help instead.

I could see by the rate sheet placed at the reception counter that hotel rooms cost three times as much money as I had in my pocket. When the manager knew this, happy to see the back of me he sent his young employee off with me to go find my hotel. Barking orders into his ear, he slid a Pusan street directory at him across the counter. So off we went again in search of Mrs. Kim.

We walked around for almost an hour, it was creeping towards 1.45 in the morning. Cold gusts of wind were blowing in off the sea and we shivered as the pages flapped in the growing breeze, drops of rain pattered on the paper which was beginning to turn soggy.

Then, in a desperate attempt to ditch his awful foreign friend, the man began pounding on random metal doors, whether he knew they were hotels, or just private houses, I didn't know, but it proved he wanted rid him of me, and fast.

A light went on, and for a moment I thought it was Mrs. Kim. Instead, it was her clone, a woman of about the same age, stature and temperament, shouting down at us from an open window. After exchanging several sentences in Korean, she finally let us into her hotel, despite the late hour.

I put on an elaborate, Oscar worthy pantomime for the new Mrs. Kim, who understood me far better than the hotel clerk; clearly, she had long experience in getting her point across with hand motions. The new Mrs. Kim gave me a room for about fifteen dollars, and I paid her quickly before she could get suspicious and change her mind. But as I closed the door to my room, she looked at me wildly when she saw I had no luggage, and even worse, no passport, and no other forms of ID.

I don't think she thought I was a prostitute checking into her hotel, but she gave my new friend a shrill earful about what she thought about being woken up at two in the morning and forced to rent a paper-less and possession-less foreigner a room without a reservation.

My hotel friend shot off a few sentences that placated the new Mrs. Kim and she smiled at me. Dripping wet and holding the ruined Pusan street directory he bowed deeply anyway and shook my hand as he stepped towards the door to return to his doubtlessly furious boss.

I almost expected him to say, 'Fuck you, man.'

But he didn't. He smiled, went down the steps and disappeared. By the time he saw the last of me, and the cold, wet adventure I had dragged him into was over, on the cold trudge back to his hotel I'm sure he wished he had understood the correct translation of those words to really let me have it.

The next morning, after a fitful, fret-filled sleep peppered with dreams of overstaying and deportation, tearful phone calls to an embassy in Seoul who would offer no help, and expensive replacements of plane tickets, I prayed for daylight.

'He prayed for daylight.' It should go on my tombstone.

As soon as the sun rose, I scrambled out of bed, pulled on my clothes, bid the new Mrs. Kim goodbye and found the street as I had remembered from the previous morning, bustling with traffic, and full of people.

More importantly, all the metal doors were now open, and in less than twenty minutes I had not only retraced my steps from the night before, but I knocked on the right door that was answered by a white faced woman, there before me, was the old Mrs. Kim who screamed shrilly, threw up her hands and hugged me like a mother greeting her long lost child.

She then bopped me on the head, and angrily handed over my room key. In five minutes flat, I had pulled off my shoes, gathered up my things, pulled on my shoes again and headed out the door to the airport. As I staggered under the weight of my bags, sweating, still pale-faced from the sleepless night, I found a taxi driver idling in front of the building and asked him to go to the airport.

'Airport?' he said, confused.

'Airport. Plane. Fly!' I shouted, searching for my Korean Air ticket to show him. When I found it, I handed it to him and he turned it in his hands over and over, admiring the pretty logo of Korea's national airline, but not understanding a word of what I meant.

Then, I made a whooshing sound like a plane taking off, matched with a hand motion like a plane lifting off a runway.

'Aaaah! Hairport,' he said, putting the car into gear and driving away. Twenty minutes later he pulled up at a railway museum and screams, 'Hairport!'

My patience was now as thin as ice on a lake in April. I hopped out of the car and found a bewildered college student standing there and asked her to explain to the driver where I needed to go.

'Domestic airport?' she asked cautiously.

'No, international. There are two airports here in Pusan?'

'No.'

'Just the main Pusan airport, please, I'm very late.'

She leaned in through the window, talked to the driver who finally understood the command. He drove off and twenty five minutes later started pointing at Boeing jets landing over our heads.

'Hairport!' he shouted, taking both his hands off the steering wheel.

'Yes! Hairport!' I replied.

And then, instead of driving to the passenger terminal, he stops in front of the Korean Air cargo office.

'Hairport!' he shouted, clapping his hands in delight.

Grinding my teeth together, I pointed to the other terminal. He drove over to it and lurched to a stop. I unloaded my suitcase, threw some Korean Won onto the front seat to cover the fare and gratefully bid the cab driver, and Pusan farewell.

I'm in Seoul airport now, flying home tonight.

Memories of my time in Japan are still fresh here in Korea, there is an obsession with Japan everywhere in this city, street fashions, food, and music too. A university student hoping to practice his English before an upcoming exam, and a self confessed patriot of his country, murmured to himself, 'But, she's so beautiful,' when he saw a girl sitting nearby on the subway who had styled her hair like a famous Japanese pop singer.

Everyone asks me if I have been to Japan, and when I say yes, their eyes widen, quickly ticking off the checklists of Japanese culture - sushi, geisha, kimonos and bullet trains. Less than a month ago, I would have agreed with them, but now I know Japan is all that and much more, including Tatami Dragon Ladies and strip searches and Disgruntled Expatriates and bone rattling earthquakes and fierce typhoons and little old ladies with crooked teeth.

Because that's what travel teaches you, including:

'Fuck you' can easily be lost in translation.

Love, Dave

Hey Annette,

I have back in the US now for only twenty-four hours after my first trip to Asia. I feel like I've returned to another country. I am stomping my feet in front of doors waiting for them to open, because in Japan they were all electric, and I'm taking change back from un-gloved taxi drivers with derision, because in Japan the thought of naked hands was abhorrent.

Maybe it's just the jetlag that is infecting my brain, but I really miss Asia, and, most of all, Japan. I'm writing this at three a.m. and in the total silence it seems like one hundred years ago since I was there.

If memory serves me right, the ferry from Pusan is just about to pull into Osaka port. I'm sure FECG is there, waiting to make some traveler's life hell. And I'm sure Mrs. Yuka is screaming 'OHAYO GOZAIMUS!' at some traveler who came home late, crashed through a spider web, and forgot to come to dinner.

I am adding a new word to the dictionary: flightmare. Any nightmare aloft qualifies as one. And they can occur on any carrier, at any time. Maybe they bite us on the ass after enjoying too much freedom. Who knows. But every once in the while the Travel Gods must get pretty bored to inflict this kind of torture while we enjoy the transport that was set in motion by the Wright Brothers, and developed into the seamless experience that maybe mere mortals weren't supposed to enjoy.

What happened on Flight 16 will frighten you from ever shrugging your shoulders about the randomness of seat assignments ever again, that faceless computer that ends up dealing seatmates to us like cards in some sadistic poker game.

While traveling through Korea I had heard many people praying in English, on buses, trains and even in shopping malls. A common question people asked, almost before your name or nationality is 'Are you a Christian?'

In fact, on my last day in Seoul, a cult called the 'Mission For The Coming Days' claimed the world was going to end on October 28th, 1992 and was papering subway stations with flyers advising passengers in English and Korean to repent now before the day of reckoning came.

Fire and brimstone, devils and pitchforks, that sort of thing. Nothing I hadn't already experienced in Japan, let me tell you.

When I ignored the hundredth person I had seen handing out flyers while screaming through megaphones, draped with sandwich boards covered with messages from God and shaking their fists into the air, a college-aged girl, irate at my curt dismissal of her leaflet, had followed me not only down onto the platform but into the subway car itself.

There, she lunged into my face, screaming about the second coming of Jesus Christ. When I still didn't want the flyer she has handing out, she angrily stepped back onto the platform, and after the door had closed and we were speeding away, she screamed at me, 'REMEMBER OCTOBER 28th!!!!'

When I boarded my Korean Air flight home to Los Angeles from Seoul's Kimpo airport, I thought I had left these deeply religious people behind. What I was to learn was that flightmares don't always have to come from disintegrating engines or cabin depressurization or an onboard fire, which those corporate safety videos prepare you for with the unnerving nonchalance of a candy bar commercial. Flightmares can come stealthily through the randomness of that computer at the check-in desk that decides who you will be fighting that armrest war with for the next twelve or eighteen hours.

Boarding for Flight 16 began with a nightmarish crush where virtually every passenger had shoved boxes full of electronics into the overheard bins, so overloaded they seemed ready to break free from the cabin ceiling. The band of sullen flight attendants, pretty but stone-faced, ignored their pleas for help and just stared back as though they were invisible.

One of them was even filing her nails as she sat at her

station, waiting for pushback. THANKS FOR FLYING KOREAN AIR!

The MD-11 aircraft was so new that all the seatbacks and tray tables creaked every time they were moved. But it wasn't the newness of the plane that was making most of the noise, it was the passengers, as the jet rushed down the runway, engines screaming, a chorus of 'Hallelujah, Praise the Lords' rose up from all over the plane.

Once we had reached cruising altitude over the Japan Alps, the meal service was underway when a tiny blue light flicked on above our heads and a sharp chime pinged five times around the cabin. The crew looked at each other in terror, abandoned their carts, and fled back to their stations.

But before they could even reach their seats, gravity evaporated.

The wide body jet plunged though a hole torn in the air, sending some of them straight to the ceiling before being flung back to the ground, I actually saw passengers several rows in front of me go straight up, like a Space Shuttle zero gravity training flight. As the plane fell further, it tilted crazily to the left and right as screams erupted from First Class all the way back to the last rows in economy.

As the plane shuddered, overhead bins popped open and the televisions and electronics that had been stuffed inside threatened to jump out. The force even dropped some oxygen masks that sent some people into hysterics.

Sitting there gripping my seat and trying to find where my stomach had gone, I noticed a flight attendant had fallen down in the aisle next to me, and was clinging to the base of my seat. I reached down to steady her as the plane kept falling towards the dark, cold Pacific, which was mercifully still tens of thousands of feet away.

But for how long?

To my right sat an older Korean woman, her hair styled in that tight permanent favored by most women her age. Staring at me with a fierce grin that seemed both childlike and evil, she looked like a character invented by Stephen King.

As a Caucasian passenger on Korean Air, you were often the only non-Asian on the entire 747, and college student seatmates treated you like a rock star, business men handed out their cards with both hands and a bow trying to invite you to get in on some shady import scheme, or some matronly lady who spoke fluent English tried to set you up with their niece studying economics at UCLA.

To avoid any sort of conversation with this woman, I smiled weakly and looked to my left, where a woman who looked strangely similar was sitting, wearing a light blue sweater. She was staring at me in the same way, her petite face framed with an identical permanent. It dawned on me that I was not only sitting between identical twin sisters, but both of them were armed, not with submachine guns, but the spirit of the Lord. Both had bilingual Bibles sitting on their tray tables in front of them.

'Don't worry, friend, if we die, we will all enter the Kingdom of Heaven,' said the Right Sister with a curt nod.

'Yes. Remember, Jesus loves you,' said the Left Sister.

I didn't know what to say, so I looked down to see if I could help the flight attendant who had fallen, but by now she had crawled up to the front of the cabin and had rejoined her colleagues at their rear facing seats in the over wing station.

I flashed a quick, polite smile to the Right Sister and Left Sister, hoping I could feign a lack of knowledge of the English language. Just then, the plane was sent into another sickening free fall, setting off fresh waves of screaming amongst the passengers as though we were riding some stratospheric rollercoaster ride.

As I bent over to feign motion sickness, my two new friends refused to leave me alone. Before I could even protest, the Left Sister and Right Sister pried my hands off the armrest, gripped my fingers as tightly as an octopus, and then they shouted in unison, 'LETS PRAY!'

As the words, 'Let's not,' flashed through my head, another bout of turbulence sent the plane plunging again, and the Sisters' grip tightened like vices.

And so we prayed. Hard.

'Are you a Christian?' asked the Right Sister.

'DO YOU ACCEPT JESUS CHRIST AS YOUR SAVIOUR???' yelled the Left Sister.

'INTO YOUR HEART??' screamed the Right one, even louder, over the sound of the engines.

Apparently to these identical twin sisters, I had a soul that needed saving.

And bad.

'DEEP INTO YOUR HEART???' demanded the Left Sister

as she beat her breast for emphasis with her free hand. The plane continued to jolt and bounce through the air, tossing drinks into the aisles and sending grandmas for the airsickness bags.

'Uh, OK,' I stammered weakly, not sure of what I was scared of more, their feverish Christian devotion or the stomach churning turbulence and imminent, watery crash.

'Hail Mary?' asked the Left Sister to her sibling.

'Yes,' replied her sister.

So the sisters tightened their grip on my hands and as we waited for the turbulence to stop, they chanted out ten Hail Mary's in a row, heads bent in concentration, as I sat there listening to words I hadn't heard since I was, oh, about eight.

When they were finished, they looked over at me.

'Jesus loves you,' reminded the Left Sister.

The Right Sister nodded sagely, cocked her head to the side, and smiled that Stephen King grin again. 'Very much.'

They refused to let go of their grip, and as the plane kept on shaking, I thought if the jet was to go down, they were going to find my hands welded to these two women, a Bible study group in the sky, praying until the bitter end.

Suddenly, the turbulence stopped, they let go, but I wasn't out of the woods just yet.

Left Sister slapped her Bible down on my tray table. 'The Gospel is a good thing to read for a young man like you,' she said as she flipped open the book to Genesis. 'Read.'

I looked at her with my mouth open.

A look of doubt flashed over Left Sister's face, and suddenly she spat out, 'YOU DON'T ACCEPT JESUS CHRIST AS YOUR SAVIOUR?'

I just kept looking at her, hoping the jet would break apart and this would all be over.

Right Sister jumped in and hissed, 'Jesus loves you. We are all Christians. You are not a Christian?'

I half expected the devil himself to saunter down the aisle and claim me as one of his own. Were these women bent on cleansing my soul of my sins, right here on this McDonnell Douglas plane, using mineral water in lieu of holy water, dunking my head in a lavatory sink in some shotgun baptism? I'm sure they wouldn't have much difficulty in finding a priest amongst the passengers, ready to baptize this infidel that innocently sat with the masses in Economy Class.

Left Sister snatched the Bible back as though it was in the possession of a demon, and stared straight ahead at the seat back in front of her.

You may not know this, but flying back to the west coast from Asia is quicker than flying to Asia by as much as three hours. Though I expected we had just a few more hours to go, when I looked at my watch, I saw there were still nine mind numbing hours to go before touching down in L.A., I snuck a look around the cabin: there was not even one free seat where I could move. It was going to be a long, cold-shouldered flight indeed.

So I came up with a plan. I pretended to sleep. I pretended to read the Duty Free magazine. I took great interest in the conversion rates between US dollars and Japanese Yen and Korean Won, and then turned my attention to the in-flight magazine, reading it cover-to-cover, over and over. Then I popped in earphones even though my batteries had died on my Walkman, and fake slept again.

Neither sister would even look at me, or even acknowledge that I existed. I felt like the second grade kid being punished by his Sunday schoolteacher. When a second though smaller bout of turbulence racked the plane about three hours out of Los Angeles, the Left Sister and Right Sister simply bent their heads to their tray tables, pressed their foreheads against the bibles, and prayed.

Without me.

When the announcement finally came over the loudspeaker that we were landing in Los Angeles, reminding us to fill out our customs forms and to have our passports handy, the last thirty minutes of the flight went by the slowest, as freedom dangled in front of me like a carrot hanging from a hook inches from a donkey's mouth.

As soon as the MD-11 touched down, reached the terminal at LAX and the fasten seatbelt sign flashed off, I grabbed my carry-on bags and fled the aircraft like it was on fire.

So there you have it, the last disaster.

If there is going to be a cast party for my first Asian adventure, FECG would be front and center providing the strip show, Mrs.

Yuka and Mrs. Tani would be providing the entertainment (a medley of wholesome John Denver hits, of course), a selection of Disgruntled Expatriates would provide the bitch sessions, a couple of earthquakes would provide the rock and roll, Mrs. Kim would be in charge of the guest list, and that little old lady on Iki would be the center of attention with her teeth pointing crazily in all directions.

Believe it or not, even after the raft of adventures and catastrophes, I want to go back to Japan. Four weeks just scratched the surface. I'm sure there are a lot of ladies with crooked teeth out there, just waiting for a lift!

I've got a huge National Geographic map spread out in front of me and covering the entire left quarter of the page is India. I am even cautiously curious about visiting that place to see the Taj and the Saddhus and the Ganges and the Himalayas.

Even if doing so would probably place me as the top story on the CNN evening news in my fifteen seconds of fame:

'On this edition of Larry King we talk to an American traveler who has just escaped from five years of brainwashing by a naked Saddhu in the high Himalayas.....Don't go away, his amazing story is coming up next!'

'American traveler found safe after wandering penniless for a decade in search of his sanity, and his passport,' the BBC headline would scream.

AM I MAD?
IF JAPAN WAS STRIPSEARCHES, WHAT WAS INDIA GOING TO BE?

No, my fantasy of visiting India proves that I am just under the mind altering influence of jetlag and forgetting the looks on all those women's faces in Osaka port when it was I who was the floorshow.

Maybe it's time I get a T-shirt printed up 'I Survived a Tatami Dragon Lady And All I Got Was This Lousy T-Shirt' or create my own clubs, like 'The Strip Searched in Osaka Club' or the 'Mistaken For An Interpol Criminal Club' or, the best of all, an honorary member in the 'Ride Givers to Women with Crooked Teeth Club.'

I hope it's the last one.

I think the old lady on Iki is drawing up the papers as I write.

Love, Dave

PS. Remember October 28th is coming! According to that mad college student in Seoul we all have less than two months to live!!

Cambodia & Vietnam

February 2, 1994
8:32 P.M.
Siem Reap, Cambodia
Welcome to the Jungle

Hey Annette,

I don't know what the owner of my hotel was so worried about. Those Khmer Rouge soldiers didn't steal his motorbike for god sakes. (OK, they might have thought about it, but they didn't in the end)

I only got to Angkor Wat this morning after a brief flightmare from Bangkok that passed through Phnom Penh. The 737's pilot announced in his Texas twang that the plane had undergone a monthly maintenance check hence the two-hour delay. Everything on the plane seemed normal until the air conditioning was turned on: hundreds of mosquitoes were blasted into the cabin in some Southeast Asian version of 'The Birds' only these beasts had blood sucking on their mind, not eye pecking.

As I filled out my customs form my seatmate slapped me across the forehead to kill a mosquito that had landed there.

He missed.

A minute later I returned the favor, smashing a bug against his forehead. It hung there for a little while before it peeled off and fell into his lap.

Touché.

Then the plane took off and the cockpit door swung open to reveal a nice view of the bright blue sky and the reassuring sight of the pilots gripping the controls.

After dozens of Laurel and Hardy smacks and slaps between total strangers to kill the flying fuckers in the cabin, the 737 landed. I gratefully stood up to get off the Hitchcockesque plane. Before I stepped outside the aircraft however, I snuffed one of the bastard mosquitoes up my nose.

Thanks for flying Thai Kampuchea Airways, and welcome to Cambodia.

Have you ever boarded a flight in a country in the middle of a civil war where there were no X-ray machines for security, but where passengers were carefully weighed in case they needed to pay for excess baggage?

FOR THEMSELVES?

After the staff asked me to stand on the scale along with my luggage, I was handed a boarding pass and pointed to the plane. There was:

No X-ray machine.
No security check.
No pat down.

Flying with a bunch of military personnel didn't make me feel any more secure. The French pilot muscled the ATR-72 into the sky and then forty minutes later made a seatbelt essential descent into Siem Reap with the nose pointing to the ground like an angry bull, ready to charge the terminal. As we sailed down the gravel runway a cow flashed past the window, and then for good measure, another cow.

Thank you for flying Royal Air Cambodge, and welcome to Siem Reap.

An hour later, after an oxcart had delivered our luggage to the terminal, (I'm not joking) I found a guesthouse, and a motorbike, and was sitting on it in the garden, sweating in the heat as I was given a stern lecture on how to drive it.

Even though it was the first motorbike I had ever driven, things were not going well. I had already careened off the pavement, Evel Knievel style, directly into the bushes surrounding the small guesthouse. Renting a motorbike was the cheapest way to see Angkor Wat and although I was failing miserably, I was still determined to learn.

The guesthouse owner was shaking his head and saying poisonous things in Khmer under his breath. Through clenched teeth he explained how his 'Golden Goose' was driven. But the bike kept leaping into the air like a bronco and flinging me off. After a final, terse demonstration in broken English and a few wobbly attempts, I was released from his custody and I took off north, towards Angkor.

Before I left, however, I was given a strong warning.

'Don't stay in the temples after three thirty. Or visit Banteay Srei. The Khmer Rouge have mined it and will kidnap you if you are out driving in the early morning or late at night.' The man wiped sweat off his brow and looked at me closely. 'Are you sure you don't want to wait until tomorrow?'

I explained again how I had first learned of Angkor Wat from an encyclopedia when I was seven years old. Black and white pictures of mysterious, eerily smiling stone faces strangled with vines had stared up at me out of the 10th century. Surrounded by suburbia, the ruins of the lost city of Angkor mesmerized me for hours. Here was a real Indiana Jones mystery, still out there, waiting.

A mystery that simply could not wait another day.

So with five hours to go before darkness, I shook my head and drove off, winding my way through the colonial heart of Siem Reap. Once I found the road leading to Angkor Wat I sped off north towards the temples. After paying an entrance fee at a small wooden hut manned by a smiling and very surprised security guard, he sucked in his breath when he saw I had no guide. In my shaky Khmer I thanked him and continued north, realizing that in just a few minutes I would be exploring the ruins that had captivated me as a child. Once again travel was bringing a 2D photo to 3D life. As I drove on through the silence, cicadas buzzed like ferocious jet engines all around me.

Within a kilometer of the famous temples the motorbike's engine coughed, lurched, and ground to a halt. Cursing, I tried to restart it, but the machine wouldn't budge. I attempted to put it into neutral but the gear stubbornly remained in first. All I could do was sit and wait. For what, I didn't know, there were no vehicles out here on the potholed road and my destination remained tantalizingly and maddeningly out of reach. My dream had suddenly ground to a halt, and Angkor seemed no closer than it had been in that encyclopedia twenty years ago.

Suddenly five young men with AK-47's slung over their shoulders jumped out from the bushes.

They had no shoes, no army uniforms and no badges. One of them pointed his gun at me and the others questioned me coldly in rapid fire Khmer. I shrugged nervously and pointed to the dead engine and then in the direction of Angkor, hoping they would realize I was just a harmless traveler.

They kept firing questions until I pulled out my guidebook with photos of the temples. As they curiously peered at the English writing that they didn't understand, they pointed and smiled at the pictures of the spires of the Bayon and it's famous faces.

Then, the tallest soldier pushed me off the bike and I thought he was going to steal it. Instead, with an expert kick of his bare foot he restarted the engine and with a smile passed the purring motorbike back to me.

One of the other soldiers tapped me on the shoulder, making a motion next to his mouth - Do you have any cigarettes? I shook my head. Great, I thought, now they really will steal my bike. But I opened my bag and showed them my Cambodian map and my guidebook again where those large color pictures of Angkor Wat were printed.

Their eyes lit up when they saw the photos once more, and I quickly tore them out and handed them over, holding my breath. They accepted them graciously before tucking them into their pockets.

We shook hands, smiled, and I took off.

Phew.

Accelerating as fast as the sputtering motorbike would allow, I looked back cautiously. The cluster of soldiers had disappeared into the bushes with the stealth of leopards.

I never saw them again.

A minute later I turned a corner and there in front of me were the spires of Angkor Wat. When I stopped in front of the long, flag-stoned causeway leading inside, the hairs on my neck stood on end - the black and white images I had seen as a child in that encyclopedia were now not only in color but right in front of me. Indiana Jones indeed.

I simply couldn't have waited another day.

I parked and locked the bike in a dusty patch at the foot of the flagstone causeway and as I approached Angkor Wat I passed not one other human soul until I reached the four long galleries of ornate carvings depicting Cambodia's rich history. There, tiny, wizened women were sweeping the floor, startled to see a westerner appear as if out of nowhere. The galleries were crowded with locals running their fingers along the carvings that were polished smooth by generations of Cambodians doing the same thing.

Friendly Theravada monks padded barefoot around the

complex, offering blessings to worshippers who were also greatly surprised to see a foreigner wandering alone around Angkor Wat. I still had, and would not see, a single foreign traveler all day.

At the urging of a wrinkled monk I bowed down to receive a blessing crouched in front of a giant weathered statue of Vishnu as incense swirled up into the dark ceilings of Angkor, populated with bats.

Driving through one of the city's main gates later that afternoon, as my wheel splashed through a puddle, a hundred frogs leaped in fright and clung to me like living suction cups before leaping off again. A couple of women carrying heavy shoulder poles saw this and laughed.

A few seconds later a dazed bat fell from high up in the rafters and a local man, tattooed across his chest with Khmer writing and symbols and carrying a satchel full of dead bats, rushed over and picked it up. Through hand signals I learned he cooked these bats into a soup.

Angkor was not a museum.

All around it, people were worshipping, growing rice meters from temples, fishing in royal ponds, eking out a living: these city wasn't sterile at all, secured behind glass or cordoned off by velvet ropes.

Angkor was alive.

This was confirmed at another temple, Ta Prom, where an old woman read the crumbling script on the walls as though it were today's newspaper. Two young school girls, facial features mirror images of the carved faces all around us led me down dank corridors choked with massive serpent-like vines to reveal rooms full of cobwebbed Buddhist statues, beheaded by the Khmer Rouge.

Sunburned and exhausted, at three o'clock I tore myself away from Angkor Wat and headed back down the main road to Siem Reap, heeding the warning I had been given not to stay out after three thirty.

Just then a low sonic boom thundered across the dry plains; a wall of coal black clouds was quickly advancing from the direction of Siem Reap, cutting off my safe return. There was no way I would make it before the storm broke and as I looked around for some kind of shelter, lightning was now stabbing the earth like jagged, silver knives.

Every bush I passed suddenly seemed a refuge for Khmer Rouge soldiers and I half expected a band of teenagers to jump out and demand my bike. A lightning bolt struck the road about one hundred meters away from me and I thought, why couldn't I have waited another day? I'm going to get electrocuted before I can even tell anyone about this amazing experience. Gunning the engine harder now, when I looked over my shoulder the clouds had advanced even closer - thunderbolts were striking the earth every few seconds and the musty smell of rain was in the air. The temperature had dropped dramatically.

Up ahead, I could see the faces of the Bayon smiling at me.

Safety.

I gripped the handlebars as dirt stung my eyes and drove as fast as the Golden Goose would allow. The wall of rain was just fifty meters away now and as the lip of the coal black clouds spilled over the edge of the clearing around the Bayon branches were ripped off crashed in front of me. When I parked and locked my bike, blinded by dust, the storm broke, raindrops the size of metal coins pelted my head as I ran up the steps of the Bayon and into the thirteenth century building.

Inside, the entire temple was completely deserted. Earlier in the day I had watched wrinkled Buddhist nuns bless large clusters of village children and monks had stopped me to practice their English. Now the place was eerily empty and my stomach fell. The locals were gone for a reason. They were well aware of the still ever present danger of murder at the hands of the young barefoot soldiers loyal to Pol Pot.

As the rain fell like a great curtain, water gushed through cracks in the ceilings, flooding the hallways and poured in through open windows. I had a flimsy backpack holding my journal and camera, and desperate to keep them dry from the water I ran from room to room, splashing through puddles, looking for a dry place. But there weren't any. Eventually I found a room that faced the inner courtyard where I leaned against the wall, sweating, panting, and dripping with water. Why hadn't I waited until tomorrow, my brain screamed.

A flash of lightning lit up the room and I looked over to see four of those iconic Bayon faces, lips curled back into that famous smile illuminated in a brilliant flash of lightning. Mocking me, or laughing with me, I wasn't sure.

After exploring Angkor, I knew it was alive, but now I could see it breathing.

Then I remembered the rule.

Be back by three thirty.

I looked at my watch. It was three fifteen. I would never get back to the safety of Siem Reap in time to avoid contact with the Khmer Rouge. I had been lucky once, but that had been in daylight. Who knew what would happen now in the darkness of this monsoon rainstorm.

As the thunderous booms echoed through the stone building, the minutes ticked by as I watched in fearful fascination as the Bayon faces dripped with water and lit up again and again. They were welcoming the first large storm of the annual monsoon season just as they had done for hundreds of years. And I was the only witness.

For more than an hour I crouched in that dark room listening to the roar of the wind through the empty corridors that earlier that day had been choked with incense smoke and packed with smiling people. I was definitely not in Kansas anymore; less than seven hours after leaving the safety of Bangkok I had come face to face with the reality of Cambodia's civil war.

The glistening faces continued to be illuminated by the flashes of lightning; one moment darkness, the next moment light, and the moment after that, darkness was followed closely by light once more.

It seemed a perfect metaphor for Cambodia itself.

The steady rush of water leaking through the porous roof tapered off and the rain finally stopped.

I gingerly hopped over puddles inside the temple and I emerged into bright sunlight and walked back to the motorbike, cold, wet, and shivering. The Golden Goose had been knocked over by the storm though amazingly the motor started on the first try.

The monsoon clouds were gone and only the wet roads and broken branches were evidence of the violent storm that had just passed. As I drove through the cool, damp air back towards the safety of the town, I looked nervously again at every bush and tree anticipating more groups of young soldiers who might jump out. And driving down that long, straight road the spires of the Bayon refused to disappear behind the thick jungle. For a long time it felt as though I wasn't moving forward at all, as though the mysterious temple was preventing me from leaving, it's invisible fingers gripping me tightly, strangling me like those vines at Ta Prom.

I could feel those Bayon faces staring at the back of my neck. With the gods watching, I twisted my head around and smiled in their direction.

I was glad I hadn't waited another day.

I am sitting on the mosquito-infested terrace of my guesthouse, swatting at the flying fuckers in much the same way as this morning's flightmare from Bangkok.

Thailand already seems like light years away.

I have just explored the tiny town here. There is nothing much to see, a few crumbling colonial villas and a lot of hotel construction sites but little else. I have seen not another foreigner, either.

Though I did find a really awesome hotel. Totally derelict of course, in the spirit of Angkor Wat. It is an old French colonial hotel, massive, imposing, trashed and abandoned, full of bat droppings, smashed furniture, and collapsed ceilings. Clearly it had not welcomed guests for many decades. I wandered around it in much the same way as I did today at the Bayon though my guidebook nor locals had any idea about the hotel's history.

> Who built this temple to tourism?
> Who constructed this pagoda to package tourists?
> Could it, would it, ever welcome guests again?

In Cambodia, you are never sure what tomorrow will bring.

So, after my rain soaked afternoon I got back in one piece to the safety of Siem Reap. When I told the long suffering guesthouse manager what had happened with those barefoot soldiers earlier this afternoon his eyes widened in acute fear.

'You should take more care!' he thundered.

I handed over the keys to his precious Golden Goose and he snatched them back. But then he smiled and pushed his two palms together and pressed them against his forehead in the traditional Khmer gesture. I mirrored it with more grace (I think) than how I drive motorbikes.

He realized at the last second that in the black and white world of Cambodia, every tourist needed to be treated like a Golden Goose because no one knew how tomorrow was going to turn out. Especially travelers who returned his precious motorbike slightly worse for wear, though at least in one intact piece.

I've got two more days here before heading back to Phnom Penh and on to Vietnam. Before that, remember:

If the gods are watching, smile back.

Love, Dave

February 4, 1994
7:02 A.M.
Phnom Penh, Cambodia
Year Zero

Hi Annette,

I'm having breakfast at the Capitol Hotel in Phnom Penh after my loop south along Cambodia's coast. I'm surrounded by some of the more colorful characters on the overland trail.

It looks like Bangkok's Khao San road has exploded.

As my first introduction to the real backpacker scene (Japan and Korea don't count, as they are shunned as being too expensive and remember the golden rule, the cheaper the paradise, the faster you are supposed to get there and the longer you are supposed to stay) and I'm overhearing conversations, talking about THE best secret beach on Bali and THE in guesthouse in Goa and which trekking route in Nepal they wouldn't be caught DEAD on and which guesthouse in Chiang Mai PROVED you were in Thailand to MINGLE with the people and NOT just follow the Lonely Planet herd.

Funny that they are all clutching the same guidebooks.

The Little Red Book for The Independent Traveler!

But there is one common topic.

You guessed it. India.

It has been two years since I've been in Asia and I hardly heard about the country since leaving Japan (even though its got nearly one billion people). I forgot. Out here, rubbing shoulders again with the multi-generational and multi-geographical mongrel tribe that is endlessly obsessed with nirvana and secret paradises and drugs and freedom, India is it, India is everything.

I'm also starting to realize just like countries have their own culture, the same thing can be said about the travelers you meet there. That being said, while Japan had the serious culture-vulture-language-student crowd cornered, Cambodia has the dreadlocks-and-pirate-pants-with-knock-off-Teva-sandals-and-other-fake-designer-brand toting crowd down cold.

I wonder what Vietnam will be like?

A side note about knock off designer brands. Japan and Korea were knock-off free zones, but Cambodia is flooded with the stuff that's sold everywhere including photocopied books and dictionaries. Lost in translation in Cambodia means Versace becomes Versuce, Gucci becomes Guvvi, LowePro becomes LovePro, and Nike becomes Nake.

Back to my trip so far: after flying back from Siem Reap, the taxi driver from Phnom Penh's airport was strangely lost, driving in two large circles that even we knew confirmed he didn't know the address of our hotel.

Who's 'we' you ask?

Let me introduce you to Jackie.

Jackie was the Australian girl who sat next to me on the plane from Siem Riep, and since she had planned to stay at the same guesthouse, we had decided to share the cab fare. Big mistake.

'The Angkor temples were the bomb, eh?' she said brightly.

I then nodded my head in silence, hoping to avoid a conversation. You see Jackie had performed the conversational feat of running a two-minute mile - she had given me a short history of her life crammed in the thirty-five minute flight. Her boyfriend had dumped her in Melbourne and she had taken off to the UK, working in London, managing a French bakery. She had saved enough to travel around the whole of Europe with three Irish blokes who 'farted their way around the continent' as she oh-so-eloquently put it. She often had to fend for herself in lonely towns where they threatened to leave her if she didn't turn up at the car park each time they took off for their next destination.

Jackie's conversation skills did sometimes come in handy. I learned from her why we had made such a steep descent into Siem Reap on my flight in. The pilot needed to avoid possible machine gun attack by Khmer Rouge soldiers...great.

'Are you from Phnom Penh, mate?' snapped Jackie at the driver. 'Seems like we've been round this way before, yeah?' She scrunched up her face and untied her ponytail.

Trying to get our bearings, I looked for street signs. But there were no signs at all, and I even saw some locals standing on street corners looking confused, throwing up their hands in frustration. What was going on?

Eventually, we drove past the vast Central Market in Phnom

Penh and by counting the number of streets on my map we found the hotel where we wanted to stay. Once inside, we were immediately given bad news by the reception staff.

'Twenty five dollars,' they said.

'Per room?' hollered Jackie, 'you must be fucking joking! C'mon Dave!' She put her backpack on, grabbed my hand and dragged me out the door.

And with that I was ensnared in that unusual travel experience that can only be described as being one half of a bickering, unstable married couple. Every once in a while, you will bump into a lone traveler going in the same direction, at the same time, and they literally hijacked your trip as Jackie was now doing. Pulling you along as a convenient, unwitting audience to their dramas, attempting to untangle yourself from this 'marriage' can be a lot harder that it looks.

We were back now in the searing dry season heat. While the monsoon had broken in Angkor, it had not done so in the capital. The air was dry, dirty and as hot as hell. We walked into another hotel, where the rate was also twenty-five dollars a night.

'No fucking way mate, no fucking way!' yelled Jackie who pushed her way into three more hotels on the same street where the prices were the same. All the receptionists were accosted with the same expletives. When we reached the intersection there was a mark on the wall where the street sign had been ripped off. I looked across the road, the plaque there, too, was gone.

My map totally useless, Jackie shouted, 'Over there!' pointing to another group of hotels up the road. So off we trotted, backpacks in tow, weaving through rush hour traffic. There we found only one hotel that would go below twenty dollars. The matronly woman behind the counter, however, would not buy my story that we were not husband and wife and refused to rent even adjacent rooms to us.

Back out into the heat again I saw the distinctive roof of the central market again. We walked around the outside, fending off motorbike drivers who kept shouting, 'Killing Fields! Killing Fields!' at the top of their lungs until Jackie shouted back, 'I'll kill you in a minute if you don't bloody well piss off!'

This made the drivers furious and as they closed in for the kill they looked at me with wrinkled brows, surely I had better control over my wife than this? I shrugged my shoulders sheepishly and they shot me a look I myself had given the frequently encountered hen pecked husbands I saw on the road.

Sweating, exhausted, and eager to divorce myself both from Jackie and this irritating hotel situation, I spotted a red and white sign up ahead for the Capitol Hotel which I had heard was a traveler's hub in Cambodia that was cheap and probably a good place to shake off my new 'wife.'

There, rooms were only five dollars, and after a quick whisper to the girl working at reception, I was taken to another wing of the sprawling hotel, waving with relief as Jackie was led off in another direction.

If divorces in Las Vegas were quick, in Phnom Penh they were even quicker.

The next morning I made a hasty, movie star exit from the Capitol Hotel: as I walked through the bustling restaurant, my sunglasses were on, my eyes were cast down to the pavement and I hurried out into the street. When I made a dash for the Central Market a gang of motorbike drivers shouted and waved, offering to take me to the river and the Silver Pagoda.

'Keep your voices down,' I hissed. 'Do you want her to hear you?'

I kept on walking, following the old map I had brought with me that was printed with the now useless street names counting off the streets as I went, an unusual walking guessing game.

At one intersection I saw a truck go by packed with UN soldiers and when I sat down for a bowl of soup for breakfast the man working there said, 'Dollars only.'

'How much?' I said, pointing to a half eaten bowl of soup at an adjacent table.

'Five dollars,' he replied with a straight face.

'What?' I whispered, incredulous.

'Five dollars, or leave.' The man swiped the menu off my table and pointed to the door. Stunned, I walked away.

Within five minutes my navigation plan of street nameless Phnom Penh went up in smoke. I was lost so I found a pharmacy where a woman was feeding her baby and asked where the Silver Pagoda was.

'Very far. You need to walk straight down that way, and then fifteen streets later, you will see the river. It is before that.'

'Why are the street signs gone?'

The woman laughed. 'We are undergoing elections now,' she said, 'and everything is being changed. Even the money.' She pulled out a wad of crisp newly printed bills.

'It's like Year Zero,' I said, referring to the time in 1975 when Pol Pot forced the entire population back into the countryside.

The woman pointed at me and said, 'Right! Like Year Zero. But no one really believes the elections will change anything. Life in Cambodia will go on as it has always had.' Then her face darkened. 'I was a little girl then. In 1975. My parents died, so did most of my relatives. The ones who survived went to Thailand and America.' She smiled sadly and went back to feeding her baby.

I thanked her and kept on walking, finally reaching the river, the Silver Pagoda and the ochre National Museum. Inside, I narrowly escaped a re-marriage with Jackie, who I heard before I saw. Yakking with a tour guide about her life in London, I flattened against the wall until the Aussie menace had passed.

While exploring the riverfront Cambodiana Hotel that afternoon a man from Nigeria stopped me and asked what the word 'political asylum' meant. I explained it and he returned to filling out his Australian visa application, ticking the box for 'seeking political asylum.'

He thanked me by buying me a beer and we sat by the river, watching kids scream and jump into the coffee colored water.

'Why apply in Cambodia?' I asked.

'It is easier than in Lagos, friend. My country is a mess, a real mess.'

'Worse than Cambodia?'

'Dead bodies lying in the streets go uncollected, friend. Uncollected.'

With that note our conversation died and we passed the time in silence until the sun set over the river. I stood up, wished him well with his application and walked back to the

Capitol Hotel, blundering along in the dark. Halfway there, even some locals asked me for directions. I shrugged and we all laughed. Even the Cambodians were lost in their own country.

Two minutes later the power cut out and as I walked on through the darkness, looking for familiar landmarks that never appeared, I couldn't find the pharmacy where the kind woman had given me directions earlier that day.

The inky darkness all around me seemed to have swallowed it whole.

I am surrounded by freaks and geeks at the moment, quickly getting high off the second hand pot smoke swirling around this place. The Capitol Hotel is apparently the epicenter of the backpacker scene here in Phnom Penh, though I am taking a big risk by even venturing in such a public place.

Jackie can't be that far away.

So far, Cambodia is far more intense than I ever imagined. You know it has been fifteen years since Pol Pot was deposed (and he is still living along the Thai border, apparently) but the past seems present here, everywhere.

Later, Dave

Hey Annette,

It's my last night in Cambodia, leaving for Saigon tomorrow. I got back yesterday from my trip south to Kompong Som and the southern beaches.

I am, of course, back at the Capitol, as it's the most affordable place in town. I am ready to leave. The United Nations presence here during the elections has inflated prices everywhere, even sandwiches on the street are like five dollars. My latest adventure just confirms that my chance encounter with the Khmer Rouge in Angkor Wat was not my last.

Read on.

The share taxi was idling in a central Phnom Penh parking lot, doors flung open, belching smoke with a portly driver squatted down beside it, Vietnamese style, sucking on a cigarette. A sour faced Scandinavian couple was sitting in the backseat, arguing. The man paused, leaned out of the window and asked me if I was going to Kompong Som. I said yes, and as soon as we had picked up one more passenger, a wild haired, rat-faced Frenchman, negotiated the price down to $40 for the whole car, the driver nodded, threw away his still burning cheroot and we took off south for the coast.

'I know good hotel for you,' the driver said as he swerved through the city's swirling traffic. 'Cheap.' He was sweating profusely and didn't stop talking. 'You tourists are very important to my country,' he said. 'Cambodia very safe now.'

'Cheap?' the Frenchman said. 'Is not possible. I paid ten dollars for a room that should have been, how do you Americans say? On the house!'

The Scandinavians also complained about their hotel room and the high cost of everything in Cambodia, and the mood in the taxi changed direction. Bitching about the cost of things in third world countries is a favorite topic amongst independent travelers. (Most of whom carry a pack of shiny credit cards in their boho-chic Nepali satchels)

Let the nose thumbing I-got-a-cheaper-paradise-than-you games begin.

This is an integral part of the Southeast Asian travel experience, believe me. If my bungalow cost $3, the other traveler will smugly declare theirs cost $2, if my flight was $500 USD, the others was $300. If my meal cost $2, I was patted on the shoulder and told it should have cost $1.

I've started telling everyone I'm on an expense account and that kills the conversation. Dead.

Three hours passed. At one particularly potholed stretch of road we passed a trundling train that the driver said took twelve hours to reach the seaport of Kompong Som also known as Sihanoukville. Then, as we rounded a bend, three private cars were stopped there, doors flung open, their drivers standing like statues, arms in the air as teenage soldiers, barefoot, angry and waving guns were shouting and yelling.

'Problem,' muttered the Frenchman as he rolled up his window.

The driver stopped the car and got out, leaving his door open. Two soldiers came over and tapped my window with the tips of their AK-47's.

'Big problem,' muttered the Swede in the back seat.

I rolled down the window, and the soldier motioned us out of the car.

'But I don't want to get out,' whined the Swedish girl.

'Just do it,' I said through clenched teeth, remembering the soldiers I had met in Angkor. My stomach flipped when I realized I had no more color photos of the temples to rip out and hand over to negotiate safe onward passage.

The driver was looking back at us, smiling nonchalantly, but I knew exactly what we were dealing with. While the Frenchmen and Swedes had just arrived in Cambodia, I had been here long enough to know what was going on.

I didn't say anything to the other passengers as the soldiers rifled through the seats, glove box, and in the trunk. As they searched I saw a wad of Cambodian Reals change hands between the driver and the lead soldier, but I acted mesmerized by the sugar palms surrounding the road, where locals were climbing to harvest the sap, to pretend I hadn't seen the transaction.

'Look!' I said, pointing to the trees, distracting not only the Swedes and the Frenchman, but also the soldiers who were still looking through the car as well.

The driver came back and we exchanged worried glances. He seemed surprised that I knew who these soldiers really were and shot me a look to keep my mouth shut, lest I screw up his guest's impressions of his 'safe' Cambodia.

In less than a minute, we were back in the car, the doors slammed shut, the Khmer Rouge soldiers waved us away with their AK-47's and the driver peeled.

'I know nice hotel for you in Kompong Som,' he said again in that high pitched voice of his, once the roadblock was behind us and out of sight, sweating more heavily now. 'Cheap.'

Two hours later we arrived at the coast. Though the scenery was spectacular, I was exhausted and sick from breathing in petrol fumes blowing in through the open windows. Bouncing around for hours like a sack of potatoes from the potholes had also worn thin. I wanted a bath, a beer, and a beach.

The bickering between the Scandinavians had also driven the Frenchman and myself up the wall and at every opportunity he gave me wicked looks of hatred as their civil war waged on in the back seat.

'We go your hotel now,' said the driver.

'Cheap, no?' said the Frenchman, slapping the driver's fat belly.

We turned down a narrow, potholed road and drove down a long driveway, overgrown with tropical vegetation, crunching over gravel. The car stopped in front of a crumbling, fourteen story building.

'Your hotel,' said the driver.

'You are joking,' murmured the Frenchman. 'Out here?'

'Someone has to stay with the car,' whined the Swedish girl, looking at me. Her boyfriend, having had enough of her, snapped out a poisonous one liner in Swedish. She returned to the backseat to make sure nobody did a runner with our suitcases.

The Swede, the Frenchman and I walked up the small hill towards the battered building which from a distance resembled a tacky 1970's resort hotel in Hawaii.

When we reached the bottom of the steps, we gasped: there were no windows at all. They appeared to have been blown out by machine guns, and as we gingerly stepped closer, we noticed there were deep bullet pockmarks in the cement walls. There was no glass in the front door either so we simply stepped through the frame, crunching on shards of glass littering the hardwood floors. What on earth had happened to this hotel?

'Sacre bleu, this cannot be,' the Frenchman said, running his hands through his wild hair.

We looked around for someone, and then went back to the car.

'Take us to another hotel,' demanded the Swede.

'This only hotel,' the driver said. 'Cannot stay in town. Only brothels.'

'Then take us back to Phnom Penh,' insisted the Frenchman.

'Cannot,' the driver wailed. 'Dangerous, shooting! Reds!' He looked at me for backup.

'I think he means Khmer Rouge,' I said as the blood ran out of the Swedish man's face.

'No, cannot.' The driver walked back to his car and put the key in the engine.

'If he leaves, we're fucked,' I told the Frenchman.

'I can't stay here!' the Swedish girl shouted, who had abandoned her job watching the suitcases, and was pointing to the ripped curtains flapping through a broken window high above her head. Whether it was to spite his girlfriend, I never knew, but the Swede marched up the steps again with the Frenchman and myself in tow.

The reception counter was covered thickly with dust. The red leather padding decorating the walls had large knife gashes slashed through it and the stuffing hung out in large wooly clumps. The elevator doors were flung open, revealing a gaping black, bottomless void, and many of the ceiling panels hung crazily off their hinges. Was this the younger cousin of the destroyed French colonial hotel in Siem Reap?

Before we could turn around the Swede rang the tiny brass bell sitting on the counter. The echo reverberated through the empty corridors while we waited, breathless, for who, or what, would come.

But nothing stirred.

'C'mon let's go,' sighed the Swede, rolling his eyes back at his irritating girlfriend waiting outside with the driver.

Just then, like an apparition, a sullen, shrunken man stepped down from a musty stairwell hidden behind the reception desk. As if we had seen a ghost, the three of us jumped in fright while the man reacted like he was used to it.

'Yes?' he asked us in slow but perfect English, his arms folded across his chest.

'Do you have rooms?' asked the Frenchman cautiously, with tremendous hesitation, as if a room was the last thing a hotel might have. (Psychotic axe murderers? Sure. Hotel rooms? No way.)

'Yeeees,' the man answered tiredly. He pulled a ledger out from under the desk.

'Have rooms. Five dollars a night per person. Follow me.' And with that, he produced three keys from his pocket and we followed him up the dark, narrow stairwell to see his rooms.

Like a lot of things in Cambodia, I had no idea what he was going to show us. After the splendor and terror of Angkor and the Bayon, and the crumbling nameless streets of Phnom Penh, what lay upstairs? Immaculate suites? An air-conditioned restaurant? A swank spa? In the unstable entity that is Cambodia, no one knew.

On the seventh floor he stopped and we walked down the dark, filthy corridor, grinding broken glass into the mildewed carpet. It felt like we were in Beirut, Kabul, or south central L.A. The man swung open the door to one of the rooms and we went inside. The view was excellent: fishing boats bobbed in a turquoise bay buffeted by waves.

A tourist minister's dream.

But the room's amenities were straight out of Stephen King. The toilet was smashed, the bathtub was filled to the brim with dark green water, the light fixtures were gone, and we could hear crickets chirping merrily away the closet. The mattress was totally ruined by the rain that had poured in the window and the mosquito nets had holes larger than dinner plates.

A tourist minister's nightmare.

'Is this the best you have?' I asked, motioning to all the

other rooms that were empty.

'Yeees,' he answered.

The Frenchman was furious and he swore under his breath. He told me he wanted to go back to Phnom Penh, immediately.

'Noooo,' the man said, making a machine gun sound and motion with his arm. At night, the roads in Cambodia still belonged to the Khmer Rouge. The driver had us in a corner. There was no way of getting transportation to the town, we were miles away.

The Swede looked aghast, not so much at the room's condition but what he would have to tell his flighty, petulant girlfriend.

So we agreed to the price, got our suitcases out of the taxi and filled our names in a ledger that had last had guests more than seven months ago.

'And your nationalities?' the man asked, looking closely at the Swede's spiked blonde hair and the Frenchman's pierced nose. We handed him our passports, and had to show him where to find our names.

Then, he ran down the list of services. Or lack thereof:

No running water.
No electricity after six p.m.
No fans.
No flushing toilets.
No restaurant.
No cleaning service.
No telephones.

'What about food?' asked the Frenchman, pointing to his stomach.

'The nearest market is eight kilometers away,' the man said. 'I have a motorbike. You can each give me three dollars, I will buy some food for you.'

With that, the Swedish girl shot a look at her boyfriend and he glared back. It was decided that the two would go into town with the man to buy food and drinks, and would return later. After saying goodbye to the driver and arranging to meet the following morning, the Frenchman and I went for a swim.

The water was amazingly clear and warm, and as we lazily swam around the lagoon, laughing as we looked at our hotel, the sun began to set over the Gulf of Thailand.

'This is mad, no?' the Frenchman said, pointing to the smashed windows of the top floors that glinted like gold in the rays of the setting sun.

When the Swedes returned with the food we prepared a simple meal of Laughing Cow cheese smeared over crunchy baguettes and they joined us for another swim. By the time we had toweled off the man had gone.

We never saw him again.

As it got dark we moved indoors and ate our sandwiches by flashlight in the huge cavernous ballroom that had suffered the worst damage. Graffiti marked the walls, the kitchen had been used as a toilet and someone had set fire to a wall but had not managed to burn the hotel down. Huge bats began to fly in, and startled by the unfamiliar light, quickly fled. They returned later that night to sleep hanging from the tilted chandeliers.

With batteries running low and exhausted after the drive down from Phnom Penh, we turned in at about seven p.m. The Swedes took the room next to the Frenchman and I. We knew when they had fallen asleep because snoring replaced shouting and threats.

But the Frenchman and I stayed up most of the night listening to the crickets in the closet, jumping at every creak and groan of the woodwork, the door to the room refused to shut and the black corridor became even darker, threatening, despite the strong moonlight pouring in through the window. Lying still on the crooked bed frames and 70's kitsch all around us, neither of us slept more than fitfully that night.

The next morning at the beach where we gathered for breakfast, the Swedes were a different couple. Not only was the girlfriend now smiling, happy and upbeat, with her boyfriend they had decided to stay at least another night surrounded by the retro seedy resort splendor, distressed to the extreme by rampaging Khmer Rouge soldiers.

The Frenchman and I, however, having had enough of this place, were relieved when the taxi driver returned at nine o'clock, crunching down the gravel driveway, sweating, even in the early morning chill. We said goodbye to the Swedes and gladly paid him the forty dollars to take us straight back to Phnom Penh.

As my last adventure in Cambodia (unless something happens tonight in Phnom Penh, which is likely, considering the wonkiness of this place) the night in that hotel was almost at the top of my list of how-the-hell-did-I-get-into-this situations, made all the more weird by another cast of cartoon characters.

More news from Vietnam.

Love, Dave

February 11, 1994
11:14 A.M.
Phnom Penh to Saigon
Machete Sandwich

Hey Annette,

Cambodia is far behind me and I'm now in Vietnam. Everything is cranked up just a bit higher here in Saigon. What I thought of Cambodia has been tempered by the chaos here. The bicycles, the heat, the noise, the pollution, the constant street vendors screaming 'YOU BUY!' the confusion and mind spinning speed of the place makes Cambodia a clockwork Swiss village in comparison. Street vendors press cold water bottles against your cheek so YOU BUY, cyclo drivers grab your arm as you walk by, and you need earmuffs just to think here.

Anyway, what follows is my first episode in Saigon, and what really, and finally, happened between Jackie and me.

You'll love it.

The bus ride to Saigon was a low altitude flightmare. Ripped vinyl seats, vomit smells, potholes large enough to swallow a lumbering elephant, clouds of choking red dust, passengers that spat constantly out the windows and diesel fumes made the twelve hour journey almost intolerable.

Make that a very, very low altitude flightmare.

My divorce from Jackie also ended aboard that horrible bus. No sooner had I taken my seat than a strong tap on my shoulder stopped my freedom cold. Even worse was the kindness of a stupid dolt of a traveler who graciously exchanged seats so my 'wife' could sit next to me. Jackie, of course, demanded the window, and I, like all hen pecked husbands everywhere, let her have it. (The seat, not a piece of my mind)

My marriage was back on.

'I was looking for you, silly,' she said, slapping me on the shoulder, then she lost no time in updating me on every detail of her time in Phnom Penh, slipping in anecdotes from New Zealand and Sumatra, describing in gory details the motorbike accident she had survived when driving to see the sunrise from a mountain peak. She had twisted her ankle and gashed herself up, but an enterprising farmer had taken her hostage for almost two days, refusing to call a doctor and insisting she pay one hundred dollars for a medicine man to heal the gash on her leg.

I didn't need to imagine the expletive laden volley of curses exchanged between this Aussie girl and that farmer because Jackie recounted each conversation in precise, anal-retentive detail.

'You're forever climbing bloody volcanoes at four a.m. in Indonesia,' she said, swerving topics as deftly as the driver lurched the bus around an oxcart slowly crossing the highway. Even after six hours her mouth was still in top gear and as we were crossing the Vietnamese border, and as the stone-faced customs officials rifled through her backpack, she shook her fist at one of them and said, 'Mate, I could report you!'

This earned her an extra long wait for her visa to be stamped and was the last passenger back on the bus to Saigon. When the gas tank that had been removed in the search for smuggled goods was replaced, we bumped along for the final five hours before stumbling off the bus at dusk in front of a Volkswagen dealership in Saigon's District One.

Saigon is like an anaconda. It swallows you whole in three seconds flat.

In the seething crowd of shouting bus passengers, bulging suitcases, pushy street vendors, eager cyclo drivers, growling motorbikes and annoying touts, we were chosen by two cyclo drivers who offered to take me and my 'darling' to a cheap guesthouse; then they would wait outside the hotel and take us to a good place for dinner.

'She's not my darling,' I snapped.

When the reception desk chick, dressed in a skin-tight blouse and jeans that looked spray-painted on her body, asked me if Jackie was my girlfriend, she got the same answer.

'She's not my darling,' I snarled for the second time in five minutes. Front Desk Chick brightened up immensely at this information and threw her breasts out at me.

'You look like a movie star,' she said as she tried to slip me her pager number. Jackie shot her a look and Front Desk Chick's note disappeared.

Maybe there was some good in being married after all.

After getting to my room I tended to the bruises from the long trip and fifteen minutes later we met our drivers, who true to form had waited patiently in the alley.

It was Sunday evening in Saigon and it seemed every single motorbike was out in the streets, honking horns, swerving crazily as two, three and even four passengers clung on, laughing and screaming a loud hello at every foreigner they saw.

'Your dahling?' smiled my driver as he tapped his fingers together like parallel chopsticks.

'No,' I snapped for the third time, shaking my head. The driver looked at me with envy, a foreign man traveling with a single woman who wasn't his wife? He called out to his friend in Vietnamese and he looked at me with widened eyes.

Jackie and I were taken to the Dinh Com Trang restaurant off Hai Ba Trung street, down an alley directly opposite the bright fluorescent pink French colonial Tan Dinh church. We paid the drivers and they pedaled off, still sucking in their breath at my luck.

Under a sagging corrugated iron roof and sitting on cracked plastic chairs next to shiny aluminum tables packed elbow to elbow, families were shouting at waiters to bring more plates of food.

We were handed a menu, ordered, and moments later were picking at grilled shrimps and yellow pancakes and spicy fish with black wooden chopsticks, sipping 333 Beer with chunks of ice floating in our glasses. The waiters began scurrying around, pulling tarps over our heads, shouting and yelling as though acid was about to drop from the sky.

Suddenly firecrackers exploded above our heads - a huge rain cloud had burst and for the next twenty minutes conversation was impossible. Jackie still didn't stop talking so I just nodded every once in a while as her mouth kept on moving. As quickly as it came, the rain stopped, the empty plates were cleared, more beer bottles were opened, and more shouts were exchanged with the waiters for more food.

Compared to the relative peace of Cambodia, Vietnam

was the loudest, brashest, in your face place I have ever been. Even Jackie, after all her travels through outback Australia and the wilds of Indonesia, looked at me with wide eyes and shouted, 'Nobody's got this place beat for decibel noise levels!'

After eating, we were stuffed and decided to walk all the way past Turtle Lake, the Notre Dame cathedral and down Dong Khoi street where bright pink, red and purple neon lights reflected off the slick streets. The 'Go Around' is Saigon's answer to small towns in the American Midwest where on Friday night high school students went cruising around their small downtown. Saigon's version was now in full swing, and traffic surged all around us like a tide, all flashing lips and shiny motorbikes and strong perfume and honking horns.

We turned a corner and there in front of us was the Apocalypse Now bar, thumping music pouring out into the street. Inside, mixed in with the eager prostitutes, rude waiters, fat Asian businessmen, bored expat housewives and a somewhat fringe-like local crowd, we found fellow survivors of that afternoon's bone shaking bus ride, and once we had bought each other a beer, we sat in the garden for several hours with them, swapping stories as one does from transits through Tokyo to Cairo and Rio to Auckland.

Out of the darkness materialized a flock of glittering creatures, Vietnamese women expertly shellacked and dressed in knock off designer clothes. Their dark eyelashes batted hungrily at me, until I realized Jackie could finally became useful.

'My darling, my darling,' I said, patting her back. The girls took a while to understand this, but eventually they evaporated like vampires before garlic, leaving just a strong smell of perfume in their wake.

Several rounds of drinks later, we stumbled out of the bar out into the cool night and into a different city, it was midnight, there were no cars or motorbikes on the road anymore, the incessant noise and traffic was replaced by some creepy cyclo drivers who were smoking cigarettes and shouting in raspy voices for customers as they pedaled back and forth through the intersection.

Jackie and I ignored them and walked in the general direction of our hotel fueled by that kind of optimism one only gets when drunk. A few minutes later, we were at an anonymous street corner where a man called out to us to buy a sandwich.

Jackie said she was hungry, so we nodded and he began to slice open a baguette, smearing pate inside, cut up some meat and vegetables, and then he wrapped it in a piece of newspaper held together with a rubber band.

'Fifty thousand Vietnamese Dong,' he said in perfect English as he handed them over.

That was the same as five American dollars, and I knew we weren't in rip-off Phnom Penh anymore.

I laughed sarcastically and said, 'I don't think so,' and then laughed hysterically as Jackie did the same, she was pointing at the man like he was a clown.

The man didn't say another word. He just grunted, leaned forward, pulled open a crooked drawer, and yanked out a massive silvery machete, which he grabbed fiercely and began to threaten us with it.

'Fifty thousand Dong,' Mad Sandwich Man growled.

'What? No way!' I cried. I was sounding more and more like Jackie by the minute.

'Five dollars!' Mad Sandwich Man hollered.

Jackie grabbed my arm. Now it was her turn to act like me.

'Dave, he's got a knife.'

I nodded my head slowly, and we stepped backwards, not taking our eyes off the knife for a moment.

My drunken brain released a wicked giggle, mistaking this for some sort of practical joke. Jackie elbowed me in the ribs. As I pulled her with me towards the safety of the street I screamed, 'Run!' and Jackie fled the scene like Mad Sandwich Man was holding a burning ACME dynamite stick.

I stayed put, pulled the two baguettes behind my head like a catapult, and fired the sandwiches right at his head. The two baguettes flew forward and bounced off Mad Sandwich Man's skull in quick succession and before they landed at his feet I too turned to flee. After a stunned silence I heard a loud shout behind us, and then a sound of of metal scraping on cement. Mad Sandwich Man had thrown the machete at us like a boomerang, but had missed.

The knife landed in the gutter with a silly clatter.

A hundred meters away, panting and white-faced, we found a cab to take us back to our hotel. Problem was, the driver was asleep in the passenger seat and we had to frantically tap on the glass to get his attention. We nervously waited for Mad Sandwich Man to appear, but he never did.

The cab driver brushed off the drool sliding down his chin and turned the engine over. I sat in the front seat, locked all the doors and told the driver the name of our hotel. Before he nodded and drove off came the usual question.

'Your darling?' he said as he poked his finger through a round hole he made with his other finger. I ignored it and said, 'Drive.'

About five minutes later, finally relaxed after the machete incident, I noticed the taxi was swerving to the left and to the right for no reason.

'What are you doing?' I said, looking over at the driver who was now slumped against the window. He had fallen back to asleep at the wheel, and his heavy foot was pressing against the accelerator. We were heading right for a brick wall.

'Whoa!' I yelled at him as I grabbed the steering wheel and slapped his cheek with my other hand. We smashed through a pile of garbage stacked by the road and a few heads of rotten lettuce bounced crazily off the windshield like in some police chase from a 70's television show, The Streets of Saigon.

The driver was awake now and slurred a weak, 'sorry,' but it was too late. Before he could start driving again I shouted, 'OK we walk!' I threw some bills across the front seat and the driver was yelling at me to forgive him.

Jackie jumped out of the back seat like it was on fire and we crossed the road to walk through the park in front of the New World Hotel. We hadn't traveled far from the Mad Sandwich Man so we kept a quick pace, looking into every dark alley and behind every bush for him to jump out with another machete, another baguette, or both.

Smack in the middle of the park was the strangest fashion show I had ever seen - transvestites in faded high heels and wilted feather boas were lining up behind an MC who was shouting in Vietnamese at the impromptu audience of drunk cyclo drivers, street vendors, guys on motorbikes, and a few children selling roses who had gathered to watch the spectacle.

Before we could even slink past this strange scene there was a scream and then Jackie and I were pushed forward to walk down the runway. Looking at each other in amazement and fear, still drunk, still scared from the machete, still shaken up from the near crash in the taxi, and still sore from the horrible bus ride, we just did what they asked, and walked, hand in hand, ever the happy western couple, bringing the house down as they clapped and sang that ABBA song, Happy New Year.

But if I was expecting wedded bliss with Jackie throughout the rest of my trip through Vietnam, I was wrong. As soon as we reached the alley off Pham Ngu Lao where our hotel was located, Jackie chose a curb and collapsed in tears.

'This place is mad!' she shouted, holding her face in her hands as her knees shook. 'I want to go home! And get away from these crazy people!' She sobbed loudly as a few prostitutes hovered nearby, waiting to swoop in and snatch me up, eager for the opportunity to help this foreigner 'forget' his darling. I patted my wife on the shoulder but Jackie slapped my hand and shouted, 'Go away!'

I waved off the prostitutes with a Cheshire cat grin, and with a laugh walked back to my hotel.

So that's how I got rid of Jackie.

Two lessons so far from Saigon:

Avoid joking with Vietnamese sandwich makers who may be armed with machetes.

Saigon divorces are quicker than those in Phnom Penh.

I have changed hotels for good measure because that girl Jackie has a nose like a bloodhound. I have two more days in mad Saigon till I head up north to Hanoi. I know I won't be ordering any sandwiches in this town.

I don't think my pitching arm will be able to rescue me twice...

Love, Dave

Hey Annette,

Our bus has broken down on the way to Nha Trang, and I'm sitting in a flyblown café squatting down on this kindergarten-sized chair, in front of a rickety table, staring at this flimsy aluminum filter where my coffee is dripping excruciatingly slow into a small Mickey Mouse glass.

Sitting on this stool I look like a cross between a cricket and a circus elephant.

The French style coffee here is pushed through this contraption that requires great skill in mastering. If you fiddle with it, you've fucked up the coffee, and every waiter tisk-tisk's you for touching it too soon. Like a lot of things I am quickly learning about Vietnam, these coffee machines are wonky, quirky, and force you to wait when you don't want to.

So here I am, starting at this aluminum pot, along Vietnam's Highway 1, coffee dripping ever so slowly in front of me, which it has been doing for fifteen minutes, and it still isn't ready. The waiters (a couple of thin as rakes punk teenage boys actually with acid washed jeans cinched up to their nipples and wearing NAKE T-shirts) are watching me like a hawk to make sure I don't fuck up my own cup of coffee.

I really think Vietnamese coffee should come with a warning label.

Let me explain my last experience with this beverage - my legs and butt are still sore from cycling like mad all around Saigon, after drinking an innocent brew like the one in front of me.

I told you how crazy noisy Saigon is, well, the second to last morning I had in Saigon began with the teeth rattling crash of a sledgehammer that sent shudders up and down the metal frame of my bed. Ripped from a cozy dream, I imagined the whole building was crumbling down in a pile of concrete dusk and twisted iron bars, or worse, the building had already tumbled down and rescuers were trying to save trapped people, including me.

Expecting the worst, I cautiously opened my eyes to find the building completely intact and the room full of grey, early morning light. All the kitschy furniture covered with bright green satin material was still there, including the Mickey Mouse towels and frilly pink curtains that jumped like Spanish Dancers when the electric fan swung past them.

A quick digression on the topic of Mickey Mouse, well, all cartoons for that matter. Everywhere you go in Vietnam it's all about Mickey or more often, Tom and Jerry, often painted on the walls of cafes and schools or standing as statues in public parks. Even the bus that just broke down had played six hours of Tom and Jerry cartoons instead of the usual Kung Fu epic passing as in-flight entertainment.

Another sledgehammer blow reverberated through the building and I could hear mortar cracking and bricks tumbling. Blow after blow it continued so close they seemed to be just inches below my bed. Was my room going to collapse into the one beneath it in some kind of cartoon? With Mickey Mouse already in the room, I wasn't sure.

I lifted a heavy arm to my squeezed-shut eyes and saw the numbers.

It was 6:37 a.m.

More blows.

More crashing bricks.

The bed vibrated.

The floor shuddered.

I leapt up and pulled on some clothes to investigate.

When I opened the door, I was confronted with a thick cloud of concrete dust, and when I pushed my way through it, downstairs I saw three tiny men, shirtless, completely covered in white paint dust like Vietnamese Saddhus calmly smoking cigarettes as they attacked the walls with their flimsy mallets, bringing down more and more masonry. I was right, they were attacking the wall right beneath my bed.

After a few hellos, head nods and an offer of a cigarette for breakfast, I went back to my room to try and sleep. Impossible, because the sledgehammer blows went on until the entire wall was gone.

It was about fifteen seconds after they took a break from sledge hammering when the brass band started playing. Off in the distance, I could hear it - mournful toots on horns, thunderous drums beating, and other, unidentifiable instruments were wheezing and screeching in a chaotic symphony.

As the noise grew louder it mixed in with the sledgehammer blows in a cocktail of noise only Saigon could produce. I lay there with my mouth agape at this orchestra that seemed straight out of Bourbon Street playing before seven in the morning. As I listened to the band play on, mixed in with it were Chinese instruments and the cries of mourners.

As I smashed the thin pillows against my ears as hard as I could press them, I wondered, was I in Vietnam, New Orleans, or simply, in hell?

Staring at the ceiling, eyes wild from my stolen, snatched sleep, the brass band got even closer, where it started to circle my building, making three, long, slow rounds of it as the sledgehammer blows and drum beats collided and clashed not only in my brain, but my bed frame as well, that was now shimmying to the beat too.

And then, the brass band marched off into the distance towards the neighborhood pagoda where the funeral was to be held, horns tooting, and drums banging. The last sledgehammer brought down what was left of the wall.

And then, finally, there was silence.

'Funerals are good luck in the morning,' beamed the owner of my guesthouse, smiling nervously to cover up her embarrassment over the construction noise. It turned out she was tearing out the walls so she could fit more rooms in her house for the growing numbers of visitors to Vietnam. Serpent green jade bracelets circled her wrists and gold dripped from her fingers as she clutched a fistful of money she had just taken from some guests who had checked out; she quickly folded it into a ball and stuffed it into her pocket. 'I can get more money,' she said with a giggle as her gold and jade glistened and sparkled.

It was now seven fifteen and too late to go back to sleep, as the sledgehammer blows were still ricocheting through my head. I decided to explore Saigon. So from the cheerful guesthouse owner I rented a Chinese made Flying Dragon bicycle that seemed a safer choice than a motorbike. Unlike Angkor Wat, where open roads were easy for a beginner, the unbelievably traffic clogged streets of Saigon didn't seem like a good place to drive for a novice. I would probably have wound up wrapped round the axles of a truck.

So off I went pedaling down the main road to Ben Thanh market, past the roundabout in front of the Rex Hotel and past the historic Continental Hotel where Graham Greene wrote The Quiet American. After navigating the hill up to the Notre Dame cathedral, I passed the former American Embassy, abandoned except for a few sleepy guards, who stood in front of the barbed wire fencing which was still pulled down in places where people had tried to escape on April 30th, 1975.

And it was that world-stopping event, and the suffering of life after it, that defined life for everyone I met in Saigon. It was a sort of Year Zero for the South Vietnamese who had needed to pull every string and favor to survive the lean years after Reunification with the north. Wrinkled men would rush forward and ask me if I knew General so and so from San Antonio Texas, another would ask if I knew Tony Nguyen in San Jose.

'He owns a mansion there,' they would say in perfect English.

It was their impeccable English that made it such a strange experience to talk with these former ARVN soldiers. Elsewhere in Saigon English was almost nonexistent and hand motions and friendly smiles were the most common form of communication. A lot of these former soldiers were delighted to practice their English skills again, though others looked at tourists as convenient couriers, one traveler I met was asked to carry a letter back to the States for relatives, but found it was a letter asking for political asylum in America from the State Department.

The slow speed of the Flying Dragon bike allowed me to take in the life along the sidewalks where postcard vendors, food stall owners and whole families sat around selling, playing, staring, fighting, laughing or just watching the world go by. This also gave children enough time to run out and shout Hello! and women to wave and vendors to yell at you to try to sell something.

Most traffic in Saigon was made up of the Flying Dragon's

cousins, i.e. other Chinese bicycles. There were no taxis, few cars, and no buses. Traffic was jammed with bicyclists carrying a staggering variety of goods from groups of squawking chickens tied over the handlebars to screaming babies to SINGER sewing machines to even jagged pieces of glass that poked out in all directions, yet seemed to injure no one.

And then there were the Eager English Students.

With bicycles the most popular mode of transport for students Eager English Students became frequent cycle mates as I drove around District One, Three, Cholon and back again. When they saw me, they couldn't believe their luck. Here was a mobile English textbook and English phrasebook all rolled into one and on wheels to boot. Eager English Students calmly rode up and asked me to explain how to recognize a dangling participle or what the word 'obscure' meant or ask me to explain how to use the future perfect tense.

In thirty seconds I will have cycled away from you.

Always smiling and friendly, their vampire like grip on my attention, and brain, was tiring, because conjugating the future perfect tense correctly was hard to recall while you're pedaling through the thick Saigon swirl trying to protect life and limb, so I was forced to become creative to get some peace.

'Is today Tuesday?' I would ask them.

'Yes.'

'Oh,' I would say casually. 'I don't speak English on Tuesdays, only Thursdays.'

And with that the conversation would end; I would turn around to see the latest Eager English Student had melted off into the traffic.

And then there were the Xin Chao Fuckers.

Saigon's answer to obnoxious brats were the arrogant packs of teenage boys who rode the streets of the city on bicycles, barefoot with shirts cracked open to reveal their scrawny chests. Upon spotting a foreigner on a bicycle, the Xin Chao Fuckers thought it their right, no, their civic duty, to taunt and tease foreigners like hyenas by swerving in front to see if they could make the foreigner crash, or shout at them and make that foreigner lose his temper, which was a grave sin in Vietnam.

'FUCK YOU!' they would scream.

'Xin Chao' being the most common greeting in Vietnamese, a pronoun like Anh for men and Chi for women is added to make it more personal. A slight twist on this greeting brought great results in fending off these dolts.

'Xin Chao Fucker,' I would say with a smile as another pack cycled next to me and started in on the theatrics to make me lose my composure.

Their faces would register confusion and they would unleash another volley of circus feats to dislodge me from my bicycle. 'FUCK YOU!' they cried in exasperation, surely the Foreigner Volcano was about to blow.

But I cycled serenely on, looked over and repeat with a smile, 'Xin Chao Fucker.'

Total silence was broken by consternation and muttering. What does 'fucker' mean in Vietnamese? Their faces confirmed they had no idea.

'WHAT?' they would yell, red-faced, trying to figure out if this foreigner was mispronouncing something in Vietnamese or just ignorant of the common pronouns used in the Vietnamese language. (The Xin Chao Fuckers had only one redeeming quality: not one ever asked me to explain transitive verbs and how to spell irregular past participles.)

'XIN CHAO FUCKER!' I would bellow as I cycled serenely on. They too, like the Eager English Students hoping for a free English lesson, would melt off into the traffic, wary of this foreigner who spoke some strange, mutant form of Vietnamese.

Xin Chao Fucker worked every time.

Anyway, with potholes large enough to swallow whole cars and road surfaces that were far from smooth, riding around all day under the weight of a six foot three foreigner was not what the engineers at the Flying Dragon bicycle factory had designed their precious vehicles for. Soon enough I had not one flat tire, but two; and at one nondescript street corner I found an unusual repairman crouching underneath a flapping bright blue tarp.

When I tried to pantomime my situation to the man who was wearing a ripped Chicago Bulls T-shirt and had wild, mad scientist hair he gave me an irritated flick of his hand. 'I know, man, I know,' he said in absolutely flawless English. 'You need me to fix your tires.'

I nodded and asked him the price.

'Five thousand Dong per tire,' he replied and before he waited for my approval he started to remove the wheels and took off the inner tubes.

'Your weight is too much for these Chinese bicycles. You really should have a motorbike.'

'Yes, I know.'

'You Americans always think you can do what you want, eh?' he said sharply as he lit up a cigarette. Then he cut two square pieces of rubber from an old inner tube with a pair of ancient scissors to use as patches.

Sweating from the heat, I watched him as he worked and asked him if he had been involved with the US Army before 1975. Expecting him to confirm that he was indeed an ex-soldier, the man looked up at me and paused, giving me a strange look as if, after hearing what he was going to say, I wasn't going to believe him.

'Wrong, brother. I worked for CBS News,' he replied with a straight face. 'I carried sound equipment for all the major journalists when they visited South Vietnam, Cronkite, Jennings, Murrow, etc.

'Really?' I looked around at the cracked pavement, the overturned helmet and small plastic chair he used as his repair shop. He was clearly just scraping by, yet his English was as good as a news broadcaster.

'Yes, I worked for other American journalists too,' he went on, 'as a translator. We traveled all over Vietnam on US Army helicopters.' As he dropped named that were now virtual journalistic royalty in America, anchoring nightly news broadcasts and interviewing everyone from presidents to popes and dictators to Dalai Lamas, he went on to say how he had made best friends with these guys who were young, homesick and away from home for the first time.

'I was a part time psychologist, too,' he smirked. As he continued to fix the tires he kept on talking, reminiscing about his old bosses, pausing to add some lighter fluid to rekindle the flames he was going to use to melt the patch onto the tires. He went on to describe in perfect detail what life was like attending the Five O'clock Follies at the Press Club across the road from the Rex Hotel in downtown Saigon. He casually told me of all the newsbreaks he was able to pass onto these young journalists that boosted their careers.

'Why didn't you leave before 1975?'

He looked up at me as he took a very deep drag on his cigarette. 'My five sons have all left the country, by boat in the middle of the night and they have all asked me to join them.'

'Why didn't you go?' I expected to hear that some official had rejected his application.

'Each time I refused, man. Vietnam is my home,' he said quietly as the traffic roared all around us, 'and I will never leave.'

Then the man fell into silence, and it was about ten minutes before he removed the two bike tires from the vices that melted the patches to the bike inner tubes. He replaced the tires, pumped them up, accepted the ten thousand Dong note for the service and I bid him goodbye. He smiled but pointed a tremulous finger at me.

'You really should be driving a motor bike, man,' was the last thing he said to me.

A few minutes later, stomach growling like thunder from skipping breakfast and my furious pedal work out, I looked at my watch and saw it was 10.45, way too early for lunch. But this was Vietnam, and food is available at any time of day: young boys were paid to clack wooden sticks together in wealthier neighborhoods to sell hot bowls of soup to housewives too busy to cook.

I was in District Three, on Vo Thi Sau street, and up ahead I could see a large crowd of people gathered under a black umbrella, a small woman in paisley pajamas was sitting on a tiny stool serving up spring rolls that she chopped up into pieces the same way the repairman had done with the bike tires.

With a pair of ancient scissors.

Intrigued, I rode up and the woman barely blinked an eye as an enormously tall foreigner loomed over her head and then sat down gracelessly as a giraffe onto one of her tiny wooden stools. I pointed at a nearby patron's lunch and she nodded.

Taking a porcelain bowl with Chinese dragons entwined around the edges she plopped in bean sprouts, noodles, mint leaves, and sliced lettuce. Then she picked up three spring rolls and sliced them sideways with her ancient scissors and put a rich, thick brown sauce on top and handed it to me with some black chopsticks.

And that was my first introduction to a dish called Bun Thit Nuong.

I dug into the food greedily so much so that the nearby patrons stopped eating, even the sidewalk traffic stopped to stare. Feeling like a circus elephant performing a clever trick, I was so enjoying this dish that I paid them no attention.

As soon as I was done, I immediately ordered another. The bowl was filled with the same nonchalance as the first, unusual in Vietnam's southern capital, where just being a foreigner almost always earned you a rock star/Jesus' second coming/super hero groupie crowd wherever you went or whatever you did. It felt like this jaded, wrinkled grandmother had experience serving space aliens.

In Saigon, you just never knew.

As soon as I had finished the second bowl the spring rolls were gone. She had just chopped up her last with her ancient pair of scissors and was already turning customers away. Then, she waited for her last customers to eat up, and pay up, she bundled up her jars, plates, chopsticks and other paraphernalia, pulled down her umbrella and headed home.

Before I had even pedaled off the delicious food stand that could have been a Michelin starred restaurant was already just an empty patch of broken, cracked sidewalk. Children had already reclaimed it for a game of badminton.

Two hours later, after visiting the pitiful zoo and poorly placarded museums I stopped at some beach chairs lined up across the street from the Pasteur Institute, founded by the French. There I ordered a sweetened condensed coffee, a ca phe sua da.

This contraption the Vietnamese serve coffee in is fiddly, made of cheap aluminum, is easy to knock over, and sits in front of you while squatting down on the ubiquitous kindergarten sized chairs. It forces you, like a lot of things in

Vietnam, to slow down, it forces you to wait, and it forces you to listen, because you never knew if the coffee would filter through quickly or slowly, and if you touched it, the process was ruined.

At first I hated it. I just wanted a cup of coffee, not a science experiment.

But slowly I have realized the beauty of just slowing down and watching the black liquid drip through and mix with the condensed milk, bcause in Vietnam, coffee and the enjoyment of it is like a science.

Even more potent is Ca Phe Chon, an unusual brew made from coffee beans either vomited or excreted from a civet cat, which partially digested the beans before they were collected from the forest floor. Sold for up to ten times the cost of normal coffee, I had been warned of counterfeit weasel coffee. Leave it to the Vietnamese to drink some beans that had taken the long way to their cup.

Well, this coffee I ordered across from the Pasteur Institute should have come with a warning label.

After a few sips of it, even on a very full stomach, the drink sent me fidgeting and jittering so much I had no choice but to hop back on the Flying Dragon bicycle to burn off this crazy, nervous, chaotic energy. I knew Vietnamese coffee was strong but this was more like an ecstasy tablet than a triple espresso.

As I was about to learn, Vietnamese coffee, like an AK-47, can and will hold you hostage.

The sun's rays were now turning golden brown, and the volume and intensity of the traffic on the roads was not my imagination or a hallucination brought on by the coffee.

I had slammed right into rush hour.

It was about four o'clock, the sun had begun to set but the heat was still out in force, and the rays of the dying sun turned buildings to gold. The growling started and grew minute by minute until by the time five o'clock rolled around the roads were jammed with five times the number of vehicles people cyclos pedestrians and children.

To fall over wouldn't have been a problem at all. You simply would have been carried along between other bicycles and motorbikes in a vehicular sandwich until you reached your destination.

In this late afternoon heat, office workers, students,

market traders, cyclo drivers, bank staff, policemen, mothers, fathers, uncles and their brothers were out in force, struggling to get home as traffic intersections surged and flooded with vehicles of all kinds, shapes and speeds. Suddenly swept up into this traffic tsunami, I literally pedaled for my life from street to street, crossing to crossing, half high from the energy emanating from the people all around me and half from the potent coffee that had sent my teeth chattering and my brain alight.

The cacophony of horns honking, vendors selling, police blowing whistles, and people yelling drowned out every other sound and sensation. This went on for almost two hours as the sun sank and the sky turned violet, pink, and finally a sort of bruised corduroy and then black.

If I had printed a transcript or a ticker tape of the thoughts going through my head while negotiating Saigon traffic, it would read something like this:

A silly inch closer and that jerk would have made us both crash - Man, that woman has two pigs tied over the handlebars - What are you doing, you moron? - There goes another Xin Chao Fucker - How can you drive with one hand and hold onto a television set with the other, like that guy? - Smile at the policeman - Shit its hot - Get out of my way, you silly cow - Think you idiot! THINK! - Can I make the next traffic light? – Move it, come on! - I'm not your friend, you dim bulb - How red is my face? People are starting to stare. - Wonder if that lady with the spring rolls is back - I'm going to have Arnold Schwarzenegger thighs from all this pedaling - Her udders were empty - Hey buddy, stop staring and start driving - Oops, almost nailed that grandmother crossing the road under her shoulder pole!

In the darkness I found myself out by the Tan Son Nhat airport, riding on and on and around and round, desperately trying to cast off the furiously pedaling legs that refused to stop as if I had put on some sort of possessed dancing shoes.

Streets all around me were printed on no map, and there was no English, people surged out of doorways to see the strange sight of a six foot tall foreigner zooming by on his very own Flying Dragon bike, pupils strangely dilated and miles from where he was supposed to be. They grabbed my arms and shouted, 'My friend!'

On and on I cycled through traffic lights both green and red and through neighborhoods both rich and poor.

Suddenly, I took a left turn, and then a right, both wrong turns as you often make when you're exhausted, riding a rapidly deteriorating bicycle in a strange country after dark, and under the influence of an over-the-kindergarten-stool drug like Vietnamese coffee.

I found myself on a strange sort of wide road, with peeling strips of reflective paint. On and on I pedaled, looking for a way back to where I had come, the ecstasy high from that slurp of coffee was wearing off, I was coming down from my rush, and I needed a place to crash.

A flurry of golden flashes flew over my head, ripping me back to reality. I squeezed the brakes and careened to a stop and then four soldiers ran towards me, AK-47's blazing, shouting at me to get off my bike.

For about five minutes I thought I was going to be arrested, but maybe it was the dazed, caffeine induced dilated look in my eyes that made these soldiers let me go, in my frenzied pedaling, round and round Saigon, I had somehow strayed right onto the active runway at Tan Son Nhat airport, which was expecting a flight at any moment.

When the soldiers relaxed and put the safety latches back on their AK-47's, they escorted me back the way I had come in. Then, the back tire popped; the sound of it echoed off the nearby buildings, like a rifle shot.

The soldiers jumped.

I winced.

Was I going to be arrested now and FINALLY get my fifteen seconds of fame on CNN?

But the soldiers still let me go, waving at me wildly, and saying brightly, 'Happy New Year!' in their limited, wonky English.

As I drove off the tire went thump, squeak, thump, squeak, thump squeak. I laughed - not one of the soldiers had asked me to explain any grammar or vocabulary. Though the thumping and squeaking went on and on, ears ringing, I was too terrified to stop and get it fixed, visions of bullets still danced in my head.

Thirty minutes later I was well off my caffeine high but my brain was still buzzing from the sensation of bullets sailing over my skull. I arrived at my guesthouse, tire thumping and squeaking, where the jade-jeweled owner shot me a horrified look similar to the guesthouse owner in Siem Reap at what I had done to her precious Flying Dragon bicycle. I giggled and just pushed it inside, back into the corral, happy to part ways with this possessed vehicle.

Then, with a wide grin I stuffed my sweaty hands deep into my pockets and peeled off one five thousand Dong bill, the cost I now knew was enough to fix a tire in her country, handed back the keys into her outstretched hands, and walked upstairs, knees still wobbling and shaking.

Though it didn't take very long to fall asleep that night, it was well into the evening of the next day before the ringing in my ears finally stopped.

I'm not waiting for the coffee anymore, waiters and Vietnamese coffee protocol be damned. (The bus is still broken down, by the way) I pushed the remaining hot water through the contraption, mixed it with the condensed milk then added some ice and I have downed the beverage in one gulp. In a few minutes, I will know if it should have come with a warning label, and I've got dancing shoes on again once more.

Love, Dave

February 17, 1994
4.34 P.M.
Nha Trang, Vietnam
The Dog Lick, Coconut Bomb, Dead Duck Beer Fest

Annette,

I got to Nha Trang eventually, (just a mere 12 hours late because of the bus breakdown) and no, the coffee was not the ecstasy laced drink I swallowed in Saigon that sent my eyeballs into cartoon popping motion.

On the bus journey here I sat in front of an American girl who spoke to her seatmate about the ONLY place to call yourself a serious traveler, the ONLY place to get more bang for your buck (read illness, death and chaos), the ONLY place to find yourself spiritually, the ONLY place she wanted to go back to.

INDIA.

I have heard this story before. Remember Jake in Japan?

Honestly, I feel like it's some marketing ploy, India. You can spend all the time you like in Thailand, or Indonesia, or Vietnam, the slogan from the commercial screams, but unless you're able to wax poetic about all things Ganges and Ghandi, all things Saddhu and Salvation, then you might as well pack up and go home.

If countries were sports cars racing towards Shangri-La, then Thailand was an ox cart, Vietnam was a Volvo and India was a Ferrari.

I have run into several travelers who are either on their way there, or on their way back from India and will tell anyone who will listen about their apprehensions, their fears, the kilos of antibiotics they are carrying. Just in case, they whisper, as though they were about to venture back into the 12th century in a time machine.

Those just spat out by Mother India are given special tables in restaurants and the bungalows with the best views where they hold court regaling others with stories of rapture and redemption, of hocus pocus tricks involving levitations and charlatans, snake charmers and healers as they shiver from lingering illnesses picked up there, while the adoring masses kiss their feet in appreciation, happy to touch someone why has BEEN and SUFFERED and SEEN.

'They've suffered enough,' the Travel Gods seemed to whisper from on high.

They've suffered enough.

And now this American girl made us all suffer as she went on and on and on about the India she loved until we all wanted to scream at her to go the hell back there. Just leave us in peace to ride safely strapped in our Volvos, thank you very much.

I'm stuck here sorting out onward travel. It's Tet, the three day Lunar New Year holiday that's like surfing a wave of even more frenzied food shopping, whizzing firecrackers and exceptionally insane motorbike drivers. For two weeks this wave builds until it crashes completely on the first day of Tet, a day bathed in total silence, a day that is reserved exclusively for intimate family visits.

All forms of travel is booked, so I'm having a hard time getting to Hoi An, my next destination. Not a bad place to be stuck, the weather is good and the seafood is amazing. I still haven't seen Jackie after our divorce in Saigon.

I'll let you know if I do run into her. (well, you'll hear the scream, anyway)

Yesterday being the first day of Tet, I was invited by a Vietnamese family to their house even though I wasn't a blood relative because they just couldn't understand how a foreigner, so far from home, could bear to celebrate such an important holiday alone.

What followed was public humiliation of the highest order.

So off I went in search of the address they had carefully written on a slip of paper, limping badly because that morning I had been burned on my upper thigh by a burst of hot water that had exploded from a water pipe in my hotel room. When I showed her the ugly, blistering burn the manager just shrugged her shoulders and flipped her hand up and down in that ubiquitous way Vietnamese used to mean they didn't know.

So trying to make the best of it and grateful for the chance to participate in my first Tet I cleaned up the wound as best I could and hobbling like a drunk man down the alley in front of my hotel, I dodged the firecrackers thrown at me by little kids in a game that could only be described as 'Terrorize the Foreigner.'

For gifts I brought with me a bunch of bright yellow flowers, which had started to wilt in the heat and tiny red envelopes stuffed with money for the children.

Searching for nearly an hour to find the house, even though the address I was searching for was just thirty meters away, no one knew where it was and just flapped both hands up and down in that already familiar gesture I was soon to copy.

When I arrived I was startled to find no ceremony at all. The house was full of people just sitting around and eating. My gifts were taken away from me without a word and I was slapped heartily on the back and handed a glass of beer with chunks of ice floating in it.

I was then seated down at a table full of middle-aged men, while the women were in the kitchen furiously cooking enough food for a wedding party of two hundred.

Cheered by my arrival they raised their glasses in a huge shout, 'Mot, hai, ba, YO!' (one, two three, YO) and then clinking the mugs clumsily together each man drained their glass completely. They had obviously been at it for awhile, even though it was only eight o'clock in the morning, all their faces glowed a bright, tomato red.

For the next few hours I sat uncomfortably on a tiny plastic chair in the blazing sun underneath a coconut tree that periodically shed coconut bombs that slammed with terrific force onto the roof, before they rolled off and crashed onto the cement, inches from my feet.

As the day wore on, and the coconuts continued their vicious carpet bombing campaign on the courtyard below it, I was urged about every ten seconds to either drink up another glass of watery beer, or empty another bowl of Banh Trung, the boiled rice cakes wrapped in banana leaves that were a revolting blend of sour, gooey rice and mung bean paste.

The burn on my thigh was leaking again and to my horror I could see my jeans were soaked through. At any moment someone would notice it and think I had pissed myself.

Though I didn't speak Vietnamese, I was not exempt from joining the conversation. Every few seconds someone would lean over, slap my arm or squeeze my thigh, and scream a question, usually obscene, in broken English, for me to answer.

Then the glasses would crash together again, a shout would go up and the horrible watery beer would be swallowed once again, followed by an ear splitting crash as yet another coconut came down onto the cement like an incoming green missile.

The only introspective question I was asked by one of the oldest men there that day, introduced to me as a poet, who leaned over and shouted, 'So, when you are in Vietnam, who is taking care of your family altar?'

I didn't want to tell them that in America, we didn't have such things, and instinctively stood up, raised my glass for another round of chugging, and repeated the chant.

'Mot, hai, ba, YO!'

The shout was followed by an intense beer chugging session, including all the men but one, a man with two missing fingers, who had glowered at me all morning. He was now standing up and pointed at me accusingly.

'You Americans left us,' he slurred, while his friends suddenly lost their smiles at the bottom of their glasses.

In the silence that followed one of the women escorted him away from the table, and took him to one of the back rooms where he passed out unconscious.

'The two ducks belonging to the owners of this house died this morning,' wheezed the poet in my ear.

'A lot of Vietnamese houses have ducks for security, right?' I asked, trying to position my leg further under the table so no one would see the spreading stain on my jeans.

'Yes, sir, they are cheap security guards,' the poet went on. 'Vietnam is shit poor,' he added with a straight face.

'What do Vietnamese eat for Tet?'

'Oh, chicken, beef, and lots of vegetables,' the poet went on. 'But today, we are eating duck.'

I nodded my head as the alcohol from the cheap beer soaked deeper into my brain. It was almost a full minute before I put two and two together and realized the family would be dining on their recently deceased security guards. My stomach squirmed, and the Banh Trung I had almost dry heaved out onto the pavement when I had swallowed it, now seemed like crème brûlée compared to the feast that was about to be served.

The remaining men still at the table lifted their glasses again for another toast.

'TO VIETNAM!' they roared. And right on cue a coconut crashed onto the roof again, landing right in the middle of the courtyard frightening the family dogs that were licking from end to end the ice blocks that a deliveryman had just dropped off. They scattered like furry billiard balls hit by a cue.

I looked down at the ice chunks in my glass and I was sure they had undergone the same treatment by the family's pack of mangy mutts. I reached down at one of them and it wasted not a second in growling and crunching down on my fingers, drawing blood.

'You are bleeding,' said the poet.

And then I saw the other men staring, not at my bloody fingers, but at my thigh, I had stood up from the shock of the crashing coconut and the dog bite and the men could plainly see what looked like a large urine stain marking my jeans in a large and spreading circular shaped pattern.

The poet muttered under his breath, 'The bathroom, sir, is inside the house,' he said, barely concealing a smirk.

The other men couldn't take their eyes off a tiny point conveniently located on the floor between their feet, and I slunk into the house like a thief. I walked past the couch where the man with missing fingers was lying down, and he cackled a hearty, 'HA, HA HA,' when he saw what looked like a young American that had pissed his pants.

I found the toilet, ducked inside and slapped my forehead in embarrassment. The germs from the dogs licking my ice were safely incubating in my stomach, my thigh was a patch of painful, singed skin, and my fingers were dripping blood. But the grotesque dead duck feast had yet to begin.

But then, my getaway plan from eating the rancid duck meat materialized - if I could feign massive, uncontrollable incontinence, surely I would be allowed to leave this dreadful party?

I have traveled long enough to know that locals often thought foreigners were crazy, first for leaving their comfortable First World lives behind, and second, for forsaking their First World dress sense by adopting odd clothes that marked them as members of some sort of rag tag international tribe. Why not play that card to my advantage for a change?

So instead of drying off my wet jeans I emerged from the bathroom with the inside of my drenched pants completely exposed for all the world to see. I found the lady of the house crouching on the floor, laying out a plastic Mickey Mouse mat (of course) where her Tet feast of dead duck meat was about to be served.

As soon as she saw my palm expertly placed in a 'distress' position across my forehead, my face contorted in an Oscar worthy performance of shock, horror and mortification, the bloody fingers, and lastly, the piece de resistance - the awful, growing stain that screamed I was a non-toilet trained adult. She let out a shriek so loud the five dogs outside let off a cascade of howls.

Within thirty seconds I was bundled in a cab and sent on my way, back to my hotel.

Fake pee stains can serve as a convenient getaway device.

My stomach is still churning from the thought of eating the meat from dead security guards. An exploded water pipe saved my ass this time.

Next stop, Hoi An.

Mot, hai, ba, YO!!!!

Love, Dave

February 23, 1994
4.49 P.M.
A Rice Field North of Hoi An
Wheel's on Fire

Hi Annette,

I have just learned that Vietnam is one of those rare countries where you can have a cultural and near death experience wrapped up tightly in one tasty, slim baguette. My legs are still trembling (just like in Osaka, remember FECG?)

Let me explain.

But first, I'm finally in Hue now, north of Danang, and the little town is bursting with people celebrating Tet. I got here by bus once again, a long low altitude flightmare where I was surrounded by Germans and Dutch screaming at the bus driver to slow down. More than twelve hours later, he did. When he pulled up with a screech of tires in the bus stop, that is, but not a moment before.

So back to near death experiences. When you travel you don't really give much thought to dying on the road, but with suicidal motorbike riders and taxi drivers that fall asleep at the wheel added to a flightmare here and there, it is a reality.

Case in point, my trip today. My knees are still shaking from it...

Speeding down Vietnam's Highway 1 back towards Hue, Vietnam's ancient capital city, I sat in the back seat of a black market taxi drinking in the earthy smell of rice paddy water and the amazing, craggy cliffs of the country's central coast. They floated in shallow water fringed with palm trees, where, in the distance, pure white cranes padded around looking for a meal.

After a full eight-hour day trip to Hoi An, we were finally free of the two loud-mouthed tourists we had just dropped off at a bus depot near China Beach. They were nightmare travelers, having bought a ton of fake designer goods in Saigon, which they draped over every square inch of their bodies, all Guvvi and Nake and Adidass, they then took on the smug attitude that customers of the real merchandise back home adopted. It's bad enough people travel paint-by-numbers, with their noses buried in their Lonely Planet's, but did they have to wear a uniform as well?

To fend off these irritating mosquito people, I had my own Royal Flush, having spend exactly four more months in Asia than them, I shut them up in sixty seconds flat when I started bragging about places I had been that they had not, that sort of thing. I have been traveling long enough by now to know how to play the travelers game to my advantage when I need to.

The driver had met their endless string of inane requests, frequent shouts at him to slow down and threatening tones whenever they were forced to pay for anything extra with smiles since seven o'clock that morning.

But I'd spent enough time in Asia to realize it wasn't the international symbol for happiness he was returning with his wide, perfect grin.

Now, free from the harassment at last, he sat in the front seat as earnest as a racecar driver, gunning his precious LADA as fast as it would go. The top speed or the level of gas consumption was impossible to tell because the car had not one dial or arrow on its dashboard as they had long since been ripped out.

We flew past more thatched roofed villages, swerving crazily from side to side. The setting sun plunged towards the flooded rice fields, turning the shallow water crimson and gold. I inhaled deeply and took in the verdant landscape that seemed frozen in time and straight out of a tourist brochure.

Suddenly the driver caught my eyes in his rearview mirror, and in slow, halting English asked me, 'Those people, they were from your country?'

I nodded, explaining they lived down the road from where I had grown up. He shook his head and muttered something under his breath.

It had been less than three years since Vietnam had really swung open her doors to tourism, and all around the country hotels and companies had sprung up like toadstools to feed the exploding demand.

Yet everywhere I went I saw conflicts between locals and travelers, sometimes heated and at least once, violent, when a tourist had gotten into a fistfight in Nha Trang with three cyclo drivers. Never before had the clash of cultures between east and west been so apparent.

The driver then peppered me with more questions about foreigners, what they drank, what jobs they had, and what sports they played, what their little blonde children ate. I answered these questions as best I could while he squinted at me in his rearview mirror waiting for that diamond of knowledge, the Holy Grail of Tourism that would make all these strangers understandable, and, of course, make his own under-the-table tourist taxi service flourish.

And then with a quick flick of his neck, he turned to me, and asked, almost accusingly, 'Just what do you tourists really want when you come to my country?!!'

His tone was split between desperation and a truly earnest desire to find out what made traveler's tick; his knuckles went white as he gripped the steering wheel fiercely, his eyes wild with confusion and frustration.

Just about to open my mouth to answer him, the car began to swerve and lurch violently as if butted by an unseen water buffalo. As I was thrown around in the back seat, the driver, swearing, cursing and shouting, desperately tried to bring his LADA under control. But in a matter of seconds we had drifted across into the left lane and right into oncoming traffic.

Through the dirty, cracked windshield I could see a local bus flying towards us at top speed, overloaded, belching smoke, touts swinging wildly from every open door and several hundred chickens tied to the roof...

FUCK. A deadly head-on collision was imminent!

With a final volley of curses, the driver, using all his strength, yanked the car out of the way of the bus with such force that the front right wheel sheared off completely. The LADA passed through a curtain of snow white feathers molted from the chickens tied to the top of the bus and with a sickening crunch crashed onto the roadway to slide on bare metal as the bumper was ripped off and silvery sparks flew everywhere.

We careened on down the road, me screaming in the back seat the driver in the front yelling his head off until we swerved right and careened straight off the road like a Russian version of the Dukes of Hazzard to land with a thick squelch in the middle of a rice paddy.

Above us, on the road, the severed wheel happily bounced down Highway 1, trailing a thin ribbon of blue smoke.

Dazed and nursing a bruised skull I tried to open the door but the mud firmly held it shut. Chicken feathers drifted into the car, and the driver sneezed. I rolled down the window, crawled out onto the roof and found a crowd of white-faced local villagers, who upon hearing the terrific crash, had expected to find a horrific, bloody car accident. Instead, they found a tall shaken foreigner standing on the roof of a Russian car as it slowly sank into the mud and the wet windshield plastered with white chicken feathers.

When the driver and I had jumped off and waded through the mud to the safety of the road, we stepped shakily back onto solid ground. The villagers had already retrieved the errant front wheel and they were pointing and admiring the deep trench our axle had carved in the asphalt.

The driver shot me a nervous grin as if nothing major had happened and said simply, 'Friend, I think you must catch another bus to Hue now.'

With that rather obvious statement he flagged down a minivan that stopped and eagerly took me inside. Having taken care of his precious customer, the driver, wiping the sweat off his brow, turned back to tend to his wounded LADA that had now settled even deeper in the soft mud.

As the minivan pulled away from the crash scene the new driver bombarded me with exactly the same tourism industry questions as the first.

Ignoring him, I looked through the back window at the old driver who was still standing in the middle of the road watching the minivan ruefully as it shrank in the distance. The poor guy never did get his most urgent tourism question answered.

As we rounded a bend and continued north to Hue I turned back to the new driver and began patiently answering his pointed questions. Explaining what a breakfast cereal was, and what a toaster did, it seemed this guy wanted to open a restaurant for tourists and wanted to get his breakfast menu note perfect.

'But Vietnamese eat noodles and soup for breakfast,' he whined.

'Foreigners won't,' I said sternly.

Though my voice was strong, my knees were still shaking. I looked down at my clothes, they were caked in mud. And decorated with a couple of snow-white chicken feathers.

With a nervous laugh I now know that Vietnam was one of those rare countries where you could have a cultural experience and a near death experience, all at the same time.

More news from Northern Vietnam.

That is, if I get there in one piece and not splattered all over Highway 1 somewhere.

Love, Dave

February 28, 1994
8.32 A.M.
Vinh, Vietnam
Now They Come in Buses!

Hey Annette,

I'm in Halong Bay. I could go on and on and tell you about the beauty of this place, like the morning mist the color of pearls, or the craggy rocks that look like bowing cranes, things like that, but you've seen Catherine Deneuve in Indochine, right? So I'll keep the focus on the offbeat stuff, the quirky stuff.

The good stuff.

Continuing north on Vietnam's National Highway One towards Hanoi, not far from Hue, our bus passed the 17th parallel where the lush palm trees and rice fields of the south vanished. They were replaced with more somber, gray buildings and dry, rocky hills.

Eventually, after a full day of driving down the highway so flooded the driver could only follow the telephone poles from preventing us from sliding off the road, we arrived in Vinh, a city completely destroyed by American bombs. It had been rebuilt in the late 1970's as a model Socialist city complete with ugly apartment blocks and wide empty boulevards, where Communist state radio was blasted out of scratchy speakers.

I spent the night in a hotel that the reception staff proudly claimed had been built with Cuban assistance. A short walk around the featureless town brought me to a market where a man was trying to sell lottery tickets.

'Ah, an Imperialist,' he said with a laugh as he wandered off without another word.

Clearly it was Communists, not Imperialists, who bought lottery tickets in Vietnam.

The next morning, after waking at dawn to the skies streaked with the screams of Russian MIG's from the nearby air base, our bus left Vinh and by late afternoon was approaching Haiphong where the bus passed a beautiful stretch of beach that made the homesick Californians onboard request a stop.

The driver agreed to a thirty-minute break and we jumped out at the chance to explore the beautiful beaches Vietnam was famous for, relaxing in the waning light, wondering when the beach resorts would arrive. A long line of basket boats were hauled out of the water and a group of young fishermen were slack jawed at the sight of two-dozen foreigners advancing down their beach in the middle of nowhere. As we approached, the fisherman's shrieks were no different than if we had been dropped from a silvery flying machine, an alien spacecraft.

Eager to talk to the fishermen we asked the driver to translate. As we told them one by one where we were from and where we were going, an old man materialized from nowhere to listen. He stood there as we talked and came in to peer closely into our eyes as though he was searching for some kind of information.

His face registered intense shock when he learned many of us were from America. Then he stepped toward the middle of the circle and raised his voice to speak.

'Those Americans,' he said, as the driver translated, 'they used to fly their planes so far above our heads we could never see them,' he pointed to the sky, and then at our vehicle. 'But now look, the Americans come in buses!'

And with that he shook our hands one by one and wandered off, chuckling to himself.

In the middle of nowhere in Vietnam this old man summed up the vast changes sweeping through his country and humbled all of us in one fell swoop. Vietnam is surging forward, eager to develop, grow rich, take their place at the world table, and judging by the smiling faces all round, it won't be long.

Love, Dave

March 4, 1994
10.23 A.M.
Hanoi, Vietnam
100 Hours in the Hanoi Hilton

Hey Annette.

It seemed innocent enough, that sip of water. (I am now wary of ANY liquids in Vietnam)

We were waiting for our chickens to be killed in a tiny restaurant on the outskirts of Hanoi. The thermos promised in the state run hotel we had left that morning was nowhere to be found and I had seen no bottles of water for sale along the road. I was dying of thirst, surely a sip of that ice water wouldn't kill me.

Jen, a girl from Iowa, saw my mistake and clicked her tongue.

'Dave, that water is filthy,' she said, making a face.

Leah, who was from California, added, 'Yeah, Dave, that water is lethal.'

I shrugged my shoulder and brushed it off. Less than five minutes before a large brown dog had come flying out of the restaurant at me snarling, white teeth bared and bit me squarely on the ankle, drawing blood. I was still nursing a scalded inner thigh and a bloodied hand, and now I had a second dog bite to contend with. Whether it was trying to get revenge on humans for eating it's relatives, (the environs of Hanoi were famous for its dog meat restaurants) I never knew, but once it had bitten me it slunk into a corner and fell asleep.

A bowl of soup was dropped in front of me but I ignored mine as I tended to my bleeding ankle. By the time I had taken care of the blood, the bus was loading and I had missed lunch.

'C'mon, Dave,' called Leah who was sitting in the back of the bus.

The traffic into Hanoi was terrible but I was feeling even

worse. It began with an innocent twitch deep in my intestines, a sort of shudder a horse uses with its skin to flick off a fly. About an hour later my stomach had begun to gurgle, squirm, and then erupt into a full-scale revolt. As my mind raced to find an explanation I had myself convinced that it was something from dinner the night before. (I had skipped lunch, and I had also eaten no breakfast.)

The stabbing pains started as the bus started dropping people off at hotels around Tran Hung Dao street. It morphed into convulsions by the time I had handed over my passport at the reception counter at my guesthouse that was managed by a sullen, angry woman, and continued with gut wrenching cramps as soon as I reached my Spartan room.

I dropped my backpack on one of the beds and promised myself a short nap before I went out to find a pharmacy. The pain was excruciating, my stomach was swelling up like a balloon, but after a few minutes of lying on the bed, I fell promptly down a bottomless, rabbit hole of sleep.

I began dreaming about all the characters I had encountered in Cambodia and Vietnam. The Swedish couple were there bickering, the barefoot Khmer Rouge soldiers were there too, speaking in English, not Khmer, admonishing me for taking a sip of that water.

'Why'd ya drink it, mon?' said one of the Cambodian soldiers in a Jamaican accent. The fingerless man in Nha Trang was there, laughing not at my stained jeans this time but my soon to be fatal disease I had picked up, Jackie was motor mouthing her way through an encyclopedia of different drugs, and that obnoxious American girl was tapping my shoulder and yelling, 'WHY HAVEN'T YOU BEEN TO INDIA?' as I tried to slink deeper into my seat to avoid the looks of derision the bus passengers were aiming in my direction, boring into my soul, proving that as a traveler without an Indian visa in my passport, I was nothing.

Even the little man who went on about Americans coming in buses was there too, wrinkling his head up in frustration, asking me in a Texas twang, 'Why haven't you been to India, man?'

The only problem with all these characters was that not only were they a confusing mixture of psychedelic colors, their heads danced free of their bodies and continued to taunt me, haunting my dreams long after their bodies were gone.

When I awoke hours later it was to a silence so deep I thought whatever I had picked up had rendered me blind and deaf.

'So this is what Helen Keller felt like,' I thought to myself ruefully as my brain frantically caught me up on the rapidly escalating civil war that left me doubled over in pain. In the pitch black I tried to move my arm to check my watch but couldn't; my arms felt like they were pressed down by monstrous sacks of cement. My head felt like it was a wrecking ball that had seen better days. Before I could scream, 'KILL ME NOW,' the pain was so great I passed out.

When I heard what sounded like North Vietnamese soldiers marching through my room, complete with a maddening medley of martial music, I opened one of my eyes a crack, fearing the worst. I realized it wasn't a military parade at all stomping through my room, it was just the neighborhood speaker system blasting the daily morning diet of Socialist radio to the early rising citizens of Hanoi.

The battery on my watch had died and I had no idea what time, or day, it was, but I guessed it to be about five a.m.

As I lay there in agonizing pain and suffering through the official sounding doctrine screaming out of the cheap speakers, I looked down in shock to see my stomach swollen like in Aliens and wondered when the evil being would burst out. I cared little.

At least the beast would end my suffering. Then I fell asleep again where I was taunted by even more terrifying dreams.

A couple of hours after the radio broadcast ended, I heard a series of doors opening and closing sandwiched between a few short grunts and the creak of wood. Hushed voices. And giggles.

Was there a pig farm at this hotel? I wondered through my delirium. I had heard about the village like atmosphere in Hanoi, but this seemed ridiculous. It finally made sense when I saw a bright red paper packet under my bed for 'OK' Condoms, a local Vietnamese brand. Just my luck, the hotel I was staying in was also a brothel.

And just then the doorknob started moving. For almost

all hotel staff across Vietnam, knocking before entering was never done, it was always at the bottom of the maid's priorities. Suddenly the door flew open with a bang.

'Aaaaaah!' the maid shrieked, dropping her bucket and crashing back against the yellow wall to cover her eyes as though they were being consumed by flesh eating acid.

I looked down and realized that I was naked. I guessed I had pulled my clothes off during my terrible night of dreams. I smiled and mumbled something lame as I feebly flicked a grey blanket over my butt as the maid, red as a beet, made a quick and embarrassed exit, leaving the room un-cleaned.

Conscious at last, for a few seconds I looked around the room, the first time I had done so in daylight. It looked like a torture cell in a James Bond film. There were two long single beds with flimsy Chinese mattresses, perfect for torture, a rickety frog green Formica table perfect for flinging a villain through in a fight sequence, a cheap aluminum chair useful for interrogations, and a small bathroom covered with swirly ceramic tiles that made my head spin.

But it was the thick iron bars on the windows that got my attention. Either installed to keep guests from jumping out to their deaths to escape this insane asylum, or to keep rescuers away in case of a fire, I did not know, either way, they did not make me feel any safer.

My tongue felt swollen to twice it's normal size and I somehow managed to slide off the bed and crawl to the bathroom. Along the way I rested on the tile floors and found the thermos with just half a mouthful of water in it. I drank it gratefully then crawled into the bathroom and promptly threw up into the toilet, my eyes so confused and mesmerized by the awful tiles, I threw up again, more out of disgust than illness.

'This is what India will be like,' I warned myself as I started shaking. INDIA is spelled H-E-L-L.

Exhausted from the effort, I took a nap on the cold tiles. It felt good for my fever, laying my cheek against the cool ceramic. I crawled back to the narrow bed, climbed up it and I plunged back into a deep, corpse-like sleep.

When I woke up sometime later that afternoon, the lights were on but the fan was off. A horrible gurgling was coming from the toilet. Water was gushing out onto the tiles and the whole commode was shaking as if it was going to explode.

I smashed pillows on both sides of my head to ward of this poltergeist but the sound still penetrated into my brain. And then the noise died down. The water stopped overflowing and the rasping noise coming from the toilet stopped. In the silence, a wooden bed was creaking. I remembered the empty pack of condoms on the floor and listened in horror for the 'performance' to end.

Mercifully, in about thirty seconds, it was.

When I drifted back to sleep I awoke to find the fan was on but the lights were off. Then, after another long tunnel of dreams where a Bollywood production recreated my impending death, all belly dancers and saris and incense, there was a knock at the door.

Looking down to see if I was clothed, the door opened again and this time it was not the maid but the sullen hotel manager herself who had checked me in.

'You must get a doctor!' she shouted at me, kicking the bed for emphasis.

I groaned and took a closer look at her. She looked, sounded, and acted like Rosa Klebb and I muttered something hateful to her, about having enough strength to fight off whatever was incubating inside my body, alien being or not.

'You are green,' she said, looking at my skin closely, breathing in my face.

'No doctor,' I wheezed.

'You stayed here two days,' she went on. 'I need money.' She started to poke my bag looking for Vietnamese currency.

I reached out and it took all my strength to find enough money to pay for the second night. As soon as she had the cash, Rosa Klebb paid no more interest in my welfare or health and left the room, slamming the door behind her.

Before I fell back to sleep, I rubbed my swollen belly, hoping that whatever Alien being was about to claw it's way out of my body, it would devour Rosa first.

Woken up again by the same Socialist morning radio racket, my swollen stomach was no better. I hadn't eaten in over two days but I wasn't hungry. The door slams, the power cuts, overflowing toilets and sexual performances in nearby rooms continued throughout the day on and on like a haunted house.

I pulled pillows around my head and slept with them stuffed as close to my head as I I could.

That afternoon a new maid barged into the room this time but there was no shriek. I was so wracked by shivers that I barely noticed her pushing the dirt around the floor. Just before she finished, I opened my eyes to find her peering at me closely, mumbling in Vietnamese that I didn't understand. I swore she was taunting me as she poked my shoulder to see if I was still alive.

I was still too weak to move out of this god-forsaken hotel and I was beginning to wonder if had been unwittingly cast in the Vietnamese adaptation of Stephen King's novel Misery. Felled by some mysterious microbe, some fetid fungus, or some vicious virus, my prison term continued.

I looked over at the maid who was still cleaning the room. I wanted to get rid of her, so I started to sing a song to get rid of this evil presence, but she cackled like a witch. So I raised my voice even higher and higher until even the Socialist radio speakers would have been drowned out. Suddenly the evil woman flew out the door, slamming it behind her.

Sometime that night, a knock echoed through the room.

'Go away,' I thundered, wondering if Rosa Klebb wanted more money.

There was another knock and then a giggle.

I realized it was a prostitute.

Had Rosa Klebb sent her to cure me?

I reached down, grabbed a shoe and threw it at the door. It bounced off the flimsy wood with a satisfying bang. A few seconds of silence was then followed by another knock, this time, even louder. I threw another shoe, even harder, but the knocks continued until it became a steady pounding.

Irritated, I flipped to the back of my Vietnamese phrasebook and selected the words for 'poor,' 'student' and called them out.

The knocking continued, so I redoubled my efforts, searching for the words for 'married' and 'old.' The knocking went on.

Then I selected the silver bullet.

'HIV,' I shouted, and the woman vanished as fast as Rosa Klebb once she got her money. Exhausted from the exchange, I fell back on the bed, unconscious.

Hours later, after more down the rabbit hole dreams, I

opened my eyes, expecting yet another long day of pain, noise, alien beings, cackling witches and James Bond characters.

But when I opened my eyes, I reached down and touched my stomach. It was flat. My fever was gone and when I was able to sit up without passing out, I ran over to the mirror to see my skin wasn't green anymore. But then, I almost collapsed from hunger, my head spinning round and round from lightheadedness.

Feeling like a lottery winner I showered and brushed my teeth for the first time in four days. While I was packing my bags, the Socialist radio sprang to life and I ran down the corridor to where the warden was waiting for her money.

I handed over the money to Rosa Klebb who was sitting behind her little rickety desk. After I paid her for my stay I gave her a full, furious dressing down about the kind of guesthouse she was running. Rosa took the money and couldn't have cared less, it was a state run guesthouse, and she just ignored my words.

'Welcome to Hanoi,' she said without a smile.

Three days later, after visiting Hanoi's sights, I was crossing the street at the northern end of the Hoan Kiem lake when a cyclo driver pedaled up to me.

'Hanoi Hilton?' he asked expectantly.

I waved him off as though he were asking me to drink arsenic. How could I go back to a place I had already been?

Love, Dave

Vietnam Airlines Flight 102
March 10, 1994
Hanoi ~ Saigon
The DMZ Freeway

Hey Annette,

Why do flightmares always happen at the end of my trips?

Is it the universe's way of slapping me back to reality after doing as I pleased for too long after forgetting to be humble and to kowtow to the Travel Gods, burning incense and joss sticks to appease their mercurial, often violent tempers?

The jury is still in deliberation but I am beginning to suspect that the purpose of flightmares is actually a cosmic slap across the face, reminding us that what has been set in motion by the Wright brothers almost 100 years ago, has NOT always become the seamless travel experience the airlines want you to think it is.

Maybe air travel today has morphed into something entirely too easy, too free, too smooth for the human race, something too easy to be cavalier about as we collect triple mileage and sip champagne at altitudes where the outside temperature is –50 degrees.

Maybe we should be cutting up our airline loyalty credit cards and cowering in the corners of airports around the world, chanting and praying and bowing to these elusive Travel Gods that have the ability to turn a two hour flight into a trip downwards into a hell without end.

So, mere mortals have to be sent a wake-up call every once in a while, and after a surreal trip through Cambodia and Vietnam, having limped (literally, 2 dog bites, a vicious stomach bug, thigh burned to a crisp, wheels falling off cars and bullets from AK-47's) across the finish line in Hanoi, I should have been expecting it.

And that's where my latest flightmare comes in.

Vietnam Airlines.
 Hanoi to Saigon.
 Tupelov 134.
 Flight 102.

The Vietnam Airlines fleet contains a curious mixture of Russian jets and rented Western planes. All the Boeings are painted white because the American embargo still prevents the carrier from showing it's flying crane logo on their fuselages. I knew it was a fifty-fifty, potluck experience flying here, I had met enough travelers and expats to know that the flight could be aboard a gleaming new jet, complete with western captain and cabin crew, or, alternatively, it could be a two-hour terror ride aboard some Soviet deathtrap with no toilet paper.

Up to this point, even despite my meetings with Khmer Rouge soldiers, touchy Saigonese sandwich makers, a cup of vicious coffee, and a stomach virus picked up near Hanoi, I thought I was safe from any real disasters, you know, the ones that make the evening news on the BBC, and not as a juicy passage in your journal.

So, off I went to Hanoi's Noi Bai airport and asked the all important question: Boeing or Tupelov? The girl behind the counter shrugged, and even the supervisor for Flight 102 was not absolutely sure.

When I joined the passengers and walked out on the tarmac we found instead of a gleaming 767, an aging Tupelov 134 was to be our ride to the economic capital of Saigon. Sitting on the runway, emergency exit doors flung open in the tropical heat, wires were sticking out of the rusted wing and liquids were dripping off the crinkled fuselage.

In the wonky lottery that is flying Vietnam Airlines, we had clearly lost this roll of the dice.

Once inside, the plane looked like a pre-war hospital: white curtains hung cross the round, Jules Verne-like windows, the thin seats were covered in itchy polyester material, scratched seatbelts were attached to tattered pieces of nylon and the in-flight reading was nothing more than a brown paper bag.

Luckily, it was going to be a short flight.

After all the passengers had boarded, the cabin crew closed the hatch with a bang. As the temperature inside the plane grew, passengers looked around in terror. Were we in a jet or an oven?

Then, pure white smoke began tumbling down from the vents like dry ice off a scientist's lab table. For years I had heard about this strange phenomenon, this travelers' urban legend, at last I knew the mythical magic show was true. Soon, I couldn't see my hand in front of my face, and the windows fogged up like a Turkish bath. As we approached the runway the Tupelov could have been twenty thousand leagues under the sea for all we knew. As we taxied on I waited for the seatbelt check and safety demonstration.

There wasn't one. We simply took off into the blue sky. The engines whined and the thin plane shot down the runway like a crumpled arrow, lurching from left to right. Seconds later, the front wheel lifted off and the passengers were flung roughly back in their seats as the nose of the plane tilted up to the sky. Was this musty aircraft dreaming of transforming itself from an ugly duckling Tupelov into a British Aerospace Concorde?

It seemed so.

The man in the seat next to me gripped the armrests so hard the whole frame started shaking.

A few minutes later the smoke cleared in the cabin and the crew came through the aisle to fling boxes of packaged food at passengers. It consisted of a disgusting sandwich filled with grey meat and butter and a banana so rock-hard it might as well have been a green boomerang. (After eating the delicious food found everywhere in Vietnam, one wonders why they couldn't cater the plane with fresh spring rolls instead of mystery meat)

The next forty minutes of the flight passed normally, except for a minor disturbance when three men began to fiddle with the emergency exit handle two rows ahead of me, curious to see if it could be opened. The crew simply shouted at them to stop.

Suddenly a woman screamed and pointed out the window, and my heart was in my throat.

Was the wing breaking off?
Was the engine on fire?
Were we going die in this Soviet death jet?

When I pulled the cheap curtain aside and looked out the window, expecting the worst, I could not believe what I was seeing: not two wing lengths away was an Aeroflot Ilyushin 96 flying so close I could actually see people waving at us out of their windows. Passengers all over the cabin began scrambling over to the right side of the plane where they pointed and gaped at the spectacle.

Instead of changing altitude, the pilot just kept on flying as though nothing was the matter. For about five minutes the two planes continued alongside each other as if in some bizarre air show display. Passengers continued to wave at us from across the way, and there was literally nothing else we could do, but wave back....

It was like watching two aging Soviet Cadillacs pass on some freeway in the skies over central Vietnam's former DMZ. The cabin crew didn't even blink an eye as foreigners on the plane clicked their tongues at yet another quirky experience in Vietnam.

About a half an hour before landing I went to the bathroom where a curtained window behind the sink revealed a view of clouds and the crumpled wing. I looked into the toilet where a comb had fallen down and had torn a hole in the plastic. There was a loud ominous hissing sound of escaping air.

Were we depressurizing?

I called one of the female cabin crew over and when she saw the comb and heard the noise, she just shrugged. What was more important to her than preventing an explosive decompression, I quickly discovered, was to rope a native speaker into helping her practice the announcements in English. 'Would I mind doing the announcement when we descended into Hanoi?' she asked.

I shrugged. What's another surreal episode on this flight from the twilight zone?

So, ten minutes later, when the nose of the plane pointed down to the ground and we began a tumbling, bumpy ride back to earth, the cabin attendant tapped me on the shoulder and led me to the back of the plane.

'Ladies and gentlemen,' I stammered into the film noir Soviet microphone, 'we are now approaching Saigon's Tan Son Nhat Airport. Please return your seatback to their upright positions, fasten your seatbelt, extinguish all cigarettes, and prepare your travel documents for arrival. Thank you for flying Vietnam Airlines.'

So strange was the flight that not one passenger turned to see why a foreigner was reading the announcements. The flight attendant thanked me and then went through the cabin to collect the trash as the cockpit door banged open. One of the pilots made a trip to the 'galley' that was a filthy counter at the back of the plane for a quick, last minute cup of coffee.

As we got closer to the ground, the scientist's smoke appeared in the cabin again, and before long, I couldn't see my hand in front of my face.

When the wheels scratched the runway and the rickety jet hugged the earth once more, as the engines slowed us down, as if on cue, every empty seat in the Tupelov 134 plane flew forward in an almost theatrical bow to the weirdness of flying the national carrier of Vietnam.

As flight 102 taxied to the terminal, I chuckled, realizing I had already been out there on the runways, riding the Flying Dragon. Ha ha.

Remember:

If you see a crinkled Soviet jet cruising a few wing lengths away from your own dilapidated plane, don't forget to wave.

I am back in Saigon after seeing the north and tonight it's back to Bangkok.

This place seems crazier and clogged with more cars than three weeks ago when I passed through after Cambodia.

I will NOT be drinking any coffee here.
I will NOT be renting any bicycles here.
I will NOT be ordering any sandwiches anywhere.
I will NOT taking any taxis after the stroke of midnight.
I will NOT be staying in any guesthouses under renovation.

Everywhere in Vietnam, Russians were out, and Americans were in, Chinese bicycles were out, and Japanese motorbikes were in, the French language was out, and English was in, Lenin was out and Colonel Sanders was in. Construction cranes scrape the sky, propaganda posters were being replaced by advertisements for shampoo, the future seems bright.

Very bright.

But there is one tiny problem.

In the words of Jackie (who I never saw again, the Travel Gods thankfully saw to that) 'THIS PLACE IS MAD!'

I doubt the Tourism Ministry would want me to broadcast my injuries or near death experiences I have had in his country too loud, but I am going to recap them here anyway. So, as I end my journey through Cambodia and Vietnam, here is my list of war wounds:

Two dog bites, one on the hand, and one on the ankle;
A burned thigh, from that hotel in Nha Trang;
A bruised skull, from that car crash in Hoi An;
A sore head from that cup of coffee in Saigon;
Oh, and add a bashed ear from Jackie's inane conversations.

And here is my list of near death experiences:

Running into the Khmer Rouge not once, but twice;
Getting shot at with an AK-47;
The Streets of Saigon near taxi crash;
The wheel's on fire near crash in Hoi An;
The Alienesque stomach bug in Hanoi;
And last but not least, Vietnam Airlines Flightmare 102.

Though I have NO plans to go to India, Indochina doesn't have the word 'India' in it for nothing. What, can you imagine, might my list of war wounds from India look like:

Run over by an oxcart and wrapped round it's axles?
Kidnapped and taken to the hills by a Saddhu?
Gored by a sacred cow?
Knocked unconscious by a piece of the Taj Mahal?
Nearly drowned in the Ganges?

WHO KNOWS. AFTER 'SAFE' CAMBODIA, AND MAD VIETNAM, WHO BLOODY KNOWS WHAT MOTHER INDIA WOULD HURL AT ME COURTESY OF THE TRAVEL GODS.

My flight tonight is NOT on Vietnam Airlines,
I'm taking Thai Airways. It was $5 more expensive. You better believe I'm paying that small anti flightmare tax! You have permission to shoot me at dawn if I ever become one of those anal retentively skin flint travelers who would choose to fly Air Gazelle to save $2.

YOU HAVE MY PERMISSION TO SHOOT ME ON SIGHT.

My flight back to Saigon on Vietnam Airlines flight 102 will always be the only reminder I need to never be like those travelers I keep running into in Southeast Asia.
Looking at the list above, I have to pause and wonder.
WHY do we leave home and put ourselves in situations that could get us killed, maimed or as the top story on the evening news on CNN? Life does burn brighter out here on the road, it is addictive, and I am steadily climbing the Lonely Planet Ladder (And always manage to be the center of attention back home whenever the topic of travel comes up) But is it really worth that 15 minutes of fame on the BBC when your bus crash takes center stage?
Hell ya.

Love, Dave

PS: This permission to shoot me on sight also applies if I am ever caught carrying a Guvvi bag or wearing an Adidass shirt.

Djibouti, Ethiopia,
Kenya & Tanzania

Hey Annette,

Oman looks like Afghanistan.

You know all those pictures you are seeing on CNN right now? And like Afghanistan, Oman is way off the overland traveler trail.

That's why I'm here. I figure it's time to jump a few rungs up the Lonely Planet Ladder and visit some countries few have been to. Oman. Uganda. Kenya. Ethiopia. Djibouti.

I lost two days getting here as my trip started with a flightmare. I'm used to trips ending with flightmares, not beginning, so who knows what this bodes for my trip. (Methinks its time for some incense to the Travel Gods again....)

It is three months since 9/11 and the mood, as soon as I arrived in Asia, (Bangkok) is palpably different. But with everyone freaking out about safety and security and terrorists, I want to fly against it and prove now is the best time to go. Scratch that. There is never a better or worse time to go.

Just go.

And arriving late last night into the Muscat airport I got a few strange looks from the immigration people as I pushed my conspicuously blue passport under the glass window.

'No problem, no problem, friend,' the official said as he stamped my passport and slid it back to me, motioning to the baggage carousel. I slunk off sheepishly and not because of my nationality: my suitcase had been trapped in the belly of a Gulf Air jet in Bangkok for two days, I had no fresh clothes, and I looked more disheveled than usual. We're talking 'distressed flightmare casual,' all stale socks and barely brushed teeth.

Fortunately, FECG was not around to strip search me and check if I had changed my underwear.

I am using an internet station in the Gold Souk not far from the Corniche, the Cannes-like waterfront here in Muscat. If Vietnam is green, and Greece is white, Oman is all brown, the buildings, the hills, the houses, everything is a dull khaki. Even the ocean is a grayish sandstone color.

Only the sky is blue.

So back to my flightmare. Here's a riddle: What happens when a dead engine, an irate Frenchwoman, an innocent chair and a plate glass window meet at a gate in Bangkok's Don Muang airport?

Read on to find out.

The check-in process for Gulf Air flight 153 to Muscat began ominously: a beaten up 'DELAYED' plaque was sitting next to the airline's transit counter. The woman sitting behind it, though, reassured me the flight was on time.

But when she saw I had checked my bags through from Saigon to Muscat, my final destination, she began to ask me a raft of questions.

'Did I have enough money for my trip to the Sultanate?'

'Where was I staying?'

'Did I have a visa for Oman?'

'You don't need a visa,' I told her with the authority of a guidebook writer. 'They are stamped on arrival in the country.'

She barely listened to me as she made a phone call and a minute later her manager stepped out from behind a nearby screen and asked, 'Do you really have enough money for your journey?'

I showed my credit card, traveler's checks, and cash to prove I was financially sound enough to visit the Sultanate of Oman.

After checking my documents and money, I was reluctantly issued a boarding pass, and assured again that the delayed sign was wrong, and the flight would be leaving in three hours. But about two hours later, when I absently checked the flight board, it read -

GULF AIR 153. INDEFINITELY DELAYED. PLEASE SEE AGENT.

I rushed back to the transit counter, and found it locked up, even the beaten up 'DELAYED' sign was now gone.

My stomach dropped..... another flightmare had begun.

I ran to the gate to find passengers milling about, mulling over the news. The two women I had seen at the transit desk were nowhere to be found, and harried staff was fending off angry questions left and right. I asked a British woman nearest to me what the new take off time now was, and she said, 'We've been told 11.45 pm.'

That was five hours away.

The next four hours passed slowly. Passengers were given a coupon for dinner that we cashed in at the Thai Airways restaurant overlooking the runway. There I talked to two Americans teaching English in Turkey and a family of Australians living in Saudi Arabia. When we walked back to the gate a frantic crowd of passengers was throwing passports at the gate agents and I asked someone what was going on.

'Flight's been cancelled, mate,' wheezed an Australian. 'We're all going to the Amari Hotel across the road.'

I quickly joined the queue and was taken to the immigration counter where our passports were confiscated and we were given a white slip of paper that served as our receipt.

Marching through the terminal was the plane's motley crew of passengers from at least thirty countries. Other luckier, flightmare-free passengers stopped to stare.

Upon arrival at the Amari Hotel, the passenger's anger was starting to boil over and was directed at the innocent hotel front desk staff. When I got my key I stepped away from the shouts and then cashed in my next meal voucher at the restaurant where the news was grim. One of the engines on the A340 was damaged, the airline's fleet was stretched to the limit, and no replacement aircraft existed to take us to Muscat.

It might be several days before the engine was fixed.

The next morning I took a train to downtown Bangkok to kill a few hours before the flight took off. When I arrived back at the lobby of the Amari Hotel I joined the Gulf Air passengers waiting there and then we were led through the departure hall, where I was stopped because I had no receipt for the airport tax, (as a transit passenger I hadn't needed it) but the woman refused to let me through.

'I was a transit passenger before leaving the airport,' I protested, finding my Thai Airways boarding pass from the previous day.

The Gulf Air rep barked at the lady in Thai, and I was finally released to the Immigration Hall where an official found my passport and then lifted it up to my face to check if it really was me.

Caught in the midst of a flightmare is like being a refugee - you have no idea when you will be free from being endlessly shunted from check-in desk to gate by airline staff and immigration agents, and back again. As I stood there, I was beginning to understand the monumental frustration of being a stateless person, handed off to yet another official, yet another bureaucrat, with no solution, no end in sight to the marathon of hurdles.

When everyone in the group had gotten their passports back we were soon sitting at the same gate, looking at the same A340 airplane and with the same angry, explosively suffocating atmosphere floating all around us.

Three hours after the flight was meant to take off we still hadn't boarded. Having read and reread every magazine, book, and newspaper we shared amongst ourselves, lunch vouchers were issued and we trooped off like school kids to the Thai Airways cafeteria for yet another free meal where the staff was now getting to know us by our first names.

Then five o'clock and seven o'clock passed, another voucher, another meal, and still, no news.

When the sun finally set passengers connecting to India banded together and began to demand information. They took their seats eventually, but not before they were threatened with expulsion from the flight.

Then it was a Frenchwoman's turn to complain and after grabbing her two children roughly by the arms and dragging them to the front of the line, she began to scream in filthy French, berating the ground staff, Gulf Air, Airbus Industrie, Thailand, Don Muang Airport and the Amari hotel in a string of expletives that bounced off the walls and ears of the passengers. Nothing escaped her venom and as the staff tried to calm her down with patronizing words and broad smiled, the exact opposite of what they should have done in that situation, the French volcano was ready to blow.

And then it did, an announcement sweetly reported that due to engine problems, Gulf Air flight 153 was to be delayed another day.

The volcano didn't just explode. It pulled a Krakatoa.

The Frenchwoman let go of her children, gave a final tirade against Gulf Air, Airbus Industrie, Thailand, Don Muang airport and the Amari Hotel, and then before anyone could stop her, she ran over, grabbed a chair, and hurled it through a ten foot by fifteen foot plate glass window, shattering it in what must have been a satisfying sound to her immense pent up frustration over the anger of spending yet another night in Bangkok.

Sitting just meters away from the window I had ducked and closed my eyes as the chair flew over my head and flinched as shards of glass bounced off my face and shoulders. A few slivers actually slid into my shoes. A fresh breeze blew through the large hole, and the entire departure lounge froze. Even the security guards didn't know what to do. In the silence, glass tinkled to the floor like notes played on an elegant grand piano.

Then, in a stream that grew to a flood, passengers began to run up the stairs and away from the mad Frenchwoman. In the chaos, a British man working on a Saudi Arabian oil field yelled, 'She'll be taken to the gaol for that. The Thais will never stand for that kind of behavior in their country.'

The Frenchwoman was then dragged off, sans kids, who stayed with a gate agent. Then, in a procedure we were getting way too familiar with, the passengers stood up like faithful slaves, extending their hands to be re-handcuffed. Repeating the process of the day before once again, we were marched off to the immigration counter where the staff were also now remembering our first names, our passports were taken away again, and on we moved to the Amari hotel where the stunned front desk staff re-checked us in and gave us our sixth meal voucher.

The next morning at breakfast there was more bad news, I was informed that the flight was liable to be leaving that afternoon, but Muscat being my final destination (I was one of the only passengers who was just going to Oman) I was told not to check out of the hotel. Only transit passengers were being accommodated on the first flight, and with two days of passengers ahead of me on the passenger list, it was likely to be at least two more days before I would get to my destination.

So I went for a swim.

That was until the Gulf Air ground staff walked by the pool, recognized my face, and started screaming. 'Get packed! You're on today's flight! If you are not out of your room in twenty minutes, you will be responsible for your hotel bill!'

So off I rushed, got dressed and raced off to the reception where the Gulf Air woman was waiting, tapping her foot in anger. She checked me out of the hotel, and then she took me to the departure hall, and there again I was interrogated for not having a departure tax receipt, and once again there was an exchange of angry words in Thai, and eventually I was let through to get my passport where I was treated once again like a stateless peasant. The gate was the same as the previous two days, and even the smashed window had been repaired.

I never saw the Frenchwoman or her children again.

Amazingly, within an hour I was sitting onboard the packed Airbus 340 jet (sitting in Crushed Peasant Class, or Stateless Peasant Class, if you prefer) that lifted off from Don Muang's main runway as passengers clapped and cheered in relief as the cabin crew stared back blankly as wax dolls. The wheels retracted into their wells and we were on our way.

IF THESE'S A CHAIR THROWING FRENCHWOMAN ON YOUR FLIGHT YOU ARE IN THE MIDST OF A FLIGHTMARE.

This trip to Africa is less than four days old and already there has been an epic flightmare to get the old travel juices flowing. Was this the Travel Gods way of making me humble and pious as I travel southward from Oman to the Horn of Africa?

'Anything can happen in Africa, anything,' a tobacco farmer from Zimbabwe had told me once on a flight to Perth. 'Anything.'

Love, Dave

From: Dave <theloweroad@hotmail.com>
To: Annette <whereisannette@yahoo.com>
Date: Jan 7, 2002 1:20 PM
Subject: E.T. Phone Home

Hi Annette,

Emailing you from here in Djibouti takes five minutes per click. The bandwidth is about as wide as a mosquito's ass. I am in Africa at last, and I am slack jawed at another flightmare so close on the heels of the Gulf Air disaster. Two in a row and definitely a first. It must be a slow week for the Travel Gods or something. Or, they just felt it necessary to send another strange tortuous experience my way.

And Djibouti is one mother of a strange place.

You would love it here. Plenty of diving, sunshine, white sand beaches and lots of French Legionnaire soldiers, too. This time the flightmare wasn't a busted engine or an aging Soviet plane or even an enraged Frenchwoman that caused it. It was simply the case of the disappearing flight, swallowed by the computer system itself. Actually both flights on Ethiopian Airlines were as smooth as could be, except for a woman's tit that made several appearances, (more on that later) but it was the ground staff from hell that made it so bad. Well, that and a malaria scare.

But that's Africa for you.

Because Ethiopian Airlines flight 810 was scheduled to leave at five o'clock in the morning for Addis Ababa from Kampala, Uganda, I took a packed Matatu minivan from my downtown hotel just before midnight, holding my breath as the minivan swerved and veered along the road to the airport, as headlight-less vehicles screamed towards us along the winding road.

When I finally reached the check-in counter the woman was talking into a telephone with headquarters in Addis and she casually informed me the flight was delayed until at least seven a.m. Then she went back to her conversation with flight control in Ethiopia.

Cursing, I stepped away from the counter and looked at my watch. It was twelve thirty in the morning, if I had known I could have stayed in my hotel for a decent night's sleep.

When I dragged my bags outside into the humid night I looked for a Matatu going back to Kampala. I learned that the last one had already left, and taxi drivers rushed in to claim an easy victim. I was quoted $30. For each direction. Adding a return taxi trip plus hotel I was looking at an $80 tab for around three hours of sleep. If I could even find a room.

It looked like I was in for a bit of terminal floor surfing, so I looked around the sparsely furnished airport and quickly claimed a raised area of floor beneath a stairway leading to the control tower. I pulled over two luggage carts to get some shelter from the fluorescent lights, and pulled out my sleeping bag, gritted my teeth and settled in for the long night.

Within seconds a team of security guards started yelling at people to leave the airport, and within minutes they had emptied the terminal using sticks to beat the people back and away from the ticket counters. I huddled behind the luggage carts and soon I was alone in the silent building.

It was about fifteen minutes later when a rising fever stopped me breathing, and it wasn't my anger against Ethiopian Airlines. The fever grew stronger by the minute, and I kicked off my sleeping bag to get some cool air. Instantly a cloud of mosquitoes closed in. For the next hour I prayed it would go away, swatting at mosquitoes constantly and checking my forehead's temperature. It kept rising.

In the second hour the shivering started. It began in my arms and then spread to my whole body. Racked with chills, my chattering teeth made me feel as though I was sleeping in an icy meat locker and not a sweaty, airless airport smack on the equator. It was in the third hour, sweating, swearing, and swatting, that I sat bolt upright in fright.

I had malaria.

I knew prophylactics were only so effective against the disease and I had been warned I could contract it in Africa. I felt the urge to throw up, and then rushed to the bathroom to do so. When I staggered back, a couple of security guards had gathered around my makeshift room, and instead of yelling at me to return to Kampala, they clicked their tongues and whispered, 'You have the sickness?'

I shrugged my shoulders and collapsed back onto the hard cement platform, eager to sleep, nightmaring about worse illnesses waiting for me in India.

'Sleeping sickness?' they said again. 'You want a doctor?'

I shook my head. I was miles from a hospital, hours from daylight, and about to fly to one of the least developed countries in Africa. I tried not to think about this, and somehow drifted off to sleep with the guards nearby keeping an eye on me.

At about three a.m. I woke and found the security guards were still watching over me. Then I managed to drift off for a short nap but was wide-awake again as another wave of shivers pulsed through me. The guards now disappeared, they were going off duty and patted my shoulder in a pathetic gesture of support. I knew Africa was going to be difficult, but this was happening way too soon in my trip. I was on my second flightmare in less than a week and I was probably coming down with malaria.

The terminal was as quiet as a graveyard.

When I woke up awhile later, the florescent lights were on now and the chills and fever had disappeared like the night, I saw the rising sun through a nearby window. I rolled up my sleeping bag, and as I stood up and staggered over to the check-in line at Ethiopian Airlines, the same woman was on the phone again, and I overheard her tell another passenger that the flight was now leaving at nine a.m. I was so weak I had to sit on the baggage cart to keep myself from toppling over.

After getting my boarding pass to Addis Ababa I was told by the check-in agent sweetly, 'You will get your onward boarding pass to Djibouti for flight 306 in Addis.' And with that she tagged my bag with a flimsy label marked, 'DIJ,' the airport code for Djibouti, and went back to her phone conversation with headquarters.

Three hours later, after sitting in an uncomfortable plastic chair, trying to stay awake, I practically crawled through the gate and out onto the sun baked tarmac where I ascended the rickety steps up to the Boeing 737.

Once onboard I found my row occupied by a family of six. I didn't even say a word and walked to the back of the plane and found a vacant row at the back where I stretched out gratefully and closed my eyes.

Two seconds later a flight attendant tapped me harshly on the shoulder and evicted me. I found my way back to my original row where I found my seat still occupied by a massive woman, nonchalantly feeding her baby from a fat breast that hung down to her waist.

'Every passenger must sit in their assigned seat,' barked another crewmember manning the exit rows. She walked over and told the woman to move in Amharic and it was a ten minute struggle to get the mother to first stow her enormous breast inside her blouse, pass her baby to a stranger (me), find her children's boarding passes and then move her four bewildered kids to their correct seats, while I stood there holding the screaming baby, ready to collapse.

When she had finished, and she had repossessed her baby, I gratefully squeezed past the woman into my narrow seat and propped my head up against the window. The woman's enormous tit made an appearance again, and her baby suckled greedily as I gratefully fell asleep.

When I woke up the 737 was whooshing down the runway, the nose wheel was lifting off and we launched right into the wide, bright blue African sky as the woman kept on feeding her baby, her breasts bouncing up and down in tune with the Boeing jet.

Moments later the plane turned right over Lake Victoria, fringed with tropical green vegetation, where fishing boats were leaving Entebbe. The ailerons retracted with a whine, and we were finally on our way, after just a brief stop in Addis, I would be in Djibouti at the latest by mid afternoon.

Fifteen minutes later the jungle disappeared and we were flying over a dark, rippling desert, the chocolate brown Lake Tarkana passed beneath the wings, surrounded by crumbling volcanic hills. Maybe it was the altitude, or the cool air, but suddenly I felt much better, thinking the nightmarish shivering and fever wasn't Malaria after all.

Thoughts of India dimished.

I even managed to eat some breakfast.

Then the scenery changed abruptly again and the desert was broken into brown shards (fields of barley) that looked like fractured pieces of a golden mirror. An hour and a half later the jet descended towards Addis Ababa and there was no sign of the city anywhere, even after we had touched down.

We seemed to be in the middle of nowhere.

After waiting for the enormous breast to be packed away one last time, I stepped off the jet and out into the brilliant sky that so far is my strongest memory of Ethiopia. I walked into the airport and found a wall of glass with a paper tag taped to it. Trasnit Desk, it read.

The 'trasnit' lady behind the glass looked puzzled when I said I was catching flight 306 later that day to Djibouti.

'There is no flight 306 to Djibouti, or even tomorrow.'

My fever flashed up and as I began to argue with her she reached for a telephone on the wall, barked a few words in Ahmaric, and then pointed me to another woman further down the wall of glass, a matronly lady who looked like a librarian, and who was also chatting on the phone.

I staggered over, feeling queasy and angrily pushed my ticket through the slot, and it took her five minutes to hang up the phone. She looked at my ticket, punched some things into the computer, made a ten-minute phone call, and then pushed the ticket back at me, and said, 'There is no flight 306 to Djibouti today. The next flight is Tuesday afternoon.'

It was Sunday. My heart sank.

'But the office in Kampala told me I was going to connect to Djibouti on flight 306 in two hours.' I pushed the ticket back at her.

'The flight frequency, sir, is twice a week. Tuesday and Saturday.

'I was told it was daily.'

'It is your fault, not that of Ethiopian Airlines.'

'It's not my fault, I was at the office yesterday.'

Then the woman started to tap her fingers on the glass like a visitor at the zoo taunting a snake. 'You have large problem. You have no transit visa for Ethiopia. You must pay for new visa. Sixty five dollars. Two nights hotel, Hilton. Three hundred dollars. And you must pay for taxi transfer, twenty five dollars each way.'

'What? The office in Kampala...'

The woman cut me off. 'You have big problem, you must pay.' Behind her on the wall hung two posters that read:

'ETHIOPIA, 13 MONTHS OF SUNSHINE!'
'BE OUR HONOURED GUEST IN ETHIOPIA!'

'No, I will stay here in the airport then.'

'You cannot, Ethiopian law prohibits this. You must leave the airport or you will be arrested.'

'No way am I paying for something I didn't do. It's ridiculous. The Ethiopian Airlines staff in Uganda showed me the flight schedule on the computer screen.' I was gripping the counter now to prevent the mystery illness from felling me like a chain-sawed tree. The woman picked up the phone and made another ten-minute telephone call. Then she turned back to me.

'Passport.'

I pushed it under the glass window, and she flipped through it. 'You have an Ethiopian visa already in your passport.'

'Yes I'm coming back to Ethiopia.'

'Coming back?'

I explained that I was taking the train from Djibouti to Dire Dawa in a week and had gotten my visa issued in Uganda.

The woman gave me a strange look and picked up the phone and a supervisor came up to the window.

'No one takes the train to Ethiopia,' he said, trying to talk me out of my travel plans.

'I know, that's why I'm doing it.'

He turned back to the situation with the flight to Djibouti. 'You sir, are in what I would call an unfortunate situation. Kind of a limbo, OK? The ET flight schedule has been reduced,' he explained, exhaling deeply, 'now it goes twice a week only, not daily.'

'And there is no other way I can do this, but to pay for a new visa, and five star hotel?'

'Yes.'

I had visions of me having an anxiety attack at the Hilton, a combination of Malaria and from being charged huge doctor's bills. I stepped aside to think this over as she dealt with another customer. It was a Japanese tour leader who was frantically trying to arrange seats for her group to Bangkok; it seemed her flight had disappeared in Ethiopian Airlines' computer system as well and here she was, en route from Nairobi to Thailand, with twenty angry guests, as she desperately tried to solve the problem.

Then, with her situation solved, the supervisor and the woman turned their attention back to me.

'Sir, do you have any proof of this person telling you the

flight was daily? It has been twice a week for quite some time now.'

Even though I felt like I was dying, I suddenly remembered the computer printout I had received in Kampala, and dug deep into my carry-on bag, and to my amazement, I found it. I pressed it against the glass and the woman peered at it and then sighed. She snatched it, scrutinized the airport codes, dates and other information, and then picked up the phone for yet another long-winded telephone conversation.

'OK,' she said with a deep sigh, resigned to the fact that due to a computer error in Uganda, I was now to be an 'honored guest of Ethiopian Airlines' until I left for Djibouti in two days.

Note - always keep useless looking pieces of paper printed out by incompetent airline staff....

Then, like a prison warden, she read off my rights as a 'trasnit' passenger, rights I had by now become very familiar with. In short, they look like the rights the United Nations grants displaced persons.

I was informed that I would be staying not as an 'honored guest' at the Hilton, but as a 'terribly unwelcome guest' at the Ethiopia Hotel. My passport would be confiscated until I left the country, so the airline would not have to pay immigration for the visa, my luggage would not be released to me, and as a final insult, I was to take the crew bus from the airport to the hotel, because Ethiopian did not provide private taxis for 'trasnit' passengers.

I wondered idly if a well-thrown chair would help my situation, but as I looked around I couldn't find one. Anyway, the woman was lucky to be safe behind glass. It might have even been installed for that very reason. So I shrugged, and waited.

She pushed a form under the window, which was full of sentences explaining what Ethiopian Airlines was not going to be liable for (international phone calls, room service, any kind of fire or damage to the room, etc). I was told to initial each line, sign the bottom, and then was asked to do it in triplicate.

Had some drugged up Brit Pop band been 'guests' of ET and smashed up their hotel room?

The woman then looked at her watch and told me a crew bus was leaving in ten minutes so I ran off at top speed, handed my passport to the immigration desk in exchange for a pink receipt, found the belching bus and sat behind a group of ET flight attendants just off the flight from Rome.

At the hotel, the front desk staff had no idea who I was, even though the woman at the airport had made three phone calls to tell them I was coming.

'Fifty dollars a night,' they told me. 'Credit card?' they asked, hand extended.

When I pulled out the Ethiopian Airlines voucher, they looked disappointed, and picked up the phone to verify the authenticity.

'Fifty dollars,' they demanded anyway.

'No, its Ethiopian Airlines fault,' I said, explaining the computer's Houdini act.

Twenty minutes later, after being sent to an uncomfortable sofa to wait while they made yet more phone calls to verify the voucher's authenticity, I was handed a room key by a maid who pointed to the stairs.

'Your room is on the fifth floor. Elevator broken.'

I trudged up the stairs, stopping at each floor to catch my breath and to disperse the ugly purple spots blurring my vision in the high air (Addis sits at over 2,000 meters) found my room, and collapsed on the bed.

What does one do in the midst of a flightmare when the earth itself seems to have stopped turning, the sun seems to have stopped rising, and time has stopped dead?

You go for a walk. A long one.

When I woke up I wandered down to get some lunch and found the Japanese tour leader sitting there surrounded by her furious customers, who were also now reluctant, yet 'honored' guests, of Ethiopian Airlines.

I took a table nearby, and soon discovered that we were all passport-less and bag-less, compensated only with a few flimsy meal vouchers.

'ET phone home,' joked an older man at the next table, mimicking the ET ground staff's phone call frequency, combined with the airline's code that matched the slang word for extraterrestrial beings.

After eating I walked to the lobby, where a security guard said, 'Transit passenger cannot leave the hotel.'

'But...'

'You must go back to your room.'

With my plans of exploring Addis dashed, and the horrible realization that I was to be trapped for two days in this Ethiopian Fawtly Towers, I walked up to the staircase, dejected.

I brightened when I found an emergency exit door flung wide-open, leading to the alley behind the hotel. I quickly ducked down it and turned a corner, and ran smack into a tall man waiting for a bus. He was a priest named Elijah and he just looked at me and said, 'You look like you need a blessing. Be careful of bad people in Addis.' With that, he pressed a thumb to my forehead, said a prayer, smiled, and walked away.

A mid-flightmare blessing. Gotta love it.

Reaching the main railway station, I saw the Lion of Judah statue that is the symbol of Ethiopia and was greeted with smiles and handshakes all round. At a café near the main square, a journalist during the Derg period, when Ethiopia had embraced Socialism, welcomed me to his country by offering me a tiny cup of rich coffee. We talked for almost an hour about my opinion of his country, though I only had an opinion about his national airline that he didn't seem too interested in hearing.

That night when I returned to the hotel, I found the same emergency exit wide open and I snuck inside, walked into the restaurant and sat down for dinner. The Japanese were there, happy now that their flight to Bangkok and Tokyo was due to leave in two hours, and they wished me well in my imprisonment at the hands of Ethiopian Airlines.

Over the next two days I explored the Mercado, Addis Ababa's main market and the outer suburbs where the university and the main museum were located. There was a religious festival going on and when I turned a corner I was surrounded by hundreds of people wearing white and carrying glittering crosses, holding Bibles over their heads. It was a kind of

Christianity, ancient, unchanged, and devoutly followed across Ethiopia that I hadn't seen anywhere else in the world.

But when I returned to the alley the door was locked tight. When I jiggled the knob, the door flew open, and there was the security guard, livid as a teased snake, who hauled me off to the front desk to expose my treachery. The two women there just sighed, then picked up the phone and made two phone calls; my flight to Djibouti was finally leaving and they would soon see the back of me. They shrugged and told me to be in the lobby in ten minutes for the crew bus.

The shuttle dropped me off at the cabin crew entrance where a team was off to work the Amsterdam flight. At the security check, a guard refused to let me through.

'No passport, no entry.'

'I am a transit passenger.'

'No passport, no entry.'

I showed him my pink receipt but he kept shaking his head. Luckily, I saw a staff member I recognized and explained my situation. I was admitted to the hall, lead to the passport counter and it was a forty-five minute wait for my passport. When it was returned to me, it was covered in dust.

Passport in hand, I marched back to the check-in line and it inched forward a few meters. Then the power cut and the check-in staff walked off the job. Thirty minutes later, the power came on and when I made it to the front of the line, the power cut again.

Fifteen minutes later I was asked, 'You are flying to Djibouti, with checked bags? Where are your bags?' She stood up and looked over the counter at my feet.

'Ethiopian Airlines refused to let me have my bags,' I explained.

'You will have to go to baggage control. Now.' Behind her a poster shrieked, 'FLY INTO THE WILD BLUE YONDER WITH ETHIOPIAN AIRLINES!'

She turned around and picked up yet another phone and called a colleague who led me down a hall, down a flight of stairs, around a corner, and down another hall, then right out under the tarmac itself beneath a 767 that was loading luggage.

'Dubai,' the man said, pointing to the jet. He led me to a shed where piles of suitcases were marked with flimsy paper flags. Amsterdam. Bangkok. Cape Town.

'Where's Djibouti?' I asked, harried. My flight was due to leave any minute.

'I don't know, let's look.' We walked around the huge piles and then the man yelled, 'Get back against the wall, jet blast!!'

I flattened against the wall as dust and dirt flew up from the jet blast from a passing 767, and gagged as that red dust caked my mouth, coughing and spluttering as I tried to breathe.

'Hong Kong!' screamed the man, pointing at the taxiing plane.

Then he found the pile for Djibouti, I dug to the bottom, sneezing from the dust, but my bag was nowhere to be seen.

'My bag isn't here!' I shouted.

'It must have been mixed up! We must look at other piles!'

As I ran from pile to pile, looking for a familiar black bag, I went through Cape Town, London, Amsterdam, Washington. Nothing.

Then I looked at the pile for Lagos and deep beneath the suitcases I found my bag, dragged it over to the Djibouti pile and asked the man to retag it. If I hadn't moved the bag myself, I would have never seen it again.

'Hurry! Hurry!' yelled the ground staff and I was ushered to a stairwell, climbed it, and popped into the tiny airport terminal. There was no computer or any staff around and I had to walk the whole length of the airport just to find the gate for the flight to Djibouti.

Twenty minutes later a boarding call was made and the crowd surged forward. When the Fokker 50 finally took off for Djibouti, flying off into the bright blue African sky and the wild blue yonder, I gratefully waved Addis Ababa airport goodbye, crossing my fingers that my luggage was safely swallowed in the plane's belly and not on it's way to Nigeria.

So, out of Africa, two lessons:

IF ANY TITS ARE NOT STOWED DURING TAKEOFF, YOU ARE DEFINITELY IN THE MIDST OF A FLIGHTMARE.

IF YOU EVER FIND YOURSELF IN THE BELLY OF ADDIS ABABA AIRPORT SEARCHING FOR YOUR LUGGAGE, DON'T FORGET TO KEEP YOUR MOUTH CLOSED.

Two flightmares in less than a week. I must have been a very bad boy indeed. Or maybe I am just getting them out of the way so I can enjoy a flightmare-free Africa....

Love, Dave

Hey Annette,

I'm sitting in front of a creaking fan and a broken window here in an internet café in Djibouti. The call to prayer is coming from a nearby mosque along with a heavy reddish dust from the unpaved streets. It is noon and I'm the only person typing. Everyone is praying. The manager just left and told me to leave the money on the table when I'm through.

That's a first.

And here's another - I had a woman smash her fist into me in the market, yelling, 'Bin Laden! Bin Laden!' the first day I was here. Getting yelled at in public and then getting FISTED by a woman in a Burka?

Definitely a first for me.

It's only a few months after 9/11 and I have already felt in certain instances a colder shoulder while traveling, not only from locals, but other travelers too. You open your mouth and suddenly lips curl and eyes narrow when they hear the accent.

But it doesn't surprise me. In the week I have been here I have not taken out my camera to take a single photo. The looks from locals and the heavy atmosphere here have been enough to convince me to take pictures with my eyes instead.

This strangeness was first evident on the flight in. Passengers on the plane included a Somali man who worked in 'the herb trade' and a shifty Brit who wouldn't explain why he was coming to this tiny country.

Well, neither could I really....

When the Ethiopian Airlines Fokker 50 touched down on the barren runway in Djibouti it was surrounded by land as barren as Iceland or the Big Island of Hawaii. Black. Volcanic.

Hot. Dusty. Africa.

We had just flown over the most inhospitable desert in the world, passing over ancient, gaping volcanic vents poking up through East Africa's winding Rift Valley, then the salty, ghost-white Lac Assal and Lac Abbe had passed like fuzzy apparitions under the plane's wings, the only freshwater for hundreds of miles.

After a short taxi ride through deserted, dusty streets, the town looked straight out of Star Wars, dun colored buildings, a camel here and there, and a few women with kohl smeared under their eyes were selling piles of tomatoes. And that was about it. Though it is the end of winter, it was already thirty-five degrees Celsius.

And it wasn't even noon.

I found a hotel near the main square in Djibouti town and the manager inspected my blue passport as carefully as a customs official. After a few phone calls, including one to the owner, he reluctantly rented me a room on the second floor. After stowing my bags, I stepped out into the harsh desert light, and walked down the street in the direction of the city's port, looking for a bank.

When I turned a corner I nearly collided with a long column of French Legionnaires marching down the road, goose-stepping in tan knee high socks, tan shorts, and matching pillbox hats.

Smack in the middle of Africa.

Taking a shortcut down a side street I found dozens of women swathed in colorful veils wrapped around their heads, leaving only their eyes exposed, marked with kohl to ward off the sun's powerful rays. Wilted vegetables and bits of fresh goat meat was all that was for sale, and as I walked down the alley, people stopped talking and turned to point, stare, and pin me to the opposite walls with piercing glares shot from their eyes.

Suddenly a woman in a black veil broke ranks and started shouting, 'Bin Laden! Bin Laden!'

No one joined her. They just continued staring at me in that way I have become used to in Djibouti, an expression of coldness mixed with curiosity and blended with awe. Whether it was the fact I was an independent traveler, and not a Legionnaire, or something else, wherever I walked in the town, conversations stopped, school children gaped, and old men pointed at me with long fingers.

Clearly this woman was no wallflower. As her rants echoed off the whitewashed walls I kept on walking, stepping over filthy puddles and potholes, still in search of a bank. Then, she ran around from behind her pile of tomatoes, rushed over to me and punched me in the stomach with a clenched fist.

'BIN LADEN!' she screamed again, smashing her fist against my shoulder.

This was not the welcome I had expected in Africa. I had been in Djibouti less than two hours at this point, and the cold stares from the people in that alley pushed me around the corner and down into an even narrower alley, where I stumbled on, looking for an escape.

And a bank.

With her shouts still echoing in my ears I finally found a bank, crowded with German sailors and chain smoking European expatriates cashing in their paychecks. Chattering away in French and Spanish and Italian as they waited for their money, I noticed they wore the same expressions as the locals, eyeing me coolly. When one man asked me which company I worked for, my bright explanation that I was in fact traveling here was met with derision, even hostility.

'Why?' snarled a slovenly Brit.

I shrugged, changed money, and when I walked out of the bank my stomach was twisted into a knot, questioning the seven weeks that lay ahead of me. After two back-to-back flightmares, I was clearly already on the Shit List of the Travel Gods; if getting fisted by a woman in a Burka was what they had in store for me here in Djibouti, what beasts did they intend to unleash on me in the rest of Africa?

After a sleepless night, I found my footing the next day.

Friday is the weekend in the Middle East, and in Djibouti, where the expatriate community is distinctly French and nearly all linked to the military they used their only day off to make the de rigueur boating excursions to the Mouchas islands off the coast in the Gulf of Aden. There, amid these dazzling white sand beaches and blue waters, they swim, snorkel and sunbathe, recreating a version of St. Tropez in Africa.

I self-consciously wandered around the bustling harbor, random French words tumbling through my head like in a washing machine as I struggled to form grammatically correct questions. Looking for a boat I was rudely told by one ugly Frenchmen that his boat was 'for French only,' but it hardly bothered me, getting the cold shoulder in this strange country was normal. (Even restaurants refused to serve me because I was not French)

So I kept on walking.

I eventually found a dive boat heading out to the islands, negotiated a price, and I was immediately asked to help them do some shopping in the only store selling foreign food.

'Could you drive a stick shift?' asked the Swiss Dive Master.

'Sure,' I said nervously, remembering it was about five years since I had shifted.

'OK, here,' he handed me a wad of money, then the keys and pointed in the direction of the supermarket. I hopped in the drivers seat and drove off right under the nose of the ugly Frenchman who had refused to let me share the cost of his boat as he yakked into a cell phone.

The cramped aisles sold outrageously overpriced tins of pate and jars of fruit preserves with baskets full of long baguettes. As I waited in line behind some scantily clad jeunes filles they sucked languidly on cigarettes as the black veiled woman added up their purchases. The girls were complaining to each other in hyper speed Parisian French about the boring life in Djibouti.

After steaming out of the crowded harbor, where sailboats carried chic French housewives carrying wicker picnic baskets stuffed with baguettes and Brie, I was paired up for diving with a German Navy captain who was stationed in Djibouti. 'Why are you here?' I asked him.

'To find Bin Laden,' he said morosely. 'We think he's planning an escape from Afghanistan and go off to Somalia. He's donated money to mosques all along the way from Kabul to Mogadishu.'

It turned out that the expatriate numbers in Djibouti was soaring due to this search for Bin Laden, and prices for everything were going up in response.

An hour later we arrived at the Mouchas Islands, donned our dive gear and were soon descending through a soup of plankton that cleared instantly at fifteen meters, like a curtain being drawn back, revealing a large shipwreck, it's masts circled with schools of large, lazy barracuda, silvery trevally, and big-eyed tuna. As we descended further, two bands of large barracuda circled above and below us and a stealth of eagle rays passed by, soaring majestically through the blue water.

The German Navy captain explained that the locals shunned the sea: the main bay in the country is called the Gulf of Demons, and they believed the seas were full of evil spirits and malevolent beings. They didn't even eat much seafood, preferring a diet of goat and camel meat to fish. The only fishermen in the country caught just for the expatriates, who consumed the lobsters, prawns and squid that cost a fraction of what they did in Europe.

As we dived again that afternoon, I had never seen seas so thick with fish, so untouched; the dive masters begged me to come back to see the whale sharks that frequented the seas in the winter.

After two amazing dives, we anchored on a deserted island, swam ashore with our backpacks balanced on our heads and ate Poisson Yemenite, a dish of grilled, salted fish drizzled with honey and served on flatbread cooked by one of the boatmen's wives.

As we sat on the beach, squinting in the blinding light reflected off the pure white sand beach, French Legionnaires, tattooed, muscled, and speaking in Arabic, French, German and Russian, sunbathed naked near us with their girlfriends, as locals watched the scene with slack jawed bemusement.

Later, I fell into conversation with a group of French engineers, building roads in Djibouti, who refused to speak English and described the crippling effect that chat, the tobacco-like leaf chewed by all in Djibouti, had on the country.

They balked when they heard that I was traveling overland into the heart of Africa.

'C'est bizarre, ami, non?' quipped one of the older ones, as he flipped his arm up and down to ward off the flies.

'L'Ethiopie est chaud,' he went on.

That afternoon, sunburned, exhausted, and my mind reeling from speaking pidgin French for hours on end for the first time in years, we unloaded the dive boat's tanks where the same chic French housewives walked down the gangways of their sailboats, sporting bored smiles, escorting their blonde, sunburned kids back to their drivers who took them back to their massive villas. And the housewives would do it all over again the next weekend, because there was simply nothing else to do in Djibouti, the hottest country in the world.

That night in town, I found a friendly restaurant owner.

'What are you doing in Djibouti, friend?' shouted the Vietnamese man running the country's only Chinese establishment, a question I could have asked him as well. I never ran into another lone traveler in the country, and neither had he served one, in six months he reported only two as he brought me my food.

The next day I packed up my bags and caught a ride to Tadjoura, a one-lane town around the other side of the Gulf of Demons, where the French poet Rimbaud had once lived. When I took my seat in the front of the car organized by my sullen hotel manager, the driver asked me my hometown.

'New York City,' I said.

He shook his head and said something in Afar to his friends in the back seat. When I turned around the four men opened their shirts and revealed Bin Laden T-shirts underneath. When I looked back at the driver, he also showed me his T-shirt: it had a picture of Bin Laden printed over a mosque.

We left Djibouti town, snaking through the Afar and Somali neighborhoods that were completely segregated on tribal grounds. We were heading towards Afar territory, and I got an earful of how wicked the Somalis were. (Later the Somalis told me how nasty the Afars were)

Within ten minutes we were out in the moon-like countryside where tiny villages of humpbacked houses looked like a movie set straight out of Mad Max. To the horizon, it looked like the surface of the moon. This was made all the weirder when I saw teams of French Legionnaires kicking up clouds of dust as they hiked across the desert, with backpacks full of rocks.

Later, we passed the craggy throat of the Gulf of Demons, where the rift valley met the Indian Ocean, where the African continent was ripping apart. The spectacular blue ocean contrasted sharply with the inky black volcanic rocks.

'We could leave you out here, friend, and you wouldn't last a day,' cackled the driver.

With this warning I didn't ask to stop the car to photograph the gulf, instead shooting it through the window. When we got to Tadjoura town, I gratefully hopped out, took my bag, and when I found the only hotel was full, I was rented a cot on the roof of the town's sole restaurant.

A half an hour later I heard a machine gun fire off, the bullets whizzing into the sky. I hit the deck, thinking of bandits, but when I looked towards the port, where people were running at a small speedboat from all directions, I realized it was something else.

It was the daily chat boat, delivering the enormously popular leaf-stimulant to the small town from the capital, the sole social activity in Djibouti. In less than a minute, the boat's leafy cargo was emptied, and as the town's residents walked slowly home, clutching long, curled branches of leaves, one by one the shops closed down, as the citizens slammed their doors shut to chew the chat.

The restaurant staff invited me to chew the chat on the roof, and I gratefully accepted. It seemed Tadjourans were friendlier than the cold shouldered residents of Djibouti town, and as we swung side to side in hammocks, we watched the ancient camel caravans that were preparing to leave that night as they had for hundreds of years, continuing the salt trade into Ethiopia's interior, harvesting salt there that was ferried back to the coast for sale.

'Bin Laden, man, Bin Laden,' said one of them, pointing to his T-shirt. His friend nodded and pulled out a pack of cards embossed with the same picture. He reached over and shoved another fist full of green leaves into his mouth, which he devoured like a goat.

Unemployment was over fifty percent in Djibouti, and the government had even commissioned a study to find out how much tax money they were losing to the weed that sucked up of everyone's afternoon. And energy. I heard men often chose the weed over the wife.

Thirty minutes later, as the chat took effect, words slurred, and talk turned to September 11th.

'Bad man, Bin Laden, bad man,' said my new found chat friends. As their words tumbled from their mouths, a sharp, mournful cry went up: the camels were finally finished being saddled, and the long, dusty caravan left the tiny, sleepy town behind for the desert, traveling through the night to avoid the searing daylight heat.

Tomorrow I'm off by train into the center of Africa: Ethiopia. If that country is as intense as Djibouti, then I know the next seven weeks are not going to be easy.

I am glad to leave Djibouti.

The oil and water local and expatriate culture and the unending heat and dust have gotten under my skin here, and into all my clothes. The inward, insular attitudes everywhere are too tough to crack, even with the assistance of a mouthful of bitter, head spinning chat leaves. For the first time while traveling I have actually asked myself, what am I doing here? The locals wont miss me, the woman in the market who screamed Bin Laden certainly wouldn't miss me.

There was however, one exception. The sullen hotel manager shook my hand this morning when I told him I was leaving, not happy to see me go, but eager for me to tell my friends about his country, so more travelers would be sent his way.

It was nice for a change to be a pioneer in a way rather than following the guidebook trail.

More news from Ethiopia.

Love, Dave

From: Dave <theloweroad@hotmail.com>
To: Annette <whereisannette@yahoo.com>
Date: Jan 12, 2002 06:14 PM
Subject: The Bullet Train

Hey Annette,

If you could only see my face right now.

The internet in Ethiopia is more than five minutes a click. THE INTERNET GETS CONSTIPATED TOO. No joke: it has taken me thirty minutes to send you this message (that's if you get it at all) I have typed this up offline here in this internet café in Harar twice because a power cut wiped out the first draft. Shit. The owner of this place informed me I was only one of two foreigners staying in his town at the moment. Anyway, here is an update on what happened on my last morning in Djibouti, and how I got to Ethiopia.

On my last morning I woke up at four a.m. to catch the weekly train to Dire Dawa, the gateway to Harar, an Islamic holy city in Ethiopia.

As I pulled open the rusty, creaky gate to the main road, the hotel's guard dog came up to me, wagging his tail. As I walked down the dark street towards the station, he followed me much to the amusement of the street vendors already up selling soup and tea by the side of the road, their customers bus and taxi drivers wrapped up tightly against the deep, morning chill.

As I entered the chaotic train station the conductor at the platform saw the dog and started to scream at me that it couldn't come with me on the train. I shouted back that the dog wasn't mine and wasn't coming. The conductor shouted at me again, and a crowd gathered to watch. When I looked at my feet, the dog had curled up into a ball.

Continuing to argue with the conductor, the crowd grew so large that more officials and police showed up. My ticket was inspected, along with my passport and when they saw that I held a ticket for this train, there were gasps all round. Was this foreigner really about to travel on this rickety railway into the heart of Africa?

As the officials handed back my ticket and passport with a head-shake straight out of India, I slipped through the heaving masses. The dog followed me to the train tracks, faithfully waiting with me until my train arrived. And when it did, right on schedule, the dog made sure I had safely boarded and found my seat. When the blast of the horn sounded, the train started to pull out of the station, I waved at him through the open window, and he stood up and happily trotted home.

The train carriage was equipped with bare wooden seats, no glass in the windows, not even doors to speak of, and when I looked above my head, I saw not one, but three bullet holes that had pierced the roof. I was hemmed in by huge sacks of Thai rice, Korean televisions, Chinese thermoses, Japanese DVD players, sacks of vegetables, all so filled to bursting, I had to sit with my knees pulled up to my chest.

The train was overloaded with an odd mixture of Somali, Djibouti, Afari, and Ethiopian traders, merchants and other businessmen transporting goods to the capital city of Addis Ababa and beyond. Now that their access to the Red Sea had been severed with the brutal war with Eritrea, Djibouti had become Ethiopia's new best friend.

Yassin, an Afari college student studying business administration in Addis Ababa befriended me at once. His eyes widened when he told him I was off to travel round Ethiopia.

'I love my country but it is full of bandits and hyenas,' he said in a whisper, pointing to the gaping bullet holes above our heads.

'You left your dog behind?' he added, motioning in the direction of the Djibouti railway station behind us.

I nodded.

Just then, four women pushed their way through the crowded train carriage and sat across from me. When they looked at me closer, they laughed and said, 'Le chien! Vous voyager avec le chien!'

Their heavy makeup and thick jangling jewelry confirmed them as ladies of the night and they wasted no time in reaching out to daintily shake my hand as they introduced themselves in fluent French, no doubt perfected by serving the numerous French Legionnaires in Djibouti.

I learned that the taller two were Somali, and the shorter pair was from Djibouti. As the train trundled through the pre-dawn darkness and once the women learned my nationality, an argument ensued, and despite my lousy French, I was able to understand that they were bargaining amongst themselves, not how much they were going to charge me, should I want their 'services' but actually how much they were going to pay to sleep with me for a passport. Insults and curses flew back and forth, and soon fists were flying too. I looked over at Yassin, and he shrugged. It was going to be a long day.

Over the next few hours the train meandered through deep volcanic valleys, strewn with dark, car sized boulders. The sun rose, staining the desert pink, and as it crept higher in the sky, it scorched the earth all around us.

Small villages appeared. Dome roofed houses were clustered together like limpets on a rock. There were no trees, no bushes, only rocks and boulders as far as the eye could see.

Soon, the wind picked up, and the glass-less windows offered no protection against the hot wind, swirling dust, and fierce sunlight. The horizon was obscured by shimmering heat rising up to the sky, and sunlight poured through the bullet holes like lasers, burning the floor of the train.

Every fifteen minutes armed guards came through on regular patrols, stopped to gawk at the foreigner already famous for the 'chien' incident in the station, who was now being bargained for by the highest bidding prostitute. They hovered above my head, fingering the safety catches on their AK-47's, ogling the elegant women across from me before losing interest and moving on.

The train turned a corner around a mountain to reveal a flat, dark brown desert, and then as it rapidly picked up speed, passengers were hurled back and forth inside the train so violently, I thought we were going to jump right off the searing hot train tracks. As the hours ticked by I watched the women across from me pull out makeup kits and lipstick, applying it with expert strokes despite the staggering train; figures were still rising in the bid to become my wife, and when one of the women traders went to the bathroom, one of the Somali prostitutes nonchalantly reached over with her long fingers and stole an orange from her sack.

As we traveled further from Djibouti and deeper into this

inhospitable land theft became the norm, until it was an absolute free for all, no one's belongings were safe, even Yassin's, who lost a wad of rolled up bills to someone when he lit up a cigarette. Accusations and counter accusations flew left and right, and passengers screamed bloody murder as they tried to resolve each dispute.

Suddenly a woman pushed her two bags out the window, walked calmly over to the open door, held onto her skirt, and without a word, jumped from the moving train. I thought she had committed suicide. But Yassin told me, 'She lives in the desert. This train never stops for small villages. Only the Ethiopian border, and Dire Dawa.'

Over the next five hours, as regular as the soldiers patrols, a woman would lift a bag over her head, and hurl it out the window, before hiking up her skirt and jumping off the train without a goodbye to anybody.

Six hours after leaving Djibouti town, the train arrived at the Ethiopian border. The dozens of rail cars crashed together as the brakes were applied and in the silence, a quiet, dusty breeze as hot as a hairdryer blew in through the window.

Two customs agents climbed aboard, and motioned for me to follow them. I took my backpack with me, despite the Somali and Djibouti prostitutes' promise to look after it. I jumped off the train into a pile of dust and walked to the small, low roofed mud hut that had a small metal sign.

PASPORT CONTRO, it said in crudely painted, misspelled letters.

Inside, it was a festival of flies, and I pursed my mouth shut and grunted as they asked me the usual questions.

'Is this your first time to Ethiopia?'

'Yes.'

'Are you a Christian?' they asked me.

'Sort of,' I said, not wanting to explain.

'Ethiopia is the land of Christianity, practiced as it was at the time of Jesus. Where are you planning to go in my country?'

I gave them a brief outline, and they nodded their heads in approval.

'Do not miss Lalibela, friend,' one of them said, 'never in your life will you see such marvelous sights. Ethiopia is the home of the wide blue yonder.'

I nodded, remembering these words from the Ethiopian

Airlines posters hanging in their office in Bangkok, where I had reconfirmed my domestic tickets.

And then one of the agents, flipping through my passport, came to the page where my transit visa had been stamped while stranded in the midst of my flightmare in Addis Ababa.

'You said this is your first time to Ethiopia, Mr. Lowe,' said the agent with a nasty scowl on his face.

'It is my first time traveling in Ethiopia,' I corrected, remembering the virtual house arrest the airline had imposed on me.

'Mr. Lowe, but you lied to us,' sneered the other. 'You have been here before.'

'I have not been here before,' I said through clenched teeth, waving my hand around the fly-blown room.

'However you have been in Ethiopia and that is the same thing, Mr. Lowe,' snarled one of the men, asking me to follow him into a smaller room where I was told to sit down.

Once I was there, the two men started the process all over again, as flies buzzed around my ears and my train, and freedom, continued sitting outside in the heat.

They then turned their attention to my passport and heavily scrutinized my Ethiopian visa issued in Uganda stamped in a British passport issued in Hanoi. After checking every entry and exit stamp in my passport, which they scribbled down on a piece of paper, they accused me of stamping the passport with the visa myself. Stunned, and remembering the stories I had heard of people being turned away at the border for small problems with their Ethiopian visa, I said nervously, 'The ambassador in Kampala, he's called Haile. I played table tennis with him, and he won.'

The man holding my passport looked up as though I had said a secret code word, and simply said, 'OK,' and there was a violent boom as he stamped 'EXPIRED' over the purple visa, which mercifully sent the flies off for a few seconds, and then he said brightly, 'Haile in Kampala is a good friend of mine. Welcome to the Land of Christians and lions.'

Within thirty seconds the name of their old friend had released me back out into the blinding sun, but not before one more piece of advice.

'Visit this man in Lalibela,' he said slowly as he handed me a business card. 'He is my brother-in-law, and a tourist guide.'

Once I was outside, blinking in the bright sun and sweating in the heat, I found Yassin and two of his friends, who invited me to a restaurant around the corner from the immigration hut. In the distance, hundreds of villagers were sitting in disorganized rows, squatting in the dust, questioned by uniformed police.

'Stateless peasants,' Yassin said as we took a table in the mud hut where Italian spaghetti was eaten the Ethiopian way, with your fingers. We ordered three plates, and when they arrived, I gingerly dug into the plate of pasta. All around us, more flies took off and landed on the table than a month of movements at Heathrow. I was starving, so I gritted my teeth and ate as the locals watched in fascination.

Each traveler has their very own Best and Worst lists covering airlines, hotels, and more. For me, this restaurant, if it could be called that, was by far the Worst Restaurant I had ever eaten in, hands down, so bad I didn't even want to know what the kitchen looked like.

After lunch we re-boarded the train and the rest of the day went by very slowly, mercifully free of flies as they were blasted out the window as soon as we left the Ethiopian border. The highlight of the long afternoon was when the two Somali prostitutes discovered their wallets had been stolen; this was vehemently denied by the women from Djibouti, and tits flew left and right as they bitch slapped each other.

The bidding war for my hand in marriage was over. The victors were the Djiboutian women, but they informed me in curt, flawless French that they each had at least three potential husbands waiting for them back at home.

And with that they lit up another cigarette and blew smoke in my face.

The sun sank towards the horizon and the cabin of the train darkened. Glowing embers of cigarette butts were the only evidence of people in the carriage, there were no lights at all and disembodied voices called out to each other in the darkness.

About an hour before arriving in Dire Dawa we encountered the first indication of civilization - huts lined the train tracks, and feeble streetlights were strung between trees. Suddenly, all the women began screeching and frantically pushing their bales of merchandise out of the window in one mass evacuation.

'The women don't want to meet the customs officials in Dire Dawa, where they must pay tax,' Yassin informed me.

The train carriage continued to empty of goods, followed seconds later by the women themselves, leaping out into the warm night as though in some Jonestown mass suicide. Even the Somali and Djiboutian prostitutes leaped, but not before blowing a puff of smoke in my face again, taking my hand in turn for the last time and kissing it gently. Eventually, it was just me, Yassin, and a French woman sitting at the other end of the carriage.

When the train lurched to a stop in Dire Dawa it was nine o'clock. We had been traveling for seventeen hours. Once out of the station, I said goodbye to Yassin. The Frenchwoman introduced herself as Anais and we went in search of a ride to Harar. All the minibuses were stopped, a local told us, and we should get a hotel in Dire Dawa and catch one the following morning. I also learned from Anais that she too, like Yassin had been robbed on the train. When I told her I had not, I smiled.

Maybe I wasn't on the Travel Gods Shit List after all.

We found a place with spare rooms and then sank into chairs at a café where we were introduced to what I was soon to discover was the best-kept secret of Ethiopia: the delicious coffee. For eight cents, a tiny ceramic cup of the richest, smoothest coffee you have ever tasted is served with tiny pastries arranged on a plate. We also ordered a large Injera, the Ethiopian flatbread meal where vegetables and sauces are piled on top that serves as a plate and utensil. You rip off pieces of bread and dip it into the sauces leaving nothing behind at the end of the meal.

As we talked about our travel plans I learned that Anais was from a small town in southern France and was also moving on to Addis Ababa. We agreed to meet at eight the next morning to sort out our buses to Harar and the capital.

'The minibuses to Harar leave at one,' the waitress told us.

'One in the morning?'

'No. Our Ethiopian clock starts at six a.m., that's zero. At seven a.m., that's one o'clock. Our clock only goes until six p.m., when the sun sets.'

With that introduction to Ethiopian time keeping, we also learned that there were thirteen months in the calendar, instead of twelve. I remembered the 'Thirteen Months of Sunshine' slogan at the Ethiopian Airlines office in Djibouti.

'You speak excellent English,' I told Anais as we sipped the sweet coffee.

'Well, I have had many love affairs with Englishmen,' she said as she looked at me expectantly.

After just surviving a whole day on the Bullet Train, tangled up with four eager prostitutes, I politely excused myself and went to my room, making a mental note to catch the first minibus to Harar to avoid Anais.

I've been in Ethiopia two days and so far I have also escaped a shotgun marriage to some prostitutes, ate flyblown pasta, talked my way through passport control and survived the journey aboard the Bullet Train. I am also quickly developing a new relationship to dust. Everywhere you step here in Harar there is a big puff of it that stains everything brown, it gets in your mouth, up your nose, and in your hair.

Since arriving in Africa I am remembering the stories of India from other travelers, wondering if that place is any worse than this. Travel pushes you to the edge, and after Japan & Korea, and Vietnam & Cambodia, Africa is squashing me closer to the precipice that is India in every way.

Love, Dave

Hey Annette.

Facial muscles are tense. I have braved the internet here again to send you my stories from Harar. Experiences are piling up so fast I have to pass them on to you before I forget them, though I am glad I am no longer writing letters to you (the finger cramps were pure hell to hammer out so many words)

I've been told Addis Ababa, my next stop is more cyber friendly, but until then, it is the hour-long ordeal to send just one email, like this one.

You better enjoy it.

On my first morning in Ethiopia, I woke up at zero o'clock Ethiopian time, and after successfully ditching Anais, I arrived here in the walled medieval city of Harar. Immediately snapped up by a guide named Haile, he had worked in Matanzas, Cuba for eleven years on an exchange program with the Communist nation when Ethiopia had flirted with Socialism in the late 1970's. As we walked to his hotel, we talked about our mutual love for the Cuban culture and people, Haile muttered to no one in particular, 'Castro is Rambo.'

'Have you ever had any Cuban visitors to Harar?'

'Only on official visits. Now I act as a guide for Spanish tourists.'

His hotel was perched on a steep hill, with an excellent view of the crumbling outer walls of Harar, and as soon as I had showered and rested, we set off for the market ringing the southern border of the town, where women were winnowing Tef (Ethiopian barley) for the ubiquitous Injera bread that comes with every meal in Ethiopia.

Brilliant vermillion baskets were piled high to the ceiling, and women wrapped in lemon yellow veils piled spices into tall cones, and shouted at me to buy some.

As we wandered farther into the maze, the lanes became narrower, darker, and like in Djibouti, the whispers turned to Bin Laden. A few fists were shaken in my direction. Though, for the record, there were no more fistings by women in Burkas.

Haile led me through a narrow door, where we went up three flights of stairs and onto a roof where a magnificent view of the city spread out before us. He pointed to a mosque in the distance.

'Bin Laden built that mosque. He wanted a safe passage from Afghanistan to Sudan, and Harar is on the way.'

I told Haile about the Germans looking for Bin Laden in Djibouti.

'They will never catch him with their big ships,' he said ruefully.

When I told Haile I wanted to wander the old city alone, he shrugged and told me to be back at the hotel at five o'clock, for the hyena feeding.

'For the what?'

'We go to the edge of town, and feed hyenas,' he said, adding, 'there are only two visitors at Harar today, you and one other fellow who was robbed yesterday, so be careful in the alleys.' He walked me to one of the massive gates before going home.

As I walked the narrow, whitewashed lanes in the thousand-year old city, I passed many of the nearly one hundred mosques in Harar. A man who looked like a tourist guide at one junction said to me slowly, 'walking, are we?'

I nodded and smiled, then continued on to the Christian and Muslim markets, which were bustling with basket sellers and children playing marbles, dressed in long flowing clothes of tan material.

An hour later, after a small boy strode up to me and warned me of thieves in Harar, a wrinkled finger shot out of an open doorway and a crone invited me inside her house. She was Harari, the native inhabitants of Harar, who call their home 'Gey,' or 'The City,' and as I pulled off my shoes, she patted a cushion for me to sit down on.

A young woman came out and began smashing coffee beans on a small metal tray, and then began to brew a cup of coffee in a dark black pot. About fifteen minutes later, she handed me a tiny cup of coffee, and we sat there in silence as we sipped the strong, sweet drink. Then, she shook my hand and led me to the door. She had nothing to sell, she didn't want money in exchange for the drink; she just wanted to invite a curious traveler into her small corner of Harar and introduce her culture to a complete stranger.

Then it was off to Rimbaud's house. I wandered the two-story structure alone with brilliant rays of blue and red light striking the floor after filtering through the stained glass arranged around the windows.

By now it was nearly sunset, and as I walked back to the Hotel, I passed through the Muslim market, sinister in the growing darkness, invaded by vultures feeding on the leftover bones, their white eyes lit up by fires burning in corners.

When I reached the hotel, Haile had a bucket full of cow bones, and with his friend, a dreadlocked tourist guide wearing a beret, we walked down the hill through a thick bunch of bushes. The sky was completely dark now, and the stars came out in force. As we walked, I heard pounding footsteps, and a high-pitched squealing, thinking they were people. Haile laughed and flicked on his cigarette lighter.

There, no more than five feet away was a wild hyena, slinking through the dark in search of an easy meal, it's eyes reflected in the light. I sprang back as if from a cobra, and he laughed.

When we reached a clearing in the bushes, Haile threw out a few cow bones and his friend began making strange cawing noises that brought the creatures to the edge of the opening, warily looking at the humans there. Before long, there were ten hyenas, including three babies, cautiously walking closer to the pile of bones. Suddenly, one lunged out, grabbed one, and tore off into the bushes pursued by a few rivals. Haile himself then stepped over to the pile, and picked up a long bone, and offered it the nearest animal. Gingerly, it approached as nearby rivals howled in fear, and when it grabbed the bone, he motioned me to come forward to feed one.

I took the longest bone I could find, remembering that hyenas have the strongest jaws in the animal kingdom, and weakly imitated the sounds Haile had made. There, in the moonlight, softly cawing, holding out an animal bone, I thought to myself, what am I doing here, in the middle of the cold Ethiopian Highlands, acting like some Steve Irwin?

A moment later, a hyena locked eyes with me, and I kept singing that strange sounding song as the hyena drew closer, I was shaking so hard I nearly dropped the bone: I could see it's teeth clearly in the moonlight, exposed, and a second later lunged at me and clamped down on the bone. I could not only feel the power of its vice-like jaws as it quickly snatched the bone away. I also could smell it's foul breath that could have easily peeled paint off a wall. Haile clapped his hands, and for the next half an hour, we fed the remaining hyenas until the bones were gone.

That night, hyenas prowled around in bushes and howled into the cold night, pacing beneath my hotel room. In my half-awake state, I thought I had forgotten to wash my hands, and had attracted these beasts to bite off my fingers. I slept only a few hours that night.

The next morning, as I stepped through the city's main gate, a familiar voice called out to me. 'Still walking?'

It was the same guide who I had seen leaning against the wall the day before, and I smiled, but kept on moving.

Sometime that afternoon I saw the same kid as the day before who had warned me of the thief. Suddenly, a teenage boy jumped out of a doorway and tried to grab my bag. I wrestled with him, a long knife blade flashed under my nose and I pushed him away in time as the young boy screamed. The teenager took off down the alley, and disappeared.

The boy came running and I thanked him, but he was furious.

'Yesterday you don't believe me, today you have thief!' he shouted.

I shrugged and apologized, but he walked off in a huff, though when I saw him later at Feres Magala square, he was now smiling at me and invited me to sit. He was holding a bag of that long familiar weed, chat, and offered me a branch. I took it and ripped off some leaves, and stuffed them into my mouth. We sat and talked and the man who had chastised me a few minutes earlier with a silky sneer, 'Still walking?' approached and told me I was lucky.

'There are two travelers here in Harar, an American, and...?' he paused.

'New York,' I said.

'Another Yankee,' he said, nodding his head. 'One was robbed, and one was not.'

The Travel Gods had looked out for me again.

The boy told the man what had happened that afternoon. The man barely reacted, and said, 'since 9/11, many travelers don't come here anymore. Last year in January, we had several hundred here a day, now, only two. Thank you for coming to Harar.' He rose, shook my hand gracefully, and walked off through the golden afternoon light.

The boy stood up and I followed him in the direction of his home. I wanted to meet his mother to say thank you, but the boy was so humble he wouldn't show me where he lived. I thanked him again anyway, and went back to my hotel, to no doubt face another sleepless night kept awake by the filthy beasts prowling around beneath my hotel.

Off to Addis tomorrow. Until then it is hyena dreaming.

I can't walk home to my hotel after dark, I don't have a Dula, those wooden sticks that look like femurs that Ethiopian men carry to ward off stray dogs and hyenas.

FYI, when traveling in Ethiopia, a Dula should be on your list below Swiss Army knife and above a deluxe snakebite kit. It should be enough to beat off any hyenas the Travel Gods send in your direction.

Love, Dave

From: Dave <theloweroad@hotmail.com>
To: Annette <whereisannette@yahoo.com>
Date: Jan 21, 2002 12:39 PM
Subject: Addis To The Blue Nile

Hey Annette.

The internet here is a bit better than Harar. Less constipated. Well, better by the width of a camel's whisker. I am now in Bahar Dar, at the shore of a great lake, after leaving Harar and passing through Addis Ababa.

I am beginning to run into more travelers here, obnoxious and loud for the most part, dull eyed and weird. I have joined the Cairo to Cape Town trail that passes through Bahar Dar, though this is Africa after all and thankfully no banana pancakes are on the menu. Not yet anyway.

Just the best coffee in the world. (Take that Starbucks)

I gratefully boarded the bus to Addis at 1 o'clock Ethiopian time, (a.k.a. seven a.m.) which picked me up right in front of my hotel in Harar. Why gratefully you ask? While I was waiting, shivering in the cold darkness, wild hyenas were sniffing around the entrance to my hotel, and by the time the bus pulled up, the filthy beasts were closing in fast.

I gotta buy that Dula.

The bus was almost full so I found a seat in the back row between two men carrying their Duals of course, that ubiquitous Ethiopian walking stick. For the first fifteen minutes, all the windows were left open to let in the cold air. But then as if on cue, they were all clammed shut, and that's when I smelled the vomit, someone had thrown up in the middle of the bus.

Ethiopians often became violently carsick in their vehicle-less country, and there was a pretty good chance in the twelve hours of traveling that at least one person would throw up; only on this journey, the vomit was at least a day old. I think you can imagine the stench?

The aroma quickly filled the bus and I reached for the

latch on the nearest window only to find stars in front of my eyes when a thick wooden Dula cracked down painfully on my skull. The old rheumy-eyed Bastard Man next to me screamed bloody murder, and I was forced to hold my breath as the smell got worse. I remembered the hotel clerk saying it was a twelve-hour trip to Addis, and I stonily settled in for my first hellish overland flightmare in Africa.

When the sun rose deep valleys were revealed where tiny villages of circular huts were clustered near wells and fields of maize. In the rising heat, the smell of vomit almost caused me to throw up myself, until I settled on a convenient mantra:

It's spilled paint.
It's spilled paint.
It's spilled paint.

About three hours after leaving Harar we made our first stop and I stumbled out of the dusty bus eager to suck in some fresh air. Walking along the road were young kids carrying water jugs who came running up to see the foreigner staggering round, inhaling deeply. The girls had an amazing hairstyle of braids pulled down their foreheads that was split and then tied behind their ears. We smiled and laughed at each other and the interaction here in Africa was very different from Asia; people see so few foreigners that you feel like you have to remind them gently, I AM NOT AN ALIEN.

The driver banged his Dula against the side of the bus.

All aboard the Vomit Express.

The rest of the day was spent fending off the blunt, expressionless stares from the passengers, even those in the front row turned around to stare at me for the entire ride. While repeating my paint mantra and trying to convince the old Bastard Man next to me to crack open the window, I got nowhere with either. Even when he fell asleep, I tried to crack open the window as he slept. But the tiniest breath of wind woke him up and he smacked my skull with his Dula again before screaming what I took to be a string of Ethiopian expletives.

Though I didn't see as serious clubs in Ethiopia like in Japan, that old Bastard Man was definitely a card-carrying member of the Miserable Old Man's Club.

It was well after eight p.m. when the bus finally arrived in Addis Ababa, and gratefully fleeing the Vomit Express I immediately caught a taxi to my hotel. The windshield was gone, replaced with slats of vertical glass that forced the driver to lean forward to see his way through the buses and trucks. When I arrived at my guesthouse, I was given a tiny, dark room where I quickly fell asleep.

At four thirty the next morning, so early it didn't even register on the Ethiopian clock, I woke up and wandered into the pitch-black streets, where I found a taxi driver who took me to the airport.

After an hour of endless security and passport checks, I was on my way to Bahar Dar, home of Lake Tana and Tis Issat, the Blue Nile Falls thirty kilometers to the east of the town.

It was the last security check that was the strangest. There was a commotion up ahead of me in the line - a man was refusing to empty the contents of his pockets. Finally, after a shouting match, he pulled out a handful of live bullets and placed them on a table. They promptly rolled off, clattered across the tiled floor and danced around like silly marbles. The bullets were confiscated, but his handgun was not. Remembering that a large number of hijacks have occurred on domestic flights in Ethiopia, I was not pleased to see the man sitting one row away from me onboard my flight.

Once again I was seated between two old guys, though thankfully, the windows neither opened, and no Dulas were in hand; they had been safely checked in the belly of the plane, along with the bullets. The Fokker 50 aircraft lifted off somewhat unsteadily from the runway, and then glided over the patchwork of brown fields clustered near villages and deep river canyons. Virtually every shade of the color brown is found in this country, from the dirt roads, to the Injera bread, to the chocolate hills, to the dark brown vegetation, to the rich coffee.

As we readied for touchdown, the plane's shadow sped across the waters of Lake Tana, and we passed over the ancient Christian island monasteries there. The wheels dropped, and we crunched down on the gravelly, undulating runway.

I was the only person getting off the plane and my bag was dumped outside of the aircraft with not even a 'Thanks for flying Ethiopian Airlines' from the cabin crew. When I dragged my bag to the terminal, I found a family of five Ethiopian Americans already there waiting for their driver after getting off a previous flight. They lived in New Jersey, and were home to visit relatives. They kindly offered to take me to my hotel anywhere in Bahar Dar, in what was to become a fond memory of traveling through Africa, the random kindness of total strangers.

They also offered to pick me up and take me to the Blue Nile Falls that afternoon. After a brief trek to the bus station to buy a ticket to Gondor, followed by a walk along the lake, I drank a strong coffee at one of the restaurants along the water. It was odd, in one of the most undeveloped parts of Africa, I would repeat the same ritual each day, sipping the strongest coffee I had ever tasted, perched on a wooden stool in front of the antique espresso machine left behind by the Italians during their occupation of Ethiopia. It was, without a doubt, the pride and joy of the owners of these establishments, whose customers included journalists, writers, and the local intelligentsia.

'The machines were too heavy to take home in a hurry,' remarked one barista.

After finishing my drink, I caught a ferry to one of the islands in the middle of the lake, where ageing priests rested on the long hike up to the top, holding their Dulas in their shaky, withered hands. At the top, the monastery there had a fantastic view over the brown lake and the town. When I was shown around the compound, Bibles that were hundreds of years old were brought out for me to look at. The elderly priests looked deep into my eyes to see how I reacted to the only earthly treasures these churches possessed.

'Beauty,' said one.

True to their word, I met the Ethiopian Americans late that afternoon and we drove to the Blue Nile following a dusty highway. The van turned down a rutted road and then continued for another thirty minutes before stopping at the riverbank where we had to catch a small reed boat to cross the murky waters of the Nile.

It was only when we reached the middle of the river that one of the captains said, 'Silence. Crocodiles.'

'Crocodiles?'

He nodded. 'And hippos. Hippos more dangerous, they bite boat, no escape. No noise. Just bite.'

Crocodiles. And hippos. Great.

I kept my mouth shut as the man punted the boat with his long stick, pushing off each time with a groan, using only the bottom of the river as an engine. Soon, we could hear the roar of a distant waterfall.

'Tis Issat,' he whispered.

When I had gratefully hopped off out of the rocking, flimsy boat, we walked along a narrow path where a group of kids suddenly appeared, selling scarves. They tagged along, and one of them introduced herself and said she was off school for the day, and wanted to be a doctor for animals.

We talked as we walked through the dusty fields, the roar growing louder until we turned a corner and there it was, the waters of Tis Issat. A deep, jade green as they plunged off the rocky cliff, we scrambled down to the base of it and cooled off in the cold mist that blew off, drenching our clothes in seconds. Lush greenery shone with diamond drops of water, and we sat there for several hours, all conversation drowned out by the sound of the water. It was such a contrast to the dry scrubby landscape of Ethiopia, it was a shock to go back to the dust once more.

It was on the walk back to the fleet of rickety reed boats when we saw two teenage kids, dressed in their best clothes, patiently waiting under a tree or us to return from the falls.

As soon as they introduced themselves, the girl began to sing and the boy began playing a reed instrument, for more than thirty minutes we stood there listening to the distant sound of the Blue Nile falls in the golden light of the setting sun, enjoying the hauntingly beautiful music made by this couple. (I learned they were seventeen and fourteen years old, respectively, and had already been married for more than a year.)

That night, I was invited by the Ethiopian Americans to share an Injera feast in a local's only restaurant with their relatives.

Several large table shaped baskets arrived, each covered with the spongy bread, and piles of vegetable dishes that we ate with pieces of the Injera we ripped off with our bare hands.

The Injera and food gone, the meal was finished, and three women laid the floor of the room with fragrant tree branches, and then began to grill a handful of coffee beans on a tiny metal tray. Then they pounded them with a three-foot tall pestle in a stone bowl, then brewed the drink in a black pot before serving us one by one with a tiny cup that was handed to us, each, with a bit of sugar, and a blessing.

So here's a fresh lesson from Africa:

LIVE BULLETS ARE NOT AN IATA APPROVED CARRY-ON ITEM.

The dust is really getting to me here in Africa, and no matter how hard I wash my clothes, the reddish color does not go away. As I wake up each day to see the wide, blue sky, free from clouds, it seems there are no end of possibilities, no end to the surprises here.

Asia, where I have done most of my traveling, seems light years away. There is hardly any infrastructure here, any highways or airports or hotels. You can however, find Coca Cola and Pepsi even at the smallest town, which reminds you the world isn't that far away after all. And India, that traveler's Mecca? I still have no idea if I will ever be ready for a trip there.

Africa, like the dust on my clothes, is staining my soul in the same way. Deep.

Love, Dave

From: Dave <theloweroad@hotmail.com>
To: Annette <whereisannette@yahoo.com>
Date: Jan 27, 2002 7:54 PM
Subject: In The Hands of Abraham

Hey Annette,

I am in Axum now after passing quickly through Gondor. The trip here is a perfect example of what Ethiopia, a country most people would never dream of visiting, is really like.

Rough.

The bus station in Gondor was not near my hotel, nor clearly marked. When I woke up at five a.m., once again off the grid of the Ethiopian clock, I turned on the creaking faucet and found there was no water, not even enough to brush my teeth. In an attitude I am quickly developing in Africa, I just closed the tap, got dressed, and went out of my hotel's front entrance, gave my room key to the startled security guard and joined the crowds of people just walking in the same direction.

It is my firmest memory of traveling so far in Ethiopia, the predawn trudge to the bus station. Freezing cold in the high altitude, the walks are long and fraught with worry. Though I was smart enough to always have a ticket, because I bought the next one as soon as I arrived anywhere, the suffocating crush of people at the station meant getting a good seat was almost impossible, especially when all the men were armed with those menacing Dulas, and the women shrieked and screamed as soon as the door of the bus swung open.

Though I have a Dula myself now, I don't fancy clashing with these men and cause an international incident over a bus seat.

As overnight buses were illegal in the country, by 1 o'clock Ethiopian time (seven a.m.) all buses had departed for their destination, and this meant a dark, lonely slog, half asleep, pounding through the dusty, unlit streets, keeping an eye out for the vicious stray dogs, wild hyenas, or bandits, all equally eager to prey on people in the dark.

At the station, normally just a dusty square, grumbling behemoths cast off from Japan, America and Europe waited for passengers, spewing exhaust and carbon monoxide out for up to an hour before leaving, making anyone waiting for a good seat sick to their stomach, choking to death on noxious fumes that clogged the narrow gaps between the buses. Tickets were cheap, mostly less than a dollar, and you got what you paid for, amenities were scarce, all the windows were hammered shut, so no fresh air came in.

Ever.

When I reached the gate to the Gondor bus station, it was chained shut. But as soon as the gatekeeper saw me, he invited me inside in a rare show of friendship and led me to the bus to Axum. His friend was the driver, and his nephew, Abraham, was also on the bus.

I was shown a seat in the front next to the driver. My bag was taken from me and tied with the chickens on the top of the bus. Above my head there was a simple plaque.

THIS BUS WAS PROUDLY MADE IN DETROIT, MICHIGAN.

I sat there, blinking in the darkness, unbelieving my good luck. No pushing, no shoving, no gagging on carbon monoxide fumes. No whacks on the skull from a Dula. The bus filled up, Abraham boarded, took a seat, and introduced himself, and we were off.

It turned out that Abraham was going home to Axum after visiting his uncle in Gondor, and made the trip about four times a year. He was nine years old, and through his flawless English explained to me the names of the villages we were passing through, and how in rural Ethiopia, market days rotated between towns, so villagers followed this schedule, taking their goods to sell in different places, depending on the day of the week. With bus tickets and bicycles too expensive, this meant that most of them had no alternative but to walk.

The stares from the passengers were so intense that Abraham turned to me and whispered, 'They are curious about you, may I pass on some information to them? What is your age? Nationality? Job? Do you have children?'

I passed on this information, he translated it into Amharic, and then he peppered me with more questions.

'How do you find Ethiopia?'

'Can you eat Injera, our national bread?'

'Are you a Christian?'

This went on for more than an hour, like some mobile game show, and I giggled when I thought of the middle class American children that had been ferried to school aboard the very same bus that was now filled to the brim with Ethiopian farmers, baskets stuffed with fresh meat, and full of flies buzzing about.

Suddenly, up ahead, the road ended. We were driving straight for a cliff as sharp as the Grand Canyon. I gripped the seat tightly in fear. It was just a few seconds before flying over the edge that the driver yanked the steering wheel to the left, and thus began the switchback ride from hell.

As we zigzagged down to the bottom of this vast canyon, each time we neared the end of the hairpin bend, the bus could not turn in one movement; the driver had to stop, back up and do a three point turn each time. Problem was, there was no railing, or any sort of barrier, and the ancient brakes were squealing like stuck pigs each time we stopped to turn.

Sitting in the front seat, my seat was actually hanging over the cliff sometimes when the driver had less than six inches of leeway each time we turned, and on more than one occasion, the front tire slipped and caught air as we drove off.

Each time the driver made a successful turn, he would look over at me and say, 'Don't worry, be happy.'

I turned around to see if there was an empty seat further back in the bus, but the entire vehicle was crammed with people and luggage. A murmur swept through the bus.

Was the foreigner scared?

My rising panic didn't go unnoticed by Abraham, and as my anxiety increased, he reached out and grabbed my hand, and squeezed it tight. Each time we neared yet another end to the road, he would distract me with some cultural fact about his country.

'Did you know Ethiopia is the Land of the Wild Blue Yonder?'

I nodded.

'Did I tell you about the marvels at Axum?'

I nodded once more.

By now, we were making a turn every minute, and even the jovial driver had stopped smiling - as we reached one very tight turn, he let the bus drift towards the edge, and then the engine stalled. He couldn't reverse, because the back of the bus was pressed against the wall of rock, going forward would have meant a plunge into a five hundred meter deep crevasse. My mind flipped through the pages of my travel insurance policy, sure that it didn't cover the recovery of my body from the depth of some canyon in Africa.

So he turned around and ordered the passengers off the bus. As soon as he pulled open the lever that freed the front doors, I scrambled off as fast as I could, glad to be off that death trap.

Then, with the bus perched at the end of the cliff, like in some still photo from Thelma and Louise, he hopped out and lifted the hood, making some clink and clank noises before he motioned for the men including me, to help push the bus back, once he had the gears in neutral. We lined up, palms sweating, as I tried not to look down, or listen to the rocks tumbling down into the abyss.

WHY HADN'T I TAKEN THE PLANE? I screamed at myself.

Then the signal was given, we pushed as hard as we could, inching the bus back towards the safety of the road. Phew.

About an hour later we reached the bottom of the valley where a strong river flowed. A huge camel caravan of about three hundred beasts was loitering along the banks as their masters took a cigarette break. A cluster of weeping families was there too, shrieking and wailing, their row of houses had collapsed without warning in the middle of the night into the cold, surging waters, leaving them absolutely possession-less. A government minister was on his way to offer assistance.

Then the reverse experience began. As the bus struggled to climb the steep hills, we all held our breaths as the driver fought with the steering wheel. After two long hours, we reached the top and then drove through some of the most beautiful Ethiopian scenery, the Simien Mountains. As we picked up speed n the flat, gravelly roads, we passed sharp, brown peaks that looked like dragon's teeth. Every once in a while there would be a troop of baboons who flipped their lips at us menacingly but gratefully accepted banana peels and crusts of bread thrown from the bus.

As always in Ethiopia, there were hundreds of people just walking along the road, the men carrying Dulas held with both hands behind their heads, and the women, carrying dark brown earthenware pots tied up in primitive backpacks.

Then the bus broke down. We piled out for the second time, and there, in the middle of Africa's highest plateau, underneath a sky as blue as eggshells, farmers and school children materialized out of nowhere to stare, point and gawk at me. Abraham translated their questions and my answers until a group of bright eyed priests, standing by the side of the road with upturned umbrellas to beg for alms, politely took my hand and invited me to join them for a drink.

Once again I was sipping a cosmopolitan coffee, freshly brewed from a dilapidated, yet loving looked after Italian espresso machine plastered with vintage hotel stickers for hotels in Torino and Roma. It was the most civilized way to wait for a bus to be repaired in any country I had traveled.

The priests asked me if I had been to Lalibela and I said not yet and they just smiled and pulled out their old Bibles and holy crosses and read passages to me in Amharic out of them. Abraham translated and then it was time to go; I shook hands with these men, whose long, elegant fingers pulsed with a devotion and elegance I had never seen before.

We hadn't traveled more than thirty minutes when there came a hideous crunch and the driver coasted fifty meters into a tiny village. It was near sunset, it was illegal to be out on the road, and we were ordered off the bus. Abraham took my hand and led me off as though he were my mother.

As I stood there, shaking the dust from my clothes in the fading light, a man invited me into a café around the corner.

Next door to it a wedding was underway and I was immediately asked inside. The guests had drunk plenty of Tej, the honey wine popular in Ethiopia, I was pressed with a glass, but it was the Kitfo that made my eyes pop.

Kitfo is raw minced meat, Ethiopian steak tartare if you like, mixed with blood and chilies and eaten with your fingers. A plate was passed to me and I was watched carefully as I gingerly took a taste of it. Though hungry after the long bus ride, bloody raw meat wasn't exactly what I had in mind for dinner, but after traveling in countries where you can't say 'no' I swallowed, surprised that it tasted so good. Even if I had wanted to spit it out, I wouldn't have had a chance. I was slapped so many times on the back it slid down my throat in about two seconds flat.

Stranger that the Kitfo was the BBC.

A television was broadcasting some BBC news report from Afghanistan and I stared at the screen as though it had landed from outer space. With weeks of no newspapers, televisions and radio contact, I couldn't believe how far away I was from home. Eating raw meat mixed with blood was one thing, but digesting a slick international news program with a bleach blonde presenter was quite another.

Abraham explained to me that because of the delay with the latest engine problem, we couldn't reach Axum that day, and as it was illegal for buses to travel at night, we were forced to stop at this small town, an hours drive to the west of our final destination.

As he led me to the only guest house, a gang of kids tried to take me to the only other guesthouse in town, twice the price and twice as far away. Abraham shooed them off even though they were older than him, and as he showed me my room, which had no running water, no lights, and a corrugated iron door that didn't even pull closed because it was stuck in the dirt, I was so exhausted, I didn't care and just turned in for the night.

It was some time during the night that I heard the hyenas. Ethiopia's countryside was full of them, and as their howling grew closer, all night I lay underneath my mosquito net trying to convince myself that the flimsy netting would ward them off, even though my door was wide open. I expected to wake up to find one chewing my foot off.

Just before dawn, one almost did.

I opened my eyes and saw to my horror, that a hyena's head was framed in the doorway, it's nose in the air, sniffing. I froze like an icicle, and stopped breathing. It took a step into the room, and began to sniff my bag. It was getting closer to my bed. Great, my foot REALLY was going to get chewed off.

Without warning I sat up and let out a blood-curdling shriek worthy of the most obnoxious Ethiopian bus passenger, and the hyena flew out the door like I had turned a hose on it.

After getting packed and skipping the usual morning shower because, like usual, was no water, I found the same band of characters gathered in front of the now repaired bus wrapped up tightly in woolen blankets against the cold. They greeted me with a hearty 'Tenestellen,' the Ethiopian greeting as if I was an old friend. They had heard about my bravery in eating Kitfo, and were impressed. Breakfast followed with another stunningly brewed espresso coffee that took the edge off my jitters from my run in with the hyena that morning.

Twenty minutes later the driver appeared and once everyone was aboard, we were off again, charging forward into the bright morning, underneath that vast, eggshell-blue African sky.

With no more canyons to pass, we arrived in Axum exactly at two o'clock, or eight a.m. With public transportation scarce, as we entered the town our bus served the locals too, and they got on and off around the town as we drove to the central bus station.

When we picked up one passenger, tears were rolling down his face, and he kept saying, 'Why? Why? Why?' over and over and over again, screaming and beating himself with his fists. Abraham told me he had been robbed.

The bus passengers shouted at him to shut up and about ten minutes later we reached the bus station.

The hellish journey was over.

Abraham and I stood up and together we stepped off the bus and down into the dirt, where we retrieved our bags. Abraham made sure I got my suitcase, checked that no one had tried to pilfer it, and then he looked up at me and smiled. 'Thank you for sharing this journey with me. These people have never traveled with a white man before. They are very happy. Welcome to my Ethiopia.'

And with that he walked off into the adult world and disappeared.

IF OFFERED RAW MEAT AT AN ETHIOPIAN WEDDING, SWALLOW. IT DOESN'T TASTE AS BAD AS YOU THINK.

Here in Africa the people are amazing. They don't shun you or embrace you like in other countries where you are often seen you as a Devil or a Saint or just a Walking Wallet. Africans look at you coolly, deeply aloof, with long unblinking stares, eyeing you intently, waiting silently to see what you are going to do and say in their country.

Waiting for you to move.

Here in Africa there are the Abrahams, who strode out of the large crowds and took you by the hand and showed you their country, no questions asked.

Here in Africa, gone are the swaggering hordes of travelers bragging about cheap paradises, drugs, and The Beach like in Thailand. They are replaced by silence. It creeps up on you, surrounding you, giving you time to think.

Here in Africa, it's as dusty a place as I have ever been, and you walk around with this clay taste in your mouth all the time.

That's Africa to me. So very glad I DID take that bus.....

Love, Dave

From: Dave <theloweroad@hotmail.com>
To: Annette <whereisannette@yahoo.com>
Date: Feb 6, 2002 10:22 AM
Subject: Eritrean Dreaming

Hi Annette,

Africa has surprised me again.

The sole computer in my hotel has amazingly fast internet. Only four minutes a click! So I'm typing as fast as I can to catch you up on my Ethiopia.

I ran into the family of Ethiopian Americans here again in Axum (about as far north as you can go in this country) and when I met them at their hotel yesterday, perched on a hill with a view of the town's central square, I also met Matt who is stationed in Africa for the US army.

As we sat in the warm afternoon light underneath that classic blue sky, exchanging stories from our trips, I told them of my overland trip the day before. They had taken the plane, and looked at me in horror.

'You took the bus?' they asked incredulously.

I told them about the steep precipice, and how we had pushed the bus back, and they shook their heads.

'If that bus had gone over the edge, there would only be a bad smell to remind us we had ever met you.'

Matt was talking with two Swiss at a nearby table that had overheard our conversation. They had a car hired, and invited us along with them on a day trip the next day, north towards the Eritrean border, where they were investigating archeological digs.

Archeological digs? Intrigued, we gratefully accepted, eager to explore the remains of the Axumite civilization said to be as great as Egypt, but less than two percent of this civilization's remains have been uncovered by archeologists.

That afternoon we visited the main church compound, believed to contain the Ark of the Covenant, where a blue-eyed guard guarded it from theft. One look at the ark and you were meant to burst into flames. We then visited the Queen of Sheba's palace, and her baths, outside of town.

At the end of the day we stopped at the Northern Stelae Field. An Eritrean wedding was underway. Thankfully, no Kitfo was served. As the sun set, the bride and groom glittered in rich, wine red brocade costumes as relatives gathered all around, clicking their tongues and singing lilting songs.

'We just wish our family in Asmara could be here,' said a young woman to me, who worked in a bank in Axum. 'There's no way we can get across the border, or call, we can only email.'

'We can only dream of Eritrea now,' remarked a college student. 'It is like the moon.'

You know, you read about conflicts in Africa, and how peace and war swing back and forth in some terrible pendulum swing of death and disaster, followed by prosperity and calm. Ethiopia is a pretty stable country compared to others in Africa, but even here a civil war has ripped the country into pieces.

The next morning I trudged up the hill to the hotel, and hopped aboard the Toyota Land Cruiser the Swiss had arranged.

'Today we get to be like Indiana Jones,' remarked the driver.

Soon we were weaving our way north, stopping at a nondescript building along a steep potholed road, that housed a 2,000 year old Stelae decorated with ancient languages, which had yet to be deciphered. The custodian unlocked the door and connected two fraying wires to light up the gloom.

Then, we drove up to a windswept hilltop, where the driver pointed to the valley beyond. 'Eritrea,' he said, as he sighed deeply. 'My home.'

He pulled out a pack of cigarettes and lit one. 'We used to be able to travel to Asmara, the Red Sea. We would go on vacation there, to bathe in the sea.' He looked wistfully towards the horizon, where thousands of mines and soldiers guarded the fragile peace that existed between the two enemies. 'At least my family is here with me. My wife is unlucky, her entire family is still in Asmara.'

He indicated with his cigarette to a hole in the ground. 'That's an Axumite tomb.'

Walking over to the car he pulled out three long beeswax candles, which he lit. Then he pushed aside a corrugated iron square covering the dark hole and we stepped down gingerly, step by step, into the darkness. When we reached the bottom we found a hallway, sloping downwards, and we followed it as the ceiling dropped lower and lower.

When we reached the end, where a stone slab connected with the stone floor, the driver jumped up and down; a hollow boom echoed through the corridor, proving there were empty chambers beneath.

'Tombs of royalty,' he whispered, placing his hand near his lips to show the secrecy of the project. 'We believe them to be as rich as King Tut's, and who knows what treasures lie beneath. Gold, pearls, diamonds are believed to be here, not yet stolen by tomb robbers.'

When we emerged from the tunnel, dusty, breathless and in awe of the unopened history beneath our feet, the driver took us to another hilltop, where we saw well-like holes with four chambers facing each of the directions of the compass. The wealthy people never gave inheritance to their children, the driver said, they believed it fostered laziness, and chose to bury their wealth instead.

The last stop was the most secret of all. A tunnel had been discovered and was believed to lead all the way to the Red Sea. It was built at the time when the Axumite civilization controlled the sea trade between Africa and Asia. We were taken to yet another hill, where a simple, aluminum sheet roof protected an entrance to another, airless tunnel.

Taking up beeswax candles once again, we ducked under the dark, stone ledge and into the dusty passageway. To the left was a small room where we saw crude stone lids covering coffins, which were to be opened in a few months time by a professional archeological team. When we inched our way to the end of the passage, blocked with rubble, there was another arrow pointing to the ground, and next to it, a crudely carved Christian Axumite cross. In the still, musty darkness, the walls shimmering from the flickering candlelight, I realized the driver was right: we were like Indiana Jones. Angkor Wat may have been amazing, but it was open, explored, exposed; here everything was closed, protected, secret. Never had I been more eager to hang around and wait for the archeologists to open up these treasures and learn the mysteries of this last civilization from antiquity to be discovered.

That night I walked up the hill and met the Ethiopian Americans for the last time, said goodbye to Matt, who was off driving to Bahar Dar and back to Addis. We ate another Injera feast and drank plenty of rich, sweet, coffee as a woman sang and a band played traditional instruments. Though I was hungry, I could hardly keep the food down. Nothing I am eating in Ethiopia is agreeing with me, and I am losing weight. Fast. Shorts are rolled up to keep them from sliding down, and even my shoes seem loose.

It's the price of Africa I suppose.

The travelers I am meeting on this continent are as diverse as anywhere I have ever been, either they are professional travelers who seem to travel for no other reason but to escape, or to brag about places and paradises they have seen and you have not, offering little in the way of conversation except for a nasty snarl and a scowl. They don't even try to play the Lonely Planet one up game I am so used to. Case closed.

On the other end of the spectrum were people like the Swiss, Matt and the family of Ethiopian Americans who shared, talked, laughed and helped fellow travelers in Africa in any way they could.

And then back to the reality of Africa. That night after the amazing archeological visit I had to walk through the darkness back to my hotel at the other side of town because there were no taxis in Ethiopia's hinterland. There was no moon, and no streetlights. Stars that were scattered across the sky offered pretty weak illumination. As I walked and walked, I thought, 'Anything could happen out here, anything.'

Frequently shunned as a no-go place, one of spells, of witchcraft, of evil and darkness, Africa, truthfully, is all this and much more: experienced travelers told me before I even arrived that I would never come closer to death than in Africa. Like nowhere else on Planet Earth was I advised so sternly to carry vast amounts of insurance, thousands of dollars in cash, even a loaded gun to rescue me in case I fell ill, was kidnapped, or thrown in jail.

Then I heard a familiar scuffling in the bushes.

Wild hyenas were lurking in the inky darkness and I had left my Dula in my hotel.

FUCK.

I barely breathed as I speed walked back to the town. By the

232

time I knocked on the door of my hotel, they were just meters away, their sharp teeth flashing at me just as they had done in Harar.

Only I had no cow bones this time.

Dealing with wild animals, real wild animals, is something I am getting used to in Ethiopia, along with a lot of other things like malaria. Hotels here have no mosquito nets, and I have to string up my own. Locals seem so used to the sickness they don't warn you about the dangers at night, but it seems a lot of lessons learned in Africa come the hard way.

After what I have seen in Axum, am I going to be able to shut up the next obnoxious traveler I meet with my stories of unopened royal tombs and Axumite crosses and Queen of Sheba's palace? My arsenal is growing.

I am at the top of Ethiopia now, and heading down to Lalibela tomorrow.

By plane.

Love, Dave

From: Dave <theloweroad@hotmail.com>
To: Annette <whereisannette@yahoo.com>
Date: Feb 12, 2002 8:29 PM
Subject: Angel and Demons

Hey Annette,

I am in the middle of my dusty trek from Lalibela to Nairobi. I'm in Addis again, the third time I have been through this city, and thankfully, my last. The internet connection is still the width of a mosquitoes ass and it's five minutes per click, as usual, but like the early morning trudge to the buses, the wild hyenas in the bushes, and those menacing Dulas, the slow internet and all the beauty of traveling in Africa are quickly being accepted as the price you pay for traveling in this part of the world.

Even my inability to keep any solid food down is no longer a problem.

Luckily there is bottled water out here and that is what makes up my 'meals' these days added to a hot cup of coffee and a handful or two of dried peanuts that I can find. I think by the time I leave Ethiopia I will need to hold up my pants all the time, I brought a mosquito net but not a belt. Hmm.

So, after leaving Axum the flight to Lalibela was smooth. It left me slack jawed. After live bullets in Addis airport, mad ground staff and countless other wonky incidents, the plane boarded, took off and landed. Just like that.

By the time my bags had been carried off the Fokker 50 plane, the airport in Lalibela was almost deserted. All the passengers aboard were part of a large tour group from Paris, and they had aggressively ignored the no smoking signs and lit up their Gauloises during the short flight.

The cigarette smoke didn't bother me.

I was grateful to avoid a two day bus ride from Axum to Lalibela, which was later described to me by a Japanese woman as 'pure hell' and ten times worse than the trip from Gondor to Axum. The thirty-minute flight had saved me from forty-eight hours of purgatory aboard some rusty American school bus sitting next to Dula wielding old men.

The Swiss were also on my flight but their driver was nowhere to be found in the parking lot. When I asked the price for a taxi into town I was quoted an inflexible price of $20 with not a chance of bargaining.

When the Swiss' driver turned up, in the spirit of the camaraderie of travelers in Africa, they kindly offered me a ride; the car was paid for they said, and no one was going to check. They just had to ask the driver, who thought for a moment and nodded his head, and said, 'no problem.'

It was exactly halfway through the half an hour drive into Lalibela, in the middle of the scrub brush plain that separated the town from the airport, that the driver suddenly slammed on the brakes and threw open the door.

'Pay twenty dollars, or walk,' he growled.

'What?' I said.

The Swiss archeologists looked at each other and told him he had said it was OK. He shook his head. 'Twenty dollars.'

Then, the mounting frustration of all those five a.m. walks to distant bus stations, compounded by the noxious carbon monoxide fumes that had poisoned my brain caused me to explode, 'You said it was OK back at the airport. I am not paying! Keep driving!!!'

The driver lunged his head towards mine until we were nose to nose, screaming bloody murder at each other, as the Swiss looked on stoically, shocked at my suddenly violent anger, and were probably wondering if they were going to be forced to get out and walk, too.

The screaming went on for about five minutes, as all my frustrations with Africa spilled out, finally the driver relented and turned back to driving. He turned into a madman in about two seconds: lurching around corners, slamming on the brakes in anger he glared at me in the rearview mirror as if he could set me alight with his stare, like the Arc of the Covenant in Axum was rumored to do.

When he dropped me off in the center of town, he unceremoniously threw my bag out onto the road as I made arrangements to meet the Swiss later on.

And that was Demon Number One.

Later that morning, after dealing with packs of other demons otherwise known as 'guesthouse owners' whose rudeness and arrogance was unbelievable as they demanded five times the rate for a hotel room compared with other towns in Ethiopia.

'Angels built these Lalibela churches!' they wailed as I walked out the door. 'Angels!'

I finally found a hotel that was only three times the price but way out of town. I knew I would have to fend off hyenas at night, but I was growing used to this. When I dropped off my bag, I walked the long dusty road towards the churches. Suddenly there was Demon Number One again driving down towards me with a German guy in the back seat of his van. Gesticulating wildly, his face tomato red, spit was flying in all directions as he screamed at me like Babu Bhatt from Seinfeld.

'Bad man! You bad man!!!! Baaaad maaan!'

Instead of walking away, I stopped and laughed. Demon Number One slammed on the brakes, and rolled down his window, screaming, 'Bad man! Baaaaaaaad maaaaaaaaaaan!'

I lunged at the window and began screaming back at him in a repeat performance of the airport road-screaming match. The German guy in the back seat was bewildered and asked me what had happened. So I explained it to him, and he just hopped out of the van and started walking away.

'He did that to me five minutes ago!' he said, laughing.

'Now, you bad man!' Demon Number One shouted at the German. We both laughed. The driver was beyond furious now, so angry that he backed his car into a pole, bending the bumper and then drove off in a cloud of dust.

The German guy and I arrived at the main entrance to the churches, where we paid the fee and parted ways. Once inside I felt immediately transported back to Narnia or the Lord of the Rings: smoothed off rock passages snaked into the hillside, leading to churches not made of carved stone blocks, but carved from the solid rock itself. The churches were the rock. So beautiful and flawless were these churches that the Ethiopians believed angels had arrived one night and left them the following morning, with no trace of where the rubble went.

And living in amongst the churches were priests with kind, expressive eyes, who spoke no English, but whose penetrating stares spoke much about the faith and devotion you found everywhere in Ethiopia.

Their cat-like movements of bare feet padding silently across the polished rock, light as a feather, looked as if they were angels walking on clouds. Once inside, it took a few moments for your eyes to adjust to the total darkness, but when they did, and the richly carved lintels and walls came into focus, the priests would gently take your hand, lead you around inside, and point out the offerings laid on the altar.

Then they would pad off and return, carrying an eight hundred year old Bible, whose pages were so yellowed they looked like they would crumble at the slightest touch. Hand copied, the colorful illustrations and artistic flourishes were straight out of the Middle Ages.

At the end of their silent tour they would point politely to the offerings box, watching you carefully as you pulled out a small wad of Ethiopian Birr and pushed a few bills inside. Then, leading you out into the bright sunlight, they would call the attendant to return your shoes, they would shake your hand for a long time, and bid you goodbye as their laser-like stare bored deep into your soul.

But lurking in between the quiet calm of these dark, cool churches were packs of predatory demons, otherwise known as 'tourist guides' petulantly calling out to anyone who was unattached, begging to be hired as a guide, shooing away priests like they were street beggars and trying to force the shoe attendants to refuse entry to independent travelers unless they entered with a guide. Church after church, encounters between the demons outside, and the angels inside went on, some turning almost as violent as my run-in with Demon Number One.

'Why don't you hire a guide?' they whined over and over, and I just smiled the way the priests did, and walked to the next church, down one of those twisting alleyways, where another priest would be standing in the stone doorway, holding a crucifix, or a Bible, or an upturned silk umbrella, beckoning to me with long, elegant fingers to come inside and explore his church.

Demons came in pint sizes, too. Small children tagged along constantly, saying they were free guides, and wouldn't ask for any money. After two hours of telling one kid I was not paying someone who should be in school, he finally had enough, screeched something hateful in Amharic, kicked me in the shins, and then ran off.

At the request of the priests in Lalibela, all the town's churches were closed each day between eleven a.m. and two p.m. so they could celebrate mass without the intrusion of tour buses and their digital camera toting herds, and no doubt to free themselves from the demons that lurked in every dark corner.

When I began to leave the last church, it was five minutes to eleven. The priest there refused to let go of my hand. I pointed to my watch and the man nodded but tightened his grip. He then pointed to a dark corner in the back of the church where I could sit and get a good view of the services. Then he released my hand and went off to get ready.

As the guides and tourists left, other priests arrived and gave me quizzical looks, but after a quick explanation from the priest who had invited me, they proceeded to start their mass, with singing, readings, and the burning of incense.

Halfway through the ceremony a younger priest broke away and introduced himself to me and said, 'You are watching a mass that is being performed like it was at the time of Jesus. Ethiopia is the only Christian country in the whole of Africa.'

He didn't say another word until the end of the ceremony. Then, he reached out, shook my hand for a long time, and just stared into my eyes, with a calm and serenity I had never seen before. He took me outside and said, 'Go. Explore my Lalibela.'

And explore I did. Wandering around the narrow corridors in front of ochre churches encrusted with bright green lichen, women sifted barley for the priest's meals. No one asked me why I was still there, no one told me to leave. They just invited me in like an old friend, showed me around and then stepped with me back out in the clear, African light, released my hand, muttered some directions in Amharic to get to the next church and said goodbye.

After the archeological explorations in Axum, and the amazing churches in Lalibela, it amazes me that the word 'Ethiopia' in the minds of most people means famine and starvation. Truth be told, famine does exist in Ethiopia, a local told me that famines are common, and farmers don't have enough food stored to survive crop failures, or enough to even walk to the nearest town to get help.

Living in the most remote valleys in the country their hand

to mouth existence is something unchanged in hundreds of years. But that is only a part of the country, the other is lush forests and thousand year old churches and civilizations from antiquity.

Tomorrow I leave for Nairobi. With plane tickets costing over five hundred dollars for the one way flight from Lalibela to Kenya I have mapped out as direct an overland journey as possible: back to Addis through the Simien highlands, down through the Rift Valley lakes near Shashemene, and finally over the flat, scorching desert through the towns of Moyale and Marsabit south to the Kenyan capital.

With a dozen days on rough African buses, what really is five or six more days? I reckon a few more kilos will be shed along the way.

Wish me luck. If the hyenas don't get me, the carbon monoxide just might.

Gulp.

Love, Dave

From: Dave <theloweroad@hotmail.com>
To: Annette <whereisannette@yahoo.com>
Date: Feb 17, 2002 11:20 AM
Subject: Seven Days, Six Fingers & Five AK-47's

Hey Annette,

I MADE IT TO NAIROBI.

I have just eaten my first solid meal in six weeks that I have been able to keep down for digestion. I am in an internet café in my hotel that doubles as a safari travel agency. It's clean, there's no dust, and so competitive is the safari business that they give free accommodation for all guests, though I am actually in a tent on the roof, as the place is full.

Kind of apt for Africa, right?

But cheetahs and lions and elephants are not a topic of conversation here. Air India serves Nairobi with a direct flight and it seems every person I am running into is either just off the flight or about to go on it. The air is thick with incense smoke and someone even hung a photo of some guru/conman with a red dot on his face above their bed claiming him as their spiritual master. Whatever.

When I told the hundredth person that I was NOT on the Air India flight, that I did NOT know the telephone number to reconfirm their flight and that I was NOT just back from an ashram or a levitation course in Rishikesh, I have earned myself the nickname 'That guy who's NOT going to India.'

I am off on safari tomorrow.

Before Ethiopia and the hot, dusty, dry and long journey from that country to Kenya evaporates from my memory, and I forget the emptiness, the desolation and the stark landscapes, here is my account of the journey after leaving Lalibela, the guns and genetic freaks I met along the way.

Day 1: Lalibela to Dessie

'Moyale has no running water,' warned Brenda, a wise friend from San Francisco who worked in the travel industry. 'Take the flight to Nairobi, whatever you do. Don't even think of traveling overland.'

But at one a.m. Ethiopian time, I boarded my first bus to Dessie, where, waiting for my bag to get loaded, I had my final, and most satisfying, run-in with Demon Number One.

'Baaaaaaad maaaaaaan!' he shouted.

But no sooner had Demon Number One rolled open his window than a priest, who had recognized me from the previous day's noon time church mass, gave him a sharp dressing down in Amharic, so vehement that the bus passengers all around me roared with laughter at the Demon, who, true to form, turned fire engine red, put his van into gear, and peeled.

About three hours out of Lalibela, after looping and swerving around steep, narrow canyons where circular thatched hut villages were tightly clustered, we entered a lush, highland forest where streams gurgled down through rocky canyons. It was the first clear, running water I had seen in weeks, after the dust bowl dry highlands and even drier Djibouti.

I stared at the lush greenery for a long time.

I listened to the water for a long time, too.

A college student pointed to the small villages below us and said, 'During the famine, those villages disappeared.'

'How?'

'They only grow what food they need, they don't store any for a rainy day. So when the crops failed in 1984, the villagers had no food to eat, not even enough to travel to a town to beg.'

It was the answer to a question that had dogged me while traveling in Ethiopia. Famous for famine and drought, and not culture and beauty, the worldwide aid sent to the country had since become an albatross. It was the same way people looked at Vietnam as simply a war or Cambodia as simply a place of genocide.

'Passengers ask us if we even serve food aboard our

planes,' a disgruntled flight attendant on Ethiopian Airlines told me. 'They even bring their own food, thinking starvation spreads even to the national airline.'

When we stopped for a break in the middle of the forest, a priest was there with an upturned umbrella soliciting donations by the side of the road. Sleeping where, eating where, I couldn't tell, but in the intensely pious country that is Ethiopia, even the poorest bus passengers dug into their pockets, flinging filthy bills into that dark umbrella until it was almost full. He blessed people as they dropped the money by pressing a golden crucifix to their heads. When he had done this to each and every passenger, including the driver and myself, we boarded the bus and kept on driving south.

Early that afternoon we arrived in Dessie. With bus journeys long, arduous experiences, I was unused to arriving in towns in Ethiopia before sunset, and darkness, so with a rare bit of extra time on my hands I followed the college student and his friends to a Tej Beat, an establishment serving Ethiopian honey wine and those bitter, dry leaves of the chat plant. Before long, whether it was the Tej, or the chat, things became really loose lipped and friendly, as the students told me stories of the evil eye, the Buda, that Ethiopians believed could turn anyone into a hyena. When I remarked that it seemed the Buda had turned many into evil tourist guides and guesthouse owners, the students laughed.

'We heard about you,' they said, wagging their fingers.

'What?'

'Lalibela is small, man, everyone was talking about how you fought with that taxi driver from the airport.'

'Really?' I giggled, the chat sinking deeper into my brain.

'Of course, Lalibela is small, man, they will be talking about you for months.'

Day 2: Dessie to Addis Ababa

I left Dessie at the crack of dawn the next morning and a few hours after leaving the town, the horrific highland roads that had rattled my teeth and bruised my ass for weeks magically disappeared, the government was building a new highway system in the country, and we simply turned a corner and drove up onto a divided, paved highway, complete with streetlights even, and wide center dividers.

Civilization.

About halfway through the day, we wound through more twisting highland roads, and flew into a tunnel with MUSSOLINI carved in Roman letters across the top, a leftover from when the Fascist dictator had invaded the country then known as Abyssinia.

Back in Addis at sunset, an Ethiopian Airlines Boeing 767 flew low over the bus as we waited for the traffic lights to change. I stared at the jet for many seconds, mouth agape.

Civilization indeed.

For old times sake, I checked into the Ethiopia Hotel, where the sullen check-in clerks and restaurant staff recognized me with shocked faces, and asked, 'Are you a guest of Ethiopian Airlines again, sir?' referring to the flightmare that had grounded me in Addis for three days.

'No,' I laughed, and handed over my passport. The woman sluggishly handed me a room key and lazily pointed to the stairs, saying, 'the elevator....'

'...is broken, right?' I finished her sentence.

'You know Ethiopia very well,' she said, and without another word picked up the phone and dialed a number. ET phone home.

When I stepped out of the hotel, the security guard who had reprimanded me now saluted me; I was a paying guest and could come and go as I pleased, without the prison cell existence I had endured before.

After many days in the middle of nowhere, the traffic, street life and people of Addis Ababa spun my head round, after hellhole towns, tiny villages, wizened priests and very few foreigners, I now gaped at blonde Dutch girls walking past, and stared at Ethiopian girls yakking into cell phones, and my ears got bashed by hip hop and rap music.

I had a coffee at the restaurant near the Ethiopia Hotel, where I had met the talkative Derg journalist, but he was nowhere to be found. It was to be my last coffee in Ethiopia; as I was to discover down south, those espresso machines vanished completely, and thought I didn't know it at the time, something in the water was going to make my trek south a living hell.

Day 3: Addis Ababa to Shashemene

Waking up before the sun had became second nature to me in Ethiopia, and on my last morning in Addis, I turned the tap, and just heard a gurgle, and a terrible clanking.

No water.

Of course.

I thought I would find a taxi, but in the darkness, I ended up walking most of the two miles to the Addis bus station which heaved with traders, bales of hay, chickens, goats, buckets full of vegetables, and when I finally found my bus, bound for Shashemene, I joined the line of people choking on the familiar cocktail of carbon monoxide, dust, cigarette smoke, and leaded fumes that spewed out of virtually every ex-American school bus.

Suddenly, the coffee I had drunk the evening before exploded in my stomach, and soon a fever erupted. It was going to be a long day. I thought I had a chance at getting a good seat, but an enterprising woman managed to get the best seat by screaming at the top of her lungs the moment the bus driver flung open the door. Frightening everyone away with evil hisses and beady eyes, she got her seat in the front.

But not for long.

A pregnant woman boarded, and the driver kicked the devil woman to the back of the bus where she scowled and swore under her breath, all the way to Shashemene. My fever grew worse as my stomach expressed it's displeasure at the poison coffee I had dumped into it, nauseous and weak, I leaned against the window of the bus, grateful that for once, that the roads were pancake flat.

The broad streets and tidy houses in Shashemene were easily explored in less than an hour. Once again I had arrived in early afternoon and immediately bought my ticket to Moyale, at the Kenyan border. With prostitutes swarming at virtually every restaurant, I retired early to my room to tend to my fever.

Day 4: Shashemene to Moyale

It was my final dark trudge to an Ethiopian bus station. Waking up in the darkness to the sound of muffled voices out the window, and the deep thud of footsteps pounding the dust, I pulled my clothes on, turned the tap in my room, and miracle of miracles, water came out. Too bad it was too black to drink. Not that I wanted to drink any, my fever still raged on, and my stomach rejected everything I tried to feed it.

When I reached the dusty plaza where the buses left, all the old familiar characters were there - the toxic fumes, the old men with their Dulas, the screaming market women, the unhappy bus drivers. I would always be nostalgic for the carved churches, delicate hands of those priests, and magnificent mountain scenery but I would never look back fondly on the Ethiopian bus travel experience. It was pure hell on earth. And life shortening to boot.

About two hours after leaving Shashemene, the asphalt ended. The bus literally flew off the end of it like a diving board, and after what seemed like many seconds careening through the air, the bus crashed down on a packed dirt track with the shape and density of corrugated iron, the bus jarred and jolted as if in some gigantic paint can shaker for hour after hour after hour.

The hell of the northern journeys was back.

Trouble was, my stomach was no better, and my fever just intensified as the sun slowly sank to the horizon. It was well after dark when we pulled into the large bus depot, I spilled out of the roller coaster, shaken, tired, and nursing a bruised ass.

In the darkness, I realized there was no power, and as my guesthouse owner told me cheerfully, 'There is no water, too, friend,' I booked myself on the first truck out of Moyale the next morning on the Kenyan side of the little town.

Day 5: Moyale to Marasabit

At four o'clock in the morning, I was taken to the border where I bought a Kenyan visa. There, a Somali woman, living in Australia, demanded that I pose as her husband so she could pass through the border more easily. She was traveling with about ten bales of clothing she intended to sell in Nairobi. Not interested in spending time in either an Ethiopian or Kenyan jail, I refused. Fending off wild hyenas in hotel rooms strengthens your ability to say no, I can tell you.

Then I was walked to the truck stop where I was introduced to my driver, who shook my hand. It felt like there were more fingers to his hand than normal, but I dismissed the thought as ridiculous.

'You,' he said. 'There.' He was pointing to the top of the truck, and it took me a couple of seconds to realize all luggage was to be tied to the roof. I struggled with it as I navigated the iron bar ladder to the top where I found a stray rope that I cinched tightly around my bag.

As we waited for the police to clear the convoy to travel south into Kenya, soldiers with AK-47's milled around, looking at me through the filthy windows. Somali bandits were spreading out farther and farther from their collapsing country, and this convoy had been established to protect the flow of Ethiopian Kenyan trade.

I was told to sit next to the driver, and no sooner had he boarded the truck than two soldiers sat to my right, brandishing AK-47's with their safety catches unhinged. Three more climbed onto the roof, for a total of five AK-47 toting guards for one truck. Were we carrying gold, diamonds, or radioactive materials? Or just Dave Lowe?

A whistle was blown, and the convoy was off. As soon as the driver gripped the steering wheel, the odd feeling that I had about his hand was confirmed.

He had six fingers.

HE HAD SIX FINGERS.

As I stared slack jawed at his extra appendage, Six Fingers turned the steering wheel from left to right and the extra digit brushed my leg. I could not move an inch to the right as the two soldiers were already smashed together against the door.

246

Each time it touched me I had to contain within me a violent, silent scream.

As the hours passed, neither Six Fingers nor the soldiers talked or even looked at me, I was treated no differently than the sacks of goods tied to the roof, just a paying customer that was giving them a bit of extra income.

The terrain out here, like much of the horn of Africa, was intense. Scrubby brush stretched in all directions, and there were no villages, no telephone poles, no markets or even settlements; occasionally women would be dropped off from trucks like those women who had leapt off the train from Djibouti. They gathered up their belongings and marched over a hill, into the desert, and disappeared.

In the early afternoon, a growing mirage approached.

'Marsabit?' I asked Six Fingers, who shook his head.

It was a small tribal village, and as we pulled in, men wearing their hair in strange, twisted shapes approached, long and lithe in the heat, carrying two meter wooden spears, clothed in material wrapped around their waists, barefoot in the sand.

As I got off the bus a group of them surged forward and I held my breath as they lunged in at me, peering at my skin, touching my hair, fingering my clothes, inspecting my shoes and watch, then they took my hand roughly and inspected it. Losing interest they moved away and watched me coolly from a distance, not blinking their eyes. I recognized scars marking their arms. They each had killed more than fifteen men in battle and could have killed me in an instant if they had wanted to.

An hour later, as the convoy moved off I boarded the truck and the warriors gathered underneath the window, emboldened by the glass between us, staring up at me with broad smiles eager as I was to connect with a human being at the absolute polar opposite to our lives.

Once we had left this village behind, the desert grew drier and even the shrubs disappeared. We truly were in the middle of nowhere. Every once in a while, we could see a village off in the distance, and even solitary people walking in the dust. Out here, in the middle of the world's harshest desert, I felt like I had landed on the moon.

'Marsabit,' mumbled the soldier to my right a few hours later, pointing to a communications tower far up ahead.

'Marsashit,' corrected the other soldier with a laugh.

If I thought Moyale was primitive, Marsabit was quite a few steps lower. When we arrived, Six Fingers uttered the only complete sentence to me in more than two days.

'We leave at six tomorrow. If you are not here, we leave anyway.'

I nodded to say I understood, and gulped.

The town looked like Afghanistan. There were just a few concrete structures, the rest were shacks tilting crazily at all angles. Luckily, we were one of the first trucks to arrive, and I quickly climbed on top of the truck, untied my bag, threw it down, and sped off to arrange a room for myself in one of the concrete buildings. Once again, there was no running water, the door didn't close, and I had to string up my own mosquito net to avoid being eaten alive after dark.

'Welcome to Africa' I could have told myself. Laughing like a hyena, I knew I was already here.

Day 6: Marsabit to Nairobi

The next morning I awoke with a start, hearing a large commotion outside of my room. Frantically packing my bags, I didn't even stop to check if there was running water. Not wanting to be left to fend for myself in Marsashit, I ran all the way to the bus station.

I found my truck, and Six Fingers; when he saw me and my bag, his face registered more than a little disappointment that I had turned up on time. Reluctantly he pointed to the top of the truck, his extra digit dangling uselessly. I climbed the iron ladder, where I expertly tied down my bag with a rope, climbed down, and found my place next to the sullen soldiers and their AK-47's.

The first few hours passed as they had done the day before: outside the windows, dull, monotonous scenery flashed past as we coasted over the bone jarring, corrugated dirt road. Inside the cabin, stony silence from the driver and both soldiers created a thick, choking mood. There was no music.

And there was no radio. The only solicitous one in the cab was Six Finger's extra finger, which scratched my leg as regularly as a kilometer marker.

Suddenly, far up ahead, an ominous black strip, as wide as the road, approached. Out here, in the middle of nowhere, it could have been anything, Somali bandits, a crashed spacecraft, a lake of oil.

As I squinted at this growing black line, I wondered: Was it a crack? A chasm? The end of the earth?

We got closer and the driver seemed not the least bit concerned as he sped towards this foreign object that seemed to stretch to the horizon. In the shimmering heat, I was sure it was a mirage, and would definitely disappear in a few moments, swallowed up by the desert.

But then we were right up at it. Even though it was meters away, I still couldn't tell what it was. The driver seemed to be fearless, was he going to kill us all by ramming this alien object?

Then, we struck it. The front of the vehicle jumped into the air and when we came back to earth, the truck was sitting on solid asphalt. We had reached the paved road at last. The teeth chattering, spine-crushing trip was over; from here, all the way to Nairobi, the journey was now to be as smooth as glass.

The driver revved his truck into gear, and sped off in a desperate attempt to reach Nairobi by dusk. Driving anywhere in Kenya's capital was dangerous at night, and he wanted to reach home without having to stay overnight outside his home city.

Late that afternoon, the desert ended as abruptly as the dirt road. We passed in the shadow of Mount Kenya, where rose bushes and wild flowers tumbled down from the snowy peak to the road, where white picket fenced houses welcomed home Kenyan school children who were riding home on bicycles, trilling their bells.

Reaching the outskirts of the city, darkness had fallen too far for it to be safe. We found a hotel and bedded down for the night.

Day 7: Nairobi, Kenya

Rising before dawn, I gratefully clambered aboard the truck for the last time. Wedged between Six Fingers and the AK-47 toting soldiers, we blew the small town behind us in about thirty seconds, returning to the dusty highway, reaching Nairobi at ten a.m.

At a street corner in downtown Nairobi I was ordered by Six Fingers to untie my bag from the roof. I attracted stares from the well-dressed businessmen and women walking along the sidewalk, and when I climbed back down I waved to the soldiers inside the truck. While Six Finger's face remained as impassive as stone, I saw the tiniest hint of a smile on the soldiers' faces.

Had I gained even a tiny bit of respect from these men?

It seemed so.

IF YOUR BUS DRIVER HAS SIX FINGERS, FEAR NOT: IN SOME COUNTRIES THIS IS A SIGN OF GOOD LUCK (JUST DON'T ASK ME WHICH ONE)

Me ass is still sore after the nonstop bus journey from Lalibela, and me feels like I have traveled between planets, the void out there, the silent desert, is just too desolate to pass through again. Once was enough.

I know you are thinking of some, but please, no six-finger jokes.

Love, Dave

Hey Annette,

I am writing to you from Nairobi again. It took three very long hot showers to remove the dust, dirt and grime from my safari. Even now, days later, the water washing down the drain is the same brown coffee color from the dirt in that country. Memories of Africa, however, are harder to wash away, and even my dreams are in color, complete with blue skies spread across my brain.

Swerving topics. Don't ever lie to anyone in the travel industry. Ever.

Because you may one day be in the middle of Africa and run into that person and be publicly humiliated amongst herds of ravenous lions and cheetahs. If it had happened anywhere else in the world, I wouldn't have believed it, but this is Africa after all.

You, my friend, have been warned.

My African bus riding days were not over. The day after arriving from Addis Ababa, I immediately booked a seven-day safari to the Nakuru and Masai Mara National Parks. So for the twentieth time in a month, and only the day after my arduous teeth chattering seven day trek from Lalibela, I boarded yet another bus, and not long after leaving the urban sprawl of Nairobi, we reached the vast, stark Rift Valley, where dark cinder cones poked up through the brown dirt, and blood red tornadoes arched down from the sky, touching the earth and stirring up dust like witch's broomsticks.

That afternoon we took our first wildlife drive in Nakuru National Park, and had to roll our windows shut as a pack of marauding baboons tore through the entrance gate. Then we drove along a forested ridge where giraffes nibbled acacia leaves, and a white rhino stepped aside to reveal a baby rhino, and saw two lions sitting in dun colored grass, looking as regal and as majestic as any shot from a Mutual of Omaha program that I had watched religiously as a kid.

Then we left for Masai Mara Park, a vast reserve bordering Tanzania, where at the gates we saw zebras and buffalo in huge herds. But about ten minutes later, the driver noticed that the gas gauge was falling fast and to his horror found there was a gas leak in the tank. The liquid was slowly dribbling away. He found a roll of tape and patched it up as best he could. But thirty minutes later, the gauge had fallen by another third, and we stopped to find the tape had fallen off. Estimating that we could just about make the camp before running out of gas, he ordered us back inside the van and he tore off through the gathering darkness.

'What happens if we finish gas?' demanded a French woman in the front seat.

'Bad. There are lions out here, leopards. They don't see difference between people and buffalo.' The driver was gripping the steering wheel like a life preserver.

With that unsettling thought we egged the driver on, and a half an hour later, we gratefully pulled into the acacia lined gate of the camp. After parking the car by the restaurant we tumbled out of the bus to find the serenity was shattered by a group of foreign tourists (whose nationality will be kept under wraps) talking loudly and smoking.

While unloading the van, where gas was still leaking out of the cracked tank, a woman from that large tour group walked over with a cigarette in her lips. Then she calmly struck a match.

One of the drivers saw her begin to toss the still burning match in the direction of the car and the leaking gas.

'NOOOOOOOO!!!' he yelled.

She was so startled that she dropped the match on her bare foot, singing her skin. She began to scream in anger, but the driver ran up, ignoring her screams, and pointed at the gas leaking out onto the ground, and chastised her in Swahili for nearly blowing up the bus, the three next to it, herself, and the entire campsite to Kingdom Come.

That would have been one hell of a Wile E. Coyote boom.

That night, after the hysteria had died down from the near destruction of the campsite from a random cigarette match, a gong sounded and dinner was served, and the French woman and her husband were unhappily tucking into their rice and beans. Both of them left their meals unfinished and retired to bed early.

They weren't going to get much sleep. The campfire was packed with that large tour group, who sang songs and linked arms in some demented karaoke sing along of 'Roll Out The Barrel' that banished the quiet of the Mara to a galaxy far, far away. The Masai tribesmen who managed the camp, barefoot, heads shaved, and dressed in their traditional clothes, tended to the fire as people rudely snapped photos with them as though they were cartoon characters.

The next morning the French couple, frightened by the furious drive to reach the campsite, the near gas explosion incident, the all night off-tune concert from the tour group, and the rustic campground, cast a vehement vote of 'NON' on the safari experience and abruptly disappeared on the next bus back to Nairobi.

The remaining eight of us boarded our bus: two Italians, two Canadians, an American woman, two Australians and me. I was sitting in the back with the Italians, and we quickly feel deep into conversation. But then I suddenly heard one of the women in the front seat say my name. When I pricked my ears up, the other woman said, 'Oh, Dave Lowe, yes, he's the reason I'm here. He helped me get the courage to travel to Africa.' Her name was Renee.

'Well, we worked with him for a long time, but his airfare prices were too high.'

The second woman's voice was maddeningly familiar, and I knew I had heard it before. As Renee and the woman continued talking I focused as hard as I could on the second woman's voice.

By the time we arrived at the first rest stop under a huge acacia tree, I recognized the second woman as Melanie.

THE CLIENT FROM HELL.
THE CLIENT FROM THE DEEPEST HOTTEST PART OF HELL.
MELANIE.

She had led me on a wild goose chase for over six months at the travel agency where I had worked. I had listened to Melanie whine about how she was a poor student, how her husband was unemployed, and how she really wanted to travel despite her limited finances. She was now blabbing on about how she was a specialized nurse, and her husband was a pilot for Air Canada, and how they saved her husband's entire salary, because living costs were so low in Edmonton, Canada.

Like many of her countrymen Melanie had a Canadian flag embroidered on her backpack; a maple leaf decorated the brass ring on her finger, and even a silver maple leaf hung from a chain around her neck. Canadians were the only people I ever came across while traveling that took their national identity so seriously. The mystery of this fervent, nationalistic North American devotion, is, in my opinion, right up there with the riddle of the Sphinx.

When we were all asked by the driver to introduce ourselves, I deliberately went last, and when I introduced myself as a former agent at a major around the world travel agency, as soon as she heard my name, Renee ran up to me and gave me a hug, thanking me for all the help.

Melanie and her husband's faces went completely ash-white. Minutes earlier, we had admired a chameleon adjust it's color to the pale bark of a tree; now their faces were doing the same thing.

In the middle of the African plains, their well rehearsed lies had come crashing down on their heads, and for the rest of their six day safari, Melanie and her husband didn't speak to anyone, they just snapped photos of leopards and lions and muttered in low voices, retiring early after dinner, not joining in any of the conversations about what we had seen that day. There were no vehicles going back to Nairobi, so they were not only stuck at the same camp, they were stuck on the same bus to boot.

The next few days were spent following the same schedule: the first wildlife drive took place at dawn until around eleven in the morning, then we returned to the camp for lunch, at two we would set out on another wildlife trek. Over the next six days I spent on the Mara, I saw every animal I had dreamed I would, from lion cubs to black rhinos, to herds of giraffes, zebras, wildebeest, ostriches, wild boar, hyenas, crocodiles and massive hippos. As it was February and the calving season was underway in Africa, all the animals had babies, from the lions and leopards, the zebras to the giraffes and even the rhinos.

The highlight was when a mother cheetah with four cubs chased a gazelle at top speed across the Mara, catching the beast at a bend in the river and then dragging it to her children who devoured the beast before our eyes.

On our last night in the camp, the large tour group was gone. In their wake, silence reigned. The roar of lions went on through the night, until they seemed to be literally right outside my tent.

Before we slept, the young Masai warriors, who had tolerated the rudeness of the large tour group and their obnoxious guide, told us stories from their villages as the firelight illuminated their young faces. They told us folk tales their own grandmothers had told them by their campfires in their far off Masai villages scattered across the vast Serengeti plains.

It was only on the last morning that I received an apology from Melanie and her husband, who crept up to my tent as the sun was rising and called out my name. As I unzipped the front door, they were crouched on their knees, heads hung in shame like school kids caught cheating on an exam. Then, in hurried, nervous tones, they spluttered out an 'I'm sorry,' before I retreated back to my sleeping bag for a few more hours of sleep, listening to the neighing of zebras and the trumpet calls of elephants, welcoming another day in the Mara.

IF YOU PLAN ON LYING TO SOMEONE IN THE TRAVEL INDUSTRY, BE PREPARED TO RUN INTO THEM IN THE MIDDLE OF NOWHERE.

You have been warned.

Love, Dave

From: Dave <theloweroad@hotmail.com>
To: Annette <whereisannette@yahoo.com>
Date: Mar 1, 2002 2:20 AM
Subject: White Sands, Dark Nights

Hey Annette,

I am in Dubai airport now heading home from Africa. Emirates Airlines put me up because my flights misconnected. In a mauve airport hotel suite. With mauve carpet. With mauve curtains. Even the toilet is mauve.

Thanks. I always did want to sleep inside a Pepto Bismol bottle.

I hate this place. Everything is fake. The marble. The five star hotels. The air conditioning. The fast food restaurants. The Gucci outlets. After Africa, where nothing was fake, where the dust not only caked your skin, but was sucked up your nose, stained your clothes and was even served in your food, this place is an Arabian Las Vegas, shrink wrapped and sterilized for your protection.

A sort of Arabian Nights Condom.

More about the last part of my trip. After the dust, illness, death, delays, carbon monoxide fumes, funerals, chaos and heat, I ended my journey in one of the least 'African' places on the east coast of the continent, the beaches of Zanzibar.

The sun was so dazzingly strong as it reflected off the white sand you couldn't go outside between ten a.m. and four p.m. unless you wanted to be blinded. Unlike the rest of my trip, where hardship and struggle has been lurking behind every bush, every bend in the road, on Zanzibar the biggest decision was what seafood you wanted grilled for dinner. But if I thought I would escape Africa that easily, I was brought up short before I even left Nairobi.

As I stepped out of my hotel to catch my bus to Dar Es Salaam, a very tall man stepped out of the crowd and before I had a chance, reached out for my hand to shake it.

'Mr. Lowe?' he said with a wide smile across his face,

without letting go of my hand.

'Yes,' I said hesitantly, remembering the Italian woman who had her watch snatched on the very same street.

'You are requiring a bus ticket to Dar Es Salaam?'

'Yes, but how did you...' My voice trailed off. I hadn't told any local or foreigner where I was heading next. 'Who told you I was going to Dar Es Salaam?'

He ignored my question, and still gripping my hand in that vice-like grip, said, 'The ticket is four thousand Kenyan Schillings. If you would like, I can go to the bus station to purchase it.'

'No thanks,' I said as I wrenched my hand free. I had already paid two thousand Schillings for the exact same ticket. I pushed my way off through the surging people, into a taxi, and slammed the door. As the taxi drove away, the man became angry and he began pointing a tremulous finger at me as he shouted, 'Mister Lowe, wait! Mister Lowe!!!'

The taxi turned a corner and the man was gone.

The bus drove through the classic Kenyan countryside, all acacia trees and villages with women pounding millet in stone bowls. The sun set and cast an orange glow on Mount Kilimanjaro in the distance.

After midnight, we passed through the most corrupt border crossing I had ever seen. Border guards were stacking American Dollars and Kenyan Schillings in neat piles next to stacks of passports that they stamped one by one. A British woman didn't have exact change for the $50 fee, they wouldn't accept her Kenyan Schillings and was about to be turned back. She was already arguing with a border guard when I walked up to her and offered to pay for her visa, offering to take her Kenyan Schillings in exchange because I was coming back to Kenya. The border guard ordered me back, but I handed the woman a $50 US note and she got her visa. When we received our passports back, our bus had already crossed a bridge, swallowed up by the darkness.

'Walk!' shouted a border guard, pointing his AK-47 at us. And walk we did, inching our way along the bridge, knees shaking, in total darkness, with only a flimsy railing to prevent us from tumbling into the river below.

'There's a hole, be careful,' I said to the British woman when I found a yawning gap with my foot. The railing was gone completely there, and all we could do was just balance as best we could as we pushed on through the darkness. The border guard's gun was still pointing at us. When we gratefully reached the other side, our passports were returned, and we boarded the bus again for Dar Es Salaam.

As we raced off under the command of a new driver, our speed increased to breakneck, and as we sped through the night, we hit so many bumps that the passengers in the back were being flung like rag dolls towards the ceiling.

They yelled for the driver to slow down, but he only increased his speed until a particularly vicious speed bump threw three men towards the ceiling, where they left clumps of hair.

'Hey, we're not cows!' screamed a man from Costa Rica, a missionary who was off to Tanzania to save some souls.

Once in Dar Es Salaam, I stepped off my last African bus trip, and gratefully boarded the first ferry I could for Zanzibar. In Stonetown, the principal town of the island, I stayed for two days, wandering the narrow passageways and admiring the bustling port, which was full of cats.

When I bent down to pet one, remembering the line from Thoreau, 'It is not worth the while to go round the world to count the cats in Zanzibar,' the slinky feline took one look at me, hissed like a cobra and scratched me on the hand and arm.

Meow.

'He got scratched by cats in Zanzibar.' It could definitely go on my tombstone.

On day three, I overheard four Swedish girls talking about a place called Mohammad's on the east coast of Zanzibar. They were looking for people to share the taxi fare. Within two hours, we arrived at a small stone village by the sea, thick with palm trees that fringed the whitest, purest sand beach I had ever seen.

Mohammad turned out to be a young man from the village who had three huts for rent to travelers. For five dollars a night the price included electricity from just four to seven p.m., a basic breakfast of tropical fruit and a fresh seafood meal each night.

Fifteen minutes after arriving, I was already swimming in an ocean straight out of a postcard as the memories of the hardships of African traveling seeped from my brain.

Cut off from the rest of Zanzibar, the village had little to offer, no shops, stalls, cafes, or even restaurants and the days were broken by the calls to prayer from the village mosque. And the rhythm of the fishermen, who left each morning, returning each afternoon in a spectacle that began like clockwork at three o'clock: elegant dhows appeared on the horizon as they had done for hundreds of years, pulled into the lagoon by the wind, and nothing more. Once there, they unloaded the fish, crabs and shrimp they had caught, selling up quickly before retiring to their village at dusk, leaving the canvas sails of their dhows to flap in the breeze as the hulls sank into the sand.

Early the next morning, with the sky still pink, the fishermen pushed out to sea again to repeat what they had done the day before.

It was at night when Africa returned.

Barely audible over strong breezes rustling the palm fronds, drumbeats reverberated through the darkness, continuing through the night. The chanting and singing seemed to come from all directions. The next morning, when I asked about the drums, and the music, Mohammad wasn't talking.

'Nothing, last night,' he said with a straight face. 'Nothing.

The Swedish girls also asked him to explain, but they got the same answer. No local we talked to would tell us anything.

The next few days passed in lazy succession. During the day, the fishermen came and went, their dhows dotting the horizon, the sun blazed off the white sand beach, and at night, the drumbeats went on and on. I did some scuba diving, and snorkeling, I watched the village women harvest seaweed exported to Japan, and very quickly, the trials of Africa disappeared like the sun did each day, behind the hills. The dust, the confusion, the terrible roads and heat all seemed like bad dreams.

One day I walked several kilometers up the beach to have lunch at a newly opened boutique resort where European tourists lazed on silk cushions scattered under a palm thatched roof that served as restaurant and chill out zone.

Though we were on the same island, and on the same continent, we were clearly on different holidays.They had arrived on chartered jets from London and Zurich, had paid for their holiday in full with their credit card before they even left home, and had no intention of exploring beyond the walls of their resort, or deep into the heart of Africa for that matter.

'Drums?' they said in horror when I told them what went on all around my room at Mohammad's each night.

'We don't have any drums here,' sniffed another.

Convinced they were sleeping too heavily to have missed the loud drums and music, I went on to describe the sounds and the rhythms in great detail, waiting for the look of recognition, or a spark of interest.

Nothing.

Then, I went on to recall my travels across the horn of Africa, sparing no details, which sent the Europeans one by one back to their room, 'to rest.'

We may have been on the same island, and on the same planet, but we were definitely on completely different wavelengths. The Europeans at that resort were clearly the polarized travelers I had met earlier in my trip, and like those, we gratefully parted ways, eager to seek out our own Africa.

It was only riding the ferry back to Dar Es Salaam when the reality of Africa returned in daylight. As I stepped across the narrow wooden plank placed there for passengers, I noticed a long stretcher being loaded. Draped in a white sheet, I could see the faint outline of a nose. When I tried to find a place to sit, I found the cabin stuffed full with luggage and gasoline fumes and was forced to choose a spot along the back railing.

Then, two workers, unable to find any room for the stretcher, put it down at my feet, right in front of me. It wasn't until a bleary eyed, weeping widow appeared, supported on both sides by family members, that I realized there was a body underneath that sheet, and that the man under that sheet was in fact her dead husband being transported to the mainland for his elaborate funeral and burial.

As there was nowhere else to stand, I was forced to stay

behind the makeshift coffin, while the widow wailed and beat her breasts with clenched fists, her eyes digging into mine, searching for answers to her misfortune. Her relatives also stared at me, thinking I had chosen to stand behind the corpse on purpose; and as we steamed for Dar Es Salaam, their stares grew colder by the minute.

As we approached the mainland, the seas got so rough I had to hang onto the railing with all my strength, and then the seawater spray began to sink into my cat-scratched hands, and they stung like mad. The sea spray also soaked the sheet and through the now translucent white cotton, the man's face began to appear, eyes wide, mouth agape, frozen in death. I tried not to look down, scrambling for my 'It's spilled paint' sanity preserving mantra I had used on that awful bus ride from Harar, but no matter how hard I tried, the searing pain in my hand prevented me from creating a new mantra or tear my eyes away from that dead man's face just a few feet below me.

The widow also now saw her dead husband's face and began to wail even louder, so loud and ear splittingly that in a vain attempt to block my ears from the shrill blast, I lost my grip on the railing completely, and to my utter, cartoon eye popping horror, went tumbling forward towards the corpse! At the last second I managed to reach out above me and grab an overheard pole. The relatives missed my horrible gaffe, but not the widow, she burst into tears again, opening up the waterworks that were badly smearing what was left of her elaborate makeup.

When the ferry arrived back at Dar Es Salaam's narrow harbor, the man's body was hoisted over the side of the boat and loaded into the flat part of a white Toyota pick up truck. The widow, giving me one last look and letting out one last mournful wail, followed her dead husband off the boat and pulled the car door closed behind her with a resentful slam.

So that was Africa.

It started with getting fisted by a woman in a Burka screaming 'Bin Laden' and ended with a widow wailing in my direction over her dead husband's fat corpse. I am still washing red dust out of my clothes, and instead of throwing them out, I'm going to keep them as a memory of Africa.

Africa is one of those places that is equally all about reality, and fiction, about dreams and disasters, about things genuine and things fake. This is what scared most of the weak travelers away, thinning out the Lonely Planet herd who went in search of easier paradises in Central America or Southeast Asia.

Life went on there in all its black and white, beauty and horror, spectacle and modesty, all day, everyday, all round. And that is what Africa means to me.

More news when I get home. My clothes may be dirt stained, but my mind is clear. In the vastness of Africa is time to think, to recall lyrics to old music tunes and long forgotten childhood memories because there is simply nothing else to do; time to think even more, because you have 13 hours ahead of you on a ramshackle bus; time to reflect on your experiences, because there is so much time and space here. Which is the greatest luxury of all. Space to think.

I'm already missing the life in Africa, stripped bare.

The trip up to Dubai on an Airbus 330 was bizarre. Fastening a shiny seatbelt inside a spotless state of the art jet was a far cry from the vomit scented AK-47 and live chicken laden buses of the previous seven weeks.

I almost cried when we took off.

And when the cabin crew dropped the virtually hermetically sealed meal in front of me, I almost cried again.

OK, they're calling my flight. Gotta wrap this up.

(Why is it that all Emirates flights land and take off between one and four a.m. in the morning? My flight home doesn't leave until the ungodly time slot of 3.45 a.m.)

Whoa.

I noticed walking over to the internet station that the gates on either side of mine are for flights to India (Bombay and Delhi) and crowding the seats and floor are hundreds of men in white, all workers off home after working in the Gulf.

My breathing has stopped.

Is this the Travel Gods way of casually informing me that the subcontinent will be my next trip?

Who knows.

At the moment, just like the French couple on safari, I am voting a vehement 'NON' on traveling to India. After Africa, my continuing bad relationship with AK-47's and endless ACME anvils, holding a burning dynamite stick marked 'INDIA' doesn't quite appeal to me.

Even if my fur DOES grow back!

After Africa I'm half expecting to breath in carbon monoxide fumes at the gate here in Dubai. And defend my seat assignment with a Dula duel. And be served a portion of flyblown pasta. And get trailed by a pack of hyenas. Or get bargained over by fellow passenger/prossies for my passport. Or get scratched by a cat on Zanzibar.

I was right. Africa really does stain your soul. (And I have the cat scratch scars to prove it.)

But hang on for a moment.

I avoided getting robbed in Africa, avoided getting malaria or seriously ill, and avoided several other nasty disasters. Maybe those fearsome hyenas were not the bloodthirsty beasts I had thought they were.

Maybe, just maybe, they had been sent by the Travel Gods to protect me.

The only thing I can smell in this monstrously modern airport city is Duty Free perfume and the oh-so-magical scent of cleaning products.

Even while looking at the floor beneath my feet, so clean you could eat off of it, I miss Africa already.

Love, Dave

Nepal, India
& The Maldives

From: Dave <theloweroad@gmail.com>
To: Annette <whereisannette@yahoo.com>
Date: Jul 30, 2004 1:27 PM
Subject: In The Grip Of Inshallah

Hey Annette…

Don't ever try to save $75 on a plane ticket.

EVER.

To get to India I booked a flight with Biman Bangladesh because it was exactly seventy-five dollars cheaper than the Royal Nepal flight to Kathmandu, Nepal. Unless that flight crashed in the Himalayas and passengers were forced to turn to seatmates as in-flight meals, nothing could have been worse than what I just went through.

Yup, you read it right.

I'm going to India.

Four months. Top to bottom. Varanasi, the Taj, Rajastan, the Himalayas, and Kerala. Bombay and Delhi have been thrown in for good measure. Camels, trains and yak or two.

Go on, say it.

Yes, I am mad. MAD, MAD, MAD.

Anyway. After being released from thirty-six hours in the evil clutches of Bangladesh's national carrier, I have realized my terrible mistake.

Arriving at Bangkok's Don Muang airport I found flight 153 to Dhaka delayed by seven hours. We were checked in anyway and were told with a shrug that it would probably be longer. No vouchers for meals were issued, and eight hours later, after watching dozens of flights leave on time, we were told it would be still four hours more.

When we finally boarded the Airbus 310 at midnight,

267

onboard were fat cabin crew dressed in vomit green saris standing at attention around the plane with arms folded across their chests, warily watching over the one hundred transit passengers from Tokyo absolutely irate after being kept onboard for almost half a day without air conditioning or food as the mechanical problem was fixed.

When we pushed back from the gate the safety video started, not with a lame blonde woman generically dressed in a branded smile and airline uniform but with blurry scenes of Hajj pilgrims circumnavigating Saudi Arabia's Ka'baa in Mecca. A scratchy recording of a mournful man wailing 'Allah Akbar, Allah Akbar!!' (God is great) replaced the usual bland 'Thank you for flying X Airlines.' When the video was finished, the crew announced, 'Inshallah (God willing) we shall be taking off shortly.'

As the creaky jet lifted off the runway, the cockpit door flung wide open and as we lurched into the night sky it banged back and forth like a Kansas barn door in a tornado, I looked directly above my head to see a large, scurrying cockroach crawling on the ceiling before it took flight itself, buzzing around the cabin, furiously smashing its head into the overhead bins, frantically trying to escape. (It's a flightmare buddy. There is NO chance of escape. Trust me....)

When the plane made a sharp left turn a large panel about five rows ahead of me fell from the ceiling and crashed to the floor. Not only did not a single passenger bat an eyelid, during the rest of the flight the cabin crew merely stepped over it and started the in-flight 'service.'

A dirty drinks cart with a dodgy wheel came round and a large hairy arm slapped a yellowed plastic tray in front of me with just a cup of water and a hunk of bread. The woman then swished off in her synthetic sari. When I hesitated, the man next to me grabbed the bread off my tray gratefully and devoured it.

As I was seated next to the emergency exit on the left side of the plane, people came with prayer mats and bowed in the direction of Mecca, indicated by a black arrow on the cabin television screens.

The praying passengers were sent back to their seats with a command shouted from the lead flight attendant, a mustached woman in a flamingo pink sari. One old man laid down to take a snooze before a female crew, face made up like a Kabuki actor, kicked him out and sent him back to his seat after a shrill dressing down in Bengali.

Sitting for three hours amongst smelly, swirly-patterned psychedelic seats was worsened by my seatmate, he removed his shoes and socks and then ripped the end of his toenails off.

That was the only in-flight entertainment.

Only until the lead attendant picked up the microphone and asked hoarsely, 'Will all transit passengers for the Biman flight to Brussels, please move to the front of the plane. Inshallah we shall be landing at Dhaka, and we need to deplane you first.'

Up stood the fifty transit passengers to Brussels who had been promised in Bangkok that their connecting flight wouldn't leave without them. They collected their carry-on bags out of the overhead bins and walked to the nearest exit door, where they gathered in bewildered clusters. They began to flap their boarding passes at every stone-faced cabin crew they saw. Even the co-pilot who had came back to the galley for a cup of water was accosted by a team of furious people, demanding to know if their bags were going to connect.

Their shouts echoed through the plane, with screaming babies in tow and dragging their plastic bags stuffed to bursting as we began to descend to Earth.

As the plane wobbled and whined to touchdown, the cabin crew pushed them aside to slap tray tables up and bark at people to fasten their seatbelts.

By now the lights of Dhaka were visible outside the window, and people were still standing in the aisles, including seven people right in front of me.

'Ladies and gentlemen, Inshallah we will be landing shortly at Zia International airport. Allah Akbar.'

The next announcement (in Bengali) sent the transit passengers to Brussels scrambling to find an empty seat. But in the chaos of the final moments in the air, most were still standing when the wheels touched down on the runway. How no one was thrown down is beyond me, but when we pulled off the runway, someone began yelling and pointed frantically out the window at a Biman DC-10 that was positioning itself for takeoff.

'It is our flight to Brussels!' shouted one man.

'Biman lied to us!' screamed another.

When we got to the gate the DC-10 plane to Brussels was long gone and as we de-boarded the smelly plane, not one, but three, fistfights broke out in the aisles as people screamed and shouted at the crew about the airline's broken promises.

I grabbed my carry-on bag and wielded it in front of me like a shield as people shoved and pushed their way off the stinking jetliner. Security guards were called and the troublesome mob of Brussels transit passengers were hauled off to a secure room (probably padded) to be given the bad news - the next flight to Brussels was in three days, and their next home would be a transit hotel two miles from the airport, and twenty miles from civilization.

All the other BG transit passengers to Kathmandu, Delhi, Calcutta and Bombay, who were going to be 'guests' of BG until noon the next day, were ordered to wait in line to get their hotel vouchers.

As we filled in the paperwork we could hear the irate Brussels passengers screaming blue murder at ground staff. Our passports were taken away from us, and we were informed of our rights, halfway through the spiel I almost put my hand up and finished it, so used to the procedures in a flightmare that it was I who could read a policeman his rights, rather than the other way round.

Then we were marched past immigration where we boarded an even stinkier bus without glass in the windows. It took us to our 'transit hotel' that turned out to be a slimy guesthouse owned by someone's cousin at Bangladesh Biman Airlines.

I was told at the front desk that I would have to share a room, I turned to find my foot-hygiene deficient seatmate from the flight grinning at me, until I started imitating the loud yells from the Brussels passengers, and a private room on the top floor magically appeared. So off I went to my room on the seventh floor, trudging up the steps. The elevator was broken.

I think in a flightmare, this is a textbook requirement.

The next morning at breakfast the front desk was empty but a whiteboard cheerfully stated that flight 751 to Kathmandu was delayed by three hours.

Thanks for flying Biman!

Despite this delay we were ordered to be in the lobby at the correct take off time, in case of further schedule changes. So we were rushed back to the airport through the flooded streets of Dhaka that were clogged with throngs of trishaws and their drivers ringing their bells.

Our travel documents were returned to us via an archaic system of bookkeeping - plane tickets had been rubber-banded around our passports, forcing each official to spend five minutes searching to find each person's documents. Then, our new boarding passes were issued, and then we were released into an airport that was about as interesting as a cattle barn.

Four hours later, one computer in the terminal said the flight was leaving at three p.m. while another said six p.m. No official knew which computer was correct. The flight was now five hours behind schedule.

It was too late to leave the airport and we were stuck watching Bangladesh fighter planes doing touch and go's as entertainment, saying goodbye to our fellow jail mates as their flights to Delhi, Calcutta and Bombay left two, four and even six hours later than scheduled.

Finally, a gate was finally assigned for the Katmandu flight. Gate 1.

I joined the horde of irate passengers as they rushed to the other end of the terminal, when I got there, I realized my boarding pass was missing. Running back to the transit desk white faced and terrified of NEVER getting out of Dhaka, Bangladesh, or Zia airport alive, I explained to the official what had happened, and he shook his head.

'No boarding pass, no flight.'

'But, I have my passport, and my ticket.'

I pushed the documents over the counter and persisted. He just turned his back on me to deal with the next passenger. Then my anger at too many sleepless hours, too many onboard flying cockroaches, too many filthy planes, and the sound of too many swishing synthetic saris, compounded with banging cockpit doors and falling ceiling panels, and too many hours of waiting, boiled over and I exploded.

'Listen! I'm on this flight! SO REISSUE THE BOARDING PASS, NOW!'

The terminal stopped moving. Two security guards started walking towards me, probably to check if I was an escaped Brussels transit passenger. But they didn't have to throw me into the padded room, because the man just typed a few keystrokes into his computer and a new boarding pass popped out. He scrutinized it and scrawled 'Duplicate' across it. New document in hand, I stepped away, but before I was out of earshot, he hissed a warning. 'I, sir, am assigned to Gate 1. If we find another passenger fraudulently using your lost boarding pass, we will hand you over to the appropriate police authorities.'

I ran all the way back to Gate 1, only to see familiar red faces huffing past me in the opposite direction. One of them recognized me and shouted, 'Gate change. Gate 21.'

It was at the opposite end of the cavernous, crumbling terminal.

Running up to a computer, I realized he was right. Not wanting to miss my escape out of this flightmare, I ran all the way to Gate 21, where the gate agent who had re-issued my boarding pass scrutinized it before waving me onboard the creaky Fokker 28 that had flown faithfully at SAS Scandinavian Airlines for twenty five years.

Amazingly, the door to the small plane popped closed, it pulled away from the terminal, and we took off into the gray monsoon sky.

Just like that.

An hour and a half later, after stepping off the jet in Nepal and bidding my fellow prison mates goodbye for the last time, my bag, and my sanity, popped out onto the carousel at Kathmandu.

I was free at last. Thank the Travel Gods almighty, I was free at last. I did however, pump my fist at the Travel Gods high in the sky and scream, 'YOU BASTARDS!'

Don't even dream of trying to save $75 dollars on a plane ticket, because once you are in the middle of a flightmare, there is no oxygen mask or canary yellow slide in the world big enough to evacuate you from that 'situation.'

You have been warned.

I'm off to India in less than a week.

When I venture into Kathmandu for the last time I am going to enter the nearest, gaudiest temple, head respectfully bowed, and with my posture submissive, I will offer as much incense to the Travel Gods as I can find. (My flight is booked on Indian Airlines, the only airline that flies the route to Varanasi) I am considering all future incense offerings as an insurance policy against a possible flightmare.

I hope it works.

Inshallah.

Love, Dave

Hey Annette,

I'm half Nepali.

FYI, 'drive by's' come in many forms - shootings if you're from L.A., but in Nepal they come in blessing form too. Some piece of work tried to speed up a slow tourist season by marking my forehead with an orange smudge of paint. While I was tying my shoes, I might add.

So, I'm half Nepali.

Anyway. Hello from Kathmandu. Got here six days ago, got one day more to go. Leaving for India tomorrow, and my mind is spinning around at what to expect.

INDIA.

The Mother Ship of chaos and confusion.

My stomach is churning in expectations of the country that lies right over the horizon.

Back to my trip so far. It took four circles over the narrow valley for the Bangladesh Biman pilot to actually find a gap large enough in the monsoon clouds to land his Fokker 70. During the flight my nose was pressed against the window on the right hand side of the plane, looking for any sign of the snow-capped peaks Nepal was famous for. But all I saw was endless gray mist, swirling clouds and buckets of rain pouring off the wing.

No Everest, alas.

When I stepped out of the deserted airport terminal I split a cab with the other passenger that had survived the hellish overnight transit stop in Dhaka, a retired fisherman from southern Japan who spoke just one English sentence.

'I am fish man from Japan,' he told everyone. 'Fish man.'

Other than muffled grunts, his only gesture to the taxi stand staff was to flash his passport like a necklace of garlic to ward off vampires. 'Nippon! Nippon!' Fish Man snarled.

As we waited for our car to pull up, Fish Man was growing stranger by the minute, flicking his fingers at invisible mosquitoes and on the ride into town, pulled out his disposable chopsticks which he had used to eat with during the flight. Now he began to mimic the Beethoven music coming out of the radio. As we swerved around police checkpoints searching trunks for Maoist bombs, random cows chewing newspapers and crashing trishaws ringing their bells, he laughed wickedly to himself at some private joke.

'Nippon, Nippon,' Fish Man mumbled.

I was glad when Fish Man motioned with his chopsticks for the taxi driver to drop him off at his hotel nowhere near the place I had booked off Durbar Square in the old town. Fish Man stuffed his chopsticks into his filthy bag, hopped out, threw some bills onto the front passenger seat, strapped his tiny backpack on and strode off into the traffic.

With just a week in Nepal, I only had enough time to explore the Kathmandu valley. But I was pretty glad to stay in the capital, the day before I arrived in Nepal the mayor of Pokkhara had been shot dead by Maoists in broad daylight, the bus lines across the country were cut off, and one of the strongest monsoons in years was underway, reducing trekking routes to mush. The increasing reports of trekkers being first detained by Maoist rebels, lectured on their movement, coerced into giving a donation, and then, being issued official 'receipts' was also a put-off.

That first afternoon, walking through the narrow medieval lanes packed with temples and scenic village life, nothing was more interesting than the numerous Saddhus I passed, the holy men who covered their bodies in ash, and wandered the subcontinent in search of enlightenment. As we eyed each other as exotic creatures from completely opposite ends of the human spectrum, the Saddhus smiled up at me serenely, carrying only their tridents and small satchels stuffed with clothes. And then they were gone, leaving a pungent cloud of hash smoke in their wake.

The next day I took a taxi to nearby villages and temples scattered around the capital, the closest were Patan and Bhakatpur, where temple complexes draped in garlands of saffron marigold flowers and trays of flickering votive candles were filled with people. I kept looking up around the city to see the snow capped peaks, but saw nothing. Random monkeys scrounged for food that was left behind, leaping down from trees into the temple courtyards where they were chased off by barking dogs.

Walking though the quiet neighborhoods I reached the edge of the city off the beaten track into quiet rice fields where women tended to their crops and school children rode bikes home, ringing their bells. With heavy monsoon rain each day it was muddy going, but every time the rain stopped I looked around to get a glimpse of the snowy Himalayas. But each time I stopped to look, they were always hidden behind the heavy mist.

By day three I was getting sick seeing the thousands of postcards for sale all over the place with pictures of snow capped peaks framed against impossibly blue skies, scenes I had yet to see.

The most interesting place I went was Pashupatinath, a suburb of Kathmandu where the bodies of both royalty and commoners are burned on Ghats perched over a small river. When I was there I watched four funerals. There was no family present and no ceremonial speeches or music, or tears. The bodies were offloaded from trucks, laid out in the open, unwrapped face up, covered with flower petals, wrapped again for the last time before being laid out on a large stack of wooden logs that were already set alight.

The Ghats are an eye opening experience made even more interesting due to the relaxed nature of the people walking along on the opposite side of the river on their way to school, the market, just stopping to watch the spectacle for a few moments before moving on. Munching on snacks, talking on cell phones, they just watched the flames do their job.

There were Saddhus here too, watching the scene and trying to convince me, the lone westerner, that enlightenment was easy - just follow them up to their caves high up in the mountains.

Sure, dude.

Let me check the credit limit on my Wile E. Coyote American Express card, and away we'll go.

When the bodies were sufficiently burned, the attendants took metal brooms and swept the burning debris into the river, where it went out with a huge boiling hiss of steam. The next stack of wood was already being put in place for the next body to be burned.

When I looked up into the sky to see if the snow covered mountains were visible, all I saw was grey monsoon mist as thick as pea soup.

Durbar Square was the best place for people watching, tailors sewed clothes out on the sidewalk, wrinkled women sold saffron garlands for temple prayers, and random cows had to be avoided as they blocked alleys of traffic. The ubiquitous Saddhus were there too of course, muttering prayers to themselves as they wandered the cobblestone streets in the rain, their dreadlocks dripping water and their calves smeared with grey mud.

When I bent down to tie my shoes, a thumb suddenly flashed out of nowhere, slammed into the center of my forehead and left behind a bright orange smudge mark. Stunned, I stood up to find a naked Saddhu standing before me, his dreadlocks wrapped expertly around his head, smiling serenely. Then, he bowed and said some prayer in Nepali. I smiled and turned to go but the Saddhu leapt in front of me and tapped his bowl for a donation. I had heard of beggars being creative to get money, but I'd never thought Saddhus had turned to drive-by-blessings to speed up a slow tourist season. I reached into my pocket, pulled out a small note, dropped it in the bowl and left the Saddhu behind to wait for more victims.

As I walked back to my hotel in the growing darkness that night, I passed a contingent of forty soldiers patrolling Durbar Square. Standing there watching the procession, I jumped when someone pulled my sleeve, expecting another random blessing from some impish Saddhu.

Instead, a well-dressed man in a business suit wordlessly handed me a business card that read, 'All Roads lead to Everest Casino.'

Putting the card into my pocket, I looked towards the horizon where the snow-covered peaks were supposed to be. But they remained hidden by clouds, out of reach.

'I'm half Nepali,' I said to the stunned owner of my hotel when he pointed in shock at the orange mark in the middle of my forehead.

The last neighborhood I visited was Bodnath, a monastic complex built around a large Stupa near the airport. When China invaded Tibet in 1959 Kathmandu harbored one of the most vibrant Tibetan communities in the world. Here, elegant silk scarves from Tibet flapped in the breeze next to prayer flags, antique Thankas, prayer wheels and conch shells fashioned into horns. It was like an authentic look at old Tibet.

Or so I thought.

When I got to Bodnath there were more tourists than pilgrims. Most of the people walking in the Tibetan tradition around the temple (clockwise) dressed in the trademark burgundy red robes were foreigners, their heads shaved and deep in discussing on meditation techniques in Australian accents, in German, and Russian. The whole neighborhood looked like a Tibetan Disneyland with Dalai Lama T-shirts, Potola Palace cafes serving banana pancakes and mango milkshakes, and hundreds of postcards with crystal clear views of Himalayan mountain peaks, still invisible behind a curtain of mist.

Beginning to think these peaks were in fact some clever scam dreamed up by some corrupt tourist minister to lure tourists to Nepal, I grumbled and found an internet place five blocks from the Stupa where three red robed monks came in calmly and sat down chatting on cell phones while their friends sent emails and surfed Britney Spears websites.

Hoping to avoid running into a Dalai Lama Mickey Mouse, I fled Bodnath immediately.

Kathmandu is also one of those places that the parents of your friends may have been to in the late 60's and early 70's heading between Turkey and Thailand on the great overland backpacker trail. While the vibe is gone for the most part, it does linger on in some ways, none more than the Snowman Café, my stop after leaving Bodnath. Around the corner from Freak Street, here, for fifty cents, chocolate cake, vanilla milkshakes and other comfort foods are served beneath psychedelic wall paintings and peace symbols dangling from lamps with Marley and Hendrix on the speaker system. Today most of the customers are young, hip Nepalis wearing tie-dyed T-shirts, smoking and sending SMS messages to their friends.

I was sitting by the window when a sixty something American man came in with his college-aged daughter. They took off their raincoats and grabbed a table by the window and then ordered a piece of apple pie each.

'This is the place, your father came when he traveled across Asia,' he said loudly.

The man's daughter just sat there and stared out the window.

'Before I met your mother, before I started the restaurant, before your brother....' his voice trailed off as the Nepali waiter dropped off the cakes. His daughter still wasn't interested and just started eating.

Her father repeated the sentences in a louder voice. His daughter just sat there and ate a few more bites. With a bellowed 'god damn it,' her dad slammed his fist on the table, dropped some bills, threw up his hands at his daughter's boredom and they left as fast as they came.

This afternoon was my last in Kathmandu.

Sitting in Durbar square, I watched the orange sun set through a crack in the clouds, but alas, snow flecked peaks were still nowhere to be seen, still veiled behind a thick gray burka of clouds.

When the 1,000th person came up to me asking if I needed a guide, after I shook my head the guy sat down anyway, bored out of his mind during the tail end of the low season during which even penniless Saddhus, I learned, earned more money than he did.

To prove this he pointed to the nearest Saddhu, dressed in ochre orange robes and clutching the trademark trident, sitting perched on a low wall accosting tourists to take a photo. As we watched, a couple from Europe was stopped, the woman smiled and posed by the Saddhu, the man took the picture, and then the Saddhu stuck out his hand and asked for 1,000 rupees, equivalent to thirteen dollars. The couple gasped, but paid up anyway and moved on.

'See,' the tour guide said, 'easy money.'

On a good day Saddhus could earn five times what a tour guide could, so much so that young guides contemplated rolling in human ash and growing thick dreadlocks just to cash in on the westerners fascination with Saddhus. He explained that most of the Saddhus weren't in Kathmandu now because it was the slow season. I told the guy the story of my drive-by blessing, and he laughed.

'To see the real Saddhu show, you have to come back in October, when the 'official' Saddhu season is here.'

'The Saddhu season?'

'Yes, the Saddhu season. They come here to make money from all the tourists here for trekking.

He went on to explain the flood of tourists in the fall, and how their hard currency kept these cool as fuck, possession-less holy men who wandered the world in search of enlightenment, rolling in enough cash, and hash, to last them till the next year.

'Where do they go?' I asked. 'In the off season?'

'Goa,' he said casually. 'Techno music. Cheap hash. They hang out with the backpackers there, on the beach.'

I guess even Saddhus need a vacation.

I never did see a single snow capped Himalayan peak in Nepal. What's printed on postcards isn't always what you find, because sometimes the tourist horde reason to come to a country isn't what you see at all.

Postcards can lie.

I did get drive-by blessed, saw bodies burn, and explored the medieval backstreets of Kathmandu, and braved the monsoon rains. I certainly have the soggy shoes to prove it. So, two lessons from Nepal:

EVEN SADDHUS NEED A VACATION.

IF YOU'RE EVER THE VICTIM OF A DRIVE-BY BLESSING, TELL EVERYONE YOU ARE HALF NEPALI.

Tomorrow I am off on the Indian Airlines flight to Varanasi. The Maoist guerillas have blocked the roads to India, and taking to the skies is the only solution.

This time tomorrow I'll be in India.

INDIA.

AM I MAD?

I have my visa. I have a hotel reservation. I have a guidebook. I have a head full of stories.

But little else. Though apprehensive, I am glad to be finally going to that giant kaleidoscopic universe that looms large in the sights of true travelers, a giant spiritual carrot that has been dangled in front of my nose ever since setting foot in Asia.

The 'proof' of being a real traveler.

India is about to be swiped off my list.

At long last.

Love, Dave

From: Dave <theloweroad@gmail.com>
To: Annette <whereisannette@yahoo.com>
Date: Aug 27, 2004 11:20 AM
Subject: How Well Do You Know Mother Ganges?

Hey Annette.

INDIA.

Everything you've heard is true. You know all the stories. The travelers' urban legends. Actually nothing can prepare you for the maelstrom of heat, chaos, confusion, cows, noise, dirt, touts, stink, beggars, holy men, suicidal trishaw drivers and more that India hurls at you from the moment you arrive.

The chaos has left me chewing on my mosquito net in my room, looking at the visa in my passport and asking...

WHY?

During my first forty-eight hours in Varanasi I was left sweaty and delirious fighting off a virulent stomach bug, topped with a furious fever, a loud, rambunctious religious festival raged on outside my hotel day and night and everywhere I went people dressed in aircraft orange threw fistfuls of Ganges water at me trying to cleanse my soul.

Whichever alley I went down a massive, stubborn cow always seemed to be blocking my way, and when a man dressed in a Kali costume harassed me along the banks of the Ganges, screeching at me to follow him to the hills, I stepped backwards right into the path of an Agori, a Saddhu who drinks water from skulls and whose body is covered in human ashes. Wasting not even a second, he gripped my arm like an iron vice as his penetrating blood-shot stare bored into my skull. I nearly had to snap his wrist to break free and as I hurried back to the safety of my room, eyes wild, I thought I had arrived in the twilight zone.

WHYYYYYY?

The chaos actually started the day I left Nepal: there had been a bombing in the Kathmandu valley, so security was tight at the airport with police dogs sniffing the trunks of cars, and searching seat cushions for explosives. Although the check-in for the Indian Airlines flight to Varanasi was easy because the plane was virtually empty, six thorough body screenings and bag searches followed before we even boarded the Airbus 320.

After take off the cabin crew handed out customs forms. Ten minutes later the chief steward came through the cabin shaking his head and peeled off another form to replace the first, which his female colleagues had given out. Upon landing, the customs agents threw up their hands and issued us a third form to replace the second, which we filled out on the tarmac before being even let into the terminal. When we handed this form to their colleagues inside, they wordlessly handed us an even larger fourth form to replace them all.

Welcome to India.

After being spat out of the sweaty terminal, the first twenty kilometers of the taxi ride into Varanasi was smooth as we sped past rural Indian villages not unlike Vietnam or Kenya, and it seemed the stories of India were exaggerated.

But they proved true the instant we plunged into rush hour traffic in Varanasi. While by no means a Mumbai or Calcutta, the streets were crammed with pedestrians, trishaws, cows, beggars, policemen, holy men and street vendors all pushing and shoving their way down to the river, through a soup of charcoal smoke, petrol fumes, cow dung, spices, sweat, raw sewage and perfume. (I don't think that concoction will ever be released in perfume form, India No. 5)

The crush was so violent that the taxi driver refused to let me out to find my hotel on my own, and called his assistant on his cell phone to come and guide me down the narrow, twisting paths of Varanasi's old city that lead to the sacred waters of the Ganges. Cud chewing cows jammed intersections, flies buzzed in clouds so thick I mashed my lips together to avoid sucking one in, and I had to navigate around elderly holy men and women who staggered by, bent double with age, their hair matted into dreadlocks and with their entire worldly possessions carried in a single cotton sack.

My room was a converted shrine that had alcoves for votive candles and arched whitewashed doorways that overlooked the Ganges. Sravana, a religious holiday celebrated each August that honors the monsoon rains so essential to Indian farmers was underway, and almost everyone was wearing orange clothes, and men were running around in a religious frenzy with small plastic cups filled with water carried on shoulder poles decorated with cobras. Balanced at each end were two ceramic pots filled with water they had dipped from the Ganges. The air was full with the smell of incense smoke, monotonous chanting, crashing cymbals and celebratory roars from the crowds of devotees went on through the night until dawn.

Of course, worshiping Shiva and the monsoon isn't the only Hindu activity in Varanasi, also known as Benares, 'The City of Light.' For Hindus, to be cremated here is to ensure salvation, and it is the dream of millions to be burned here, though many can't afford it. Here in Varanasi the simple act of bathing in the river purifies the soul, and thousands come to the city to do just that.

At both ends of the city large cremation Ghats burned twenty-four hours a day, seven days a week, smoking the horizon by day and lighting up the sky at night. Cremating only Hindus at the south end, and all other religions at the north end, the Ghats are operated only by the Untouchables who form the lowest caste of Indian society. As you approach the Ghats the smell of burning hits you first, then the silence of your footfalls, because as you get closer, you are not walking on cement but on thickly compacted ash and wood shavings from the firewood. Almost every person you pass reminds you not to take pictures. 'No photo, no photo, sir,' they say over and over, and as you reach the lookout where no more than five meters away a dead body is being reduced to ash, they look into your eyes curiously and deeply to see what your reaction is going to be. No doubt they were used to tourists who were shocked by the spectacle.

'No photo,' they reminded me again before patting my shoulder and wandering off.

Workers constantly carry dead bodies down to the Ghats where the bodies were prepared for the final sacred funeral rites. Chopped firewood was quickly stacked, the fires were lit and flames quickly consumed the body, as onlookers, none of whom were even related to the deceased, looked on. The Untouchables had grown immensely wealthy off the business of death and the bosses supervising the operations had gold jewelry dripping off of every appendage. The surrounding neighborhoods near the burning Ghats had an otherworldly, alien feeling, completely disassociated even with India, in fact, I wandered round most of the time feeling off balance, unwell, and disoriented, as though I had fallen through a trapdoor.

THAT is what traveling in India is. Like falling through a trap door into another world.

At the burning Ghats you saw taxis pull up with bodies tied to the roof, and random men carried deceased people to be burned. I wandered for hours there, talking to people, watching them work, taking in a scene people in many countries would pay dearly to never, never, NEVER see.

Even Indians visiting the city for the first time were in shock at the scenes on display everywhere. 'This is shocking, truly shocking, man,' mumbled an IT professional as he videotaped the morning Puja where garbage and trash floated around people as they went about their sacred bathing ritual.

I spent a lot of time walking along the shore of the Ganges where stone steps leading to the river were exposed because of the low waters of the dry season. I watched people bathe, dogs fight, and street vendors sell their wares to people sunning themselves from sun up to sun down.

At one Ghat I lingered longer than normal, snapping pictures, and a crazy man came out of nowhere and vigorously shook my hand up and down and said coldly, 'Yes, shit. You take picture of shit. Shit river. Shit city. Come,' he said, trying to pull me away by the arm like that Agori, 'I take you to my shit shop.'

A lot of time in Varanasi was spent just dodging the predatory touts, who pecked you like vultures at a dead carcass. Wherever you went, no matter what you said or did, everyone had something to sell you, either reams of silk or a boat ride or a head massage or an internet connection, and despite your real name printed in your passport, forget it, because in India it will change to:

'Hello, Hashish.'
'Hello, Massage.'
'Hello, Marijuana.'

When a ten-year old kid asked me my name, I replied casually, 'Marijuana.'

And when he wrinkled his nose, no more than ten seconds passed than a bleary eyed tout wandered up and wheezed with a bone-weary head-shake-roll, 'Hello, Marijuana.'

The kid burst out laughing and whenever I pass by him or his friends they shout, 'Hello!! Marijuana!!! Hello!!' which earns me strange looks from the western tourists wandering past.

And each morning I rose before dawn and hired a boat to slip along the Ganges to watch the morning Puja ceremonies commence, where, all along the city's expansive waterfront facing the yellow rays of the rising sun, people of all ages and walks of life came to bathe, say prayers, wash clothes, fish, take a nap, consult with a holy man or just take in the scene. They never minded being watched, I sensed a feeling of pride from the people of all ages that went on doing what their ancestors had done for generations.

When I looked at a picture I had taken along the Ganges one morning, I gasped. Tucked into the top right hand corner was a sinister Saddhu, back straight, body ash grey, dreadlocks tied medusa-like around his head, staring down from the top of a Ghat, trident pointing at me.

He had been invisible when I had snapped the photo.

In the evenings, I would also hire a boat and in a complete reversal of the dawn ceremonies I watched people light small candles placed in flowers that were set afloat in tiny boats. As it grew dark, large clusters of these candles floated downstream on the Ganges like ever changing constellations, mirroring the real ones in the dark, vast sky above.

With so much drugs and enlightenment everywhere, Varanasi is bound to attract its fair share of crazies. And it has. All you have to do is walk down the Ghats and you will see them, Agoris smeared with human ash, comparing their dreadlocks with an equally bleary eyed Saddhu from Santa Cruz, groups of Japanese religious students, heads freshly shaved bathe in the Ganges urged on by a gnarled guru standing high and dry above them on the platform, and a white Saddhu well known in both Kathmandu and Varanasi wanders around carrying a tattered umbrella in all weather shouting in Swedish and saluting people as though in a military parade.

Whole clusters of others crash out for days on the Ghats sleeping off their latest hash binge ignored by all except for the numerous pigeons and stray dogs. The canines nor the birds could give a fuck about enlightenment; the birds snapped up stray crumbs left behind by pilgrims, and the dogs just curled up next to these convenient bodies for warmth to ward off the overnight chill.

Everything is a racket in India.

When I stepped off the boat from my last trip down the Ganges, one Saddhu, lucid now as he awakened from yet another drug fest, eyed me coolly as I paid the boatman and stepped onto dry land.

'How well do you know Mother Ganges, the river that is sacred to all Indians?' he asked in perfect English with all the crispness of a Shakespearean actor and the seriousness of a customs official.

'Oh, OK,' I answered lamely with a tired smile as I walked away, hoping to avoid yet another lecture followed by a blunt request for a donation.

Just when I thought I had escaped him, he swiveled his head around and thundered, 'HOW MUCH?!' smacking the concrete angrily with his hands for emphasis that sent molting pigeons and stray dogs scattering away from him in all directions.

NO MATTER WHAT YOUR PASSPORT SAYS, IN INDIA YOUR NAME WILL BECOME 'MARIJUANA'

Seventy-two hours after landing in India, I am still not over the fever or the ACME anvil of culture shock that struck me the moment I arrived.

And I am freaked by these Saddhus all round.
WHY do I look like someone who's soul needs saving?
Maybe in the next four months I will find out.
But there is something wonderful here.

The Gods talk to you in India, in fact, just like in Cambodia.

This afternoon a massive tornado wind blew through Varanasi as the monsoon tore through the city, skies turned charcoal black, and the rain washed off the dust and extinguished the heat. The colorful chalk drawings of the Universe some Saddhu had done beneath the window of my room was gone, but no sooner had the sun come out when he was back, effortlessly drawing the Universe once more.

In Africa dust coated you in a reddish film, but here it's the whiff of open sewers and incense smoke and sizzling chapatis and burning cow dung that wraps it's fingers around you and won't let go. I am glad I am not writing letters to you anymore or I would have massively cramped fingers if I was.

I'm leaving for the Taj Mahal tonight on my first overnight train in this country. I have already learned one tip - send someone from your hotel, who for about thirty rupees will buy your train ticket for you to avoid a sweaty, four hour wait.

All the faces of all those traveler who prophesied to me about India in Japan, Vietnam, Cambodia, and Africa are now floating in front of my face.

INDIA?
I'M HERE.

Love, Dave

From: Dave <theloweroad@gmail.com>
To: Annette <whereisannette@yahoo.com>
Date: Sep 09, 2004 11:20 AM
Subject: Guru Shmuru

Hey Annette,

I think my hotel here in Agra was formerly a prison.

It was not until two nights of hellish heat that I realized the roof was painted BLACK, making the room hot enough to broil a pot roast. When I staggered out at dawn, sweaty and delirious a few kilos had been sauna-d away.

Twilight zone indeed.

If there is a war between the traveler and the tourist then Agra, home of the Taj Mahal must be a key battlefield. There are not many places in the world where Jesus booted backpackers rub shoulders with khaki clad Sony camcorder gripping tourist herds in such concentrated numbers, but the Taj Mahal is certainly one of them. All day and everyday the beauty of India's most amazing monument plays second fiddle to the Indian tourists who gawk at the Western Haves and the Have Mores whose vastly differing styles of dress is puzzling to the extreme.

'You must have caste system in your country too,' wondered a young man who was visiting the Taj with his new wife.

'Is this what it means to be filthy rich?' asked another, who was proudly off to San Diego State for a degree, trying to make a joke out of the tie dyed shirts with cigarette burns and worn out flip flops whose owners probably carried American Express cards.

And all the while, the two opposing armies of westerners tried their best to ignore each other, one with their noses stuck into their Lonely Planets, the other straining to hear their guide's commentary blasted out of a megaphone.

'Oh my gawd therz a caow lickin' mah leyg!' shouted some woman who was beet red and frantically waving a fan to keep off the heat as her behemoth tour bus was being turned around for trip back to Delhi. A calf was in fact licking her leg and her husband was nowhere to be found to shoo it away.

'Do you take dollars?' shouted a man at the ticket booth. 'AMERICAN DOLLARS?' he thundered, waving the bills as though they would open any door in the world.

'Walter. Walter. I can't get the focus right on the camcorder. Walter....'

If you are deemed to be a 'half caste' i.e. someone who falls somewhere in between these two oil-and-water groups, then expect to get asked lots of questions by visitors milling around the Taj, and more importantly to those asking them, politely requested to pose in their holiday pictures. In less than three hours, I was snapped more than a dozen times, standing next to grandmothers and uncles and babies, winding up in family scrap books as far away as Bangalore and Chennai.

Others came from even further away, during the day I mingled with mustached, turbaned Rajastanis, fierce, bearded Sikhs, middle class Delhi families with wizened grandmothers in tow, fat businessmen from Kolkatta, Diesel clad teenagers from Mumbai, a troupe of Kathikali dancers from Kerala, and even a Bollywood model was there, pouting prettily while having her picture taken in a designer sari.

It was like a microcosm of the subcontinent.

The monsoon actually broke over the Taj Mahal today. The fierce morning heat scorched the white marble and the glare was so bright you could barely look at it; but once the thunder and lightning moved in, the cooling showers drenched the monument and turned the Taj almost translucent. The weather that day was also a strange metaphor for what is going on in India at that moment: a fierce drought was expected in Rajastan, while to the east, record monsoon flooding in Assam had killed hundreds and left millions homeless, all in the same week.

A little side note on Indian newspapers.

Each day the Times of India's front page has some tiny blurb, never more than 50 words, about either a suicide pact between two sisters because their parents couldn't afford their dowries, or a student who hanged himself because he was caught reading porn by his teacher, or a husband and wife who had drowned themselves to avoid being a burden on their kids. Whether an Indian print version of Ohrah Singh or Rajiv Springer, I don't know.

But it is the first thing I read each morning right along with my cup of sweet chai.

Which brings me to chai. Chai wallahs are some pretty cool dudes. Clogging train stations and carriages they taunt you to drink their tea served in earthenware cups which are just chucked out the window when you're through drinking. With train tracks popular outdoor toilets in India, a well aimed chai cup can go far in reducing the stress and that I-want-to-rip-that-fuckers-head-off feeling when yet another dolt screams at you in Hindi or acts like a fuckwit when you ask for directions. You might not hit the target every time but it does make for some cheap fun. (The train has pulled away fortunately before the hail of swear words is hurled in your direction anyway)

Unlike Varanasi where the attraction of the place is the worn edged down at heels feel the town exudes, Agra's charm ends at the front gates of the Taj Mahal - the city is polluted, concrete ugly, and the touts particularly vicious, claiming their meat the moment their prey step off the train until the moment they leave, earning commissions from restaurants, souvenir stalls, internet stations, and more.

Even worse are the auto rickshaw drivers, who were as deft at snatching up tourists as the flying monkeys were in The Wizard of Oz. No one stands a chance once they emerge from the safety of the Fort railway station, where they get leeched onto immediately.

And, of course, this being India your name abruptly changes too:

'Hello, Change Money.'
'Hello, Visa Cash Advance.'
'Hello, ATM, over here.'

Outwitting these vampires was all travelers talked about in Agra and actually it is easier than you think. Once they know you aren't interested in being dragged to their cousin's gem shop, or to buy some hideous marble model of the Taj, you get dropped like a millstone, and may experience what happened to me: when I made an appointment to view the Taj from across the river at six a.m., my driver simply disappeared, happier to sit at the train station at dawn, patiently waiting to vampire himself onto next wave of fresh arrivals.

Thanks dude, thanks very much. A well-aimed chai cup will be sent hurtling in your direction very soon. I guarantee it.

Thankfully, his colleagues were numerous and I was only slightly delayed for the sunrise. As I watched the Taj's domes turn pink and orange in the morning light, it was one of those skin tingling moments when yet another world wonder leaps from the pages of National Geographic and stands before you in 3-D.

That's the miracle of travel. Full stop. From 2-D to 3-D in 6.3 seconds.

A troupe of villagers was crossing the river, carrying brass pots filled with water on their heads. A few hundred meters away, a fight broke out between four dogs. They had found a windfall - an unidentified carcass had washed up on the opposite shore and for a moment I thought it was human, especially after coming from Varanasi, when one morning a human body did indeed float past my boat. I was relieved to see a pair of horns.

Further up the river I watched a grandmother supervise her grandchildren wash the family water buffaloes. When she saw me, she said something to her grandchildren, who stuck their hands out and shrilly screamed, 'Money!'

Though huge, like a lot of countries India is also one of those places where you travel and see the same faces in different places. Though I have only been here a week, many of the people staying in Varanasi had moved on to Agra. Five Spanish nuns who were taking a break from Mother Teresa's hospice in Calcutta. An American woman living in Rome who had just arrived in India to shoot her first silent feature film. Six Scottish students who were studying the Koran in Pakistan and were doing a comparative religions project in India. A British couple who were DJ's in Ibiza. A French woman who was traveling with her Indian boy toy, a sitar player at Baba's School of Music in Varanasi. And last, a Chinese guy from Shanghai who had bathed with the locals each morning in the Ganges and who spoke passable Hindi.

Oddly, the beauty of the Taj was never a topic of conversation, though the nauseating hierarchy persisted there. Those having spent less than three months in India were banished to the kiddie traveler table. And even after Japan, Korea, China, much of Europe, East Africa, Australia, and South America, all that mattered was India.

So you know where that left me.

Even at the kiddie traveler table, the treachery and deceit at the hands of the town's touts was all that was talked about. Well, that and what color your bowel movements were the previous evening. Seriously. In India, a kind of spell falls over you and no topic here is taboo, not even potty talk. So, in India you sit, swathed in a silky shawl of humidity and swatting at mosquitoes, discussing the inner, intimate workings of the lower intestine, your deeply profound experiences with antibiotics and marveling at the geniuses working for GlaxoSmithKline.

Sickness it was deemed, and seemed, somehow tightly linked to the suffering of travel. Especially in India. Rushing to the toilet every fifteen minutes brought you closer to god, to projectile vomit was to prove your loyalty to the tribe, and to have Malaria, well that was the Holy Grail. Many travelers seemed to reveal this malady as though they had earned a Purple Heart in battle, not while passed out trashed on a beach on Zanzibar, too wasted to apply mosquito repellant.

Eventually there was no more wind left in the talk of illness and crap, and I did something very brave. I stood up and sat down at the grownups table. Just like that. When a stringy haired Kiwi girl swiveled her head round and asked me how long I had been in India, my brazen smile and complete ignorance of the English language earned me a place at the table.

I'm sorry, I don't speak New Zealand.

Here, the conversation turned to the other topic in India - spiritualism. It's what kept most of these at the adult traveler table talking to each other, despite such diverse backgrounds, cultures, and their haughty love of travel. All, it seemed, had come to India to soak up the religious vibes that India was famous for. The question was then posed around the table, what sect do you follow, who is your spiritual advisor, in short, 'Who is your guru?'

The talking went on for endless hours, trashing Catholicism, reworking Judaism, rewriting Buddhism to include Christian elements, reviving Pagan rituals merged with crystal therapy. It went on and on and on. Each person, it seemed, had smugly found their spiritual drug of choice, in the form of ashrams, gurus and spiritual leaders, which in most cases were the sole reason these people had come to India in the first place.

The American lady swore by her ashram, she'd been there as a child, dragged halfway around the world by her mother who had ended up meeting her second husband in the ashram south of Goa. The Chinese guy wanted to start his own, and the British couple started talking enthusiastically about their ashram that was somewhere west of Chennai.

'Do you want my guru's email address? I have it if you want it.'

'My parents think I'm crazy, but my ashram never asks for money, just donations.'

'Just because these places make you take an AIDS test doesn't mean people sleep around there, we meditate most of the day anyway.'

'My ashrams just got a new flash website, you can find it through Google.'

Only the Scottish Six were unconvinced and argued fiercely against these places claiming them to be shams, scams, and actually worked to remove people from the country they had come to visit. They went on bragging how they were in India with 'real' intentions, eating with the people, living with the people, and learning the language. Nothing they said or did ever compromised these principles, and one intended to spend at least two more years in Pakistan at the University in Karachi, despite the recent violent attacks on westerners there. To further prove this point, they pointed to their clothes and shoes, all made by Pakistani tailors and craftsmen.

The next morning the Scottish Six had moved on, and the hotel manager came in at breakfast laughing. 'Hey, your friends left behind some interesting stuff in their rooms. Five boxes from Pizza Hut!'

Next I'm moving westward to Rajastan as temperatures continue to rise. It was 42 degrees today here, meaning my room tonight will probably be about 60.

Ding. The turkey is done.

Love, Dave

From: Dave <theloweroad@gmail.com>
To: Annette <whereisannette@yahoo.com>
Date: Sep 21, 2004 11:20 AM
Subject: The Great Railway Bizarre

Hi Annette...

A STERN word of warning if you decide to travel by train in India because -

Even if station agents point to a train to confirm the train is going to Jaipur,
Even if the train is leaving from the platform the sign says is going to Jaipur,
Even if two conductors wearing identical upside down Ganesh nametags tell you the train is going to Jaipur,
Even if two passengers nod their heads and confirm the train is going to Jaipur,
Even if the only empty seat in the coach matches the seat number on your ticket to Jaipur,
Even if the train leaves at the exact time that is printed on your ticket to Jaipur.

DON'T EVEN THINK OF GETTING ON THAT TRAIN.

Reporting from somewhere in Uttar Pradesh...

The morning started with a very Africa-like five a.m. trudge through the cold murky morning air to find a rickshaw in Agra to catch the six a.m. train to Jaipur. When I found a driver, I told him to go to Agra Fort train station.

'Yes sir, yes sir,' he answered and we drove off lurching and jumping over potholes, swerving around cows and ambling pedestrians. Twenty minutes later he pulled up at the Agra Cantonment train station, and the day's first misunderstanding unfolded.

'Your mistake sir,' the driver said merrily, his head rolling in that half-nod, half-shake that meant everything and absolutely nothing in India.

'Look, just go to Agra Fort station, I have ten minutes to catch my train.' I got the head shake-roll again, and we lurched off, weaving through herds of cows, swarming pedestrians and dozens of cycle rickshaws ringing their bells, back over the bridge, where, off in the distance, the Taj Mahal sat glowing in the light from the rising sun.

Pulling up at the Agra Fort station I had exactly two minutes to catch my train. By the time I had even reached the railway cars, sitting on the platform marked in the lobby as the one going to Jaipur, I had asked four people about the train, including two different conductors wearing identical 'Ganesh' nametags, which were hung upside down.

'Yes sir,' they said, pointing at the train and smiling as their head shake rolled. Reassured, I boarded the car, and found just one seat empty: number six, the same as the one printed on my ticket. I confirmed the destination again with two men sitting opposite me.

'Jaipur?'

'Yes sir.'

The train pulled away almost immediately. But ominously, we were heading east, over the bridge, instead of west. As I sat there puzzled, I saw the Taj Mahal for the second time that morning.

About an hour later, after watching groups of peacocks foraging for food intermingled with views of naked butts of villagers who had dropped their pants to shit on the tracks, the conductor came through and when he saw my ticket, he started to laugh, then guffaw. 'You, sir, are on the wrong train.'

'Where are we going?' I asked, looking out the window, the ominous wrong way trundle over the bridge finally sinking in.

'Calcutta.'

I smiled ruefully at the two good Samaritans that had confirmed the train was going to Jaipur. Luckily for their necks, they were now fast asleep, snoring, heads clunked together like Tweedle Dee and Tweedle Dumb after a suicide pact. I wanted to strangle them, but the conductor interrupted me, giving me no time to kill them.

'That,' the conductor shouted, pointing at a train hurtling past, 'is your train to Jaipur.'

'But...'

'This train is coming from Jaipur and we are due to arrive at Calcutta Central Station at 11 p.m. Wednesday.' That was sixteen hours away. Luckily, that meant it wasn't a Super Express and at the next station, I was unceremoniously dumped off and told to catch the next train back to Agra.

The name of that station? Tundla. Not on any map, nor in any guidebook, it seemed quite simply that I had fallen right off the map. When a few minutes had passed, I had begun breathing again from the fecal stench wafting up from the tracks, and shaken off that what-the-hell-do-I-do-now anger, I found the station's ticket window. It was locked shut.

'A tea-break will occur at 6.45 to precisely 7.00 each morning' read the sign over the window, and encircling that were hand painted signs written only in Hindi. It was 7.30 and there was no sign of any movement.

'Will there be a train to Agra soon?' I asked the only official standing around.

'Yes sir,' he answered, spiced with that head roll-shake. When I asked him what time, he just smiled and his English trailed off.

A predatory crowd of taxi drivers had now gathered around me, unused to the sight of a sweating foreigner chucked off the train in the middle of nowhere. It wasn't even eight o'clock in the morning, and it seemed the free entertainment had arrived. (That would be me)

'How much to Agra?' I asked around desperately, hoping to at least have the chance to catch the train I saw fly past, in case it was delayed in Agra.

'Six hundred rupees.'

'I'll give you two hundred.'

I got the head shake-roll again and after throwing my

bag in the back seat of the Ambassador car we were off. The ubiquitous white taxi driven all over India was now flying past villages and towns that had each been hijacked by advertisers that had painted every available wall with lurid advertisements. It alternated between three: a village plastered with ads for women's bras, the next for men's underwear, and the last, a village taken over for ads for Kama Sutra condoms.

At least someone had their priorities in order. (That or the Birth Control Agency was hell bent to prevent unwanted pregnancies caused by racy underwear adverts)

Forty-five minutes later we pulled over the bridge in Agra and I saw the Taj Mahal for the third time that day. Back at the Agra Fort station, trying to make sense of the next departure to Jaipur, bumping through munching cows and people staggering under loads of luggage, a new trishaw driver approached me and said it was better to catch the bus to Jaipur.

'There's a better way to get to Jaipur?'

'Yes sir. Air-conditioned, luxury bus, leave every hour. Get to Jaipur by five o'clock.'

Realizing this would put me into Jaipur at the same time as my first train, I happily obliged, turning my back on the sweaty, smelly station and we ploughed through the touts outside, the ambling cows, and the crowds, hopped into his rickshaw to the bus station. Once there, it turned out the air-conditioned buses only left at night and the only ones left were rust buckets with half flat tires.

'Go back to Agra Fort train station,' I said through clenched teeth for the third time that morning and all I got in response was the head-shake roll again. I wanted to rip his head off and drop kick it into the Ganges at this point, but in the spirit of non-violence, I sat back and took a deep Ghandi breath instead.

So off we went back to the Agra Fort train station where I unloaded my bag and ploughed back through the crowds, the cows, the touts, and the shouting taxi drivers and found a place in the line for today's tickets.

'You sir, you just missed the most recent train to Jaipur, it left five minutes ago.'

The man was luckily protected by iron bars so I couldn't punch him. So I smiled, asked him when the next train was (three hours!) bought a ticket, found a bench, and stayed there until the train arrived. During my wait, three shoeshine kids felt sorry for me, and after I pantomimed in hand gestures the back and forth I had been through since five o'clock that morning, to make me feel better, they broke out into a dance routine they had seen in Namaan, the latest Bollywood blockbuster taking the country by storm. It told the story of an army man haunted by his evil twin brother, the movie had actually been filmed in Switzerland to resemble the Himalayas.

Also hanging around were two of the Agra train station crazies.

'Hello, model man,' wheezed one of the more insane ones.

A husband and wife team selling newspapers with their two year old daughter introduced me to a couple of chai vendors who gave me free cups of tea served with their deepest sympathy. We laughed at the stilted Hindi phrases in my guidebook, I was shown how to bow correctly to the pictures of the garish gods plastered on their magazine cart and I was taught a few choice Hindi swear words that I had regretfully learned too late. They would have definitely come in handy a few hours earlier.

They also had a copy of the Times of India, where true to form on the front page was the latest tragedy. An elderly woman had killed herself in fear of being sent away by her daughter-in-law, but the daughter-in-law, distraught at her husband's belief she had caused her mother-in-law to kill herself, had killed herself as well. The son killed himself soon after.

When I finally boarded my train (which left on time) from the right platform my motley entourage waved goodbye to me from their part of the platform. As we pulled away from the station and trundled over the creaky bridge yet again, I saw the Taj Mahal for the fourth and final time that day.

ALWAYS BE SUSPICIOUS OF ANYONE WEARING AN UPSIDE DOWN 'GANESH' NAME TAG.

More news from the rest of Rajastan. I am in Jaipur now but it feels like Delhi, concrete, polluted and ugly.

Love, Dave

From: Dave <theloweroad@gmail.com>
To: Annette <whereisannette@yahoo.com>
Date: Sep 30, 2004 11:20 AM
Subject: Pamplona, Rajastan

Hey Annette,

No, I am not in Spain.
With so many cows in this country I was bound to have a 'run-in' with some of them eventually, and here in Jodhpur, I did.
Olé.
More on that later.

I am typing to you from the world's filthiest keyboard. A dusty fan is sweeping the room. Two men simultaneously hacked up a lung and spat them out on the floor. Where they are now twitching. Who's going to hack up the other?
And we have a winner.
The man on my left.
I am keeping my long legs carefully tucked under my chair expecting to get electrocuted at any moment. There are tangled wires under the desk, I saw a spark already, I can smell smoke and I really don't want to be electrocuted in India.
I am also crammed in between two 'Xin Chao Fuckers' if you can remember the idiots in Saigon that taunted me when I rode the Flying Dragon. While I have the innocuous Gmail loaded on my screen for the teenagers on either side it's hardcore porn. Animated. Oh, and there's music, too. Not cheesy porn music, but a shimmying Bollywood soundtrack that is giving me a massive headache.
If I so much as see a hand go down beneath the keyboard I am OUTTA HERE.
Well. Being penned in by porn has its advantages with the 'horny' story I am about to tell you it does seem rather

appropriate.

But before I get to it, another lesson:

DON'T EVER WEAR BLACK IN INDIA.

Walled, medieval, and awash in blue paint, Jodhpur resembles a town in Mykonos lost in a sea of golden sand. In it's meandering, cramped passageways you come across turquoise veiled women leading their kohl-eyed children to the local school, wrinkled Saddhus with tridents sitting under Banyan trees muttering prayers, packs of dogs dozing in the shade and massive cows freely wandering about accepting 'donations' from passer-bys who offer them any leftover food they may have. The occasional roaring of motorbikes tearing through the alleys is about the only indication of the time or date and you feel like many centuries have vanished.

And perched high above the town encircling a sheer cliff is the Fort, one in a string of defenses that were built in Rajastan by the Maharajas to protect themselves from attack. Handprints located at the spiked gates were made by all their wives who committed suicide when their husbands died in battle, and whole rooms are filled with shotguns, swords and daggers.

The whole state of Rajastan is rich in feudal history, some bloody, some amazing, and many of the towns there resemble something you've read about in Arabian Nights. I passed quickly through Jaipur, which was a traffic-clogged mess, but it is here along the border with Pakistan that the romantic image of India comes to life.

Just as I was thinking what a relief the town was so far to anywhere I had been in India, and that the place resembled the safety and security of a clockwork Swiss village, I heard a strange rumbling and thumping approaching from up ahead of me in the alley.

Suddenly four men appeared, all wearing Metallica and Marilyn Manson T-shirts, running as fast as they could towards me, shouting and yelling blue murder. One of the pointed at me and screamed out in a British accent, 'Run man, run! You with the black shirt, run!!!!'

And right behind them were four huge, irate bulls, running fast, heads bowed and sharp horns angled forward ready to gore. Looking down at my shirt I remembered the Swiss man who I had seen get his chest viciously butted by a massive steer in Varanasi because he was wearing a black T-shirt.

SHIT.

The alley was too narrow to avoid the enraged bulls. There were neither doorways to hide in nor any safe alleys to duck down into. It was run or get trampled by the three hundred kilo beasts. Shoving my camera into my bag I turned and ran as fast as I could, joining the four who were now nearly out of breath, and suddenly the five of us, all dressed in black, eyes widened in acute fear were running down the twisting blue painted alleys of Jodhpur, chased by some of the meanest, angriest bulls I had ever seen, in some sort of twisted Indian version of Pamplona.

How does one say olé in Hindi?

I think it goes something like 'FUUUUUUUCCCCKKKK!'

We ran as fast as we could for about four hundred meters: dogs howled, children screamed and traffic stropped as we flew down the alley, desperate for somewhere to hide. Fortunately the alley widened, then split, and we were able to lose the behemoths by ducking into the courtyard of a large house that doubled as a restaurant. Panting, and wide eyed with terror, we watched with relief as the bulls thundered past, no doubt searching for other prey dressed in black.

'This place is mad!' said one of the four. (Taking the words right out of Jackie's mouth)

'Bloody hell, ripped my jeans,' said one of the others.

They turned out to be cousins from the UK visiting family in Delhi, and had decided to come to Rajastan without them to escape the suffocating rules and regulations put upon them by these distant relatives. Between us there were two scraped knees, a gashed elbow and a partially twisted ankle. As we laughed off the experience, an old man shook his fist at us.

'You should never wear black in India!' he yelled before slamming his window shut.

What I want to know now, is that if getting Malaria is the Purple Heart for travelers, what is getting chased by bulls? A Medal of Honor?

Hey, this morning's Times of India had a story about some dolt brothers in Bihar who aren't speaking to each other because they are competing for the same bride, and their parents have yet to decide which bachelor will get the girl.

Drama in the countryside of Bihar. Gotta love it.

After this introduction to Rajastan camel trekking was next on my list and I caught a night train last night to Jaislmer to start one. (That's where I am now, surrounded by medieval walls but hemmed in by porn. I KNEW India was the land of contrasts but this is a bit much)

In my compartment traveled a French photographer with his taciturn niece. He happily flipped open his Apple PowerBook to show me his latest work, an exhibition on Varanasi's burning Ghats featuring revealing and sometimes gruesome scenes of people's last moments before their bodies were reduced to ash.

As we watched the slide show a rich Indian man sleeping in the next row sat up, furiously shoved on his shoes and pointed at the Frenchman, 'I am disturbed!'

'Yes, you seem to be,' said the photographer coolly a moment later with a laugh, looking him up and down, smirking at his enraged expression.

'I am BEING disturbed!!!' shouted the rich man, his gold chains jangling around his neck like a fat Neil Diamond. He lunged towards the photographer, and poked him in the chest. 'Turn off your machine! I sleep now!'

'No, we are watching theez show. You can go to sleep over zhere, without being, how you say, DISTURBED,' the Frenchman shouted back, waving the man off with a Parisian flick of his arms.

This set off the rich man like an open flame to a stick of dynamite. He pushed closed the Apple laptop, dragged the Frenchman up to his feet and began wagging his finger up at him, screaming in Hindi, while the Frenchman unleashed an irate string of swearwords, brandishing his laptop like a shield. A pitched battle ensued, and just as I began imagining filling out a police report detailing how an Apple PowerBook was used as a murder weapon, along waddled in the conductor.

He pushed the men apart, snatched their tickets, scrawled new berth numbers on them and banished the two men to opposite ends of the train carriage. Then he killed the lights and slammed the door shut, sending everyone to sleep.

APPLE POWERBOOKS CAN BE USED AS MURDER WEAPONS.

Where's an efficient train conductor when you need them?
He could sever the internet connection to these Xin Chao Fuckers and end the Bollywood meets Playboy mansion feel in this internet café. (The moans of ecstasy are not from customers getting a free chai with every hour of internet, I can tell you.)

I'm soooooo outta here.

Love, Dave

From: Dave <theloweroad@gmail.com>
To: Annette <whereisannette@yahoo.com>
Date: Oct 07, 2004 11:20 AM
Subject: Cow Crap Sandwiches

!!!

AFTER READING THE FOLLOWING STORY YOU WILL NEVER EAT ANOTHER SANDWICH FOR THE REST OF YOUR WHOLE LIFE WITHOUT CHECKING WHAT'S INSIDE FIRST.

I never expected that what's attached to the FRONT of a cow (HORNS) was going to come flying at me like in Jodhpur, but for two travelers I met, what comes out the other END?

SHIT?

First of all, I swear it didn't happen me.

Scouts Honor.

I heard this from a very trusted source. (Please, we snorted sand for two days, pointed out scorpions to each other, treated each other for heatstroke, total foxhole buddy stuff, so believe me, it's a trusted source)

Confused? You should be.

Go on.

Read it.

After absorbing this latest story you will be checking EVERY sandwich you will ever eat for the rest of your life. Paging members of the Travelers Tribe: a brand new urban legend has been born.

Cigars all round, not pink nor blue, just BROWN.

In Jaislmer I left with a couple of Austrians on a pre-dawn jeep ride to Philoda, a village forty five kilometers away where I was matched up with a petulant, moody camel named Raj. I was later to find out Raj was horny as well. He tried to buck me off immediately after I sat on him.

'Oh, he don't like smell, you know, soap,' explained the guide. 'No worry, it will be windy soon.'

We then took off, traipsing across sand dunes, walking across rubbly cliffs, visiting remote water wells where women carried earthen pots on their heads back to their villages, farmers came to chat and exchange gossip dressed in brilliantly white turbans and faces decorated with handlebar moustaches. The mood was somber though, there was a drought on, the monsoons had failed, and widespread suffering was imminent.

No one smiled.

To avoid heatstroke, we rested through the middle part of the day at a dry creek bed where we watched peacocks forage for lunch and saw hawks circle far above us in the white-hot sky. The silence out there was straight out of outback Australia, or the highlands of Ethiopia.

The silence that screams.

At three o'clock we took off for our overnight camp spot, but it was still too hot, within thirty minutes the horizon melted, the camel beneath me transformed into a dragon, and I was frantically gripping the creature's neck to prevent my body from falling off.

For an interminable amount of time (in these situations, it feels like forever) I was positive I was going to do a header over Raj, land headfirst in a sand dune and be laughed at by the smug camel trek organizers, two farmers who must have gotten sick of planting crops and decided to win big by escorting European women out into the desert.

In various countries, winning the lottery means different things...

I looked down at my arm. I was sweating so heavily there was salt on it. I had already drank three liters but it was not enough, and by the time I went to sleep, I had swallowed five.

At sunset we arrived at our campsite (I use this term VERY loosely) on some sand dunes that stretched to the Pakistani border. When we unrolled our blankets, incredulous that the promised facilities were, well, just sand, the guide started to make strange finger motions with his finger.

'Finger puppets?' asked the unsmiling Austrian with a heavy Schwarzenegger accent.

'I think he means scorpions,' I translated.

'Yes. Scorpions. Cobras. Snakes, spiders.' The guide smiled, and happily stowed away his finger.

'What?!!' cried his girlfriend, a Swiss Miss look alike with shoulder length blonde pigtails.

'Scorpions. Cobras. Snakes, spiders,' he repeated, making that finger gesture again.

Schwarzenegger and Swiss Miss traded pained looks and began rapid-fire exchanges in German that flew right over the guide's head like a hail of bullets.

'Lets go up on top of the dunes,' I ventured, hoping that it might be a less risky spot to sleep. So the three of us dragged our stuff to the top of the hill and made a makeshift Bedouin tent up there. Even without proper blankets, firewood, a roof, or anything, it was still the perfect place for watching the Milky Way spin and shooting stars streak across the sky later that night.

Until about three a.m. I woke up, freezing cold, lying on my mattress (cold sand) and sneezing sand as well.

There was dead silence. Except for some weird thumping. Groans. More thumping. Louder groans. Swiss Miss sat up, her pigtails sticking out sideways Pippi Longstocking-like in the darkness. Schwarzenegger sat up too, and the pair rattled off more light speed German.

'Don't worry,' came the guide's voice out of the darkness. 'It is only Raj, he likes to find new girlfriend. He will be quiet soon.'

Schwarzenegger and Swiss Miss were unconvinced, and continued sitting up, listening as the two camels bumped pelvises down below us. At least their frantic, heavy humping would scare away the cobras, spiders, snakes and scorpions that might be lurking there.

When Raj's sex show was over, that's when the wind started blowing. I mean hard. My eyes were squeezed shut and sand STILL got in, the blankets became useless and it was totally freezing. Dawn seemed like a century away and all we could do was try to shield ourselves from the wind; when

I woke up the next morning the camel trek employees asked ruefully, 'Did you sleep well?'

The guides began cooking breakfast with eggs that had been left out in the sun in a box, baking in the forty-five degree heat for almost a day. Were they forgetful, or were they deliberately trying to poison us?

Swiss Miss and Schwarzenegger exchanged some machine gun German again and by the time the food was ready we had our story perfectly rehearsed.

'Sorry, in our country, we don't eat eggs,' said Schwarzenegger.

Swiss Miss nodded her head sagely. 'No eggs.'

The man looked at them strangely. 'Australia people eat eggs. I know.'

'AUSTRIA! We are not from Australia. Austria,' growled Schwarzenegger.

Swiss Miss threw back her pigtails and added, 'Yes, Austria, no eggs.' She made the sign of the cross for emphasis.

The guide turned to me with a disappointed look on his face, eager for me to eat. I smiled and said, 'My country, too, no eggs, too. Our religion.'

He shrugged and muttered some Hindi under his breath. It turned out the guide didn't eat eggs either, and he gave up and tossed them to the camels. Even they wouldn't touch them.

Maybe it was against their religion, too.

And now for the urban legend part.

Drum roll please.

I ran into the Austrian couple two days after the camel trek. (I was still sneezing sand. 'He sneezed sand.' It might just go on my tombstone) They told me they had ordered a hot vegetarian sandwich and though it was delivered to their table toasted, it was beyond stone cold.

So the Austrians asked the waiters to take away the vegetarian sandwich they had ordered and heat it up. The waiters smiled and took it away and returned fifteen minutes later with it, grinning, dropping off the now re-grilled sandwich.

The Austrians dug in and the waiters retreated to the

safety of the kitchen, giggling. When the unusual taste and heavy weight of the returned sandwiches made Swiss Miss suspicious she peeled back the top piece of bread and found to her horror, pulverized cow crap had been mixed in with the tomatoes and onions.

Vegetarian indeed.

After hearing this story, I frantically flipped back through my meal memory and realized I had thankfully NOT eaten a single sandwich, vegetarian or otherwise in India, and had, more importantly, NOT pissed off any waiters in the subcontinent enough for them to fuck with my food.

Or so I hoped. Gulp.

Might I too have been served the tasty excrement of India's most sacred animal as payback from some disgruntled waiter?

Only the Travel Gods know for sure.

Onwards with my trip through Rajastan.

The temperature got hotter as I moved around the state and by the time I left Jaislmer it was forty-eight degrees Celsius in the shade.

My bus to Bikaner (where I am now) was scheduled to leave at four p.m., but a breathless man came running to my room and pounded on my door, the bus was now leaving at two thirty. It was just past two twenty.

'How far away is the station?' I asked calmly, as though I had been expecting it.

'Twenty minutes.'

The familiar head-shake roll reared it's head again and I threw everything into my bag and hopped into the back of the jeep that idled outside. By the time I got there the bus was pulling away and the jeep lurched up next to it and the driver hung out and slapped the side. The bus driver stopped, I hopped out and ran around to the door.

Suddenly Annie Lennox popped her head out of the window and screamed in a Swedish accent, 'Don't pay for the bags! Whatever you do, don't pay for the bags!!!'

Annie withdrew her head and I was now standing in front of two touts, no doubt recent graduates of the world famous Taj Mahal Tout University.

One wonders about their coursework.

Beat Them Down 101?

Rip Off Tactics 101?

How to Drive Your Taxi to Increase The Fare 101?

Wander the halls of this great learning institution, and you'll overhear their lecturers scream, 'You WILL not take no for an answer. NEVER!'

With their turbaned heads and gold rings hanging from their earlobes the pair looked like extras from the Pirates of the Caribbean film set. They held the key to the baggage compartment and shooed Annie's comments away with their hands, like flies, hoping for some fat baksheesh. I threw my bag in and refused to pay them any money, and asked for a receipt. They laughed ruefully, tobacco stained teeth exposed, and before spitting out a torrent of betel nut juice, said, 'No guarantee sir! No guarantee!!'

I jumped on the bus grateful for the fact that there was a bus and not a dust cloud as it tore off towards Bikaner without me. I found my seat but it was the assigned place printed on the ticket for the four p.m. bus, not the two thirty bus. It turned out Annie Lennox, her sister, two Dutch travelers and a lone Turk were also supposed to be on the four p.m. bus as well, and re-organizing the confusing array of seat numbers proved to be the challenge of the ticket collector's career.

First, he took our white tickets away and handed us a blue one with the same seat number written on it. But then chaos reigned as passengers for the two thirty bus continued getting on. So he reissued us all with red tickets for the few empty seats remaining on the bus, sweating profusely as he furiously scribbled new tickets, confiscated the old ones, and motioned to us with his fat hairy arms.

When even more people boarded, he threw up his hands, muttered something hateful in hideous Hindi, kicked out the two stragglers sleeping on the bus' last row and ordered all the foreigners to the back.

So off the six of us went, filling the back row like some comic dreadlocks-blonde-redhead police line-up, this time without tickets at all, where the ticket collector could keep an eye on us. All except for a petite Korean girl who sat near the front, who the conductor had overlooked, she sat still and catlike, looking back at us, wild eyed with terror, as though she were in some Iraqi hostage crisis.

Within five seconds the conversation turned towards what it always did in India, the can-you-believe-this-is-happening-to-us-in-India thread that by now I was getting really tired of.

But the mood quickly changed when a ticket blew out of a woman's hand and the ticket collector bent over to pick it up revealing a butt crack as wide as the subcontinent. This brought the house down, the Police Line Up roared with laughter right along with the last four rows of the bus who had seen the man's hairy ass up close and personal.

With that, the mood swung towards camaraderie and friendliness all the way to Bikaner. Babies were happily loaned to sit on our laps, the Turk's dreadlocks were admired by all, and Annie Lennox's blonde hair was the subject of intense scrutiny by some grandmothers with gnarled hands who tugged at it to see if it was real.

This town is as concrete ugly as Agra, but there's no Taj Mahal here. For humans at least, no. But for rats, yes. Tomorrow I'm off to Karni Mata, the temple you may have heard about where rats are worshipped.

Only in India.

Before I get to the rats, remember:

SANDWICHES SHOULD NEVER TASTE LIKE COW CRAP.

Love, Dave

From: Dave <theloweroad@gmail.com>
To: Annette <whereisannette@yahoo.com>
Date: Oct 17, 2004 11:20 AM
Subject: Rats Gone Wild

Hey Annette,

I have now seen everything.

After seventy countries I can wrap up this road show, stop the wandering, cut up my frequent flyer cards and go home. Give it all up, tear up my passport and put myself on a 'no fly' list.

I never would have thought that a rodent reviled by millions could be God. But this is India after all.

After seeing Karni Mata I can understand people's puzzlement at the tear filled reverence expressed at Graceland, or the irrationally ecstatic behavior displayed on Abbey Road. I mean, I was born in the Year of the Rat, but even I was creeped by the spectacle of overfed rodents lying around like stoned hippies at Glastonbury...

A half an hour outside of Bikaner sits the Karni Mata temple, a rodent's Nirvana, Mecca, and Heaven all rolled into one - if you're a rat, and you've won the lottery, or your furry arm has pulled down the lever to win millions in Las Vegas, this is Beverly Hills, too. While most rats around the world are battled with poison, traps, and cats, these rodents are sacred, so special in fact that eating or drinking any food or water chewed or slurped by their teeth and tongues is deemed to give luck and good health.

As soon as you enter the inner sanctuary of the temple your shoes need to be removed and your bare feet slide across the marble floor where fifteen thousand scurrying rodents, their mangy tails dragging behind them, run between your feet, to and fro this way and that leaping in glee as yet another bowl of milk is placed before them.

In short, a holiday resort/luxury spa for rats.

Karni Mata is decked out like a Four Seasons Hotel to pamper and feed these animals, thought to be descendants of a goddess. Believe me, some of the spiritual travelers you meet in India who brag about traveling third class for 45 hours and sharing dorm rooms with 20 other travelers, live worse than these lucky rats. Large aluminum tubs filled with saffron rice and meat are placed along the walls where rows of rodents cling to the edges, their tongues furiously lapping up the free food and drink. And if you look closely into their beady eyes, I think even the rats there just can't quite believe their fortune. I'm sure even deep in the sewers beneath New York, City Karni Mata is spoken about in whispers, with deep, deep reverence.

Even shorter, Rats Gone Wild.

Small holes in the temple's walls lead to warrens of dens and burrows, and fierce fights break out all the time as the rats wake up and come out to feed. Most of them are so full of food they lay around unconscious. Women stoop to kiss the floor where the rats are sleeping, motioning for their children to do the same.

I hadn't been at Karni Mata for more than five minutes, taking in all these animals when I nearly dropped my camera as a violent, involuntary shudder pulsed through me.

It was, quite simply, a massive, unstoppable attack of the willies.

'What happens to the dead rats?' I asked a man shakily a few minutes after I had recovered a bit of my composure. He was there with his wife and two daughters. 'You know, the ones that get old and die?' I imagined some miniature burning Ghats hidden somewhere behind the temple, like in the Frenchman's photos from Varanasi, solely reserved for rats with tiny funeral pyres and midget garlands draped across their furry bodies before they were cremated. Maybe there were Saddhus that rolled in the rat's ashes too, like the Agoris that rolled in human ashes for enlightenment?

'Die?' the man asked with his eyes widened. 'Oh no sir, these rats don't die, when they get old, they disappear in a puff of smoke, and are taken straight to heaven.'

The fact that I had seen several dead rats lying in a corner didn't seem to bother him.

'They are sleeping,' he answered coolly, the subject closed, 'after enjoying too much rich food.'

All around us squirmed, squeaked and scurried rats that happily ran off to eat food from a tray that had just been put down for them.

'These rats are very special, very special indeed,' the man went on. 'Can you feel the power?' he slurred, his mouth now full of betel nut as we watched his wife bend over to pet one, revealing generous folds of fat that oozed out of her silvery sari.

I nodded my head weakly. No I can't, my brain screamed as I resisted an urge to yell out: a rat had just run over my foot and I froze to the spot like I had been Tazered.

'You are blessed, my good man!' he said, slapping my back as I stood as still as a block of cold marble. 'You will be rich!' he roared.

Today is my last day in Rajastan.

I went to a museum housed in the Maharaja's palace here in Bikaner that was crammed with the elegant relics from the Maharaja's life, photos of him posed next to his white Cadillac in 1960, having dinner with Jackie Kennedy in Udiapur, and lots of photos posing next to dead elephants, tigers and rhinos he had killed in the jungle, wearing silly Panama hats and white tropical suits posing oh-so-colonially next to half naked natives.

As I walked around looking at photos and cabinets filled with vintage motorcycle goggles, cameras, spectacles and business cards printed with 'The Maharaja of Bikaner, and Member of Parliament,' I got chills up my spine and felt like someone was watching me. I looked behind me, but there was no one there.

Then, as I entered Room Number 13, and as my size 13 footfalls echoed off the walls, I saw three carved chairs facing the impressive throne of the now deceased Maharaja. Huge portraits of the dead man looked down at me from three putty colored walls, the fourth wall being a row of windows.

The temperature outside was about 45 degrees, but there in room Number 13, it felt like a freezer. The hairs on my neck stood on end again and suddenly one of the windows slammed shut.

Only, there was no wind at all.

It was time to go.

As I leave Karni Mata, remember:

IF A RAT RUNS OVER YOUR FOOT, RELAX. YOU'LL GROW RICH.

Tonight I am off on a train to Amritsar, in the Punjab, via Delhi. Unfortunately there is no direct train or bus there, though thankfully I will only be in Delhi station for two hours.

My hotel here is owned by the private secretary to the Maharaja, a home/hotel filled with dusty volumes on 'Hunting in India' and 'Hindoo Holidays' and such. While the chai wallahs and taxi drivers wail on outside the window, India is very far away inside the house.

The sitting room, hallways and guest rooms are decorated in a style not unfamiliar to a Surrey country estate, and the distasteful looks I got when the owners saw my backpack was hilarious, even the cook turned up her nose.

I know I won't be ordering a vegetarian sandwich here or anywhere in India, and maybe anywhere else in the world. Ha ha.

Love, Dave

Hey Annette,

I'm finally starting to get high.

I am climbing up into the Himalayas and I have a view of the vast steamy plains below from my room that I am lucky to have at all here in Dharmsala, because the Dalai Lama is giving one of his Teachings. The town is like a spiritual freak convention, but more on that later.

After Varanasi, Agra, Jaipur, Jodhpur, Jaislmer, Bikaner and Amritsar, it feels as though I have been to five different countries, not one. Every time I step down from another overnight bus or train I feel like I've had my passport stamped. But I haven't. That's just the reality of India.

First, the Punjab.

The Golden Temple that is the cornerstone of the Sikh faith in Amritsar resembles the Kabbah in Mecca, the Golden shrine in Kyoto, and the Taj Mahal in Agra - a blinding white marble square inlaid with black stones surrounds a shallow green lake in the middle of which sits a central shrine covered in over one hundred kilograms of pure gold. It glitters fiercely as people come to walk around it, clockwise to worship.

Nearly destroyed in the siege of the temple complex in the early 1980's, the damage has been repaired, but since then Sikh pride has only been strengthened. Blending Hinduism and Islamic elements, the religion is open to all, it preaches equality between men and women, and unlike stratified, segregated India, Sikhism has no caste distinctions in its ranks.

Sikh pilgrims come to Amritsar in a Varanasi-like act of devotion to bathe in the pool that surrounds the temple, watched over by fierce looking, spear-gripping guards who stand around, eagle eyed, watching you carefully to see that your head is adequately covered, your facial expression is pious, your shoes are off and your head is respectfully lowered. And overlooking the temple complex is an Airtell mobile phone advertisement that screamed, 'EXPRESS YOURSELF!'

Even with India's staggering array of religious structures, the Golden Temple is one of the most moving and profound religious buildings you can visit in the country. All around you are Sikhs from New Jersey and Sydney and London and Hong Kong, returning home to visit the temple that is so central to their faith. The old people wear scraps of red and blue to cover their heads, while their children, eager to set themselves apart from their country bumpkin cousins, wear neckerchiefs embroidered with Chicago Bulls and Nike logos.

Just outside the temple grounds, free food is also served to all visitors. Everyone is welcome, even non-Sikhs, and it's considered extremely rude not to eat there when you visit the Golden temple. People praying there continually pause politely and point it out to you in case you forget, and several fearsome guards strode towards me and tapped me on the shoulder to remind me to do the same.

So once I had made my round of the complex I went there. As soon as I pulled off my shoes I took a metal cup, plate and spoon, taking a seat self-consciously at the end of one long row of pilgrims where attendants came around to serve flatbread, white rice and dhal.

The proper way to receive the flatbread is with outstretched hands, like a beggar, to reinforce humility, a central tenet of the Sikh faith. As the attendants walk past they motion for you to stick out your hands, which you do, self consciously, and then a second later, plop, down drops a piece of flatbread.

After I had received the bread, and the rice and dhal, it was more than a little disconcerting being the center of so much attention, the five hundred people eating in the hall had swiveled their necks around to see if I was dipping the bread correctly into the dhal, to carefully check if I was using the spoon the right way, and whether I was drinking the water I had been given.

On the way out, a huge turbaned man armed with two huge silver swords that could have cut me in two saw me walking out of the communal hall; with a black beard down to his waist and over two meters tall he smiled down at me, the only foreigner at his temple that day.

Before I had time to even breathe in, the Giant reached out his arms had crushed me in a great bear hug and then lifted me completely off the ground.

Express yourself, I thought. (The Giant must have seen the Airtell advert.)

'How do you feel here?' the Giant asked me after I had gotten my breath back, the question that had followed me doggedly not only in the Punjab but during my entire stay in India. India is really one great big religious Hypermart, where you can browse and buy your salvation and religion in bulk. (Which makes me a very picky shopper)

'Great,' I nodded feeling somewhat a loss for words and air after being squeezed. 'Do you live here, in Amritsar?' I asked.

'No, Queens. Jackson Heights. New York City.'

When I told him that Jackson Heights was the exact neighborhood where I had been born, I was lifted off the ground again and squeezed once more for good measure.

EXPRESS YOURSELF INDEED.

Was Dharmsala just another franchise of McNirvana where people came from near and far to soak up and tank up on spiritualism and religion, and nothing more?

As I got off the bus from Amritsar, it seemed just that.

Perched high on a spur of the lower Himalayas, Dharmsala is decked out with the usual Lonely Planet Strip Mall of internet cafes, banana pancake breakfast joints and bhang (marijuana) lassis on the menu. Everywhere I looked flyers advertised Tibetan massage, Tibetan cooking, Tibetan meditation, Tibetan Thanka painting and Tibetan enlightenment courses offered to the crowds of pirate pants wearin', Nepali cotton bag totin' members of The Tribe, the mongrel international-set of travelers that pounded the town's pavement in search of either spiritual sustenance or a natural high trekking amongst the world's tallest mountains.

Beyond The Tribe I found the spirit of Dharmsala to be much deeper. I lingered at street corners talking to friendly

Tibetan monks eager to practice their English, I waved back at lively Tibetan grandmothers who wore broad smiles at any time of the day and talked to whole Tibetan families running shops and businesses and always ready to say hello, and finally His Holiness The Dalai Lama himself who had lived here since 1959 with his government in exile after being driven out by the Chinese.

Though over seventy years old he kept a very active schedule of preaching and teaching. As soon as I checked into my hotel I learned that there was a specially scheduled Teaching going on while I was in town.

Everywhere I went people were talking about it.

The Teaching.

Sixteen tour buses of Taiwanese Buddhists, who, after giving a hefty donation to the Tibetan cause had been granted a ten-day lecture series by his Holiness. It was open to the public as well, the English translation of which was broadcast on the only local radio station.

'Oh, I'm just waiting for my friend,' a British woman told the waiter in the restaurant primly as he stood at her table to take her order. A few minutes later she checked her watch and stood up to go. 'I will be back after the second Teaching,' she said cryptically to the same waiter who nodded his head sagely in deep understanding in a scene straight out of a spy movie.

'Do you know what time it is?' asked an Aussie girl even though I wasn't wearing a watch.

'Around eight fifteen,' I told her.

'Oh,' she slurred, 'my Holy Man told me it was eleven o'clock,' she laughed as though this was hysterical. Then she turned serious. 'Are you here for The Teachings, too?'

As I walked to the temple following the crowds down the hill, I saw a lady who had been on my bus from Amritsar walking along in front of me, conversing in rapid fire Korean with the stray dogs that lived in the town. She was feeding them rice paper snacks that she tossed like birdseed from a plastic bag stowed in her backpack. But they refused to eat them, getting more and more aggressive towards her, wanting meat, anything more substantial than flimsy crackers. This made the woman furious and she slapped her thighs in disgust, spitting out more angry Korean bursts that left the dogs more perplexed and wary of this mad woman. And still hungry.

'Oh, hello,' she said to me kindly when she recognized my face. 'You go to the Teachings, now?'

At eight thirty sharp the lecture started and while the inner sanctum was reserved for the deep-pocketed Taiwanese, large crowds of Tibetans gathered outside to listen, prostrating themselves on the floor in front of the monastery as they lifted their clasped hands to their heads, face and hearts.

As the Dalai Lama's voice trailed off into the forest of pine trees behind the complex, it was eerie watching the monsoon clouds crash silently into the hills. It was poignant to think how much his people in Tibet would give to be able to hear him lecture directly from the Potola Palace, his ancestral home.

When the lecture was over, the Dalai Lama made his way back to his private residence. Suddenly over five hundred Tibetans, many of whom where dressed in traditional clothing and draped in chunky turquoise jewelry, sank in unison to the ground as though in the presence of a king, and it was impossible not to be moved as the tears flowed down their cheeks as their hands were clasped over their heads.

I was lucky to be standing right where the Dalai Lama swept down the staircase and was one of the few people he shook hands with before he stepped into his tan colored Suzuki SUV. He smiled at me through the glass and pressed his hands together.

I bent, smiled back, pressed my hands together and briefly felt like Richard Gere.

Over the following days I kept meeting the semi-permanent foreign residents of Dharmsala, many of whom had skipped The Teachings altogether. Perhaps because their spiritual gas tanks were already full and therefore didn't need any more spiritual wisdom, or maybe because they had already had been filling their heads with enough knowledge of Tibetan painting and Tibetan cooking and Tibetan Healing of their own, I never knew. But some of their own Teachings were posted on the walls:

'My Fellow Dharma Brothers and Sisters, I implore
you to please read the Golden Light of Sutra
1,000 times in the next twenty four hours, to alleviate
the violence, pain and suffering in Iraq. Our positive
energy flowing from India will therefore will
immediately reduce the suffering there.'

If anyone is catching the train to Delhi from
Pathankot tomorrow, and wants to share a taxi to the
train station, please contact Tenzin Chorghi, the
(very tall) American nun formerly known as Sharon.'

Looking for someone who answers to the name of Xi. Of
former British nationality, has been living in India for 7
years.
Please contact Rinpoche Smith at the Shangri-la Hotel.'

The rest, however, were strictly off the wall:

'How much longer will you be traveling in India?' I asked a
French girl as we watched the parade of monks and nuns
walk past and back to their monasteries after The Teachings.
    She scratched her head and said, 'I dunno, my passport
expired three months ago...'

An Israeli grandmother of twelve had decided to stay in India
forever.
    'It will never change,' she added happily, 'and I will never
leave,' as she knitted a hideous purple scarf at the foot of a
waterfall, just outside of Dharmsala. 'Why should I go back
where my children can, how you Americans say, put me in a

home?'

'But where do you plan to go?'

'Everywhere. Everything is possible in India. Look, even the Dalai Lama is here, who will be next?' Her conviction was so strong, it seemed that she expected the Pope to relocate to the Subcontinent at any moment.

'Have you been to Kerala, the south?'

'No, not yet. I keep being distracted. I don't know, the spiritual energy keeps pulling me north,' she said with a straight face, 'like a magnet. I've never been south of Delhi.'

A Spanish girl in a café leaned over to me and pointed to a word in her Ayurvedic Massage Handbook.

'What does this word mean?' she asked dreamily, as her finger touched the word 'hibernate.'

When I told her what it meant, she smiled, thanked me, and returned to her manual.

'How long have you been here?' I asked the blonde haired Dutch girl who sold me her bus ticket to Manali, because her new Tibetan boyfriend was now taking her to Srinagar, Kashmir, for the Peace Festival there and she was off the next morning to cling to the back of his motorbike for three days.

'Oh, about a month.'

'You are here for studying?'

'Yes.'

'Have you been to the Dalai Lama's for his Teachings each day?'

'I went, like, the first day, and it was very interesting, don't get me wrong, but once I'd seen him, well, that was enough.' Her voice trailed off. 'But since then, I've been so....so busy.'

'With what?'

'Classes,' she said vaguely as though she was struggling to remember exactly what she had been studying. 'One was for Water Therapy,' she said brightly. 'We sat in circles, drinking water for hours, and were told of the healing power it had on the body, the importance of drinking enough water each day, and the spiritual dangers of not drinking enough.'

'I think that's called dehydration.'

'Oh no, it was developed over thousands of years, this Water Therapy.'

'How much was the course?'

'Two thousand Rupees.' ($50)

After collisions with Spiritual Tourists left and right in India, I am beginning to think this country is a gigantic Lost and Found Department.

Let me explain.

Half the travelers are The Lost, smiling sheepishly as they lug round backpacks full of spiritual books and juggle schedules overloaded with classes and seminars and teachings and lessons and more, devouring all that they can in the hope they will someday join ranks amongst The Found.

The Found, on the other hand, travel light. Backpacks half full (clothes only) and day packs empty (journal only) they are smug, self centered and aloof as they move about India, languidly informing travel mates of dietary and spiritual requirements that have secured their place in the Universe.

'Why are you in India?' demanded a girl from Scotland bluntly when she sat down next to me on one train journey, asking me The Question as I fumbled for an answer, scratching my head.

Just where DID I fit in, anyway?

Nowhere, I realized, and hung my head, expecting to be excommunicated by The Tribe, sent home, ashamed. 'He dared to be a real traveler in India but failed,' my obituary would read. But when I overheard an Irishman talking to his mates in one café, I knew exactly why I was here.

'Sod enlightenment and trekking, I'm here for the pies,' he scoffed, surrounded by his soccer-playing mates on the terrace of a restaurant run entirely by twelve-year old school kids on school holiday. The Irish blokes were in India for nine months and couldn't stop dreaming of all the western food they had eaten in Kathmandu.

'I am here for the pies,' I now give this answer to The Question when it is posed to me by The Lost or The Found.

This sends The Lost and The Found off scratching their heads in puzzlement. Is 'pie' some kind of secret code? Some kind of new Teaching they haven't heard about yet?

I am soooooo here for the pies.

My last encounter in Dharmsala was the most hilarious.

A Canadian girl with long blonde hair (The Lost Girl) was talking to an Aussie girl (The Found Girl) that worked at a Tibetan bookstore perched in a pine forest high above Dharmsala in the Tushita Meditation Center blessed by the Dalai Lama himself.

'Can you tell me the four noble truths?' The Lost Girl asked her new friend.

'Uhhh....no, not all of them,' The Found Girl replied sheepishly. Though she had been studying Buddhism for nine years and spoke nearly fluent Tibetan, she could remember just two.

'Did you get The Teaching His Holiness gave yesterday?' The Lost Girl went on, unperturbed.

'What, the one about women's bodies being disgusting?' asked The Found Girl.

'Yes,' The Lost Girl sighed, running her hands through her hair in frustration. 'I'm having so many conflicts here. I'm thinking I should go home, leave this place. I mean, its no good to the other students in the class when I am so confused.'

'I think it was a metaphor for male monks to reduce their desires,' The Found Girl offered, hoping to calm her recently acquired, and increasingly agitated friend.

The Lost Girl nodded her head violently. 'I know, I know. I am, like, devoted to more than one species, in this lifetime, you know, and I don't know how the Dalai Lama, who doesn't have a vagina, can sit there and tell me, a woman, who has a vagina, that its evil. I mean come on, women, with their cycles, and vaginas, are connected to the earth...'

Tonight I am off to Manali on the overnight bus, the jumping off point to Ladakh.

After three months in India, after the overdose of Spiritual Tourists, The Lost and The Found, the cows, the Saddhus, the Cow Shit Sandwiches and Dalai Lamas without female genitalia, I am ready for a break. I mean really ready.

I have been told that Ladakh is a Saddhu and Sacred Cow free zone so that is my next destination. Maybe the thin air scares them away?

Before I sign off from here in Dharmsala, remember:

THE DALAI LAMA DOES NOT HAVE A VAGINA.

Love, Dave

From: Dave <theloweroad@gmail.com>
To: Annette <whereisannette@yahoo.com>
Date: Oct 26, 2004 11:20 AM
Subject: The High Road

Hey Annette.

If I thought I was going to escape India easily, I was totally wrong.

Immediately after stepping off the night bus from Dharmsala the bad news hit me like a lightning bolt out of a clear blue sky, a bridge on the road to Ladakh had collapsed, landslides had blocked ten kilometers of roads and the highway would be out of service for at least five days.

'Is there any other way to get there?' a Japanese girl asked the travel agency manager the question he had answered for the millionth time that morning.

'Well, the only way around the bridge is to hike nearly 1,000 meters straight up the mountain, with no trail. Only rocks. And mud. If you slip, you'll fall straight into the river, and no one will ever find your body.'

Remembering that travel insurance didn't cover the collection of my body from canyons in either Africa or India, I settled in for the long wait in Manali, the Himalayan equivalent of Goa. Perched in the foothills like Dharmsala, the town was spread out, filling a large valley that looked straight out onto snowfields 6,000 meters high, waterfalls plunged in the distance and the monsoon mist and clouds drifted in and erased the town as swiftly as an avalanche.

Manali's visitors were strung out too, shops vibrated twenty four hours a day with trance music, nightly techno raves were organized in the woods, and odder still, marijuana grew wild everywhere between rosebushes in hotel gardens, by the side of the road and along river banks choking pathways so thickly you felt like you were invading some pot growers farm in Northern California. You didn't even need to smoke the stuff because the air was so heavy with pot fumes you could get high by just sniffing the air.

Cows munched it freely.

'If this was Santa Cruz, we'd have been shot by now,' whispered Brandon, the Bostonian who was living in San Francisco, who had also been on the night bus from Dharmsala, as we pushed through the marijuana bushes trying to find the river.

Brandon was a rare breed of traveler in India. He wasn't a spiritual freak, he didn't gush about ashrams, and as far as I knew, he hadn't bathed in the Ganges. In short, he too didn't fit into The Lost or The Found, and like me was on his way to Ladakh.

We were not just surrounded by The Lost or The Found anymore because Manali was all about The Tribe.

Though it sits at 2,000 meters, looks like a Himalayan Aspen or Boulder and smells like an illegal California hashish farm, it felt most like Little Tel Aviv. The place was crawling with newly discharged Israeli soldiers, dread-locked college students and retired couples. Many were stoned out of their minds, happily picking the free marijuana leaves that grew like weeds everywhere, getting High up High.

There were more shop signs in Hebrew than Hindi and waiters in cafes greeted you not with 'Hello,' but 'Shalom,' and also remarked, 'You speak very good English, my friend, for someone coming from the Middle East.'

I learned that the freak season in Goa was over until December, and until then the Goaites had drifted north like flocks of migrating Club Kids eager to recreate Ibiza in the Himalayas. And following right behind them were the Tibetan, Nepali, Indian and Kashmiri traders that earned their living off them. Their shops were crammed with hand stitched day-glow club wear, rainbow woolen stockings, Rajistani puppets and kitschy Tibetan religious objects. Restaurants served whole menus dedicated to marijuana milkshakes and I overheard a woman from Berkeley telling her newfound friend a recipe for hash brownies.

'I got this recipe of someone who knew Abbie Hoffman,'

she beamed as she wrote it out for a girl with a Jiffy Pop hat stuffed with her dreadlocks.

On my first day in Manali I saw an Israeli girl lope past with black army boots pulled up to her knees, bra-less in a tank top, her head shaved as bald as a monk with a chunky Ladakhi silver necklace decorated with old coins and turquoise draped around her neck like an Egyptian breastplate. Her boyfriend held her hand, his purple dreadlocks down to his knees squelching by barefoot in the mud, his nose pierced with exactly the same kind of metal piece I had last seen poking through Raj the camel's nose in Rajastan.

If you were one of the few travelers who didn't sport any of The Tribe's accessories you were given The Look by all Israelis who lounged around the town smoking chillums and plopping ground up ecstasy tablets in their mango lassis at breakfast. As soon as they saw you weren't wearing the de rigueur tie dyed cheesecloth pants, endless strands of antique Tibetan jewelry or beaten up leather bags embedded with lapis lazuli stones from Afghanistan, you were stared at with narrowed eyes, branded an enemy and treated with heavy suspicion. The Look followed you constantly and in the four days I was trapped in Manali it never got any less annoying.

The Look was everywhere.

'If I see another person matching Pirate pants with a pair of Teva sandals, I'm going to beat them to death with a prayer wheel,' hissed a Delhi fashion designer in the internet café where I sat with a view of the Himalayas. She was there to attempt to finish her fifth Vipassana meditation course, but had left early from the previous four, unable to stop speaking for ten days.

Hanging out in Manali grew tiresome and finally we heard that the road was nowhere near being fixed, it was climb the 1,000 meters or continue watching the endless parade of Israelis, dragging their Kashmiri wool shawls and their drugs, behind them as they shot The Look in all directions.

Five people were found to share the jeep journey. Brandon, and two Israeli women: one, a kindergarten teacher who we called Steven because her family name was Seagal, and the other was Yael who was a computer programmer. And then there were two other travelers who due their bad behavior their nationality will forever remain anonymous.

After meeting Steven and Yael on the bus from Dharmsala they had swiftly taken Brandon and me under their wings and began to teach us to travel The Israeli Way.

Steven and Yael knew the price for everything in India, from flight tickets to toilet paper rolls. They had met twelve years before in India and traveled together for five months around the country, and they actually had people standing by in Tel Aviv who had just come back from the subcontinent who they texted SMS messages to confirm that all the prices they were getting were in fact correct.

The pair was so efficient that when the two went shopping in Manali for waterproof bag covers they ordered one for each of us and told us where to pick them up; when I told them my hotel was three hundred Rupees they clucked their tongues and said it should cost two hundred, and when we found a travel agency to hire a jeep to Leh the first price of ten thousand Rupees was met with some wicked Hebrew sentences and then furious negotiations started, as a volley of cell phone conversations and an avalanche of SMS messages between India and Israel commenced.

Finally, hours later, the price of eight thousand Rupees was set and we were cleared to leave Manali, The Tribe and The Look behind. At three o'clock in the morning there was a knock on my door. It was Brandon who informed me the two anonymous travelers had sheepishly decided to bail out and travel to Kashmir, in the opposite direction, instead.

With the loss of the two the price became too high for the rest of us and it seemed the Escape From Manali (a.k.a. The Escape from India) was off.

Yael and Steven came over, angry words flew back and forth in the darkness and the two travelers just turned their heels like vampires before crucifixes and fled the hotel.

The Travel Gods will curse you both.

Within an hour the travel agency manager, named Om, found not two replacements but four. A group of sullen Spaniards. (Known from here on as 'The Replacements') Despite the discomfort of cramming eight people in a jeep for two days, we even gratefully accepted another Israeli girl named Dorit (who we christened Dorito).

And then there were nine.

Right on time, at six in the morning, and in a jeep painted with 'ACME Adventures' on the side, the Escape From India was on.

'ACME Adventures. ACME anvils. ACME disasters,' moaned Brandon.

Half an hour later we arrived at the washed out bridge and after negotiating with porters we set off. At first it was a romantic walk through the woods, as sweet as a slice of cake from a Kathmandu bakery.

I'm here for the pies, I thought.

Soon after the steepness escalated until it was impossible to ascend without hanging onto the branches of small trees. We joined Kashmiris gripping briefcases, and actually carrying on cell phone conversations while squelching in the muck, Ladakhi families in their best clothes returning from a wedding, Tibetan monks who smiled the whole time, and lots of porters who were carrying down the half rotten vegetables that had been stranded between the collapsed bridge and landslides for almost a week.

What had started as a nice alpine Bambi stroll quickly turned into a mess of muddy shoes, slipping down backwards as you tried to get a foothold in the goo, and trying to avoid grabbing the thistles as a means of support.

'Merdes!' screamed a Frenchman when he grabbed one by mistake.

About halfway up I suddenly ran into two passengers who had shared the hellish Bangladesh Biman experience, proving that misery really does love company. Stopping to catch our breath, we talked for awhile, joking heartily about the unbelievable coincidence of sharing yet another nightmare.

And then Steven screamed - up ahead was a childhood friend who was now running a Kibbutz in Israel and was traveling in India with her new husband. They all exchanged email addresses and moved on.

The mountain got steeper and more treacherous and indeed the rushing river the man had spoken of did exist. It was pouring straight off the mountain and down the path we were meant to take. Remembering vividly the insurance fine print that reported the company didn't cover the recovery of dead bodies from Himalayan canyons, my mantra became 'Don't look down,' and ploughed on. A few paces later the glacial river plunging down the mountain became the path and we were forced to step through the icy water as we slogged skyward.

'He slogged skyward.' It should really go on my tombstone.

When we stopped for a break, gagging in the thin air, throat dry, muddy, and sweaty, I wailed to the Travel Gods high in the heavens, 'IS LADAKH REALLY WORTH ALL THIS?'

Steven and Yael waited until my scream had stopped echoing around the surrounding peaks, looked at each other and said nothing. Then they bent over, stuck their fingers in the mud and painted three striped across my cheeks.

I was officially initiated into The Tribe.

When we finally reached the precarious cliff where the road had been, a tremendous boom shook the earth and small rocks crashed down all around us, the army had just dynamited what was left of the road and that meant an even higher detour around the newly collapsed section. Echoes reverberated off the distant mountain peaks, and we stopped in awe as we listened to them dissipate. Looking down over the crack, not one hairpin bend of the road, but four had been completely washed away by the monsoons.

When we took another break from the climb, in the rain and caked in mud, the view was amazing, Swiss like mountain peaks stretched to the horizon with glaciers and snow clinging to the tops with green fields underneath.

When Brandon screamed, 'Ricola!!!!' at the top of his lungs, the Indians, Tibetans, Ladakhis and Kashmiris looked at him like he was mad.

'You know, like the commercial?' he tried to explain.

No one smiled.

When we finally reached the next jeep we were hopping up and down in happiness that the nightmare was behind us. We then began the two day journey through the high Himalayas to Ladakh, also known as Little Tibet, (and even believed by some to be Shangri-La) which had only opened to outsiders since the 1970's.

For half a day we wound our way through alpine valleys

crusted with glaciers and soon we were above the tree line in a wide, barren wilderness almost totally empty of people. The scenery quickly changed to even more dramatic peaks and mountains, all draped in heavy snow and wispy clouds that curled off them.

Suddenly up ahead there was a sight that none of us had seen in monsoon season India up to that point.

A clear blue sky.

The mountains of Ladakh act as an enormous rain shield and almost all the monsoon clouds and rainfall is deflected off the Himalayas so while the rest of India is buried in murky, ashen clouds Ladakh is left sunny and dry as a summer day in Arizona.

We passed through tiny towns where hay was being forked on top of the roofs to prepare for the long winter. But in an instant the little civilization there vanished completely as we entered the desolate and stark landscapes that stretched to the horizon, one of the world's highest deserts. As we reached mountain passes four and even five thousand meters high, vistas spread out before us so vast and beautiful they looked like they had been painted as a movie backdrop. Totally unreal.

We snapped photos in the thin air, gasping for breath, each step an ordeal.

As we drove on, swerving up and around canyons, rounding bends with 1,000 meter drop offs we had several fights with our driver who took great pleasure in navigating the mountain passes while looking for his favorite Bollywood soundtrack tapes in the glove compartment, taking his eyes completely off the road. Steven refused to let him even light his own cigarettes and like a doting mother confiscated them and handed them over, lit, one by one, after had learned the Hebrew word for 'please.'

Often we were the only humans for miles except for solitary yak herders and nomads permanently wandering the high desert. That evening we drove through the darkness to Sarchu Serai, a tented camp in the middle of nowhere established to serve travelers to Ladakh. The night sky was so clear it seemed unbelievable and so was the cold. During the day it had been thirty-five degrees Celsius but by morning, there was ice covering everything.

When we woke at dawn we found ourselves in a stark, steep valley completely surrounded by rocky hills, the tops of which were lit up like gold by the rising sun. Did it look like Mars, or the moon? We couldn't decide, but even after the passport changes of the numerous states I had visited in India, I seemed to have stepped off the continent into somewhere else entirely.

A twilight zone indeed.

Just after breakfast a herd of yaks and their wide-eyed minders wandered through the camp, crunching over ice and frost as they went off, appearing from nowhere and going off into nowhere once more.

As the ice melted we took off towards Pang, a Tibetan settlement on the banks of a grayish river where we had lunch. The landscape became even more desolate and empty, so much like the highlands of Africa that I thought I was back in Ethiopia again. I was half expecting someone to serve me Kitfo, the Ethiopian-Raw-Meat-Treat.

After long hours in the jeep surrounded by sweeping vistas and glacier scoured canyons so beautiful that the nine passengers were silenced by their majesty, we drove over the Tang Lang La pass, the second highest in the world. We stood there, gasping for breath at nearly 18,000 feet as prayer flags flapped in the wind all around us, the snow flecked Ladakh ranges loomed in the distance, underneath a sky that was the deepest blue I had ever seen. All I could think was: LADAKH REALLY IS WORTH ALL THIS.

Even The Replacements smiled.

Three hours later we arrived in Leh the capital of Ladakh and gratefully spilled out of the jeep.

Brandon and I said goodbye to all but Steven and Yael, who, like adoptive mothers everywhere, continued to keep us tightly tucked under their wings. They searched for decent hotels for all of us, bargained the price down for us, and arranged a trek for us.

I did escape India after all.

The skies here in Ladakh are blue, not monsoon gray; the streets are full of jeeps, and not trishaws, and I haven't had a stomach upset or fever since I set foot here.

There is also not a blood-shot-eyed Agori in sight.

Or a cow crap sandwich. (or so I hope)

So hard to believe is it that I am still in India, I just opened my passport searching for that passport stamp.

But I never found it.

Love, Dave

Hi Annette,

I'm back to Africa-slow internet here in Ladakh, though I have enough to tell you to make the ten minutes per click wait worth it.

Leh, the capital of Ladakh was once a stop along the vast Silk Road that stretched across Asia. It is a tiny, Buddhist, mud-walled town hiding in the shadow of the royal palace that clings to a rocky hill directly above the jumbled labyrinth of the Old City's narrow lanes.

Ladakhi Buddhist monasteries, called Gompas, are perched even higher, with golden yellow curtains flapping against whitewashed walls where lines of prayer flags are stretched across the deep blue, crystal clear sky.

With the year's high season in full swing, the town's Bazaar hummed with whole Argentinean families in trekking gear, blonde Swiss mountaineers, more stoned, stone-faced, and dread-locked Israelis than Manali, British social workers doing farm projects in Zanskar, and clusters of chain smoking French package tourists.

Ladakh, with its similarity to Tibetan culture, and all the exoticism westerners drew from it, made it sometimes feel like a human zoo. While the locals tried to go about their daily lives with dignity, tourists snapped them rudely in photographs if they wore any turquoise or were carrying prayer wheels and even school children walking home from school had to carry newspapers to cover their faces when tourists tried to take their photos.

'You!' shouted a bearded man at me in the main Bazaar. 'We met. Kabul Bazaar. Remember? You were traveling with the German puppeteer?'

'I've never been to Kabul, sorry.'

'Kabul! We met in Kabul, last year. It was summer.' He lifted his hands in frustration.

'I told you, I've never been to Afghanistan.'

'I'm sure of it. You bought a lapis lazuli necklace for her.'

No matter what I told the man while I was in Leh, he was absolutely convinced I was the guy who married the German puppeteer from Bremen, and every time he saw me he greeted me like some long lost friend.

'You! Kabul!' he shouted each time, so often that other travelers who saw me yelled rudely, 'You, KABUL!' to which I replied, 'I never bought a bloody necklace in Afghanistan!'

That experience summed up perfectly what Ladakh was like because Leh was packed with people escaping the monsoons in the south and hardly a day went by when some character you had seen on a train, bus or plane in India didn't walk past you in the Bazaar:

The crazy Frenchman from the Rajastani train fistfight,

The ditsy Australian from Dharmsala who had now divorced herself from her holy man,

The Austrian couple that had gotten cow crap served in that restaurant in Jaislmer,

The Scottish Six from Agra, still decked out in their Pakistani wardrobe made a brief appearance at a Tibetan restaurant one night, but left quickly when they couldn't get a table,

Even the two anonymous travelers that had bailed out of the jeep trip to Leh were found sitting in a corner table of a restaurant and still smiling sheepishly, after arriving from Srinagar.

That was until the dagger sharp looks from me, Yael and Steven scared them away like vampires from daylight.

With the phones never working, the power always off more than it was on and the internet eternally clogged, Leh was great for catching up on our individual Indian journeys while feasting on Tibetan and Indian food and watching the sun creep up the hills as it set behind the glacier capped mountains, drinking mint tea and fresh apple juice from Kashmir.

'Hello, friend,' said a tall blonde massage therapist from L.A. (who I will call Phoebe) at my guesthouse the first morning I arrived, shattered from the two day slog from Manali. 'Welcome.'

She had just arrived in India, was here as a Spiritual Tourist and had not only done a three week camel trek in Mali, during which she had completed a native American rite of passage, where she meditated on a mat and only drank water for a week, she had also completed, she said with a smug smile, four ten day Vipassana no-talking meditation courses in Big Sur, California.

Phoebe had her Jesus booted feet firmly planted amongst The Found.

Having been in Ladakh only a week she was already an expert on where the best trekking company was and where the best vegetarian food was and where you could stay in a monastery for free if you didn't mind cold showers.

'Come to Summer Bounty, tonight, friend,' Phoebe said slowly, referring to the veg/chill out restaurant on Fort Road. 'There will be some groovy people there.'

There were groovy people there that night, but it felt more like that Intergalactic bar in Star Wars with practically every nationality represented and freaked out to the extreme. A poster on the wall announced a séance later in the week for channeling the 'Great Spirit of Bob Barley,' Janis Joplin was on the sound system, and even the Ladakhi waiters had dreads down to their knees.

A Swiss woman was warning her new found friends of the bacterial dangers of sharing joints mouth-to-mouth and was instructing them on how to stick it in their noses to inhale; a lone stray Yak had wandered into the restaurant and was eating the flower arrangements off an empty table, and when a German woman asked a man thought to be a native of her country where he was from, the Caucasian man stared back at her and growled, 'Goa.'

The whole place was horizontal.

People's bodies were scattered all over the carpeted floor, lying stretched out on pillows smoking chillums and talking in low voices. As soon as I walked in I felt very vertical and self-consciously crouched down until I recognized Phoebe crashed out in the corner showing off her Masai warrior scar to some stringy haired Kiwi girl.

'Hello, friend,' Phoebe said as she introduced me to her 'smoking' buddies who peered at me sagely through a haze of a thousand lifetimes smoking hash. No one even acknowledged me, and even Phoebe went back to explaining the meaning of her scar/tattoo.

When the waiter took my order a girl across from me blew pot smoke in my face and started to cackle like a witch. Maybe it was the altitude or the choking incense, but before my drink, or food, even came, it was time to for me to leave the Rabbit Hole.

And the altitude was fierce. The town sits at over 4,000 meters and on my second day in Leh I was crouched down for a few minutes buying some apricots. When I stood up suddenly the world spun around like a washing machine, went black and I was falling through a tornado-hole in the ground.

When I came to I was staring up at the sun, a Ladakhi grandmother was screaming in my face and fanning me with her silk hat and my now useless legs were blocking traffic, both bovine and vehicular: a huge cow and a massive army jeep loomed over my head and somehow I managed to crawl out of the way before being first trampled and then run over.

Yael, Steven, Brandon and I left one morning before dawn and caught a bus to the Tikse Gompa seventeen kilometers from Leh where the dawn Puja ceremony takes place in a musty room holding an enormous bronze Buddha statue, with walls painted with scenes from hell, amid the strong stench of rancid yak butter tea.

The Gompa complex covers an entire hillside and is modeled on the Potala Palace in Lhasa. The stunning views of the glacier covered mountains across the Indus river valley are enjoyed by over one hundred and fifty monks in residence. They rise each day at dawn to the sound of two yellow mohawk-hatted monks who blow bone-white conch shell horns encrusted with turquoise stones and silver work from the wooden roof and they come in, one by one, smiling at each other and saying 'Ju Le!' (Greetings!) before filling the rows of straw mat covered benches in descending lines of age, from eighty down to just eight years old.

When the venerable Rinpoche of Tikse is seated they strike a yak skin gong, and the chanting and meditation of the Puja begins. Slowly, as the daily ceremony gets underway the monks began to rock back and forth in their seats, eyes squeezed shut, hands at their sides as the Rinpoche, wearing the same yellow robes and 70's-esque John Denver style sunglasses favored by the Dalai Lama who conducts the pitch and tone of the mantras and phrases repeated by all in attendance.

Except for two.

The youngest monks sitting right in front of me whispered continuously back and forth so much that when a senior monk walked past he bashed their shaven heads with prayer books. The youngest, a.k.a. Problem Child, was the worst and he acted as though the whole Puja was just a joke and all the monks were there just for him to laugh at. Even more funny were the foreigners sitting with their backs to the walls, appropriately sitting as far away from the Buddha as possible, directly beneath fierce portrayals of blue headed demons smashing the skulls of the wicked and deceitful. (According to tradition, the older you get the closer you get to the Rinpoche, and heaven, so tourists eager to watch the Puja were forced to sit in the Hell Bleacher Section)

During the three hour Puja Problem Child didn't close his eyes for a second. He just hummed some nonsense song that clashed with the monotone chanting and in punishment got himself assigned to tea duty - he had to lug huge brass teapots around, filling all the senior monks bowls with tea in penance, bowing to them deeply as they continued their mantras and chanting.

When the Puja was over the monks spilled out into the thin desert light and continued the chores they were meant to complete before the next Puja at noon. Problem Child took off down the stairs shrieking like it was the last day of school.

Perched high over the town, Shanti Stupa was built with Japanese donations and features a shiny round Buddha statue facing in the four sacred directions of the universe. With more staggering views over Leh and the Indus river valley, it's a favorite place to watch the sunset, and like everywhere in Leh during the high season, there was a battle to deal with the crowds of people jostling for space.

Steven and Yael were leaving on the flight to Delhi the next morning and we decided to brave the 600 steps at about 5.30 p.m. when the sun's fierce rays had finally died off. We took about fifteen steps and practically collapsed, gasping for air in the thin atmosphere as Ladakkhi school children laughed at us and scampered up them easily.

By the time we reached the top the sun had slipped behind the mountains and the valley floor now darkened stretched before us. We could see a Ladakhi polo match on, we could hear the distant calls of prayer from the Kashmiri mosque in town, (where a Pakistani flag fluttered, defiantly, most days) and watched great armadas of Indian Army trucks and vehicles trailing even greater dust clouds as they drove off to their distant army bases near the Chinese and Pakistani borders.

The platform in front of the Stupa looked like Rome's Trevi fountain in August, awash with two camps, the Tourist Cows and the Mad Meditators. The place reverberated with the usual Tower of Babel languages you hear everywhere from Angkor Wat to the Tower of London to Ipanema Beach; the Tourist Cows there for the view, the Mad Meditators there for the serenity.

We dropped our voices immediately, hard for Yael and Steven, who shouted most of the time anyway and crept around the lotus-seated Mad Meditators with care watching out not to smash any fingers. We avoided the herds of Tourist Cows and their guides who looked at us contemptuously like we were AWOL soldiers without our 'General' to tell us where to eat and what to see in their country. We used hand signals to communicate and found an empty place near the precipitous edge where we could shoot our photos without disturbing the Tourist Cows or the Mad Meditators.

All around us was silence.

'Click,' went Steven's camera with the precision of a rifle.

'Hum,' went Yael's with the shriek of an AK-47.

'Whine,' went mine as though magnified through loud speakers.

There was a murmur of disapproval from the Tourist Cows, and rustling of angst among the Mad Meditators, so we exchanged glances and hand motions to cut the photos out.

It was too late.

A tour guide snapped his fingers at us, and a tall blonde foreign woman sitting amongst her fellow Mad Meditators went a step further. Emerging from her bliss she swiveled her neck around like a Buddhist Exorcist, shot us a look of pure hatred, and then screamed, 'Can you take your god damned cameras and jump off the mountain. Sod off!'

Most evenings here in Leh the power is dead and the 'nightlife' consists of Bakery Hopping from the English to the Swiss to the German to the Dutch and around again, sitting around before flickering candles, draped in our hideous purple and blue $2 wool Kashmiri shawls, talking travel and drinking the only, and most awful, beer available in Ladakh, Kingfisher.

Made by an Indian multimillionaire from the south that likened himself to Richard Branson, The Times of India reported he was planning to start a low cost airline the following year. (His vision was to create a cross between Southwest Airlines and Hooters Air)

Sometimes Phoebe is around with new friends in tow, other times it is clusters of Israelis who were friends of Steven and Yael who drowned out English with Hebrew in the predominantly Israeli company that was all around us. Other times it was travelers we met while visiting Gompas and other times it was Nepalis and Sikkimese who had cornered the bakery market in Ladakh, distributing every chocolate croissant, apple crumble, and peach cobbler to the highest bakeries in the world.

Though Leh wins hands down over Manali for freakdom, as always in India it is religion that defines the odd Masala mixture of the transient visitors to Leh - Islamic Kashmiris are always ready to strike a bargain for a pashmina shawl over bottomless cups of mint tea, Ladakhi Tibetan Buddhist monks who are on pilgrimages visiting historic Gompas in the Indus valley, Jewish Rabbis flown in from Israel by their government to celebrate the Sabbath each week at the Leh Jewish House to keep the newly discharged, and very disgruntled soldiers, Jewish, Catholic cross wearing Europeans, celebrating masses at a different hotel each week. Even a few hardy naked Saddhus that hung around the main square, looking for alms to fall into their hand.

And day and night all around Leh on swirled the World's Finest Freak Show, free, weird, surreal, and always entertaining.

'Whee!!!!' shouted some French girl as she spotted a stray cow chewing on some garbage. 'Une vache sacré!!' she wailed to the night sky, bowing down before the bovine creature reverently as though she were in the presence of some great celestial being, as the cow, now wary of this mad woman, munched on.

FOR THE RECORD, I NEVER BOUGHT A LAPIS LAZULI NECKLACE IN KABUL.

Love, Dave

From: Dave <theloweroad@gmail.com>
To: Annette <whereisannette@yahoo.com>
Date: Nov 4, 2004 11:20 AM
Subject: Lightless in Little Tibet

Hi Annette,

I can now add 'Able to Drive through the Himalayas in Total Darkness Without Headlights' to the Special Skills section of my resume. This is India after all and when renting anything here, kick the tires, check the brakes.

Just don't forget to check the headlights.

I did.

Brandon and I rented a vintage Vespa each one day, and after filling our gas tanks in the 'World's Highest Petrol Station' south of town, we puttered west of Leh through the stunning Indus River valley so deep sometimes it made the Grand Canyon look like child's play. The sky was a bright, wide blue, and not a cloud was in sight. What could go wrong?

Stopping off at Tibetan monasteries in Likkir, Alchi, Spitok and Hemis, all hidden behind dry, cracked, Martian looking mountains, we watched elaborate Puja ceremonies. Ancient paintings hung on the walls of darkened rooms where Buddhist monks dressed in wine red robes shuffled around, sweeping the earth, tending to their apple orchards, or happily sitting to talk in the bright sunlight about their experiences traveling abroad with the Dalai Lama and the marvel of the Western Groupies who fell at his feet in airports, universities and independent bookstores from Berkeley to Recife to Sydney.

We rested in tiny, lush villages where the bells from spinning prayer wheels sounded off over the whispering barley and sunflower fields buffeted by hot breezes, hemmed in on all sides by tall, shimmering Aspen trees. After four p.m., when school was out of session children sold fresh apple juice along the road in the Ladakhi version of the suburban American lemonade stand.

With a conspicuously free seat on your motorbike on Ladakh's empty roads you invariably served as a free taxi driver to uniformed school children, friendly monks, fierce looking Sikh soldiers, stern policemen and wizened grandfathers all of whom sat behind me for many kilometers, clinging in ones and even twos as I struggled with clutches and gears up, around, down and through the deep gorges and passes desperately trying to deliver these total strangers but fast friends to their police posts, schools, homes, and fields without crashing.

Brandon and I became so used to strangers asking for lifts that when we weren't asked we felt a pang of disappointment. Though it was a relief because being overloaded on such treacherous roads would have spelled out c-r-a-s-h eventually.

And there is a lot of crashing in Ladakh. Many trucks miss the very tight curves of the roads and go right over the edge, one such accident I saw involved a truck that had tumbled down into a deep, rocky valley, the tires still spinning, bloodied sheep carcasses splattered all over the place.

The Himank Corporation are the self described 'Mountain Tamers' and having built the world's highest roads, have also devised clever but ultimately annoying slogans and sayings to keep the drivers and their bad driving in check:

IF YOU MET GOD, WOULD YOU HAVE ANYTHING TO SAY?
IF MARRIED, DIVORCE SPEED
BRO DON'T LOOK BACK
SAFETY ON ROAD MEANS SAFE TEA AT HOME
FALL ASLEEP, YOUR FAMILY WILL WEEP
WHY HURRY?

The signs were so frequent and so lame that I imagined truck drivers swiveling their necks around to read the sign, 'DON'T WORRY, BE HAPPY' before 'happily' sailing right over the precipice to their deaths. I knew quite a few trishaw drivers who I would have not shed a tear over if they had tested my theory and met this fate. The steepness of the drop offs and the unpredictable nature of our Vespas that often accelerated without reason and brakes that mysteriously stopped working when you needed them most left both of us white faced and terrified of flying off the edge ourselves.

So most of the time we drove like old grandmas, navigating each hairpin bend as if it was our last because out here in the high Himalayas it could have been.

Traveling as far as we could go without staying overnight away from Leh, Brandon and I decided to head back in the late afternoon beating the deep chill that would soon come.

I flipped the switch on my headlight.

It was dead.

CRAP.

Leh was more than three hours away. The sun was already gone and the inky tentacles of black shadows were creeping octopus-like ever higher on the canyon walls. In the dark crevasses of the ravines the temperature began to plunge.

I realized I was going to have to drive home completely in the dark. Cursing and remembering that in Ladakh, roads were potholed, twisting, rutted, always under construction and without any street lights whatsoever, I made a plan with Brandon to share the feeble arc of light spilling out of his motorbike which seemed to be working.

For now.

It was weak, but Brandon's headlight should have been enough to see a monstrous hole in the road or a deadly hairpin bend in time to swerve. Or so I hoped.

So off we went driving slowly and cursing loudly. (AREN'T I HERE FOR THE PIES? my brain bellowed.) We passed no gas stations and no repairmen; we had driven through the last village and though mountains towered all around us, they disappeared completely as darkness fell like a velvet curtain.

Gritting my teeth I gunned the engine as fast as I could to cover the last one hundred kilometers back to the capital that sat beyond three huge gorges. The road had no barriers and cliffs dropped straight down into the seething Indus River choked with glacial melt water.

'Pray for a moon,' I thought.

But there was no moon at all and the stars, though bright, didn't help at all. I started to shiver violently from the icy air; after days of warm, hot weather, and because we had left at midday, I was only wearing a light T-shirt, and thin shorts. No jacket, no sweater, nada.

For thirty minutes I was able to sense where the road slipped off the edge. But as the sky turned the color of dark corduroy and then black as coal, Brandon's headlight could only do so much and the place where the edge started disappeared completely. In the inky darkness, even my spatial orientation was sent off kilter.

Inching along, and in the middle of nowhere, the nightmare was only eased when the few approaching trucks lit the way with their headlights. But these behemoths soon passed, and the darkness that returned seemed even blacker.

Finally, after a few last minute swerves away from the deadly canyon and a few crashes through potholes that rattled my teeth and jolted my arms, we saw a thin horizontal sliver of lights far up ahead.

Leh.

As we yelped out of happiness it still took us almost an hour to reach the safety of the town, where we parked our bikes and ordered ourseelves a round of that awful Kingfisher beer to calm our rattled nerves.

In Vietnam cultural experiences go hand in hand with near death experiences, but here in India, they seem divorced from each other. I can't imagine learning any deep revelations into Ladakhi culture as I sailed over the edge and into the Indus River to my death.

Luckily for me, I didn't.

Love, Dave

From: Dave <theloweroad@gmail.com>
To: Annette <whereisannette@yahoo.com>
Date: Nov 16, 2004 11:20 AM
Subject: Into Thin Air

Hey Annette,

In the space of the Himalayas was time to THINK. Here in Delhi, there is no such luxury.

Before the memories of the Himalayas and Ladakh slip away I'm sending you the last part of my trip there. I am in New Delhi's Connaught Place, not far from the train station where I'm waiting for my train to Bombay. Navigating the cow-clogged streets again, ignoring the filthy trishaws, beggars and touts has been a shock. How can I think with all this racket? Half of me wants to turn right around and get back to Ladakh, but the Maldives is my next country and it is my carrot to the proverbial donkey.

Gotta keep heading south.

But first, the rest of the north.

No matter what time of year you come to Ladakh there are always toothpaste white glaciers hanging from just about anywhere you look in the mountains, outside your hotel window, perched behind some thousand year old village, or sliding down a ravine towards a seething river, the country is so high, and the air so thin, they just never melt.

Snow and freak blizzards are also possible at any time of the year, especially in the mountain passes which can be snowbound even in the middle of summer. And surrounding Leh are three of the world's highest passes where ancient trade routes from central Asia had no choice but to climb them to reach markets and civilization. The beautiful names of the passes rolled off your tongue like names in some fairy tale.

Kardung La was the highest, at 5,600 meters, followed by Tang Lang La, at 5,400 meters, and then there was Chang La, at 5,100 meters. With autumn fast approaching, snowflakes were already starting to settle on the higher elevations around Leh and the mountains were quickly turning silver and white overnight. But the human flakes in town had yet to be chased off to southern, warmer climates and herds of them continued to gather in the main square of the town, mostly just chilling out eating the Nepali-made cakes and pastries and also trying to arrange group trips over some of the world's highest roads to places off limits just a few years ago - Nubra Valley, Pangong Lake, the Zanskar Valley, and Moriri Lake.

Posters carpeted the place with urgent requests to join jeeps to Kashmir, Manali, even Delhi and to share costs for eight to ten day camping treks. All the travelers seemed eager, responsible, and reliable, but the reality one learned was that for whatever reason, the altitude, the heat, or just something that was seeping into the water supply, 90% of travelers flaked out, backed out, and just plain disappeared.

'I could have strangled that Japanese girl, friend,' said Phoebe in a rare show of anger one day at lunch as she dug into her vegetarian Tibetan soup. 'That girl simply vanished like a ghost.'

At first I could hardly sympathize with her, having had just one nasty experience with the bad behavior of two travelers in Manali. But once I began to arrange my own trips the problems mounted like the mountains all around us, and by the time I left Ladakh, I swore I would never rely on another traveler EVER again.

One of the closest places to go was Nubra Valley, the furthest north you can go in India, off limits for foreigners until just recently where I went with Yael and Steven, another Israeli couple with shaven heads, a couple of Italian astronomers, two British guys from Manchester, two Polish social workers and two Swiss chemists.

The main 'religious' draw for travelers to Nubra was not the spiritual pull of Dharmsala, or the ashram that was Rishikesh, it was the cathedral-like mountains, icy blue rivers and lush green valleys that resembled the scenes of Afghanistan flooding the international news programs now.

The trip nearly collapsed when the four long haired and ear-ringed Israelis complained that the jeep they found that morning was not the 'big jeep' they had been promised and the trip nearly was nearly called off, as the travel agent desperately tried to explain that the 'big jeep' was a small one for environmental reasons.

The arguments flew back and forth, discounts were offered and the British barmen laughed at the 'transvestites' that were causing the delay, and tried to remember the lyrics of the Eurovision song contest won the previous year by an Israeli trannie.

The trip finally left four hours late. Kardung La Pass sits between Leh and the Nubra Valley, and at just under 5,600 meters, or 18,300 feet, it stands as the highest road in the world.

Take two steps up there and you're already gasping for breath but the Sikh soldiers who were stationed at Kardung La, oblivious to the amazing so-close-you-could-touch-them view of the snow swathed Karokorum mountain range just behind the pass were playing a tense game of cricket in the thin air, possibly the Worlds Highest Cricket Match.

A French film crew, smoking, of course, sucking even harder on their Gauloises in the high altitude, filmed away as some French mountaineers group hugged and cheered 'Bravo!!' and some Aussie rugby blokes were trying to chat up some wasp-thin Dutch girls on puttering Vespas and some dread-locked Japanese were posing Easy Rider style on their 500 cc Enfield motorbikes as their friends recorded it with a shiny Sony.

The scenery after passing Kardung La was much like the road from Manali to Leh - lots of huge mountains, steep, stomach churning drop-offs, bone-white glaciers, and deep river valleys full of gleaming Buddhist Stupas with Ladakhi settlements and their complex irrigation systems channeling cold, clear glacial melt water to their barley fields, potato fields, and apple orchards.

Ignoring the scenery, most of the people in the bus talked Europolitik with each other, trashing the Euro currency and bemoaning the impending addition of ten new states which set off the Poles like a bucket of water dumped on a cat to defend their motherland and the honey pot of money they would get to build up their country.

The British guys, dressed in black track suits, sent poisonous looks at the Swiss and their perfect alpine gear and accessories, while the Italians had gone shopping before we left, expertly matching their new Indian Pashmina shawls with their dark brown leather shoes.

'Look,' the British guys said sarcastically to the Italians when the driver pointed out a herd of pashmina goats munching on some grass, 'There crawls your next season's pashmina!'

'Si,' the Italians countered coldly, serene as monks behind their gold Dolce and Gabbana sunglasses, 'Versace winter collection.'

During the trip I was kept firmly under the wings of Yael and Steven and throughout the bumpy journey they lectured me sternly on the cheapest way to travel in Israel, introduced me to Hebrew food including an Israeli inspired dessert, (but that was not eaten in Israel) oddly called Hello To The Queen. It was made of chocolate sauce covering a bowl full of chalk-dust-dry cookie crumbs and cashew nuts. They perfected my Hebrew pronunciation that consisted of long sessions practicing hacking up an imaginary phlegm ball to get the special sound that I heard constantly in India.

'Indians can reproduce this sound as expertly as any Israeli,' I said to them brightly, referring to the constant spitting and throat scouring that went on all day and night, in train stations, streets, and other public places.

Like the Queen, they were not amused.

Our accommodation was in a traditional Ladakhi farmhouse, large and rambling, constructed of mud bricks with hay bales stored on the roof for the long, cold winter where temperatures would soon plunge to minus 30 degrees Celsius.

We all pitched in for dinner to make the dough for the Ladakhi momos that are pasta shells stuffed with peas and spinach and then helped the matron of the house steam them over a fire lit in her tiny courtyard. Her husband invited us inside afterwards and happily sent round cup after cup of chang, fermented barley wine that tasted like sour, watery orange juice but was as strong as rubbing alcohol.

Tibetan food is bland and plain, and while it fills you up, you tire of it quickly.

'Where's the barmaid with my mead and victuals?' joked the Brits as they turned their noses up at the same food we had all eaten for weeks.

But the Poles lauded the cook for momos that resembled the large plain dumplings they ate at home, while the Italians picked at their food diva-like and talked endlessly with the

Swiss Italians about the swish fusion restaurants they missed from Milan. The Brits got pissed on some Kingfisher beer they had brought along in their backpacks but had forgotten to pack a single shred of warm clothing.

After dinner we walked to the family's dike where cold water gushed through sluices into the fields of barley that were already turning brown. The sun had fallen behind the mountains and the shadows that stretched across the valley were one of the reasons Ladakh was so amazing: great stretches of darkness crept across the land erasing the deeper river gorges first, then the dark green settlements stretched along the river, then the Gompas higher in the hills, and the final act being the slow crawl up the mountains, the waning light tingeing the tops pink and gold several hours after the sun had slipped behind the icy Himalayas.

The temperature plunged immediately and the stars were so bright the sky was still light when they appeared. Even shooting stars were visible way before darkness fell.

Except for the Israelis who quickly grabbed the entire indoor room set aside in the farmhouse for travelers, the rest of us slept outside under the brightest carpet of stars outside of the horn of Africa or outback Australia counting as many as three shooting stars per minute streaking simultaneously across the sky.

The voice of the river, which first put us to sleep, grew louder during the night and as the Ladakhi's intricate network of canals and sluices sprung to life after midnight, with the opening of the floodgates to irrigate the land at dawn, the rush turned into a roar.

When we woke up the square patch of land we had slept on was now surrounded on all sides by gurgling streams leading to the thirsty fields.

After breakfast and on our way back to Leh, we stopped off at dark sand dunes where double humped Bactrian camels, left over from the ancient silk trade from China, grazed on grass in the valley floor, and now were harnessed by enterprising Kashmiris to give rides for travelers in the one of the world's highest deserts.

Three quarters inside Tibet and only one quarter in India, Pangong Lake is as far east as you can go in Ladakh. A deep turquoise blue that stands shimmering, and calm, in front of 7,000 meter mountains permanently snow bound, you could actually see the beginning of the Dalai Lama's home country and even higher snowfields than those around Leh.

It's also a place where even India's bureaucracy stretches, even to the high Himalayas, you need a permit to visit and border guards snap to attention stiffly when your car approaches, taking the copy of your permit and taking a very good look at your face when you pass through.

'How far away is China?' I asked the driver.

'Two kilometers.'

'Two?' I replied. 'Can't you drive down to it?'

The driver laughed but made machine gun noises with his hand; like the problems with Pakistan in Kashmir, border tensions existed between the Indians and the Chinese, too.

My last trip got off to a bad start. Two Israeli brothers, heirs to a Tel Aviv furniture fortune, claimed they had been told it was a strictly out and back trip, with no overnight camping involved.

Fabienne, the no nonsense, French-Algerian journalist from Radio France, who had been among the first teams to arrive in Kabul and Baghdad after they fell to the Americans, was adamant camping was going to be part of her vacation and having already lost three days waiting for other travelers to make up their minds, argued fiercely with me to convince the guys not to puss out and come along.

Arguments flew back and forth and finally the trip was off. As a last ditch effort I huddled with Fabienne for one last time and convinced her we should let the guys come back alone and we would brave hitchhiking or the local bus back to Leh. Fabienne agreed and the trip was back on.

We left at seven the next day and during the long drive and waits at checkpoints, the conversation swerved towards Israel and the Israelis bristled as Fabienne explained how she had interviewed Arafat and had been in Gaza and Ramullah dozens of times. One of the Israelis had been a soldier stationed there and she asked him if he knew about The Grandmothers, who were retired Israeli women who cross questioned soldiers who held up innocent Palestinians without cause when crossing the checkpoints.

'No,' he said coldly.

'Oh, I'm dreaming of my Kabul,' Fabienne said to me when we passed over Chang La Pass completely snow covered and freezing cold as we waited to go though yet another check point. When she saw the Indian soldiers wandering around brandishing weapons on the 3rd highest pass in the world. Later she became even more homesick for 'her' Afghanistan when she saw solitary road crews smashing rocks to make the roads that kept the Indian Army running.

'Just like my Khandahar,' she said dreamily.

The last hour of the road to Pangong was amazing: a deep, verdant green moss grew along the river valley and we stopped to listen to our voices echo around the purple rocks and crags that rose above our heads.

In the afternoon we laid, Cannes style, on towels by the shimmering lake, watching the blues change with every passing cloud and watching the mesmerizing shadows creep and crawl across the rocky scree slopes that tumbled down from the glaciers.

When it was time to go back to Leh the Israelis tried to convince us to go with them but Fabienne and I stayed firm. The driver, eager to get home, told us a bus was leaving at 12.30 and that we couldn't buy a ticket until eleven the next day.

We said goodbye to the nervous driver and the lame Israelis, found an abandoned field outside of town and pitched our tent as the sun set. While Fabienne read her book I hiked up to a nearby Gompa built into a cave and watched the clouds turn to gold with young monks who said little but smiled a lot.

The next morning we learned the Jammu & Kashmir (J & K) bus we thought was scheduled to leave at 12.30 was now leaving at eleven. Fabienne and I ran back to the field, collapsed our tents and found the bus was almost about to leave. We hadn't even bought tickets and were still on the roof of the bus when the driver just lurched into gear and took off with us hanging like monkeys frantically clinging to the pitching roof while tying down our bags. Then we crawled down the bus' shaky and cracked aluminum ladder and inched our way along the bumper to the back door with our teeth chattering wildly where we slid inside to find the bus passengers smashed inside as tightly as chicken feathers in a lumpy pillow.

Totally packed.

Somehow the conductor took pity on us and found us some seats by moving around some bundles and bags, right between five Indian soldiers carrying rusty AK-47's. They looked at my French companion with contempt and sat there smiling like Cheshire cats at her as we bumped along, barely able to contain themselves.

Fabienne was tired of the male chauvinist 'eve teasing' she had experienced in India where men leer, sneer and make hissing noises at women so she grabbed one of the guns, cocked it and aimed it out the window at a mountain, first earning the respect of the soldiers, and then a new seat next to the driver who regaled us with stories fighting the Taleban factions in Kashmir that fled over the border after the Americans attacked, while Fabienne told him stories of riding the American's 'toys,' the Black Hawk helicopters and Hummers in the Iraqi desert and how she the first time she had met Arafat at a conference he had patted her head affectionately, like a puppy.

At our lunch break at some lonely restaurant tucked in the shadow of a high mountain pass, a friendly Tibetan monk behind me tapped me on the shoulder and handed over a heavy wedge of raw, runny barley dough with a hunk of yak cheese in the middle.

Fabienne flatly refused the bread even though she hadn't eaten solid food for six days due to the altitude, and watched me, smirking, as I discovered that not only was the yak cheese runny, a generous amount of yak fur was mixed in with the dough. With my entourage happily waiting for me to swallow the Tibetan delicacy, Fabienne could hardly contain herself.

'Bon appetit,' she said facetiously, pursing her lips together to stop from laughing.

Braver than I had been in the past, I picked off as many yak hairs as I could see and tore off a piece. I took a deep breath and popped it in my mouth. It was not only as sour as the chang I had drunk in the Nubra valley, but there was way more yak fur inside than I thought, and as I swallowed, I almost dry heaved as the yak fur stuck in my throat. Fabienne came to the rescue and handed me her water bottle as she collapsed in laughter. The monk slapped me on the back, grinning, thinking that it was my enjoyment of his food that made me grimace so strongly. When we stopped for the next break, the yak-fur-sandwich went straight into the bottom of a ravenous stray dog's stomach sleeping by the side of the road that inhaled the food like a furry vacuum cleaner.

Just as we accelerated towards the straighter roads of the Indus Valley a deafening explosion ripped through the bus and we thought a gas canister had blown up on top of the roof.

Actually it was a tire blowout and we nearly rolled off the cliff while the bus driver tried to control the lurching vehicle. It took thirty minutes to fix it and we were back on the road after the truck tire on the roof was dusted off and cinched into place.

Three hours later we pulled into Leh, passing a restaurant where the Israeli brothers were sheepishly sipping strong apricot juice. Then we went to the travel agent that had rented us the camping gear who grinned at us even more, relieved to see that we had come back in one piece.

Between trips to the far corners of Ladakh I had short stays in Leh where the Freak Wheel spun on, bearded Euro Trash walked bare-chested and barefoot through the town banging cymbals, their girlfriends trailing behind them twirling their hair, the Kashmiris patiently asking me again and again to sit with them and drink mint tea to hear about the problems in their country and how buying a Pashmina for my dahling would help solve them, French girls drew long drags on their Gauloises in cafés that oozed nothing but Parisian stink, not chic, and sunburned Brits came back from ten day high altitude trekking trips raving about the Premier League football matches they had missed on Sky Sports.

A notice was posted for a three day trip to Moriri Lake twenty kilometers from China with a couple whose nationality, due to more bad behavior, will also remain anonymous. Before I left for the Pangong trip I met them with a British traveler who was also keen to go. They shook our hands and promised to wait till I got back and we all put the money down for the permits.

When I returned, the couple had disappeared and taken their permit (with my name on it!) with them. With a bit of sleuthing, which wasn't hard because Leh was a one yak town, I found where they were staying and discovered that not only had told their landlady they were going to Moriri that morning they had said nothing to me or the other traveler even though they knew we were waiting to share the car; not to mention the three agencies who were waiting for them to pay for their previous trips.

Furious, I wrote them a carefully crafted note calling them on their treachery and left it in the hands of their landlady to search the town's notice boards for any and all trip to Moriri even calling in at the Israeli House where Shabbat was underway to see even if some Israelis were going to Moriri.

I finally gave up, the British traveler was so mad she left the next day for Manali.

I had two days left in Ladakh and as the flights to Delhi were packed, I was going to be stuck in Leh waiting for the next confirmed seat. Moriri was off and I was livid at the fourth time a trip in Ladakh had come to grief because of other travelers.

Then I remembered my Nepali contacts in town that ran the bakery racquet and knew everyone. It turned out there was a local guy heading to Moriri the next morning. Clutching my new permit I tracked him down, paid the deposit, found a tent, sleeping bag and mat and instructed them to pick me up the next morning at seven.

Moriri was on.

While the drive wasn't as spectacular as Nubra or Pangong, I learned more about Ladakhi culture in those two days than in the previous three weeks in the country; I heard from Sonam, the driver, about their witch doctors, the funeral rites, and the Yeti myths and footprints that circled around the place. I also learned the phrase, 'Om Mani Padme Hum,' a Tibetan mantra that is very difficult to translate, and also how his relatives had traveled on the passes before there were roads. When we reached a chorten that was draped on prayer flags we circled it in the jeep three times, and the driver gave me a white silk scarf to tie around it for good luck on the rest of our journey.

While their devout Buddhist sensibilities ensured our safety on the twisting roads, their taste in music was nowhere near as inspired. The music swerved between:

Acid Trance from Goa: a gift from some Israelis
Tibetan Monk Chants: a cassette from his uncle
Lobo: including the classic You Me and a Dog named Boo
Milli Vanilli: left behind by some German man's wife

'My grandfather went to Tibet on his ass,' Sonam said with a straight face referring to the convoys of donkeys that were used as transport. Later in the trip I saw a group of trekkers, half French, half American; one American had obviously set his sights on the Isabelle Adjani look-alike on the trip and I overheard him say, 'My ass is bigger than yours,' he told her with a shy smile, referring to their transport, while she stepped away and struck up a conversation in French with someone else, using hard words he couldn't understand.

Along the way we passed through a deep gorge carved by the Indus river, where solitary families were preparing for winter and hoisting hay on their roofs, and where rocks and boulders surrounded Gompas and schools where red cheeked grandmothers walked home from classes with their grandkids.

The last hour, we entered a valley so broad and flat it felt like Mongolia, and then we passed little Moriri, a gem-like lake that reflected the clouds like a cool, blue mirror. Marmots stood up to greet us as we passed through the final barrier to the large lake and when we descended to the valley floor great gusts of wind blew mini tornadoes around the car as Tartar horsemen drove their animals home, followed by dogs that looked like Alaskan malamutes.

It was truly remote, truly Himalayan, and truly Ladakh.

That night I camped near the village in an open field where shadows from curve horned goats loomed on the walls of my tent as they butted heads with rivals. Large packs of vicious wild dogs sniffed around my tent too, looking for food as I shivered, remembering the Yeti myths.

During the night I could barely sleep because the altitude was 5,200 meters, so high every time I drifted off to sleep, I woke up, gasping for air. Breathing as deep as I could to stave off oxygen starvation, I prayed for daylight.

'He prayed for daylight.' It could go on my tombstone.

The wind picked up so strongly that the tent nearly blew over and by the time dawn came I was ready to leave for lower ground. Though I had escaped India for three weeks, I was now very eager to get back to it, even braving the filth, the noise the chaos and confusion that now paled by comparison to the cold and oxygen depravation.

When the sun did come up it was two hours before it cleared the mountains around Moriri and I had enough time to get down to the shore where the suns rays spilled over the top of the mountains, illuminating the glaciers behind me in gold and pink. It was so cold that the ground was solid ice and each step was crunch-crunch-crunch in the thin air. Painted ducks from China were feeding in the shallows where strangely shaped brine shrimp cruised through the water, even though the ocean was hundreds of miles away and thousands of feet beneath my toes.

In my last few days in Leh the seasons finally clicked in Ladakh. Summer was over, with fall and the bitter winter on its way, the Aspen trees had suddenly turned yellow overnight, frost covered the ground in the morning and though the sky was clear the sun's rays were now weak. Prayer flags that had flapped to the north now flapped to the south as the chilly winds shifted from the warm Indian Ocean monsoon to the cold northern winds sweeping off the Mongolian plateau.

And more than the physical seasons were changing in Ladakh, as Kashmir was deemed too risky to most travelers and with Nepal's Maoist woes scaring off more and more tourists, Ladakh has become the center of the Himalayan Trekking Trade. Over 40,000 trekkers were expected in a country that had received just 3,000 people only two years before. The invasion has brought along with it problems and headaches the country had long been free from.

For centuries the average Ladakhi bartered for everything and no one went hungry or lived in slums, now the young flocked to the cities to get jobs and garbage and crime were rising: a foreign girl had been raped in Leh in broad daylight; a group of German tourists had lost all their money from a trekking company when the employees, and their money, went missing; and even the most remote Gompas now had to padlock every room to avoid theft from not only the foreign tourists that flocked there but from their own people.

All around town the elders were preparing a mid-winter gathering to devise new restrictions for the next year's tourist season; bed taxes and flat minimum charges per day for trekking were to be implemented, and it seemed that 2004 was going to be the last year for unchecked tourist arrivals in Ladakh. The Israelis, having gotten wind of these developments, were already outraged, and desperately looked for other cheap places to crash in India.

On my last night in Leh I rounded up people I had met there for a Freak Free dinner, no bland momos, no banana pancakes, just some of the best Indian food I had even tasted, at a restaurant ironically called Baba's Little Italy - some New Zealand travel agents, a group of Aussie surfers from Margaret River, a sociology couple from Stanford, a Thai classical dancer traveling with her American English teacher husband, two retired Israeli school teachers, two stock brokers from London, a pair of Korean photographers traveling with their French Canadian English Lit teacher, and a Kiwi mother daughter team traveling around the world. It was a mini United Nations around the table, and not a Freak to be seen.

That was until Phoebe turned up.

Cool and distant now that her newly minted relationship with her muscled, tattooed Lenny Kravitz look-alike Israeli boyfriend Shlomo had been sealed on a recent, and very carnal, two day camping trip. She no longer called me 'friend,' and curtly told me that she too was following the seasons and was off the next day to travel southward towards Goa. With Shlomo in tow, or course, following the flocks of migrating Club Kids and Hash Heads south for the winter, away from Ladakh and the hauntingly beautiful Himalayas.

Three hours from now I am heading south from Delhi, hitting Bombay, Goa, Bangalore before ending my trip in the Maldives. Can't wait, some blue water and palm trees are the carrot luring me south.

You can see by the length of this email alone how much I was moved by Ladakh. I hope the energy I gained here, free from the monsoon clouds and rain, will sustain me until I leave.

Om Mani Padme Hum.

Love, Dave

From: Dave <theloweroad@gmail.com>
To: Annette <whereisannette@yahoo.com>
Date: Nov 23, 2004 11:20 AM
Subject: Beware the Delhi Dog Shit Man

Hey Annette.

Got to Bombay from Delhi two days ago. Two overcrowded, stinking polluted cities in two weeks.
　　Oh joy.

　　The calm absorbed in Ladakh was trampled first by the 400 passengers trying to get to Delhi on the flights out of Leh and then squashed flatter than a chapatti by that one of a kind Delhi cocktail - leaded car exhaust, the smell of cow shit (probably about to get served to some travelers in some episode of Punk'd, set up by some irate waiter) spitting touts and putrid cooking oil fumes from street vendor carts. When it came time for dinner, I passed. I had already dined on gasoline fumes laced with ginger and spice and not everything nice.
　　My stomach was full.

　　I did see my first snake charmer today.
　　No, the snake didn't bite me.
　　Actually it was a bit of a let down. The guy was at the Gateway to India and the snake looked more lively than he did, waving in the air as some Xin Chao Fuckers tried to get it to slither towards me.

　　I am in a firetrap internet café reached through a trapdoor no less. As I choke on carbon monoxide fumes belched by every self-respecting bus in Ethiopia that are seeping in through the window, it's the usual menagerie of customers. They are all surfing porn sites. I mean XXXXXXX porn. I seem to have stumbled across the Bombay chapter of the '1970's Gay Moustache YMCA Porn Club' or something. There are some very hairy beasts being drooled over all around me.

Great. I am understanding the reason for the trapdoor now.

Let me catch up on the end of Ladakh and mad, marvelous Delhi.

After the freak-free dinner in Ladakh it was one o'clock in the morning when I stumbled and blundered back to my hotel. There I found the power was out my landlady nowhere to be found and I nearly cut my head off when I walked into a razor sharp clothesline stretched across the garden.

Without flashlight, candle, or even matches, in the inky darkness, there was no way I could get the rusty Indian-made lock to open.

Barred from my room, I was forced to wait in the pitch-dark garden for nearly an hour until the matronly landlady returned with a flickering candlestick so I could pack up my things for the six a.m. Jet Airways flight to Delhi.

When she lit the candle she told me soberly that in fact the 'whole town was out of power' and I had no choice but to borrow her noisy alarm clock so I wouldn't oversleep, because both my watch and alarm clock were broken, and the power had been out for so long, my laptop's battery was nearly dead and there was no way of checking the clock on it. If I missed my flight there would be no refund and no second chance, the flight was overbooked for weeks and it was that or a five-day overland slog to Delhi instead of a one-hour flight. Though I loved the scenery in Ladakh, my ass wasn't too keen on repeating the spine-crushing trip.

My landlady sheepishly gave me a candle and I fell asleep with it burning nearby with the noisy alarm clock tic-tocking next to my ear. Each time I woke up I saw that the candle was lower, the night sky was still dark and I realized the candle wax wasn't going to last until three thirty. I desperately tried to find a spare candle in the hallway, groping in the darkness for any that might have fallen down behind the stairs but I gave up and I fell back asleep, hoping for the best.

At about two a.m. the candle went out completely and the room was beyond dark. There was more light in a deserted mineshaft. Remembering the nerve rattling, moonless night drive I had experienced with the Vespa, I cursed and lay there, hoping that the sun would soon rise and I could check the clock.

It didn't rise because the sky was full of clouds, and all I could do was to use the nearly dead laptop battery as a 'candle.' When I turned it on I realized with horror that the time was five ten a.m. though my taxi was due at five o'clock, I hadn't packed and worse had only the feeble light of a laptop to act as my 'flashlight.'

Frantically shoving things into my bag I swung the laptop around the room, science fiction style, as though I was looking for aliens or radiation, searching for things I had missed, and scraped them together. The shrill beep-beep-beep of the low battery alarm came on as I zipped up the final zipper and then the laptop died completely, plunging me into that deep sea darkness once more.

Inching my way down the hall I had to find with my foot the place where the stairs where (it was just a hole in the floor with rickety wooden slats for steps) I found it, banged my way down the steps and groped my way blind drunk man style along the downstairs wall nearly knocking off picture frames as I struggled for balance. I eventually found the way out, crashed through a field of sunflowers before finding the path leading to the road, where I saw that other houses and the streetlights were on and realized my landlady had lied, covering up the fact she had either not paid her bill, or she had somehow angered the powers that be at the Ladakhi Electric Company.

There was no time for bitterness, my taxi was nowhere to be seen. But in the darkness I found some Poles waiting down the road for their taxi to the airport. Hoping to share their cab with them I used the basic Polish greetings I had learned in the Nubra Valley to quickly win them over.

But I didn't need to, my taxi driver, the one who had brought me to Moriri Lake and back finally showed up and I gratefully piled in, worriedly asking him about the raindrops that were now pattering off the windshield.

'Maybe, flight canceled,' he said with a smile.

When we got to the airport the gate was guarded by sullen soldiers. As a military airport barbed wire and cement-bagged bunkers were everywhere. I was first out of the car, the first through security and the first to check in at Jet Airways. Within five minutes the place was packed with Europeans white-faced and worried because over two hundred names were on the waiting list. It was typical of the Ladakhi trekking high season to face such stress and annoyance. At every turn it was packed restaurants with two hour waits for food and hour long waits at the bank; and after seeing more Europeans in the market than Ladakhis. I was actually looking forward to get back to India, because after the peace and quiet, I was ready for some noise, color, and surrealism.

While downing a cup of chai I met the grandfather of Ladakhi tourism, whose father had climbed Everest, and whose ice pick was in a museum in Nepal, and whose wife was a famous German documentary filmmaker, who split her time between Ladakh, Munich, and the world, which she traveled around constantly filming Napoleon docu-dramas, Ghandi life histories, and Sony and BMW commercials, to pay for all the documentaries she was not able to sell.

As we talked the mango lassi I had downed at the Freak Free dinner the night before, made by the matronly lady related to the Ladakhi royal family, suddenly revealed itself to be nothing but poison and went off without warning in my stomach like a grenade leaving me dizzy, queasy and fighting to keep from throwing up as the boarding announcements rolled on.

After we had identified our bags in the rain, passed through two body searches with a pat down by a very 'thorough' soldier and finally a question and answer session where we were sternly asked if we had packed our bags ourselves. (No, I let some Xin Chao Fucker pack it for me, I thought to myself. As I was heading back to India, my sarcastic sense of humor, like the stomach upsets, was back)

I boarded the plane to find an enormous and completely immobile Indian woman in a red sari taking up my window seat, which I had reserved strictly to take photos of the Himalayas. It seemed that only the Jaws of Life would move her so I grumbled to myself and accepted the center seat instead.

The 737 backed away almost immediately, raced down the undulating uneven runway and took off towards the south passing within one hundred meters of the Spitok Gompa at the end of the airport. The monks could not have appreciated the mid-Puja scream of the 737's jet engines as the Boeing roared overhead.

The flight path followed the Indus River valley and as we passed over the Tikse Gompa, where I had seen Problem Child crack jokes about his fellow monks, the monsoon clouds swallowed the countryside below.

Ladakh was gone.

I ignored the food that was served and asked the Jaws Of Life women at the window to take some photos. But Sky Bitch (a.k.a. the in-flight supervisor) who had seen me take a photo as I walked up the ramp and had shouted at me to put my camera away was watching me like a hawk. No sooner had I leaned over to ask the Jaws Of Life woman again to snap a photo of a lake reflecting the clouds, I hadn't even explained how to shoot it when Sky Bitch tapped me on the shoulder, and snapped, 'Take another photo and the captain will report you to the police when we land in Delhi.'

Fortunately the clouds were so thick there was nothing else to shoot and we were soon descending through the thick monsoon swill. When we touched down at Indira Ghandi airport we were spat out into a chaotic terminal, where, after being at 12,000 feet in Ladakh, the lower altitude in Delhi made no difference to my ability to breathe, the pollution soup that swirled around the city was so thick it was like being at 18,000 feet and crawling up a mountain with a backpack full of cement.

I pushed through the crowds of pushy taxi touts and shared a cab to the train station, left my bag there and walked outside where a billboard from the Times of India bellowed, WELCOME TO THE FUTURE.

Walking south I reached the teeming sidewalks outside the underground Palika Bazaar where men were selling leather whips menaced me with the ugly things that they cracked like S & M professionals, inside piles of pirated software and fake

Louis Vuitton handbags were piled to the ceiling and cigar fumes was so thick there that it looked like a Buddhist temple swathed in incense smoke.

I walked further, going through the Tibetan Market crammed to the gills with prayer flags and prayer wheels, dusty Buddha statues hawked by Muslims and Buddhists selling copies of the Koran.

As I walked by a man said, 'Excuse me, sir...' in the same tone of voice you hear all over India, which means please-come-to-my-shop-and-buy-something-friend. Without trying to be rude, I waved him off with a smile, but all I got was a barrage of abuse.

'I'M A HUMAN BEING!!!' the man screamed at me, waving his arms about his head. 'WHY CANT YOU REALIZE I'M WELCOMING YOU TO MY COUNTRY?'

Stunned, I turned around and told him that if he knew what it was like being a foreigner in India, and being accosted at every turn in tourist towns to buy, look at, and rent this and that, then he might understand.

'I HAVE BEEN, ABROAD.' he thundered, 'I'M NOT TRYING TO SELL YOU ANYTHING!!!!' he went on. I apologized and shook his hand, and smiled again.

No sooner had I walked on, when he scampered up and whispered, 'I do know where you can get some realllllllyyyyy good hash. If you want some, you know my faaaaaacecccccee.'

Next, I grabbed a coffee in Barista, an Indian knock off of Starbucks where teenagers in low-slung jeans and briefcase toting business types yelled into their cell phones above the music videos blasted by Channel V.

An hour later I went back to the Delhi station and my stomach was still whirring around like a washing machine. I was so much taller than the people waiting in line with me that several beggars actually sat down at my feet as though they were taking a rest in the shade of a great Banyan tree. When I got closer to the ticket window behind it sat a gnomish Ghandi look alike perched on a tall stool, his eyes magnified comically by his Coke-bottle glasses. He was shouting at an

English girl who was nearly in tears.

'No ticket!' he screamed, waving his arms before folding them across his chest.

'But why?' the girl pleaded, guarding her backpack with her foot and wiping the sweat off her forehead.

'No clean money!! No ticket!!' he grinned at her fiercely like a gargoyle and refused to assist her any further. He pushed her bills back at her and turned his back, case closed. The crowd, that had gathered like they always did in India whenever some incident was taking place broke up like a flock of birds and melted into the chaos that swirled all around us at the New Delhi Railway station.

The girl turned to me with tears in her eyes and said the man refused to sell her a ticket because the bills had staple holes, made by the bank, she didn't have enough time to get to a bank to exchange them, and her train was due to leave in thirty minutes. She shrugged, lifted up her backpack, and was gone.

Nervously I greeted the old man in shaky Hindi, 'Namaste,' and pushed the correctly filled out train reservation form under the sill, hoping the man would be kinder. He reviewed the form and all seemed to be going well until he started to yell at me.

'No ticket!' he shouted, flinging spit against the glass, waving his arms and tapping on the window like a child trying to antagonize some aquarium fish.

'Why?'

'Train number. Wrong!' He pushed the form at me as though contaminated with Anthrax.

'I can't know the train number because I don't work for Indian Railways,' I countered, pushing the form under the window again. 'What is the train number?'

'No!' he shouted, tapping on the glass again with his gnarled fingers. 'No train number, NO TICKET!' With that he shoved the paper back through the sill so quickly it fell on the floor and as I reached down to pick it up, five people had already taken my place, shoving forms and money at the man.

Dejected, I picked up my bag, stepped around the beggars and stalked off, defeated. As I walked around, doing the head shake-roll and thinking like an Indian, 'What to do?' I saw a pair of small hands move towards my shoes and I stepped back instinctively. A plop of dog shit missed my foot by an inch and landed on the steaming cement. The small perpetrator looked up at me, grinning evilly.

I paused and looked at Delhi Dog Shit Man, then said with a rueful smile, 'Better luck next time dude,' as I patted him on the back as Delhi Dog Shit Man scraped the dog crap off the sidewalk for his next victim, hoping for a large sum of money to clean it off.

Two madmen in two minutes flat.

I was DEFINITELY back in India.

You know, while Japan was clubs and bureaucracy, and Vietnam was chaos and madness, and east Africa was dust and death, INDIA IS EVERYTHING.

A few minutes later I saw two Germans come down a dusty staircase gleefully clutching train tickets and mumbling 'Gott sei Dank,' I got directions to a foreigners only booking office upstairs. There I found the English girl still guarding her bag and still shaken up about the man downstairs. 'Evil, evil, evil,' she muttered under her breath to herself, shaking her head as she nervously counted her staple holed bills.

'Hey, at least the Delhi Dog Shit Man didn't get you,' I told her as her face fell.

'What?'

'Beware the Delhi Dog Shit Man,' I said cryptically as I went on to explain the racket I had just avoided. She stood up when her number was called and eventually got the ticket she wanted, waved goodbye and promised me she would keep her eye out for any dwarves armed with dog shit.

When I got to the front of the line I told the lady not about the Delhi Dog Shit Man but about the mad man behind the window downstairs.

She looked at me and laughed. 'Oh, that man, yes, he's famous for giving foreigners a hard time, been working here for forty years. He's actually retired, but he has no one at home, so he keeps coming to work, without even getting paid. We can't get rid of him.'

A few minutes later just when she was about to push the final click on the computer to issue my train tickets from Delhi to Bombay, and Bombay to Goa, and Goa to Kochi, killing three birds with one stone, the computer died, the lights went out, and the fans began slowing down, like jet engines spooling idly after shut down.

'Maybe tomorrow,' she said, pushing the forms back at me across the counter. 'It's the monsoon season. No power, twelve hours. Just go on the train, give them this.'

She wrote out a note for the ticket to Bombay, similar to a note to excuse me from gym class, I paid her the fare and off I went, grabbed my bags from the bonded baggage room, bought some mineral water, popped some pills for the still exploding bomb reverberating around in my stomach, and was glad to see the back of Delhi as the packed express train sped off towards the bright lights of Bombay.

The next time you are in India's capital city:

BEWARE THE DELHI DOG SHIT MAN.

I will email you shortly with news from Bombay. My head is still on spin cycle from Delhi, though my stomach is calm for once. You'll hear from me in a day or two.

Love, Dave

From: Dave <theloweroad@gmail.com>
To: Annette <whereisannette@yahoo.com>
Date: Nov 29, 2004 11:20 AM
Subject: Ganesh is My Co-Pilot

Hey Annette.

Thanks to Air Deccan I am saving twenty-four hours aboard Indian Railways. By flying from Bombay to Bangalore via Goa, each for $40, this will leave me with just one more overnight trainmare in this country.

Rolling the dice one more time will be enough.

So, on to Bombay.

'Sorry for the delay, sir, but the police are looking for terrorist bombs,' said the taxi driver to me, a recent migrant from Kerala as we waited in a monumental Bombay traffic jam just meters away from the Gateway to India where over one year before two bombs had killed nearly sixty people, set off by perpetrators the police had yet to catch. Nervously he scanned the cabs around us, reminding me in a hushed tone that it was two cabs like his that had been packed with explosives and driven into crowds, then detonated.

Half an hour earlier I had jumped off the overnight train from Delhi, and you know you're now in a westernized city when you see a McDonalds inside the station, the taxi driver is sending SMS messages, and more women on the sidewalk are wearing jeans than saris. Policemen were walking car to car, screaming into walkie-talkies, searching for suspicious packages in back seats, and questioning random people. Sniffing dogs lunged at open windows, snarling and barking.

Despite the delay and the air of danger I was glad for the 'fresh' air. The train compartment from Delhi was filled with champion farters and the noisiest, piggiest snorers I had ever heard, and I had hardly slept during the eighteen hour trip; fumigated first by the farters and then left deaf by the snorers. It seemed IMPOSSIBLE that anyone's intestines could hold so much gas.

As we passed the last roadblock the driver began weaving as fast as he could in the traffic, the bright blue Ganesh idol hanging from his mirrors jangling around and around, the elephant god's face frozen in a plastic smile, the cone of incense he had burning mixing with the car fumes, cigarette smoke, and a cocktail of other smells that seeped up from the monsoon clogged drains. When he lurched to a stop for a red light we watched a woman with a pile of grass accept five Rupees from pedestrians to feed the massive, black cow sleeping beside her who was happily chomping down on the free food.

'This city is full of rackets,' the driver said ruefully as he furiously tapped more SMS messages in his cell phone held inside a protective purple plastic Ganesh cover.

Of course.

It was great to be back in the tropics with humidity and palm trees. In a matter of days I had gone from being breathless in the high Himalayas to bathing in the sweltering heat blowing off the Arabian Sea.

And from what I saw cruising down from Victoria terminus station, Bombay resembled an Indian Hong Kong, New York, Cairo and London combined - there was a container freighter clogged harbor, high rise residential apartment buildings, hundreds of black and red taxis like the Egyptian capital, and rusty double-decker red buses that replaced the stinky auto rickshaws and bicycles Delhites used to get around.

And, once again in India, I had 'changed' countries without crossing an international border, from the deserts of Arabian Nights Rajastan; to Tibet in Ladakh; to the surrealismo of Varanasi and the blinding white stones of the Taj Mahal, each time you moved in India, whether it was stepping out of an overnight train, or a short plane ride, it felt like you were in some other country, something I had never experienced before.

When I reached my hotel in Colaba, the driver whistled when he heard the price and said, 'I can get you a room for 500 rupees.' I declined knowing full well the high percentage of commission that price included, and how awful the budget accommodation was in Bombay - airless cells in firetraps.

'You need taxi now,' he spluttered while he hung around the lobby as I checked in, still hammering away at his cell phone's keys.

'No,' I told him wearily and with a grunt he still wouldn't go away.

'You stay Bombay for Ganesh festival?' his eyed lit up as he showed me his prize possession cell phone for the 15th time. 'Very interesting, Chowpatty Beach, we give Ganesh a bath.'

'No, I only have a week here.' His smile faded, he slammed his phone in his pocket, and was gone. With a huge marble bathroom and a view of the Gateway of India, I wasn't moving. No more power cuts like in Ladakh or freezing cold rooms like in Manali, or touristy hotels with banana pancakes on the menu like in Rajastan. I was looking forward to some satellite TV, room service and steady air conditioning.

That afternoon I walked down the pirate DVD and software crammed alleys where the whips of Delhi were replaced with goat skinned drums. Beaten by shop attendants to drum up business, I suppose. Nike shops competed with designer sari stores while many homeless slept, begged and sold their wares to the menagerie of wealthy Indians, Nigerian drug dealers, Chinese businessmen, Italian housewives and Sri Lankan cricket players who browsed and dug through the piles of fake goods sold by some of the most persistent salesmen I had seen in India. No doubt all very, VERY recent graduate degree holders from the Taj Mahal Tout University. (Now opening our Khao San Road Campus! Classes start NOW!)

And all along the alleys hung up in corners in windows or hung around necks and decorating T-shirts was the thick trunk nosed Ganesh, holding his arms up and looking like a Buddha in need of a nose job. Bombay was definitely enamored with the Elephant Baby God that you hardly saw in Delhi.

YESSSSS!!!!!!!' they cried as they watched you walk past, hands extended to shake your hand, 'WHAT ARE YOUUUU LOOKING FOORRR??'

'FEEL ME!!!!' sleazed a salesman to a group of blonde

Germans who he wanted to touch his pashmina that he held out. 'VERRRY SOFTTTT!!!!!'

'I can get these in China for forty rupees,' I told a DVD salesman who started screaming at me when he wanted 300 rupees for a single disc.

'YOU LIE!!!!' he screeched as I told him that 40 was the retail price in Shanghai. 'No wayyyy!' When he realized I was telling the truth dollar signs clouded his eyes and I became his new best friend. 'We go into business, you and I, please, leave me your email, I want to know more about this.'

'I'm your friend!! Remember, your friend!!!' screamed another salesman after another woman who was trying her best to just to squeeze through the Hong Kong-like night market crowds and was not interested in buying some tacky mirrored bedspread pushed rudely in her face.

'Why am I looking at shoes made in Vietnam when Nike is American?' shouted a South African with a six person entourage in tow at a salesman in Bombay's only Nike outlet where I was sheepishly buying a pair of shoes to replace my pair that was shattered after three months in India.

'Almost nothing in USA is made in USA,' I said to him sarcastically. The salesman nodded in agreement. 'Indonesia. Vietnam. South Korea. India.'

The South African began to shake his head angrily and shouted,' I have AMERICAN MONEY to spend here, DOLLARS, and I want AMERICAN PRODUCTS. Show me your AMERICAN MADE SHOES!!!'

The salesman shook his head, and said, 'I'm sorry sir this is all we have.'

The South African huffed loudly and then stormed out, his entourage in tow.

'It's unbelievvvvabble,' screeched an Indian woman at an intersection across from Victoria Terminus, talking to her friend in a sari the color of solid gold. 'Can you imaginnnneee living at home with such a mother-in-lawwwww? Its positively crrriminallll what she's done to my sisterrrrr.'

Her gold saried friend clicked her tongue in agreement. 'Talk about a trageddyyy. Forcing her to cook and clean in this day and age, and she's been to America!!!!'

Negotiating Saigon-like traffic was worsened because crosswalks and crossing lights were non-existent and street signs had either been stolen or completely missing. Bombay's soul may have been Indian, but it's skeleton was British, bone white, brittle, ancient and decorated with gargoyles, Queen Victoria statues and rusting signs for Cadburys and Guinness. The city's twisting streets were fringed with Gothic cathedrals, British Railway stations and colonial buildings.

'I've never seen such a city's newspapers so different from the reality of the streets,' said an Indian woman who was living in Princeton, New Jersey, visiting home with her husband and kids for the first time after ten years away, as we watched the Bombay skyline grow larger after our three hour trip to Elephanta island.

She was right. The Bombay Times was so stuffed full of Bollywood blockbuster news, model movements, and fashionista articles that it was hard to believe it was the hometown paper of a city where thirty percent of the population lived and died on the streets, nothing was even mentioned of the plight of these people, only the news of the rich and connected, with advertisements for the launch of the new 'Manhattan' credit card printed with skyscrapers and yellow cabs to remind one of what Bombayites dreamed their city could be. And all day long the tables at Barista, India's knockoff Starbucks, was full of college students drinking fake frappacinos as street kids hovered at the exit, looking for pens and any loose change.

Unlike the Times of India, there were no sensationalist stories of suicide and on the front page. Here, it was money and power and supermodels and racecars.

In India where wealth and poverty went hand in hand in most towns and cities, the disparity was especially magnified in Bombay where the more the wealth, it seemed, the greater the poverty, and everywhere you walked, especially at night, it was around rows of sleeping bodies, whole families cooking in the gutters, taxi drivers sleeping in their cars and stray dogs and cats yowling at each other in the darkness, and above them, the shiny billboards for Air India flights to Los Angeles, and bright photos of luxury apartments more costly than London or Hong Kong.

When I took a taxi to get to Chowpatty Beach, the scene of the upcoming Ganesh Festival the driver thought I was mad to miss the festivities that would bring thousands of pilgrims to the beach carrying their favorite god on their shoulders to dip in the sea for good luck.

'He gives us EVERYTHING,' the driver went on, pointing to the faded and peeling photo of Ganesh on the dashboard. Where most cab drivers have their own photo to identify themselves, in India, most likely it will be their favorite deity, and in most Bombay cabs, elephants greatly outnumbered Krishna twenty to one.

'Are you SURE you can't stay for our Ganesh?' asked salesmen and hotel bellboys and taxi drivers and random people on the streets.

The night before I left the city, I went out with a Chilean lawyer living in Auckland, two British exchange students living in Chengdu, and a couple from Delhi who were here as wide eyed as we were at the spectacle and speed at which Bombay moved compared to sedate and dour Delhi.

We hit some bars in Colaba. It was a Saturday night, and we climbed down dank stairwells to places dimly lit and so full of people it seemed a fire marshal's nightmare, and squeezed past mini-skirted girls and guys wearing Travolta hair swept back severely with Bryl cream. We struggled to make sense of the common door policy where single men were barred but single women were allowed in without question.

'In China, the women are kept out in droves, especially in Shanghai, where most are pros,' screamed the British over the noise.

Here in India it is eve-teasing that kept the men out and to protect the dignity of women, not only were they given free access to bars and clubs, they had women's only train cars on suburban rail lines, and even a line of taxis exclusively for women.

The streets of Bombay may be 1920's Victorian, but inside the bars and clubs the atmosphere is very 1980's with Depeche Mode and vintage Madonna on the sound systems. There was even a break dancing contest going on at one place. We hadn't been at one bar for five minutes when a business-suited guy handed us all his name card, requesting us to act in some Bollywood movie being filmed the next day.

'Its got Miss Universe in it,' he shouted, but none of us were going to be around and told him no thanks.

My last morning in Bombay was a Sunday, and Colaba's roads were deserted of traffic, the street sellers were still out, however, setting up their stalls, and even at this early hour they were eager to make a deal.

'YESSSSSS!!!!!' a man shouted at me from thirty meters away who wanted me to buy a chess set made of coral.

I ignored him, but it didn't make any difference because all his neighbors got into the act and a chorus of 'YESSSSS's!' followed me for four blocks.

As I ducked down a small alley to take a short cut back to my hotel to get away from the noise, the hawkers, and the traffic, I stopped to cross the street. A tugging at my shorts made me think it was someone who wanted to remind me of the upcoming Ganesh festival, and I shook my head.

But when I looked down it turned out not to be a person at all but a blue-eyed goat, about to make breakfast out of a chunk of my shorts.

The lights changed and I leaped out of the way of the animal's jaws before it tore off a piece.

Getting a taxi this afternoon to Goa airport, off to Bangalore next.

Love, Dave

From: Dave <theloweroad@gmail.com>
To: Annette <whereisannette@yahoo.com>
Date: Dec 11, 2004 11:20 AM
Subject: From Freaks to Geeks and The End of India

Hey Annette.

I can't tell if I am in Vietnam, Mexico or Brazil.

Trivandrum is yet another passport stamp-less change here in India, and I am rubbing shoulders with nuns and cows and trishaws in the streets.

I am leaving in four hours to the Maldives. Can't wait. White sands will replace rubbishy ankle twisting sidewalks and palm trees will replace mangy bushes.

I will have slayed the beast. India will be just memories. Captured in photo and journal form. (Do you hear that Jake???) Already, even though I have 240 minutes to go, my mind is flipping through those memories like a departure board at an airport, all clap clap clap clap as each destination in my journey re-reveals itself. Then I can tell all those smug travelers I have met since beginning my travels: INDIA? HUH. I HAVE JUST DONE IT.

Below is the last of my trip snowboarding down the west coast of India to the toe of the country.

I am here for the pies but I am so ready to jump off into the Indian Ocean.

My flight was on Air Deccan, India's newest low cost carrier, and was completely unlike Bangladesh Biman Airlines; it didn't mean cabin cockroaches and planes with missing ceiling panels. Their aircraft were brand new ATR-42's with great ground staff and cabin crew whose airline didn't charge more than $40 for each flight. With the top class on trains costing nearly $20, and a twelve-hour journey each to boot, spending two hours in a plane seemed a better option than twenty-four hours as a guest onboard yet another Indian Railways train. My lungs and ears (after being gassed and blasted) gave a huge sigh of relief.

The flight from Bombay to Goa took off from the main airport passing over luxury condominiums and swathes of slum areas that went straight to the horizon. Seconds after rotation we slammed into monsoon turbulence and as we ascended and during the hour flight, it was a nonstop roller coaster of lurches and stomach-churning plunges that suspended cabin service and kept the seat belt sign permanently on.

Our cruising altitude was 16,000 feet.

Two weeks earlier I had been STANDING on solid ground 3,000 feet HIGHER in Ladakh. On landing at Goa, once again, it was like you had stamped your passport into another country. Now it was like a mixture of northeast Brazil, southern Vietnam, and hilly Mexico with red roofed colonial villas, white-washed churches straight out of Europe and beaches and scenery straight out of Cuba.

Like everywhere else in India cars and taxis became showcases for local religions, and Goa was no different, the Bombay taxi driver's Ganesh statue had now been replaced with ivory rosaries that jangled from the mirror, and Virgin Mary statues, too, (glow in the dark, the driver told me) on the dashboard her arms outstretched and her head tilted to one side. And not only dashboards were spouting religion, because all along the roads were signs like these:

JESUS LOVES YOU
SIN IS NOT IN
MARY'S VIRGINITY IS PURE

I stayed in the Fontainhas area of Panjim town on the river where I got a room filled with a dark four poster bed and huge creaking cabinets set next to lace curtains that opened onto a small latticed balcony, it felt like Florence, or Spain, but sacred cows and chai wallahs calling out and walking through the streets below were reminders that I am, in fact still in Mother India.

I took a local bus to Old Goa where churches and cathedrals sit on a muddy river surrounded by lush coconut plantations. St Francis Xavier is buried in one of them, and the gold decorating the naves, crypts and altars remind you of the ornate churches of Innsbruck or Vienna.

That evening I wandered down a cobbled lane, following the golden light, rays from the setting sun that struck the colonial and art deco houses, churches, and government buildings in the town, watching women hanging washing, artisans paint tiles in outdoor studios on street with names like Rua Sao Tome and Rua Vasco De Gama and Rua San Jacinto, crowded with glassed in art galleries selling water-colored paintings straight out of Mykonos or Provence while kids in the street played cricket and football as nuns in starched white smocks walked school kids home in the gathering dusk.

When I boarded my second Air Deccan ATR 42 I arrived in darkness at India's own Silicon Valley, the IT center of Bangalore. Instead of Krishna, Ganesh, or Jesus, it was Larry Ellison and Bill Gates who ruled that town, all along the streets were booksellers hawking books on:

HOW TO GET RICH- NOW!
RELEASE YOUR INNER MANAGER
BE A CEO, FOR LIFE

There were no books on Buddhism; no street sellers hawking Krishna kitsch, and no Hindu Holy Men begging. The streets were filled only with business-suited locals, yakking into cell phones, mostly in English and mostly with people twelve time zones away.

And the newspapers were full of ads for self-fulfillment seminars and business networking functions and software job fairs and three step processes to getting a US resident visa and how to immigrate to Canada with 25,000 US dollars. And all over the city empty walls were plastered not with spiritual Gods but with the Gods of the IT generation: geeky Bill and sneering Larry, both looking like heads of state in three piece suits and looking very out of place in the steamy, Indian heat.

But they weren't the only ones out of place, everywhere you went, mixed in with crowds of locals you passed khaki wearing American IT professionals bragging to their Indian colleagues about nightlife in Atlanta, expat wives bored to tears in Barista reading battered fashion magazines, tech kids from San Francisco wearing Craigslist T-shirts and skateboarding down rutted roads, and polo shirted ad execs from Chicago, wide eyed at the cows munching leaves from overhanging tree branches at bus stands.

And all around you are Yahoo and IBM campuses and Singaporean tech parks and high rises that are taller and plusher than anything you can see in Delhi or even Bombay, and shiny shopping malls have popped up all over the place selling even more self-fulfillment and get-rich-quick books than you could read in one hundred lifetimes.

I never saw a religious building or any sort of sidewalk salvation offered in Bangalore, not a single Indian Saddhu. But I did see western Saddhus, a.k.a. 'management consultants' handing out resumes at street corners, looking for jobs and even weirder, a white beggar sitting on the sidewalk sticking his hand out at pedestrians.

Even the auto rickshaw drivers had photos of Bill and Larry in their cabs, and one was taking evening HTML classes in his free time.

My last journey aboard the Indian Railways network was an overnight train from Bangalore to Trivandrum. And like previous train journeys this one was another memorable one.

I had only been able to get a wait-listed seat on the Kaniyakumari Express, #2625, and when I had booked the journey in Bombay I was not quite sure where I stood with my ticket.

'You have a 120% confirmed ticket,' the man smiled at me

from behind the window after I had paid for it and he had pushed the ticket through.

'If its 120% confirmed, than why does it say, 'RAC' waitlisted?'

'It's waitlisted now, but it will be 120% confirmed before departure.'

'But all the trains are booked, what if I don't get the confirmed space?'

'120% sir, 120%.'

'Why not 200%, and confirm it now,' I asked, pushing the ticket underneath the window again, not really liking the probability of showing up at Bangalore, boarding the train, and then being told there were no seats, no way was I going to get chucked off the train again like in Agra.

The man tapped at his keys on his computer a few more times, and then pushed the ticket back to me.

'150% confirmed now, you are waitlist number four.' His smile was gone and he motioned to the grandma in Coke bottle glasses standing in line behind me who grunted and gladly pushed me aside to shove her Rupee bills under the window.

Giving up, I walked away and forgot about it. When I was finally in Bangalore station, I found the right platform for #2625, and asked for train coach number 'RAC.'

It was only after I had dragged my forty kilograms of luggage up and down three flights of stairs that I was told I had to go BACK to the reservation office to get a stamp confirming I had been granted a reserved berth. The man in Bombay had forgotten to tell me that confirmed tickets could not be checked at the platform.

How revoltingly careless of him.

'But it says berth seventy on the ticket,' I whined to the ticket collector who was busy pasting the train reservations to the outside of the train compartment.

'Just go the reservation office, sir,' he said angrily and waved me off.

So off I went back up and down the three flights of stairs huffing and puffing grateful it wasn't in Ladakh that I was doing this, or I would have blacked out from the altitude. Finding the reservation line snaking around the corner, I had learned enough after over three months in India to just cut to the front, shove the ticket under the window, screech a little, and get what I wanted.

And that's what I did.

Reaching over the heads in front of me, I shouted, 'RESERVATION!!! BERTH!!!' I tossed the ticket under the window.

I had to only wait five seconds for the man to tap a few keys on his computer, watch him scribble a car number on it, grunt and shove it back to me.

And then I saw a Caucasian woman behind me, face pulled back in a sickening sneer. She had seen my American Football Linebacker Approach to the Indian Ticket line, and she was clearly NOT impressed.

'Wait,' my face screamed, but it was too late. Clearly the woman had just arrived in India, and had not mastered the art of winning the gold medal in the Olympic Indian Train Ticket Confirmation event. When I marched up the three flights of stairs again now gasping for breath, suddenly Mother India and her billion inhabitants made a lot more sense.

Then I triumphantly found the rude conductor again. He scrutinized the train number in the darkness and then with a reluctant wave he sent me off with a dismissive flick of his hands, 'TRAIN FULL!!! HURRY!!!!'

I ran back to the right car, practically dragging my bag by now, boarded and then collapsed in my berth, exhausted, with exactly three minutes before departure.

I realized the berth I had been given was not big enough to hold all my luggage, and started to chain my bags to the wires provided for just that purpose at a berth right across from it, then when the person came along for that berth, I would just switch with them, no problem.

When we pulled away from the station the berths were still empty and a minute later the same ornery conductor came through, snatched my ticket away, scrutinized the car number, the berth number, looked at me over his glasses, twice, then again, and then screamed at me to move my bags, the train was not only full, it was overbooked, and I had to be in the correct bunk.

'MOVE!!! NOW!!!!' He kicked my bag with his foot for emphasis.

Tired and used to more flexible conductors in the past who easily switched seats with a flick of their pen, I pointed out that the berth I had been assigned was too small for my luggage, and all I had to do was switch with who ever came, no worries.

'NO!!!!' he shouted, thundering at me as though I were deaf. 'MOVE NOW!!!! THERE ARE THREE PEOPLE COMING!!!!'

He started to drag my bags away but confounded by the chain, pulled harder and harder while I sat there, still red faced from the double hike over the railway trestle.

Gathering all my strength, I performed a perfect Oscar Worthy 'Head Shake Roll' expertly crafted after seeing it thousands of times, pointing at the three empty berths all around me. Then, four months of frustration boiled over and I stood up to scream at him hurling all the Hindi I had learned in a chai-cup bile-full stream of abuse.

The scene was so funny, this conductor screaming in English, the foreigner yelling in Hindi, that even the jaded chai vendors stopped and stared as words ricocheted back and forth. Eventually I sat down, hoarse, my point made, delivered yet another Oscar perfect Head Shake Roll for good measure, and folded my arms across my chest.

The conductor, angry at the laughs from the chai vendors, screamed at me for the key but I refused to budge as stubborn as a sacred cow blocking a Varanasi alley, swishing its tail languidly. I had learned from the best beast of all.

The chai wallahs pleaded with the conductor to just change the berth numbers, but the conductor stormed off, and with an angry flick killed the lights in my side of the carriage. (and there wasn't even an Apple PowerBook in sight) Not wanting another argument, I just wanted sleep. Two chai wallahs came over, grinned, and said sarcastically as they giggled uncontrollably, 'You, sir, we can see you been in India long time. You win sir, you win!'

When I woke up the next morning the three berths around me were still empty, the blankets unmoved. The three people had never even shown up.

At the Trivandrum train station a white Toyota sedan was waiting for me. The driver got out and loaded my luggage into the trunk. There were to be no more trains, no more planes and no more buses in front of me - it was my last full day in India and my final destination before my flight to the Maldives was Kanniyakumari, the very tip of India where the Bay of Bengal, the Arabian Sea and Indian Ocean mixed.

It seemed like an apt place to end my Indian journey, having stood at the end of the road in Hundur in the Nubra Valley, as high geographically, and physically, you could get in India, now I was at the tropical, polar opposite.

The scenery on the eighty six kilometer drive felt like Sri Lanka, but even more so, like Vietnam, as the only Communist state in India, it was a surprise to see so many hammer and sickles painted on walls and red flags fluttering in front of police stations and the lush palm tree studded countryside reminiscent of the Mekong Delta.

When we passed a line of Chinese fishing nets imported from North Asia by sea traders and adopted by locals to catch bait fish, Stalin, my driver, asked me if I was amazed by this spectacle. I told him they had the same things in Vietnam and he brightened.

'You know Vietnam?'

'Yes, for several years.'

'Then you are a Communist then?' Stalin asked happily, taking his eyes completely off the road as he lit his cigarette.

'Oh no, I'm not a Communist.'

'Are you sure? I am a Communist! My mother is one! My brother is too! My father is dead, but he was one too!!'

I nodded my head as Stalin rambled on, changing topics, telling me how the book, the God of Small Things, was a sham, and a bad reflection on the good people of his home state.

'We don't like this book,' he said, shaking his head angrily. The next minute, he was talking about David Beckham; the minute after that, the outlook for the Indian economy after the poor 2004 monsoon season.

On and on the conversation swerved as the car lurched around cows, random bicyclists, and school children, between the corruption of Tamil Nadu politics, Bollywood films, which Keralans didn't watch because of the language barrier, the truth to the virginity of Britney Spears and the treachery of President Bush.

When we reached Kanyakumari the sea was roiling with huge breakers that rolled in and smashed themselves to death on the rocks, the sun was high in the sky, so brightly reflecting off the sea you had to squint to look at the water. Indian women, young and old, dressed in bright saris were bathing in the sea, an informal football match was being played on the beach, and dozens of young couples and families were sitting along the battered sea wall eating grilled peanuts and drinking chai from tiny earthenware cups emptied and then crushed underfoot in the sand.

'You did it!!!' screamed Stalin as he joined me in the shallow waters for a dip. He lifted my arm above my head as though I was Rocky Balboa. 'You've been from end to the other end of my country!!!!'

I didn't need some train chai wallahs to tell me: I WON.

We laughed and said yes when some people, who, like at the Taj Mahal, wanted a photo with a foreigner and we happily smiled and hammed it up for the camera as the waves crashed in, the sky burned from the strong equatorial light, and the long familiar smells of Indian tea, curry, charcoal smoke, car exhaust, perfume, and incense swirled all around us.

It was a fitting ending to India indeed.
I am about to jump off the continent I have called home for a third of a year and straight out into the Indian Ocean.

Just did it.
I did India.

INDIA.

You've heard all the horror stories, the hushed tones travelers adopt when they talk about the place, the evil touts, the vicious camels, the choking pollution, the filthy gutters, the bowel churning food and the Bladerunneresque cities. A spiritual playground where the world's major religions cut their teeth, a train system that actually works, towns where bodies burn all day and night, temples where the world's luckiest rats run free, cities where silicon is king, a golden temple patrolled with scimitar wielding guards, and remote mountain caves where holy men roll in human ashes.

Excuse me, Mother India, but just WHERE is your place on planet earth?

Even after four months, I have absolutely no idea.
And that is the greatest thing.
I don't know.

I DON'T KNOW.

And something tells me even all those smug 'The Found' know-it-all Indiaphiles don't know it either.

In an instant, India took my breath away, and not because of that open sewer grate. The festivals, the street life, the beaches, the forests, the temples, the monuments and the characters that surrounded me from the moment I arrived until today, when I set foot on my state of the art jet (and not a moment too soon for half of me, and a moment I've dreaded for the other half). India, quite simply, sent my head spinning as quick as a Bhang Lassie.

After flightmares, that Agori in Varanasi, charging bulls, horny camels, cow shit sandwiches, the Delhi Dog Shit Man, the collapsed highway, Sky Bitches, farting train mates, that blue eyed goat, Stalin the driver, and much MUCH more, I am ready to leave.

SOOOOOOO READY.

Love it or hate it, India got under my skin faster and deeper than any other cultural chigger; and there it will stay, fueling me with enough stories of bravery, adventure, horror, rapture and redemption to last a lifetime.

Make that several lifetimes.

If you're a culture vulture, search no more.

Welcome to India.

Welcome to you Mother Ship.

Love, Dave

From: Dave <theloweroad@gmail.com>
To: Annette <whereisannette@yahoo.com>
Date: Dec 23, 2004 11:27 PM
Subject: Tea with Tattoo

Hey Annette,

If you've ever wanted to imitate Tattoo from Fantasy Island and croak, 'Da plane, da plane!' as your red seaplane lands in a turquoise lagoon, where you exit to shake hands with Mr. Roarke in a white tuxedo, then the Maldives is definitely the place for you.

India is about 600 kilometers away but I have almost completely forgotten the dirt the noise the chaos and the cows. The Maldives is heaven - cows are illegal here.

ABSOLUTELY ILLEGAL.

I love this place already.

With 1,200 islands, ninety resorts, 99.6% water, .4% land, and all less than two meters above sea level, the Maldives is not your average country. Five star is the norm here, and with daily rates rising from $500 plus per person per day, to the sky's-the-limit resorts where the room alone costs $10,000 per night, plus service charge, most independent travelers would be bankrupted within hours of arrival and sent packing on the next flight to Sri Lanka.

However, if you are able to afford the sticker shock of the accommodation, the country is one of the most unique on the planet. As a completely independent archipelago, the country has its own language and culture, the Maldives is where the concept of shell money was invented, even the word 'atollu' in the Maldivian language became the English word 'atoll,' a perfect metaphor from a country that virtually is a picture perfect icon for paradise.

It is the only place I have ever been where the photos in brochures simply fall short of the reality: there are no roads or highways here and there is so much water and open space that you have to get almost everywhere by seaplane. Gone is a horizon interrupted by mountains because the sky comes straight down to the sea in all directions, similar in a sense to a blue desert rippled with waves. The country's airport is an aircraft shaped island with water on all sides and an aborted takeoff here would mean a dunk in the Indian Ocean. Now that would definitely qualify as a flightmare.

On the surface the Maldives is paradise in the classic sense, Robinson Crusoe excursions visit sandbanks with exactly one palm tree on it, water bungalows have retractable glass floors to feed the colorful fish, buffets serve mountains of seafood and fresh fruit three times a day, and water temperatures are a perfect 29 Celsius every day of the year. A 'cold' day is one where the air temp drops by more than four degrees.

But there is a side to the Maldives guests don't see. The water in the sink and in your glass is desalinated; even the Coca Cola bottling plant here uses seawater to make soda, all trash has to be removed on time each day to avoid burying the island; sand is pumped from the lagoon to preserve the sugar white sands from the rising sea levels; and every food item from Dom Perignon champagne to sea salt has to be imported.

The biggest danger is getting hit on the head by a coconut, in fact, it's the leading cause of death in the Maldives.

Spending two weeks on board a live aboard affords a view of the other half of the country, the part that lies underwater. There, reefs are full of fish, manta rays and even whale sharks are so common in some places that encounters can be guaranteed year round. Diving each day before breakfast, we surface in water so calm and clear it felt like bobbing in the middle of an alpine lake. Frequent night dives at unnamed reefs were punctuated with lightning flashes spreading out from massive anvil shaped thunderheads, passing overhead like antique Clipper ships.

In between the diving were visits to the many luxury resorts scattered across the country. Perfectly manicured pathways, gracious staff, luxury water villas and blinding white beaches were strange oases in the deep blue ocean, morgue-like and quiet on the expensive ones, (Soneva Fushi, Banyan Tree) and rowdy and boozy on the cheaper ones (Club Med, Fun Island).

Even the staff was weird.

Most at the expensive ones went about their jobs with the efficiency of those at a villain's lair in a James Bond film dressed in flowing head to toe, space station robes or black silk jumpsuits that swished as they walked, a vacant, yet brochure perfect smile spread across their lips. Nothing was too great, or two small a request for them to do. Towels scented with peppermint were pressed into your palms as soon as you stepped off the toothpaste white speedboat and a frangipani flower wrapped in a silk ribbon was handed over to you like it was the Hope Diamond. Everywhere you went, wide smiles, polite nods and patronizing words followed you like a fragrance, each staff you passed offered you the same, note-perfect 'Good morning, sir,' that you began to wonder if the Stepford Wives had expanded into the hotel industry.

But all was not quiet in the staff quarters, and more than one were quietly questioning their workplace that offered them no escape: they lived, ate with, and drank with their work colleagues, that could be heaven or hell depending on how well you got along with them.

'Can you believe the hotel handbook actually has a chapter about the ban on sexual relations not only between guests and staff, but between staff and other staff?' whispered a Japanese girl with rose red lips at one resort, her eyes wild from months of forced abstinence. She confided in me that she was planning to quit and go back to Osaka, but she couldn't.

'All staff must hand over their passport when they arrive,' she said. 'The GM won't let me go until they find a replacement who speaks Japanese, and for three months now, no one. This place is a golden prison for staff, but heaven for guests.'

Life for staff at the cheaper resorts swerved to the opposite end of the spectrum. Sex with guests or staff went on without any reprimand from management, and with all staff HIV negative, because a positive result of an AIDS test would have been followed by a speedboat to the airport, where they would have been kicked out of the country, this meant that unlike at home, STD risk was literally written across potential sexual partner's foreheads.

Or at least in their HR file.

More than one GM had been sent packing after rumors of orgies and three ways with couples were picked up by the resort's owners.

Truthfully, the release was necessary: cast adrift in the Indian Ocean with little contact with civilization for months on end, staff was imported along with the food and the furniture. While many I talked to moaned about being far from home, for some, it was precisely this that attracted some to the

Maldives in the first place, including a London party girl at one high-end resort, who needed some more extra distance from her pushy coke dealer.

'Lots of sand around but none to snort,' she said ruefully as she tucked into her dinner one night while everyone looked away uncomfortably.

Many of the staff in the Maldives was rumored to be on the run from something: ex-wives, debtors, the police, the Mafia, ex-business partners, Interpol, and more. If so, it was the perfect place to do it. Water separated each island as perfectly as a bottomless canyon.

'Shipwrecked,' whispered a French guest at one resort as we drank at the bar, watching the staff dance underneath a pulsating strobe light. He pointed his finger at them again and whispered once more, 'shipwrecked.'

The antidotes to the resorts were the local islands where dive liveaboards stocked up on essentials and gave their guests some time to get off the boat. Completely off limits to overnight stays for foreigners, it was only on these islands where you can experience the country's culture that unlike almost every other country you have ever visited in the world, was tucked away behind a veil, in some sort of tourist apartheid.

Often ignored by the luxury resorts where a weekly Bodu Beru drum performance was the closest guests got to the people, life on the local islands was as fragile as the coral reefs themselves: over hundreds of years, the Maldivians had learned to survive with meager vegetation, water and animals; learning how to use coconuts for food, shelter and even clothing, they had learned to tap toddy, go fishing for marlin with just a hook attached to coconut rope, or navigate their elegantly decorated dhonis at night just by the position of the stars.

The locals were always willing to teach you how they built their traditional dhonis without plans, saws, or even nails; and I couldn't believe that months before I was telling bewildered Ladakhis what it was like to swim in the ocean and now I was explaining to Maldivians the concept of a mountain to people that have never seen snow, a hill, a cow, a skyscraper, or even a dog because canines were banned throughout the country.

Most of the guests and many of the staff turned their noses up about the local islands which they thought were breeding grounds for witchcraft and superstition, choosing to spend their days off at the pool rather than taking time to get to learn another culture or language.

And it is out here, in between visits to the resort and the local islands, in all this blue emptiness where my experiences and memories from India come flooding out, so much so that more than once I left people slack jawed at my blabbering, my mumbling and ramblings about the horrors and rapture of the place. Finally, after encounters across India with Spiritual Tourists and The Found and The Lost, interested in only talk that revolved around the Dalai Lama, Levitational Meditation, and past lives, here in the Maldives the conversations were deep, intense discussions about seafood, suntan oil and sand.

Turning away from the banality of these people, it was to the locals I had long conversations with. Tourism is less than three decades old here in the Maldives, and many locals derided the young people who knew more about Hip Hop than traditional fishing, leaving in droves for Male and jobs with hotels there. Despite these fears, the Maldives was now threatened with extinction by a far more sinister force than package tourists.

It is threatened by the very sea itself.

The Maldives is famous for being a country that won't exist in less than one hundred years. Even though the unthinkable is decades away, the sunken future of the Maldives has already arrived. A few weeks before Christmas, a strong tropical storm arrived during the highest tides ever recorded in the country, waves and wind heavily eroded beaches, leaving resorts with washed away coconut trees and collapsed water bungalows. Sand pumps worked overtime to repair the damage. The work was finished quickly and the white sand, blue water paradise that attracts 700,000 people each year was quickly restored.

Christmas is in a couple of days, and New Years. It's funny, with India now far away, memories are clogging my dreams, and conversations. Photos on my laptop already seem like they were taken by someone else.

Love, Dave

From: Dave <theloweroad@gmail.com>
To: Annette <whereisannette@yahoo.com>
Date: Jan 3, 2005 4:27 AM
Subject: (No Subject)

Annette I have been getting literally hundreds of emails since the 26th.

To cut it short, I am lucky to be even writing to you. I'm back in New York, jetlagged, still shaking, and unable to watch the TV news.

Dying while traveling is not something you think about, even after climbing Himalayan canyons in your bare hands and wheels snapping off cars and AK-47's shooting at you and Khmer Rouge soldiers and being charged by angry bulls.

It always seems impossible.

But not anymore.

It started with shrill screams, pounding footsteps and the sound of splintering wood. More ominously, with a distant roar that sounded like a line of approaching 747 jets, flying low. More screams. And the roar was only growing louder.

It was 10:30 a.m., the day after Christmas, and we were still reeling from our hangovers from a late night drinking session in the bar.

What the HELL was happening?

Cold, dirty seawater started pouring in under the door. In seconds there are sparks popping out of the power outlets and then they explode. I leap for the exit but I can't get it open, there's too much water pouring against it. The roar continues growing louder along with the screams. Using all my strength I smash my way out and by now the water is knee-deep freezing cold and surging faster and faster like a washing machine gone mad.

'The children! The children!' a staff member was screaming and I joined him to ferry kids who were drifting past us in the rushing water that was pouring over the island. As I run to the beach I look out at the ocean to see that clean to the horizon it has turned a greyish, dishwater brown, and there were whitecaps like a stormy North Sea. The turquoise Maldives blue had completely disappeared.

With the last child off the beach I ran to the opposite side of the narrow island and see water surging towards me, I turned to see the island was now completely submerged. Champagne bubbles dribbled up from the sand beneath my feet. For a split second I think the island is sinking because the level of the ocean is rising so steadily that it seemed we were dropping down, and fast. I look around and see people standing like wax figures frozen solid.

The first wave sweeps in and smashes me against the wall. I am gasping for breath, barely breathing, tasting gasoline and raw sewage mixed in with the salt. Keys shoes sunglasses wallet and cell phone are sucked off me.

Another wave slams into my stomach and I am smashed against the wall again and I grab a pole for support. I hear staff and guests in the reception area who are screaming for God, Allah and the Buddha. Surrounding me are televisions and computers that are tumbling over and over, in front of me, a wall of glass implodes sucking desk chairs and office equipment underneath into the swirling currents. Watching deckchairs mattresses and lamps fly past I feel for a moment that I am on the sinking Titanic.

With the words 'This can't be happening' rushing through my brain seconds later the main wave hits and blackness replaces the bright sunlight, surging boiling white water rapids swallow me and an interminable amount of time passes. Another wall collapses metal and wood are smashing into me and I see a huge palm tree hit the ground in a silent crash.

When I come to I am gasping for air and the sound of water is rushing through my ears. A huge piece of wooden deck is smashing into the poles holding up the roof and it seems determined to crush its way through the island and slice me in two.

I squeeze my eyes shut again, clench my jaw tight, and wait.

Suddenly it's as if someone has flushed a toilet; the water is gone the wave had passed but it had sucked the ocean out along with it. Tropical fish are flopping frantically in the sand.

I run to the beach and see that thirty meters of vertical ocean have completely disappeared.

If time had stopped I could have walked along the rim of the atoll.

There wasn't time for that because in the confusion of screaming guests, distraught mothers and overwhelmed staff I knew that the missing water was going to come back. And fast.

And standing there waiting, not breathing, it did.

Another wave smashed into the island surging in from the opposite direction full of furniture and debris.

When it was gone only silence is left behind but in the quiet injured people come hobbling in from all directions bleeding and mumbling incoherently; staff began to count heads but there was no dry paper no electricity no radio no telephone no cell phone coverage no contact with the outside world. We had no idea what had happened or what was to come but when another train of waves approached and the hissing roaring sound that none of us would ever forget was back again people began to use the word tsunami.

Actually it was a group of Japanese.

They had somehow found some lifejackets which they quickly pulled over their heads formed a circle and ran around, yelling, 'Tsunami! Tsunami! Tsunami!' until an Australian man snapped at them, 'Shut the fuck up!'

As I struggled to put my sluggish brain into gear revolving through my brain like on some viciously ironic merry go round was the Bee Gees song Staying Alive that the DJ had accidentally played twice the previous night. We plunged ahead to help the injured keeping a very, very nervous eye on the sea expecting death at virtually any moment. Pausing for a second I looked out at the ocean to see gigantic whirlpools forming eddies and currents around the island. The sea had gone completely mad, and the surface spent hours swaying back and forth like a huge bathtub.

It was early that afternoon after more waves hours of uncertainty rumors threats and tears all played out under the hot burning sun when people began to start checking out of the hotel.

Mentally speaking that is.

A man salvaged a briefcase and a saltwater soaked cell phone and sits staring out to sea, a staff member found a tin of lip balm and is running around yelling at people that they need it, and a young receptionist shrieks in Dhivehi and then faints right in front of me.

Then a French woman, hands at her throat, starts yelling at no one in particular. 'Mes bijoux, mes bijoux!' she cried pointing to her room now gone.

And then an Austrian was demanding where her plane was.

And an Italian woman wanted a refund. Immediately.

The staff point to where the buildings once stood, decimated by the waves.

'Wait,' says one as he stalks off, disgusted.

The hysteria gets worse: it was the end of the world, moaned one lady, we were now going to starve to death screamed another. On and on it went. The little civilization that been imported to the island had been wiped clean in an instant and the terrifying void that remained was now filled with rumors and speculations that swirled on and on, out of control, more ominous than any wall of water.

That night the moon was as full as I had ever seen it, illuminating the horizon with a silvery mercurial light. We were grateful, more waves were predicted and no one wanted to be caught off guard in the darkness.

Not taking our eyes off the horizon for a second, slapping mosquitoes and still tasting gasoline in our mouths we counted our losses in the darkness. Cameras. Cell phones. Clothes. Money. Books. Heirlooms. Jewelry.

'The reef,' murmured a French dive instructor hoarse after so much screaming who was in the water when the tsunami struck and had completed her first emergency ascent in her fifteen year career, 'saved your lives.'

She was right. We didn't have time to lament our losses. Or sleep. We had to keep our eyes on that horizon.

Our lives depended on it.

The next day was very long and incredibly hot. As the sea slowly returned to normal the tides went it went out again and we passed the long hours salvaging for our things. Passports clothes shoes suitcases books and resort debris was mixed with smashed wood doors television sets air conditioners and more scattered about. Every once in a while, there would be a sharp cry as someone found something that belonged to them.

A DJ, flown in to perform on Christmas Eve has lost 2,000 CD's from ten years of work. An American woman is looking for her wedding ring. A German man was looking for his cameras.

It was sometime that afternoon when the screaming starts again and people begin to run.

'A wave! A wave!' someone is shouting at the top of their lungs. Heart in my throat I bolt for a tree and climb it heart racing barely breathing acting like a shell-shocked soldier when he hears an innocent firecracker explode.

It was time to go home but beneath the relentless equatorial sun stomachs rumbling from hunger and tongues swollen from thirst we had no idea when that would be.

The second night was longer and darker than the first. And not just from the fact the moon was gone, making it almost impossible to see the waves, I remember the story that a guest has told me of the three spirits dressed in jewelry that had visited him in the middle of the night before the tsunami, warning him strongly of some impending mortal danger.

By day three morale was rock bottom and we settled in listlessly for more waiting. Movements became slow, speech slurred and energy evaporated from the dehydration. My clothes hung off me like I was a skeleton. A raging headache pulsed through my head like a freight train. I began to visualize Kali in front of me and Agoris and Sacred Cows and more, floating on the turquoise waters. The blue Indian Ocean was now the murky Ganges, reeking from the smell of death, the scene of carnage.

But all of a sudden a buzzing seaplane circled the island. When it lands and taxis, the cabin door pops open. The

Canadian pilots, stunned at the damage, start to snap pictures as though they were on holiday.

'Get us off this godforsaken island,' snarled a Sri Lankan accountant.

And get off we did.

In a carefully choreographed convoy, seaplane after seaplane took everyone back to the capital where we were dropped off barefoot sunburned exhausted and starving where locals ran up to us and asked us where we had come from. When we said the name of the island they gasped.

'We heard everyone was dead there,' one woman said, shaking her head.

But we weren't.

We were alive.

The next day I boarded a Singapore Airlines 777. As it lifted off from the runway still covered in beach sand left there by the tsunami the cabin was full of passengers crying and quietly sobbing. The crew looked at each other bewildered; clearly their training at one of the world's best airlines had covered serving drinks and food. It had not covered how to handle survivors of one of Asia's worst natural disasters.

During my short transit stop in Singapore where I watched fireworks burst on New Year's Eve I had terrified a young sales girl at a shopping center where I had greedily snapped up underwear and socks and flung them onto the counter, eyes bulging, happy to wear some clean clothes at last.

'What happened to you?' she said, carefully checking my signature with the back of my credit card to see that she wasn't helping some wanted criminal steal underwear.

When I told her, she burst into tears.

On a bright New Years Day I boarded a brand new Airbus A340 that lifted off gracefully from the runway at Changi airport for the long flight to New York. I was seated in the last row between an American couple whose driver had saved their lives in Sri Lanka when he drove their taxi into the hills as soon as the sea withdrew, and another American who had tossed a coin to choose where to spend Christmas. Koh Samui or Phi Phi. The coin landed on Samui and he and his friends were spared a hell that tens of thousands of others hadn't.

Despite our ordeal, and lots to talk about, we quickly slipped into silence, the weight of what we had experienced finally sinking in.

In the airport at Newark New Jersey I went through customs with suitcases leaking seawater that a startled customs agent unzipped, releasing a gasoline stench into the terminal.

'Welcome home,' he stammered, waving me on after I told him where, and what, I had come from. I caught a cab downtown wearing flip-flops and shorts. The temperature was about zero, and even jaded Manhattanites stopped to stare at the sunburned man slipping on the icy streets.

I now know what homeless people feel like.

The next morning, walking the cold, crowded streets of Manhattan, people kept asking me if I was all right. Surely I was shaken up, traumatized, damaged, unable to sleep. I'm OK, I nodded, saying I was sleeping fine and things were good, all considering. Donate as much as you can, I told everyone, even total strangers. DONATE. But I kept ignoring this nagging feeling deep inside me that something was different.

Forever different.

It wasn't until hours later when I turned a corner and slammed into the neon, noise and nutcases in Times Square that I realized what it was.

New York City felt small.

Annette, I loved the Maldives as soon as I arrived but that paradise is about as deep as a lagoon. Shallow.

Not like India.

India was deep.

Remember my first three days in Varanasi, when I trembled

in fear, fighting off a virulent stomach bug, topped with a furious fever, stepping backwards right into the path of an Agori whose body was covered in human ashes and who grabbed hold of me and refused to let go?

As the days and weeks passed I grew to appreciate the kaleidoscope of colors and cultures all around me but all in an unusually detached way. I moved about the country in as methodical way as Mother India would allow, losing my usual happy go lucky nature, replacing it with a clinical schedule, timed down to the hour, carefully arranged and rigid, a personality I had never known I had.

Even so, I didn't miss a thing, slipping off my shoes I walked amongst the holy rats at Karni Mata, I climbed aboard a horny camel in Rajastan, I wandered around the burning Ghats in Varanasi, I uncovered the greedier side of Bombay, and gasped for breath on icy Himalayan mountain passes.

I took lots of pictures, asked lots of questions, tried lots of food, but my demeanor, to my disappointment, remained distant, detached, and aloof.

...if India with all her religions tucked under one roof was like some vast Salvation Hypermart, I wasn't buying...

....and if India was one vast Spiritual Buffet where enlightenment redemption healing and inner peace were just an ashram away, I wasn't hungry...

Maybe I am a slow learner or maybe it was just the sheer weight of all the knowledge available in India that clogged my brain, making it take longer for it all to sink in, but even after several months there very little of the country's richness was absorbed; it seemed to bounce off my brain like Teflon.

When it came time to leave the country I gratefully boarded that Indian Airlines Airbus 320 for Male and almost cried when I stepped out onto a spotless un-cracked tarmac where there were no holy men eager to save my soul, no mad cows blocking my way, no stomach bugs to send my bowels into convulsions or any mad railway officials to send me on the wrong train.

It was there, though, in that placid, tranquil picture-perfect island nation that is the Maldives where I seemed least likely to learn one of life's greatest lessons. The country's resorts, though beautiful, were artificial paradises, carefully landscaped, expertly decorated with Thai silks and high thread count Egyptian cottons, and staffed with smiling, patronizing people. In that artificial world where everything down to the salt had to be imported, and where even the water had to be desalinated, the more you paid, it seemed, the less you learned.

A shrink-wrapped paradise.

Sterilized for your protection.

And the guests there were pretty happy to keep it that way, shunning India completely as a pariah, a leper.

But it was in the Maldives where the unthinkable happened out of the blue and swept across Asia on that bright warm day right after Christmas.

Sitting dazed and wide-awake on the long, turbulent flight home yesterday, head still spinning from watching the sea act like it had been possessed by some malevolent, evil spirit, the Airbus 340 jet flew on through the inky darkness passing over the North Pole.

A brilliant display of Northern Lights lit up both sides of the plane and it was in those vivid green blues and pinks that my experiences from India resurfaced. I realized that my exposure to such extremes of shock, death, hatred, love, surprise, life, horror and wonder had prepared me for this experience.

Travel had delivered it to me.

Like FECG and the old lady with crooked teeth and that INTERPOL line up and the Khmer Rouge soldiers and that vicious cup of coffee in Saigon and Rosa Klebb in Hanoi and getting fisted by that woman in a Burka and Six Fingers and that Agori and Raj and Cow Shit Sandwiches and the Delhi Dog Shit Man and much, much more.

The passengers all around me on the Singapore Airlines plane actually turned their heads away from us, refusing to listed to our stories, acting much like the guests in the Maldives, shutting anything out of the ordinary out.

You have my permission to shoot me if I ever get like that.

Extremes teach you things, and India has that in spades. After first hearing about the place way back in Japan, and the repeated delays of my plans to explore that place, all the myths and urban legends (to which I can now add a few colorful ones of my own) that had scared the shit out of me, falling down that Rabbit Hole and the exposure to the polar opposites of the human condition on the sub continent it reminded me what travel is really all about.

To live.

And for that lesson Mother India, I am most grateful.

This isn't all of it of what happened, as you can probably tell. I am haunted by the one German girl who asked me one night in the bar a week before the tsunami.

'Dave, what would happen if there was a wave in the Maldives?'

I looked at her as my blood ran cold, and said simply as I shook my head, 'Impossible. We would be drowned like rats.'

But we lived.

When I turn on the television I can hardly watch the news at all right now. MILLIONS lost everything. I lost so little. I'm home though, and you can call me here, it would be good to talk. My cameras, journal, 3,000 photos, guidebook and clothes are all gone. Even that laptop that miraculously survived climbing the Himalayas in India is gone.

The emails I sent you are all I have left from my trip.

Wait.

The memories are still seared into my head where they burn even brighter, branded into my brain cells like nothing ever before.

That's India for you.

The Travel Gods wouldn't have it any other way.

Love, Dave

Epilogue

When going through Japanese customs, make sure to wear fresh underwear.

You will never be sent an invitation to join the Middle Aged SalaryMan Club.

If you don't like John Denver songs, never be a guest of a Tatami Dragon Lady.

If you come across an old lady in Japan with crooked teeth, give her a lift.

'Fuck you' can easily be lost in translation.

If the gods are watching, smile back.

Saigon divorces are quicker than those in Phnom Penh.

Avoid joking with Vietnamese sandwich makers who may be armed with machetes.

Fake pee stains can become a very convenient getaway vehicle.

If you see a crinkled Soviet jet cruising a few wing lengths away from your own dilapidated plane, don't forget to wave.

If there's a chair throwing Frenchwoman on your flight, you are in the midst of a flightmare.

If any tits are not stowed during takeoff, you are definitely in the midst of a flightmare.

If you ever find yourself in the belly of Addis Ababa airport looking for your luggage, keep your mouth closed.

Travel insurance does not cover your body's recovery from canyons in India or Africa.

If offered raw meat at an Ethiopian wedding, swallow. It doesn't taste as bad as you think.

Live bullets are not an IATA approved carry-on item.

If your bus driver has six fingers, fear not: in some countries this is a sign of good luck. (Just don't ask me which one)

If you lie to someone in the travel industry, be prepared to run into them in the middle of nowhere.

If you board a flight and see crew wearing synthetic vomit green saris, be afraid.

Even Saddhus need a vacation.

If you're ever the victim of a drive by blessing, just tell everyone you are half Nepali.

No matter what your passport says, in India, your name will become 'Marijuana'.

Be suspicious of anyone wearing an upside down 'Ganesh' nametag.

Don't ever wear black in India.

Sandwiches should never taste like cow crap.

Apple Power books can be used as murder weapons.

If a rat runs over your foot, relax: you'll grow rich.

The Dalai Lama does not have a vagina.

For the record, I never bought a Lapis Lazuli necklace in Kabul.

Yak fur comes up easier that it goes down.

Ignore that impish retired railway official in the Delhi train station.

Beware the Delhi Dog Shit Man.

Acknowledgements

To my family for first introducing me to the road.
To my size 13 shoes that have taken me down that road.
And to friends who I have encountered along that road.

Thanks to my editor Alex Sarelle for helping with the voice, direction and point of view of the book, keeping the feel raw and real. And to all those who offered encouragement and suggestions including Doug Lansky, Lori Burke, Donna Burr, Brenda Semrow, Catherine Chapman, Neeka Wilson, Aaron Morris, Michael Henman, Christine Bui, Annette Bouvain, Cousin Isaac, Debbie Masamori and many more.

Thanks also to Susi O'Neill for first publishing my work on the Pilot Guides Globetrekker website, and to Helen Roberts for keeping it up there. Thanks to Jay Koren, whose adventurous career at Pan American World Airways he wrote about in The Company We Kept helped sow the first seeds that eventually became this book.

And special thanks to Annette Spörel for being a kindred spirit with a writer's soul whose glittering prose really pimps my ride, and to Brandon Roy who was held co-captive by a faulty headlight high in the Himalayas that became the story 'Lightless in Little Tibet' and who snapped the photo from which the book's cover was created, and to Sebastian Serandrei for capturing the mood of the book in the cover design.

To all the characters, human and inhuman, named and unnamed who appeared in Sandwiches Should Never Taste Like Cow Crap after crossing paths with me, thanks for jumping into this tasty word stew of adventure, chaos, humor, horror and beauty.

And lastly thanks to the very road itself.

You've been good to me.

About the Author

Dave Lowe was born in New York City, grew up California, and is currently based in Southeast Asia, where he is involved in writing and marketing. Work has taken him to Australia, Vietnam, the Maldives, Thailand and Hong Kong, while life has taken him to more than seventy other countries.

His earliest memories of travel include taking clattering subway trains beneath the streets of Manhattan, flying shiny Boeing 707's across the Atlantic, and riding around in the back seat of a fire engine red Volvo 244DL across the wild American West.

Favorite places include the Malecon, Havana, Big Sur, California, Harajuku, Tokyo, and the upperdeck of a 747 at 30,000 feet up high in the blue sky.

This is his first book.

Dave can be contacted via email at theloweroad@mac.com or through his website: www.theloweroad.com where he blogs the travel industry, uploads photos and other stories from his travels, and where release dates for future books are posted.